Learning to Lead Together

Learning to Lead Together

The Promise and Challenge of Sharing Leadership

Janet H. Chrispeels Editor

Gevirtz Graduate School of Education,
University of California, Santa Barbara

SAGE Publications
International Educational and Professional Publisher
Thousand Oaks ▪ London ▪ New Delhi

For information:

Sage Publications, Inc.
2455 Teller Road
Thousand Oaks, California 91320
E-mail: order@sagepub.com

Sage Publications Ltd.
1 Oliver's Yard
55 City Road
London EC1Y 1SP
United Kingdom

Sage Publications India Pvt. Ltd.
B-42, Panchsheel Enclave
Post Box 4109
New Delhi 110 017 India

Printed in the United States of America

Library of Congress Cataloging-in-Publication Data

Learning to lead together: The promise and challenge of
sharing leadership / [edited by] Janet H. Chrispeels.
p. cm.
Includes bibliographical references and index.
ISBN 0-7619-2885-5 (cloth)—ISBN 0-7619-2886-3 (pbk.)
1. School management teams—United States—Case studies. 2. Teacher participation in administration—United States—Case studies. 3. Educational leadership—United States—Case studies. I. Chrispeels, Janet.
LB2806.3.L43 2004
371.1′06—dc22 2003027726

04 05 06 07 10 9 8 7 6 5 4 3 2 1

Acquisitions Editor:	Diane McDaniel
Editorial Assistant:	Margo Beth Crouppen
Production Editor:	Melanie Birdsall
Copy Editor:	Sally M. Scott
Typesetter:	C&M Digitals (P) Ltd.
Proofreader:	Mary Meagher
Indexer:	Sheila Bodell

Contents

Preface

The impetus for this book, *Learning to Lead Together*, grew from six years of research about the formation and functioning of school leadership teams. Over the course of this longitudinal study, several notable findings surfaced, which informed and guided the formation of this book; these included the following:

- The ability of the principal to work with a leadership team made a difference in what the team could accomplish in building a strong collaborative culture, improving classroom practices, and enhancing student learning.
- Principals who shared leadership successfully found ways to work with the contradictory expectations of being simultaneously in charge and giving authority to the team to make decisions.
- Through learning how to interpret data with their team, principals often found ways to collaborate with teachers to distribute leadership and empower teachers to be leaders of change in their school.
- A focus on team building and problem-solving skills promoted greater teacher and principal collaboration; lack of such skills undermined the distribution of leadership.
- District cultures can be strong countering forces that prevent or weaken distributed leadership. Just mandating site-based management does not make it a reality in the day-to-day lives of the local school community.

As I explored the field, I met other researchers investigating how principals and heads of schools share and distribute leadership and address the challenges of leading their schools collaboratively. Furthermore, I realized that the push for shared leadership, a product of both legislation and informed practice of the past two decades, now seems to be going head to head with a new emphasis on accountability. The demand for results creates pressures for quick action and increases individual liability, two actions that are counter to practices of collaborative leadership. My work and the work of others suggest that the material in this book—which presents recent research-based examples of principals, including many who have and some who have not negotiated the quagmire of distributed leadership—is needed to document the pathways and pitfalls that may be encountered in the process.

Learning to Lead Together, through numerous case studies, addresses how principals and their staff struggle with the challenge of shared leadership and attain some of the promise that leads to teacher growth and development and higher levels of student learning. The cases allow us to explore how shared and distributed leadership is socially constructed across contexts and, as such, illuminates the ways teachers and principals share leadership. We identify unique features as well as commonalties across sites, and through analysis we identify a variety of theories in action used by those working to share leadership in schools.

Acknowledgments

Although I did not know it, the seeds for this book were planted more than 30 years ago when I joined the League of Women Voters of San Diego. Through my years of work with the League, I learned what shared leadership means through living it. The League of Women Voters not only defends democracy; its members practice it on a daily basis. I am deeply grateful to the many League colleagues who taught me what it means to be a citizen in a democracy.

This book also would not have been possible if it were not for Don Davies, founder of the Institute for Responsive Education, who provided me, as a parent and community leader, with the opportunity to write about my experiences of working with district advisory committees and school improvement councils. Those early writings have continued to give shape and meaning to the work and research I have pursued ever since.

In my journey to understand shared leadership, the founders and leaders of the California School Leadership Academy have contributed profoundly. No words are sufficient to thank Karen Kearney, Larraine Roberts, Albert Cheng, Bill McKeever, Elaina Hershowitz, Janis Millett, and the many other dedicated regional CSLA leaders and team members who allowed me to study their work and learn at their side. California educators and citizens lost a state treasure when funding for CSLA was dropped from the state budget in 2003.

I also wish to thank Janet Brown and former graduate students Salvador Castillo, Marisol Rodarte, Kathleen Martin, Itamar Hararri, and Cheryl Strait, who contributed greatly to the exploration of the School Leadership Teams in California; and Barbara Taylor and the Olin Foundation, who supported our work.

I am indebted to the Sage reviewers whose thoughtful comments and suggestions helped to take each chapter to greater clarity. The editorial staff at Sage is outstanding and has made the process of publishing easy. My sincere thanks to Diane McDaniel and Margo Crouppen for their editorial assistance and gentle reminders that the project was worth finishing, to Sally Scott for her careful copyediting, and to Melanie Birdsall for steering the book into production. Jane Ready and Sally Grubb also deserve my thanks for helping with the details of readying the manuscript for submission.

I would like to give a special note of thanks to each of the chapter contributors, who have stayed with this project through its many delays, and to the educators who allowed each of us to tell their stories of struggle and triumphs in learning to lead together.

About the Editor

Janet Chrispeels is a professor in the Educational Leadership and Organizations emphasis at the Gevirtz Graduate School of Education at the University of California, Santa Barbara. She serves as director of the Center for Educational Leadership and the California Center for Effective Schools, as well as directs the administrative credentialing program at UCSB. She earned her B.A. from Michigan State and Ed.D. from the University of San Diego. Her research interests include school change and restructuring, school-home collaboration, leadership, and professional development.

As a faculty member at UCSB, she conducted a six-year study of the California School Leadership Academy program (CSLA), a three-year development and research project focusing on district-wide implementation of the Effective Schools process. Prior to joining the faculty at UCSB, she worked as a curriculum coordinator with the San Diego County Office of Education. She has written numerous articles on school leadership teams, professional development of administrators, and school-family partnerships, and she authored *Purposeful Restructuring: Creating a Climate of Learning and Achievement in Elementary Schools* (1992). In addition, she has served as chair of the Board of Directors for the National Center for Effective Schools Research and Development Foundation; she has been president of the International Congress of School Effectiveness and School Improvement; and she is on the editorial board of the *Journal of Effective Schools,* the *School Effectiveness and School Improvement* journal, and the *Leadership and Policy in Schools* journal.

About the Contributors

S. David Brazer is Assistant Professor in the Education Leadership Program at George Mason University in Fairfax, Virginia. He teaches aspiring principals and Ph.D. students in a variety of courses. His research focuses on school site decision making in both site-based management and more traditional systems. Prior to his appointment at George Mason University, he served as a high school assistant principal and principal in the San Francisco Bay area. He received his Ph.D. in Administration and Policy Analysis from Stanford University.

Edwin M. Bridges is Professor Emeritus of Education and Past Director of the Prospective Principals Program at Stanford University and is a two-time recipient of the Excellence in Teaching Award in the Stanford School of Education. Prior to joining the faculty, he held academic appointments at the University of California, Santa Barbara; the University of Chicago; and Washington University, St. Louis. He is a former vice president of the American Educational Research Association. His research interests are teacher evaluation and problem-based learning. He emphasizes the importance of creating a supportive classroom environment in which mistakes are regarded as learning opportunities and in which the instructor models the practices and philosophy that he espouses.

David Burke is the principal of Portland Secondary College, Portland, Victoria, Australia. He has 30 years of teaching and 12 years in the principal class (i.e., assistant principal and principal positions), and continues to teach mathematics and engage in pastoral care as part of his principal duties. His school focuses on engaging staff in professional learning teams to improve classroom teaching and learning. He has facilitated professional development activities for various schools and teacher groups in Victoria. His strong interest in the developing role of principals as educational leaders has led to presentations at the American Educational Research Association annual meeting (United States) and work with principals and administrators in Canada.

Peggy H. Burke is an assistant professor in Teacher Education and Professional Development at Central Michigan University in Mt. Pleasant, Michigan. Her primary instructional and research focus are in middle-level education and organizational change. Prior to coming to Michigan, she was the Director of the New England Turning Points Network and was on the Board of Directors for the National Turning Points Network. Turning Points is a national design for comprehensive middle school change focused on improving learning, teaching, and assessment for all students. In her tenure at Turning Points, she worked as a coach with urban and rural middle schools in Massachusetts, Rhode Island, and Vermont. She has 15 years of school-based experience, ranging from director of parent involvement to teacher, administrator, and curriculum director, which provide the foundation for her beliefs in organizational learning and shared leadership.

Joseph I. Castro is Executive Director of Campus Outreach Initiatives and Adjunct Associate Professor in the Gevirtz Graduate School of Education at the University of California, Santa Barbara (UCSB). As the Chief Outreach Officer at UCSB, he has responsibility for overseeing outreach programs that help to diversify the campus student body. As a faculty member, he teaches seminars and conducts research on K–12 leadership, policy, and equity issues. Prior to his appointment at UCSB in 2001, he served as Founding Director of Academic Programs at the University of California, Merced; Assistant Dean of the Richard and Rhoda Goldman School of Public Policy at the University of California, Berkeley; and as a Policy and Legislative Analyst for the University of California Office of State Governmental Relations in Sacramento. He has a Bachelor's degree in political science and Master's degree in public policy from UC Berkeley and a Ph.D. in educational policy from Stanford University.

Mary Cavalier has been the principal of the Amherst Regional Middle School in Amherst, Massachusetts, for the past six years. Prior to her work in Amherst, she was a mathematics teacher and administrative intern at the Magnet Middle School in Stamford, Connecticut. Guided by her leadership, the Amherst Middle School has transformed from a traditional junior high school to a middle school fully embracing the philosophy put forth in the Turning Points model of educational reform. In 2001, the school was named the first demonstration school for the National Turning Points Network. In addition to her leadership at the school level, Mary has worked with principals across the country to help them develop collaborative leadership capacity and a deep understanding of the work that is necessary in order to transform schools.

Robin Endacott Doerr is a graduate student researcher with the Center for Educational Leadership at the Gevirtz Graduate School of Education at the University of California, Santa Barbara (UCSB), currently working on her doctoral dissertation. She earned a B.A. in Psychology from the University of Denver, a B.A. in Marketing Education from Central Washington University, and an M.A. in Educational Leadership and Organizations from UCSB. She served as a qualitative researcher for the California Center for Effective Schools and for the Equity in Mathematics Education Leadership Institute. She has teaching, outreach, and administrative experience in a variety of educational contexts in both public and private schools and universities.

Judy Durrant is a senior lecturer at Canterbury Christ Church University College, United Kingdom, working within the Centre for Education Leadership and School Improvement (CELSI). As a secondary school teacher she became involved in school-based research and is now director of a school-based Masters program that supports teachers' leadership of development work. She coordinates a professional network that is based around the program and edits its teachers' journal, *The Enquirer*. She has also been involved in a national initiative to support teacher research, the Best Practice Research Scholarships Program. In collaboration with David Frost, she has been involved in research and publication on teacher-led school improvement and in particular its impact on pupils, teachers, and schools. She is currently involved in further research focusing on teacher leadership.

David Frost is a member of the School Improvement and Educational Leadership team at the University of Cambridge Faculty of Education and a cofounder of "Leadership for Learning: the Cambridge Network." Since the mid-1980s, he has worked with teachers, schools, and LEAs (Districts) in the United Kingdom to provide frameworks of support for school improvement. His research has focused on strategies for facilitating teacher leadership and the question of how the quality of teaching and learning in schools can be improved through teacher-led development work. His most recent book, *Teacher-led Development Work: Guidance and Support,* is coauthored with Judy Durrant. His previous book, *Teacher-led School Improvement,* was published in 2000. He is currently involved in an international "Leadership for Learning" project and has worked with teachers and principals in a number of countries including the United States, Austria, The Netherlands, and Greece.

Alma Harris is Professor and Director of the Leadership, Policy and Improvement Unit at the Institute of Education, University of Warwick, United Kingdom. Her most recent research work has focused on improvement in schools facing challenging circumstances and the relationship between distributed forms of leadership and organizational change. She is nationally known for her work on middle-level and teacher leadership, focusing particularly on ways in which these contribute to school development and improvement. Her most recent books include Harris and colleagues (2003), *Effective Leadership for School Improvement;* Harris and Lambert (2003), *Building Leadership Capacity for School Improvement;* Harris (2002), *School Improvement: What's in it for Schools?;* and Harris (2002), *Leading the Improving Department.*

Vishna A. Herrity is Executive Director of the Gevirtz Research Center at the University of California, Santa Barbara (UCSB). As the Center's director since its inception in 1997, she has been responsible for establishing collaborative university, school district, and private sector partnerships that promote community outreach and programs that lead to high levels of academic achievement for all students. Prior to her appointment at UCSB, she spent 25 years working in school districts as a bilingual teacher, elementary principal, and district coordinator of Bilingual, Title VII, Migrant, and Preschool programs. She received her Ph.D. from the University of California, Santa Barbara, in educational leadership and organizations. Her experiences as a school district administrator and a researcher have focused on school-leadership issues related to the design and implementation of appropriate educational programs for culturally and linguistically diverse students.

John L. Keedy, after receiving his doctorate in education administration and supervision from the University of Tennessee in 1983, was principal of Brookfield Elementary School, (Massachusetts) and assistant superintendent for instruction in Galax City Schools (Virginia). Keedy held positions at the University of West Georgia and North Carolina State University before assuming his current professorship at the University of Louisville in the Department of Leadership, Foundations, and Human Resource Education. He has published in the *Canadian Administrator*, the *Journal of Educational Administration*, *Teaching and Teaching Education*, *Journal of Educational Research*, *Journal of School Leadership*, and *Theory Into Practice*, among others. His research interests include studying norms within institutional settings, school reform, personal theories in practice and the superintendency. Professor Keedy's teaching interests include qualitative method, organization theory, and action research for administrators. His service accomplishments include coordinating University of Louisville's application to the University Council for Educational Administration, which he now serves as U of L's plenum representative, serving on the editorial boards of the *Journal of School Leadership*, the *Journal of Thought* and *Education and Urban*

Society. He is coordinator of the cooperative doctoral program with Western Kentucky University, and is part of the State Action for Educational Leadership Project, a Kentucky consortium of administrators, educators, and policy specialists in cooperation with the Southern Regional Education Board and the Wallace Readers Digest Fund.

Kathleen J. Martin received her Ph.D. from the University of California, Santa Barbara, with an emphasis in Educational Leadership and Organizations, and Culture and Language. Since 1999, she has collaborated with Janet H. Chrispeels on articles investigating school-leadership-team functioning. She is a lecturer and coordinator in the Administrative Services Credential and Joint Doctoral Programs in Education at the University of California, Santa Barbara, and a lecturer at California Polytechnic State University, San Luis Obispo, in the Ethnic Studies Department. She brings to her research a rich knowledge of diverse cultures as well as organizational and group dynamics theory.

Deborah H. McDonald is Kentucky State Director and Associate Director of the Mathematics and Science Consortium at Appalachian Educational Laboratory (AEL). Her experience in regional and national education includes working as a school improvement specialist with the U.S. Department of Defense, as a Distinguished Educator with the Kentucky Department of Education, as a design team member with the Prichard Committee Commonwealth Institute for Parent Leadership, and 20 years with Kentucky public schools. McDonald also serves as Chair of the National Center for Effective Schools Research and Development Foundation Board and is a member of the editorial board for the Journal of Effective Schools. Dr. McDonald's research interests include leadership for distributed and collective accountability, high performance culture, and data-driven research for results-focused school improvement. As a child in the Eastern Kentucky section of Appalachia, Debbie McDonald observed the life differences afforded by educational choices she and her peers made and became dedicated to "narrowing the gap" for cultural as well as ethnic diversity. While her school-improvement reach is international, she reports the greatest honor of her career as being invited to give the keynote address for her home Jackson County, Kentucky, Schools Millennium Commencement.

Ian Mitchell spent 23 years as a secondary teacher; for the last 14, he has also worked half-time in the Faculty of Education at Monash University, Melbourne, Australia, where he is currently a senior lecturer. In 1981 he began research in his own classroom into ways of improving how students went about learning. This began what has been a career-long commitment to teacher research and the unique and essential contribution it can make to the knowledge base of education. In 1985, Ian cofounded the Project for Enhancing Effective Learning (PEEL). The PEEL teachers shared concerns about passive, dependent learning and intended a two-year teacher-led collaborative research project to improve the way their students learned. This project proved so rewarding for teachers that it has subsequently spread to hundreds of schools in several countries. He convenes the PEEL network and is editor and author of a range of publications that have flowed from PEEL.

Pat Morales has been involved in education as a classroom teacher, as a mentor teacher, and as an administrator for the past 30 years. She is currently principal of Peabody Charter School, and under her leadership Peabody became a teacher training site for the University of California, Santa Barbara, and a charter school. She increased parental involvement, developed portfolio and performance assessment, implemented an integrated visual and performing arts program, and received a Title VI grant to develop a dual-language program and meet the academic needs of the English-learning students. She holds an Administrative Services Credential, a Masters in Administration, a teaching credential, and a Bilingual Certificate of Competency. During her tenure, Peabody received two distinguished school awards and was named a top-performing school in California in 2002.

Shiou-Ping Shiu is an assistant professor at Shu-Te University in Taiwan where she teaches both preservice teachers and administrators. Her current research interests are teachers' collaborative work to improve instructional practices and school change through leadership teams. She recently earned her Ph.D. at the Gevirtz Graduate School of Education at the University of California, Santa Barbara. She is a former early childhood education specialist and teacher.

Maureen Yep is currently assistant director of the Center for Educational Leadership, Gevirtz Graduate School of Education, University of California, Santa Barbara. The Center is engaged in innovative work with school district teams of all stakeholders—district and site administrators, board, union, parents, teachers, and classified staff—to work collaboratively on effecting systemic change that supports high-level learning for all students. She has 35 years of experience as a teacher and administrator in Australia, and she spent a year as an exchange principal at an inner urban school in Cleveland, Ohio. She has extensive experience in professional development of existing and emergent leaders in both Australia and the United States. Her interest and current research is in shared leadership and developing school- and district-wide leadership capacity.

PART I

Providing the Context

1

The Dynamics of Sharing and Distributing Leadership

Janet H. Chrispeels

I would like to put forward the revolutionary idea that all teachers can lead. If schools are going to become places where all children and adults are learning in worthy ways, all teachers must lead.

—Barth (2001, p. 85)

For children, there is no shortcut to becoming thoughtful, responsible, and intellectually accomplished adults. What it takes is keeping company with adults who exercise these qualities in the presence of adults-to-be.

—Meier (2002, p. 3)

Principal leadership is central to school improvement; when principals share leadership with teachers and community, schools become more effective learning environments for children and adults.[1] But how do principals share leadership? When faced with pressures from above that hold them accountable for the performance of their school relative to other schools, and with pressures from teachers who are reluctant to abandon their traditional autonomy, how do principals make the transition from chief executive officer to a leader of leaders? How do principals share responsibility for learning with the entire school community so that the adults who work there have the opportunity to model being thoughtful, responsible, and intellectually accomplished adults? A major development in educational policy and practice that started three decades ago is to involve teachers in the process of school reform. Many educational reform programs require that school leadership councils or teams[2] be created to provide structures for involving teachers. Not well documented are the ways principals learn to share leadership and shift their roles and responsibilities to include teachers, parents, and students in the messy and challenging work of achieving educational excellence. This book addresses that knowledge gap.

Part I—this chapter—provides an overview of *Learning to Lead Together: The Promise and Challenge of Sharing Leadership.* In Parts II and III of this book, I have assembled single and multiple case studies of elementary, middle, and high schools that investigate the dilemmas that principals face in engaging teachers and others in the school community in shared leadership. Part IV describes three approaches to enhancing the skills of teachers, future principals, and current administrators to lead collaboratively. Collectively, the empirical cases in this book illustrate that experience-produced knowledge combined with "research-produced knowledge are essential to the practice of schooling and its improvement" (Cuban, 2003, p. 4). The case studies are unique in several regards. First, they describe the work of principals and their staff who, in the words of Alma Harris in Chapter 11, "face challenging circumstances" and are striving to raise the achievement levels of students who have not always been well served by schools. Second, many of the cases are longitudinal and trace the developmental process of principals learning to share and distribute leadership to others. These cases do not present formulas but rather capture the nuances and challenges as well as the promise of shared and distributed leadership. Third, the cases examine the significant tensions and inherent conflicts (a missing dimension in many studies of effective leaders) between top-down bureaucratic directives and structures and bottom-up initiatives by teachers and principals to change their school practices. Fourth, the cumulative findings of the cases suggest that much more attention needs to be given as to how to bring about system congruence and coherence in ways that do not crush the initiative shown by teachers and principals who have committed themselves to the process of change. Fifth, the cases illustrate the role of policy levers (e.g., the Kentucky Educational Reform Act and charter school legislation) as well as outside supporters of school change (e.g., universities, foundations, support agencies) as critical resources that can assist principals and their schools. Finally, the volume makes a contribution to the field by describing three programs from different contexts designed to develop the collaborative skills of leaders.

Shared and Distributed Leadership

We define *shared leadership* as principals, teachers, support staff, and in some cases community members and students who come together in leadership teams, governing bodies, or committees to jointly make decisions required to manage the school and improve the learning environment. This opportunity to share decision making, closely aligned with the idea of democratic leadership, is usually supported through board policies or legislative requirements. Building on democratic principles allows schools to develop the social capital of trusting relationships, networks, and shared norms needed for collaboration and shared leadership. Democratic schools also foster the development of intellectual capital, which is essential if teachers are to acquire the knowledge and skills that will enable them to take all students to high levels of accomplishment. Leadership team composition, the range of decision-making authority, and how decisions are made (that is, through consensus or voting) may be determined by the group, or it may be spelled out in policy documents. Both formal decision-making bodies established by policy and more organically developed, locally grown decision-making teams are reflected in the case studies in this book.

The term *distributed leadership* has surfaced relatively recently in educational literature and is being widely used to represent a more encompassing and less structured form of collaborative leadership. In a recent study of the concept of distributed leadership, Bennett, Wise, Woods, and Harvey (2003) assert that "distributed leadership suggests that many more people are involved in the leadership activity than might traditionally be assumed . . . and should not be limited to a small number of people with formal senior roles" (p. 3). Distributed leadership is an *emergent property* that arises from individuals joining their expertise in ways that allow the group or collective to accomplish more than the individual could alone. "Distributed leadership, then, is group activity that works through and within relationships, rather than individual action. It emerges from a variety of sources depending on the issue and who has the relevant expertise or creativity" (Bennett et al., 2003, p. 3). As Darling-Hammond, Bullmaster, and Cobb (1995) assert, "teacher leadership is inextricably connected to teacher learning; that teacher leadership can be embedded in tasks and roles that do not create artificial, imposed formal hierarchies, and that such approaches may lead to greater profession-wide leadership as the 'normal role' of teacher(s)" (p. 87). Many of the individual and cross-case studies in this volume illustrate the power and potential of distributed leadership, as groups of teachers (as distinct from officially mandated councils) come together to solve problems or improve practice such as through the work of interdisciplinary or grade-level teams. An important aspect that emerges from several of the case studies is that designated shared leadership teams often foster and structure multiple avenues for further teacher collaboration so that leadership truly becomes a property of the organization and is distributed throughout. A synergistic relationship appears to exist between strong formalized structures and the emergence of more informal networks and committees that widely disburse leadership to teachers and, at the secondary level, foster greater student-teacher collaboration around learning goals.

The Complex and Multiple Roles of Principals

Principals are expected to be professional managers who guide staff and students to master externally set standards. They must also be community builders and entrepreneurs who form business partnerships and raise funds to address unmet needs. The new directives to involve others, however, are enacted within the context of existing hierarchical structures and district policies of centralized authority. A survey conducted the United States in 2001 by Public Agenda (Frakas, Johnson, Duffett, Foleno, with Foley) revealed that principals increasingly feel they are held accountable for a wide range of tasks and achievement expectations without the concomitant authority. As a result of these conflicting messages, principals face considerable tensions and dilemmas as they try to manage and lead their schools. Furthermore, teachers themselves often have little experience with collaboration and shared leadership in a system in which top-down authority and management are the norms.

The case studies in this book illustrate how existing bureaucratic structures and policies can both impede and assist principals in sharing and distributing leadership, and they document the personal and organizational challenges principals confront when they are committed to shared leadership and believe it is essential to improve student learning. Leading from the top and leading through others require principals to engage in a delicate balancing act. This volume of empirical studies adds to our knowledge of how principals and heads of schools manage this balancing act when they are caught in the middle between district administrators and teachers. This book examines, through a series of individual and cross-case studies in the

United States, Australia, and the United Kingdom, how principals and staff (and in some cases parents and community) struggle to build schools where leadership is shared and distributed. The book is unique in that the cases reflect longitudinal studies that illuminate how the process, and often the struggle, of learning to lead together evolves and is socially constructed by the participants, frequently in politically charged macroenvironments. The case studies will help educators and policymakers see the interactive process of principals and teachers negotiating new roles and responsibilities to improve student learning. The studies show that building good relationships that allow shared leadership and accountability is achieved only through hard work, high energy, and considerable social and political skills. The majority of these accounts document that striving to lead together can result in increased opportunities for learning by staff and students. In addition, student outcomes on publicly valued measures (e.g., standardized tests in the United States or external exams in the United Kingdom) improved. The cases also illustrate that the process of sharing leadership does not always work.

A Historical Perspective of Shared Leadership

Over the past 30 years, shared leadership became a valued mantra. It gained vogue in the late 1970s as policymakers implemented school councils and site-based management in an effort to close the achievement gap of children from diverse and low-income backgrounds through involvement and participation of stakeholders in local decision making. In the United States, federal Title I legislation required parents of disadvantaged children to be consulted, and it established either district or site Title I parent advisory committees. A few states also passed similar legislation establishing school councils (Zerchykov, Davies, & Chrispeels, 1980). For example, in 1973, California passed early childhood legislation that established parent and teacher councils, which later became known as School Site Councils (Chrispeels, 1980a). The state of Victoria in Australia also began experimenting with school councils about the same time and passed path-breaking legislation to establish self-managing schools in the 1980s (Caldwell & Spinks, 1988; Chrispeels, 1980b).

Two concepts guided these early efforts at shared decision making. One was the idea that those who are most impacted by the decision need to be involved in the decision-making process. With such involvement, it was assumed that better decisions were likely to be made and that they were more likely to be implemented. A renewed commitment to democratic principles and the rights of parents to be involved was also behind many of the early efforts to establish advisory councils, which brought parents and teachers together with administrators to govern their schools (Zerchykov et al., 1980). As Murphy and Datnow (2003) remind us, the same era that brought increasing implementation of school councils was also coupled with many top-down government remedies such as increasing graduation requirements, setting minimum competency levels, developing curriculum frameworks to guide instruction, increasing the length of the school year, and mandating shared governance.

These early efforts to establish school councils flowed into ongoing decisions in many districts to implement site-based decision making and to push school restructuring initiatives, a second wave of reform (Murphy & Datnow, 2003). Ogawa (1994) discusses the surprising speed with which site-based management was implemented in school districts throughout the United States. The results of site-based management as a way to involve teachers, and sometimes parents and students, in more active decision making and to place more decisions at the site level are mixed. Reformers' expectations that site-based management would directly lead to student achievement gains were not always realized (Leithwood & Menzies, 1998). As David Brazer shows in Chapter 10 of this book, the implementation of site-based management can vary considerably even within one district. This variability rests in large measure on the clarity of guidelines, roles, and responsibilities, as well as on the principal's ability and willingness to share leadership.

During this time, the concept of teacher leadership also emerged as a parallel path for schools wanting to improve student achievement (Lieberman, 1995). It became embodied in mentor teacher programs, a focus on master teachers and differentiated salary scales, team teaching efforts, and teacher participation in leadership teams for school restructuring. Repeated studies show that teacher leadership is key for both short- and long-term school improvement efforts. Wohlstetter, Smyer, and Mohrman (1994) argue that "there is evidence that a high-involvement approach, where control over power, knowledge, information and rewards is decentralized, can boost organizational performance and productivity" (p. 81). Growing evidence also suggests that principal and teacher ownership and leadership of the improvement process is critical to long-term sustainability in school change and student learning (Darling-Hammond, 1997; Murphy & Datnow, 2003; Short & Greer, 1997; Southworth & Lincoln, 1999; Teddlie & Reynolds, 2000). In other words, distributing leadership and sharing accountability throughout the school are essential practices if teachers are to be able to learn the knowledge and skills that will enable them to engage all students in intellectually challenging standards-based work. In spite of the mantra of shared and now distributed leadership, the road to its implementation remains poorly understood. What do actual efforts of shared leadership look like in practice? How do principals and teachers socially construct distributed and shared leadership? How do they identify and differentiate their decision-making roles and relationships? How do principals and teachers decide what decisions and leadership activities are distributed and to whom? What are some of the consequences for teachers, principals, and students in adopting efforts towards shared and distributed leadership?

Exploring answers to these questions and investigating examples of principals who share leadership is critical, given the current cycle of school reform. Recent policy initiatives in the United States, United Kingdom, and Australia have centralized leadership at state/national levels through the passage of curriculum standards, the implementation of high-stakes testing, and the requirement for passing school exit exams to receive a high school diploma. In the United States and England, schools are ranked on the basis of student achievement gains, and reforms are now being accompanied by a new orthodoxy of teaching and learning that includes a narrow range of textbook adoptions, scripted skill-based lessons, as well as mandated professional development for principals and teachers to match the required texts. Political leaders call for full responsibility and accountability for results to be placed on school leaders, with rewards or sanctions for their schools to follow if targeted outcomes are not reached. School leaders are experiencing greater bureaucratic and institutional forces that direct their actions (Ogawa & Bossert, 1995). These traditional command-and-control directives, designed to preserve the perceived legitimacy of the school system, often inhibit the implementation of shared and distributed leadership and leave teachers and their leaders with little decision-making authority or autonomy and a lack of confidence in how to proceed with involving their staff.

Why Is Sharing Leadership So Difficult?

The immediate challenges of the policy arena, as well as a variety of cultural, organizational, and personal factors, make it difficult for principals or heads of schools to share leadership. First, as middle managers in the hierarchy, school leaders must fulfill their institutional role of attending to the external (district and other governmental) expectations to demonstrate direction and coordination of the school's internal environment. At the same time, they are expected to smoothly manage the internal functioning of their school. As van Vilsteren (1999, p. 172) points out, this relationship can result in a one-way leader-to-follower direction. The leader gives subordinates a voice in decision making only as deemed helpful to maintain organizational legitimacy. As a result of district expectations and policies, principals may feel they cannot share leadership because they regard themselves as ultimately accountable in this era of high-stakes testing and public ranking of schools. They perceive leading as having *power over* subordinates and are reluctant to let go and allow others an equal voice; they fear that the group may make a wrong decision for which the designated leader will subsequently be held responsible.

Second, school leaders may find themselves caught in the middle as they implement many site-based school reform initiatives that encourage or rely on shared leadership, and at the same time they feel constrained in implementing school-based teaching and learning decisions that may be counter to the new mandates (Chrispeels, Strait, & Brown, 1999). Boyd, Banilower, Pasley, and Weiss (2003), in their study of schools implementing the Local Systemic Change Initiative to improve instruction in science, math, and technology, found that it was essential for local project coordinators to help principals see the alignment between their initiative and state curriculum mandates. The tension caused by overlapping mandates and conflicts between pedagogical approaches seems to be increasing as state and national centralizing and prescriptive policies continue to be enacted. The stronger the institutional norms of hierarchy and control, the less likely the leaders will sense agency and authority to act to distribute leadership. Educators "can feel infantilized or respected, collegial or alienated, depending on the dominant climate of values sustained at the district level" (Tyack, 2002, p. 23). Furthermore, if principals feel they are unable to influence the organization in the upward direction, they may also feel diminished in their ability to exercise leadership downward (van Vilsteren, 1999). As McLaughlin found in her analysis (cited in Tyack, 2002), school boards and district administrators "can do much to enhance coherence, morale and trust—or the opposite" (p. 23). As several of the case studies presented in this book show, without coherence, high morale, and trust, shared leadership is difficult to implement and harder to sustain.

Traditional views of teaching and the roles of teachers is a third reason why it is so difficult for principals to share leadership. Teachers can neutralize a principal's actions to share leadership through the persistence of institutional patterns such as the norms of teacher isolation, autonomy, contract provisions for equal treatment, and limited time for meeting outside set classroom hours. These norms and practices are likely to be especially strong among those teachers whose tenure in the organization far exceeds that of the principal. Reynolds (cited in MacBeath & Mortimore,

2001, p. 17) found that schools that have failed to improve faced problems such as the following:

- teachers projecting their own deficiencies onto children or their communities
- teachers clinging to past practices
- defenses built up against threatening messages from the outside
- fear of failure
- seeing change as someone else's job
- hostile relationships among staff
- seeking safety in numbers (a circle-the-wagons mentality)

These critical issues must be addressed if shared leadership is to be effectively realized. Several of the case studies here illustrate that principals cannot overcome these blocks to shared leadership alone, and efforts to eliminate systemic inconsistencies and lack of system coherence have to be made simultaneously.

A fourth factor that impedes shared leadership is the uncertainty of teaching and uncertainty about how to achieve the outcome of high levels of student learning. In the past two decades, however, a growing body of knowledge about effective instructional practices that impact student learning has emerged and can be used by teachers and leaders to ensure greater student success (Marzano, Pickering, & Pollack, 2001). Compounding this uncertainty has been the response of teachers' unions, especially in the United States, and their efforts to maintain teacher autonomy and equality. Local unions often resist shared leadership because they see other teachers taking leadership roles within a school as a threat to the distinction and division between teaching and administration. The threat or actual filing of grievances against principals for involving some teachers in leadership can quickly undermine the confidence of a principal's attempts to build a collaborative culture.

Fifth, principals may find it difficult to share leadership because they themselves have not experienced its power and potential as teachers or administrators in their district. The traditional institutional patterns, values, and expectations of how to behave as an *in-charge leader* are implicitly understood, taken for granted, and reinforced by existing hierarchical structures. Many district administrative meetings do not give school leaders an opportunity to learn how to debate and discuss issues, reach consensus, or work as a team of equals. In fact, most administrative meetings serve only to reinforce a command-and-control mentality.

Finally, school leaders may lack the intra- and interpersonal skills needed for shared leadership. Their path to a leadership position is usually through the teacher ranks, with an emphasis on autonomy and *solo* leadership roles.

In addition, their administrative preparation programs often focus more on the content knowledge needed to manage the school than on the group process and problem-solving skills essential for effective collaborative decision making with multiple stakeholders. Thus, Part IV of this book addresses examples of programs that have been designed to enhance future or current leaders' collaborative skills. As Chapters 7 and 10 show, principals can interpret the concepts of site-based management and shared leadership quite differently; therefore, principals need time to explore the concepts. Principals need a range of skills and abilities to facilitate shared leadership. These include how to work effectively with a variety of stakeholder groups—teachers, parents, community members, business leaders, district administrators, and students. As Leithwood, Begley, and Cousins (1992) have shown, principals need skills for problem solving alone and with others. Knowledge of group dynamics, effective listening skills, treating others with respect, and keeping one's perspective and humor are important skills in group collaborative problem solving. In the United States, these essential skills are not part of the new national standards for school leaders, but they may be as critical to school and student success as instructional and management skills.

Why Is Shared and Distributed Leadership Important?

Middle managers in industry have always had to cope with pressures from bosses above them and from employees below them, who with the support of the union bureaucracy may file grievances against them. The school leader as middle manager is caught in a similar squeeze. Why is this dual pressure on the principal from district and union bureaucracies a critical problem for education? Numerous studies in the past three decades show that the successful implementation of innovations and improvements depend on the principal as the key school leader (Beck & Murphy, 1996; Murphy & Datnow, 2003; Scheerens & Bosker, 1997; Southworth & Lincoln, 1999; Teddlie & Reynolds, 2000; Waters, Marzano, & McNulty, 2003). Other studies indicate the principal's primacy in creating the climate and conditions so necessary for robust professionalism of teachers that can lead to increased student learning (Boyd et al., 2003; Chrispeels, 1992; Lieberman, 1995; Scheerens & Bosker, 1997; Teddlie & Stringfield, 1993). Principals or headmasters cannot do it alone, however. Even with the best of visions and ideas for improvement, if school leaders do not involve their staff, the school will soon be in crisis (MacBeath & Mortimore, 2001).

Research also suggests that principals are vital to the process of facilitating the delegation, sharing, and distribution of leadership, especially instructional leadership, throughout the school and cultivating teachers as leaders (Chrispeels, 1992; Chrispeels, Brown, & Castillo, 2000a; Darling-Hammond, 1997; Lieberman, 1995; Little, 1993). When principles structure and facilitate teacher participation in site-based leadership committees that make decisions about teaching and learning, student achievement improves (Smylie, Lazarus, Brownlee-Conyers, 1994; Waters, Marzano, and McNulty, 2003; Weiss & Cambone, 1994; Wohlstetter, Van Kirk, Robertson, & Mohrman, 1997). When principals help the leadership team learn how to use data, the school increases its focus on teaching and learning (Chrispeels, Castillo, & Brown, 2000b). When principals distribute leadership through teacher-led action teams, teacher and student learning are enhanced. Without shared and distributed leadership, it is unlikely that schools will achieve or sustain the outcomes that policymakers and the public want from its schools, yet too little attention is being given to shared leadership within the context of hierarchical and bureaucratic systems. Previous leadership studies have investigated the traits, behaviors, and practices of school leaders that support school improvement and effective schools. Although this approach is helpful, it often keeps the focus on individual leaders as well as promotes a technical-rational view of leadership and fails to illuminate the context and struggles that principles confront as they try to lead their schools collaboratively. This book helps to illustrate the urgent need for realignment of districts and their schools to democratic principles of shared governance, and the need for support and assistance to leaders and their staff to develop the skills and knowledge to lead together.

Chapter Overview

Part II: Single Case Studies of Principal's Work to Implement Shared Leadership

The five chapters in Part II present the struggles that individual principals have encountered in coping with the tension of instituting heterarchical and shared leadership within the confines of hierarchical systems. How do school leaders engage teachers in collaborative work and distributed leadership and at the same time respond to centralized policy directives? Chapters 2 and 3 help to answer this question by describing in detail how two principals, who had clear visions of what they wanted to accomplish for their students, teachers, and parents, were able to engage their faculties in bringing the visions to life. Both principals established a variety of mechanisms for sharing leadership. Particularly important to the process were the Leadership Team and interdisciplinary teams in the middle school case and the Governing Council and grade-level meetings in the elementary charter school case. The principals created not only the structures but also the time for teachers to lead. Both of these principals were resourceful in using outside policy instruments to help them accomplish their goals—goals that would have been difficult to implement if they had both remained functioning within the district system in a traditional way. The national middle school reform initiative in one case (Turning Points), and charter school legislation in the other, gave the principals the leverage they needed to distribute leadership more broadly in their schools.

Chapter 4, through a first-person narrative, recounts an Australian educator's 16-year journey of collaboration. He emerged early in his career as a teacher leader and then assumed more formal positions of leadership (curriculum coordinator, assistant principal, and finally principal). This chapter illustrates the central role of the principal in facilitating or blocking teacher leadership and provides specific insights on ways to facilitate a community of learners. It also illustrates the fragility of shared leadership when policy and leadership changes, and the importance of sustaining practices such as learning teams over time. In addition, the chapter shows the benefits of linking with a university that supports teacher action research as a means of examining one's own practice in collaboration with others in ways that enhance student learning.

Chapters 5 and 6 document the challenges of sharing leadership. Principals often have not received specific training in problem solving, group dynamics, shared decision making, and strategies for distributing leadership. In these two case studies, training was provided for the principals and core staff to collaborate and improve their schools. The leadership teams, however, continually felt buffeted by pressures from the district office in ways that undermined teacher and principal efforts to collaborate. These two case studies show that, given outside training and support, principals and teachers can learn to work together in new ways. Nevertheless, district, principal, and teacher worldviews created tensions and dissention that limited progress, especially in the early stages.

Part III: Cross-Case Studies of Shared Leadership

Part III moves from single case studies to cross-case analyses of shared and distributed leadership. Chapter 7 presents interview data from 13 principals on their perspectives of the challenges of sharing leadership. This chapter is important in documenting that although principals agree with the concept, how they actually define and implement shared leadership is varied and in some cases quite limited. The principals differed considerably in their comfort; for many, the conflict between the ideal and the reality of what is possible is a dichotomy not easily bridged.

Chapter 8 examines the problem of guiding whole-school change in a large urban district from the perspectives of four middle-school principals. How do you share leadership in a system that grants limited building autonomy and discretion over instructional programs, time, and financial resources? The chapter highlights the importance of a principal who clearly articulates the school's core purpose, engages in double-loop learning, and facilitates dialogue across the school community. When confronted with shifting district policies, the case makes clear why it is easy for teachers to put up defenses, see change as someone else's job, and assume that "this too will pass."

Chapter 9 presents a more hopeful picture and confirms that in every system there are outliers who outperform their peers in spite of the odds to do so. This case study of three Kentucky principals is unique in documenting how these principals conceptualized the development of teacher leaders within the Kentucky Education Reform Act of 1990 (KERA). These principals realized that, without close collaboration with teachers, they would not be able to fulfill the requirements of KERA and achieve the improvement targets set by the state. This chapter shows how these principals established clear communication systems around common goals, embedded a culture of professionalism in the school, and institutionalized the basic tenets of KERA. The principals were found to be analytical guides who provided appropriate internal and external resources, supported teachers as leaders, shared leadership, and distributed accountability to achieve student success.

Chapter 10 is valuable in illustrating how mandates to involve teachers in shared decision making can be interpreted quite differently. Based on their own experiences and comfort in working with staff, the principals in this large district in a county in Virginia constructed their own meaning of site-based management. The study documents the sustaining nature of site-based management once a district adopts it as policy, and at the same time shows that the implementation and the range of decisions in which teachers may be involved will vary based on each school's unique culture, context, and principal leadership.

Many urban school districts around the world, with their concentration of pockets of poverty and students from diverse cultural and language backgrounds, face challenges in bringing their students to high levels of achievement. Chapter 11 makes an important contribution by focusing exclusively on the successful leadership practices in such schools. Drawing on the case-study evidence from 10 schools in England, the chapter outlines the key features of successful leadership practices and focuses on how distributed leadership was achieved. This chapter, together with Chapters 8 and 9, provide rich descriptions of the critical strategies principals and their teachers use to improve their schools in ways that lead to increases in student performance and achievement when faced with challenging circumstances.

Part IV: Preparing School Leaders for Shared Leadership

The chapters in Part IV take up the issue of preparing future and current administrators in ways that will assist them in sharing and distributing leadership. The past five years have seen increasing worldwide interest and pressure to develop new administrative preparation programs or to improve those that exist (Hallinger, 2003). For example, Brian Caldwell, one of the world pioneers in promulgating site-based management, also helped found the Principal Center in Melbourne, Australia. The National College for School Leadership reflects a major shift in English policy to greatly expand the opportunities for leadership preparation and ongoing professional development for lead teachers and headmasters in England. In the United States, the recent adoption by many states of the Standards for School Leaders proposed by the Interstate School Leaders Licensure Consortium is serving to redefine most university administrative preparation programs. The focus of many of these initiatives is away from the more traditional emphasis on management knowledge and skills, such as finance and school law, to leadership with attention to the importance of articulating a vision of learning that is shared and engaging in culture and community building. The ethical and moral roles of the leader are reinforced, as is the centrality of the instructional guidance role that keeps the school focused on its core purpose of teaching for learning. The challenges confronting school leaders, which are given scant attention in the standards, are the skills and dispositions needed to collaborate and share with others the ever-expanding job of leading a twenty-first-century school. Collins and Porras (1994) found in their study of high-performing companies that their performance was sustained over long periods of time because their leaders helped to develop them as visionary institutions. The leaders of these outstanding companies overall were not charismatic and visionary, as is often assumed, but rather they knew how to build the capacity of staff and to distribute leadership throughout the organization. Given the frequent turnover of school leaders, especially in many high-poverty schools, shared and distributed leadership may be the only means of sustaining school improvement. The three chapters in Part IV share ideas and approaches that can be used to help current and future leaders develop the knowledge and skills needed to foster leadership in others.

Teacher development, especially the enhancement of content knowledge and instructional skills, is the foundation for lasting school improvement. One promising approach to such development is teacher-led development work. Chapter 12 presents teachers' ideas and views about what principals and headmasters can do to empower teachers as leaders. Their recommendations about the support that teachers need—including creating a culture that is conducive to teacher-led development and action research, providing time for collaborative work, promoting access to external resources, and serving as critical friends to teachers—are key components of this chapter and have not been described in most school leadership literature.

Chapter 13 describes a university leadership institute designed in partnership with local school districts to assist school leaders serving high-poverty rural schools to develop their leadership skills and to cope with the isolation that many of these leaders face. A key feature of the program is the network-building and collaborative process among school leaders, which in turn gave them the ability to collaborate with others. Through the institute they gained a deeper understanding of the need to trust colleagues and more actively engage them in the process of change. The study also highlights that one institute, with follow-up sessions, can help but is not sufficient to address the many challenges faced by these young leaders in developing their schools as high performance systems.

Part IV concludes with a chapter on problem-based learning. The approach to professional development pioneered at Stanford University's administrative preparation program by Ed Bridges highlights the need to prepare future leaders to engage teachers, staff, and parents in shared decision making. Through membership on teams established to address real problems that these future leaders are likely to face, students experience what it means to be a leader and to guide the work of a team. Students are taught explicit skills for leading groups.

Part V: Conclusion

The final chapter of *Learning to Lead Together* draws together the lessons learned from these cases. It highlights that principals, teachers, support staff, and community are at work on a challenging problem of reinventing schools so that all children may learn and prosper. They must collaboratively engage in fundamental, adaptive, or second-order changes if shared leadership is to be implemented successfully. Although each case study reveals unique features and nuances that shaped shared leadership within the context of that particular case, important themes cut across the cases. From these themes, implications for policymakers, central or district administrators, school leaders, and teachers are discussed.

Notes

1. Different terms are used to denote the position of school leader in Australia, the United Kingdom, and the United States. In general, in this book we have used the more common American term *principal.* However, we have also referred to them as "school leaders" or "headmasters."

2. Although many site-based management committees or school site councils involve parents as members, this book focuses primarily on the dynamic of principals and heads of schools sharing and distributing leadership with teachers. This is not to minimize the important role that parents and community play on such committees and councils, but rather to give this book a sharper focus that addresses the relationship of power and authority between site administrators and teachers. We believe that if principals and teachers learn to work together effectively, the opportunities to widen the circle to more meaningfully involve parents and students in schools are more likely to arise.

References

Barth, R. (2001). *Learning by heart.* San Francisco: Jossey-Bass.

Beck, L., & Murphy, J. (1996). *The four imperatives of a successful school.* Thousand Oaks, CA: Corwin Press.

Bennett, N., Wise, C., Woods, P., & Harvey, J. A. (2003). *Distributed leadership.* Retrieved April 5, 2003, from The National College of School Leadership Web site: *www.ncsl.org.uk*

Boyd, S. E., Banilower, E. R., Pasley, J. D., & Weiss, I. R. (2003, February). *Progress and pitfalls: A cross-site look at local system change through teacher enhancement.* Chapel Hill, NC: Horizon Research.

Caldwell, B. J., & Spinks, J. M. (1988). *The self-managing school.* London: Falmer Press.

Chrispeels, J. H. (1980a). School level decision making: Problems and possibilities. *School and Community News, 5*(2), 26–36.

Chrispeels, J. H. (1980b). The Victorian Home/School Interaction Project. *School and Community News, 5(2)*, 37–47.

Chrispeels, J. H. (1992). *Purposeful restructuring: Creating a culture for learning and achievement in elementary schools.* London: Falmer.

Chrispeels, J. H., Brown, J. H., & Castillo, S. (2000a). Leadership teams: Factors that influence their development and effectiveness. In K. Leithwood (Ed.),

Understanding schools as intelligent systems, Vol. 4 (pp. 39–73). Greenwich, CT: JAI Press.

Chrispeels, J. H., Castillo, S., & Brown, J. H. (2000b). School leadership teams: A process model of team development. *School Effectiveness and School Improvement, 11*(1), 22–56.

Chrispeels, J. H., Strait, C., & Brown, J. H. (1999). The paradoxes of collaboration. *Thrust for Educational Leadership, 29*(2), 16–19.

Collins, J. C., & Porras, J. I. (1994). *Built to last: Successful habits of visionary companies.* New York: Harper Business Essentials.

Cuban, L. (2003). *Why is it so hard to get good schools?* New York: Teachers College Press.

Darling-Hammond, L. (1997). *The right to learn. A blueprint for creating schools that work.* San Francisco: Jossey-Bass.

Darling-Hammond, L., Bullmaster, M. L., & Cobb, V. L. (1995). Rethinking teacher leadership through professional development schools. *The Elementary School Journal, 96*(1), 87–105.

Frakas, S., Johnson, J., Duffett, A., Foleno, T., with Foley, P. (2001). *Trying to stay ahead of the game: Superintendents and principals talk about school leadership.* New York: Public Agenda.

Hallinger, P. (2003). *Reshaping the landscape of school leadership development: A global perspective.* Lisse, the Netherlands: Swets and Zeitlinger.

Leithwood, K., Begley, P. T., & Cousins, J. B. (1992). *Developing expert leadership for future schools.* London: Falmer Press.

Leithwood, K., & Menzies, T. (1998). A review of research concerning the implementation of site-based management. *School Effectiveness & School Improvement, 9*(3), 233–285.

Lieberman, A. (Ed.). (1995). *The work of restructuring schools: Building from the ground up.* New York: Teachers College Press.

Little, J. W. (1993). Teachers' professional development in a climate of educational reform. *Educational Evaluation and Policy Analysis, 15*(2), 129–151.

MacBeath, J., & Mortimore, P. (Eds.). (2001). *Improving school effectiveness.* Buckingham, UK: Open University Press.

Marzano, R. J., Pickering, D. J., & Pollack, J. E. (2001). *Classroom instruction that works: Research-based strategies for increasing student achievement.* Alexandria, VI: Association of Supervision and Curriculum Development.

Meier, D. (2003). *In schools we trust.* Boston: Beacon Press.

Murphy, J., & Datnow, A. (2003). *Leadership lessons from comprehensive school reforms.* Thousand Oaks, CA: Corwin.

Ogawa, R. T. (1994). The institutional sources of educational reform: The case of school-based management. *American Educational Research Journal, 31,* 519–548.

Ogawa, R. T., & Bossert, S. (1995). Leadership as an organizational quality. *Educational Administration Quarterly, 31,* 224–243.

Scheerens J., & Bosker, R. (1997). *The foundations of educational effectiveness.* London: Pergamon.

Short, P., & Greer, J. T. (1997). *Leadership in empowered schools.* Upper Saddle River, NJ: Prentice Hall.

Smylie, M. A., Lazarus, V., & Brownlee-Conyers, J. (1994). Instructional outcomes of school-based participative decision-making. *Educational Evaluation and Policy Analysis, 16*(3), 181–198.

Southworth, G., & Lincoln, P. (Eds.). (1999). *Supporting improving primary schools: The role of heads and LEAs in raising standards.* London: Falmer.

Teddlie, C., & Reynolds, D. (Eds.). (2000). *The international handbook of school effectiveness research.* London: Falmer.

Teddlie, C., & Stringfield, S. (1993). *Schools make a difference: Lessons learned from a ten-year study of school effects.* New York: Teachers College Press.

Tyack, D. (2002). Forgotten players: How local school districts shaped American education. In A. Hightower, M. S. Knapp, J. A. Marsh, & M. W. McLaughlin (Eds.), *School districts and instructional renewal* (pp. 7–24). New York: Teachers College Press.

van Vilsteren, C. A. (1999). Leadership in schools. In A. J. Visscher (Ed.), *Managing schools towards high performance* (pp. 163–212). Lisse, The Netherlands: Swets & Zeitlinger.

Waters, T., Marzano, R. J., & McNulty, B. (2003). *Balanced leadership: What 30 years of research tells us about the effect of leadership on student achievement.* Boulder, CO: Mid-Continent Regional Educational Laboratory (McREL).

Weiss, C. H., & Cambone, J. (1994). Principals, shared decision-making and school reform. *Educational Evaluation and Policy Analysis, 16,* 287–301.

Wohlstetter, P., Smyer, R., & Mohrman, S. (1994). New boundaries for school-based management: The high involvement model. *Educational Evaluation and Policy Analysis, 16,* 268–286.

Wohlstetter, P., Van Kirk, A., Robertson, P., & Mohrman, S. (1997). *Organizing for successful school-based management.* Alexandria, VA: Association for Supervision and Curriculum Development.

Zerchykov, R., Davies, D., & Chrispeels, J. (1980). *Leading the way: State mandates for school advisory councils in California, Florida and South Carolina.* Boston: Institute for Responsive Education.

PART II

Case Studies of Principals Sharing Leadership

2

Changing the Culture of a Middle School

A Narrative Examination of a New Principal's Implementation of Shared Leadership

Peggy H. Burke

Mary Cavalier

Using portraiture, this chapter traces how implementing shared leadership at Amherst Regional Middle School in Massachusetts enabled the principal to guide her school through the transition from a traditional junior high school to a middle school that fully embodied the principles of a school reform model, Turning Points 2000. In the process, teachers, administrators, students, and parents built a learning community. This case study illuminates the challenges and hard work required to create learning organizations. It illustrates the importance of focusing first on personal mastery before leveraging change in other areas to support the whole organization in moving toward its shared core purpose (Senge, Kleiner, Roberts, Ross, & Smith, 1994). The chapter begins with the principal's clarification of her vision for a middle school and the development of her own capacity to create what she truly wants to occur. Through the process of looking inward, she is able to articulate her core beliefs and orient herself toward the school's core purpose before she attempts to engage the whole staff. Particularly helpful is the application of the "ladder of inference" (Argyris, 1990; Senge et al., 1994) to surface underlying beliefs and assumptions held by representatives of the school community on the leadership team. Through the unfolding of the leadership team's development, this chapter explores the cost and benefits of learning to lead collaboratively.

Context of the Study

The Junior High School Before Mary Cavalier's Arrival

When Mary Cavalier started as the new principal at Amherst Regional Middle School in the fall of 1997, it was a traditional junior high school, grades 7–9, under top-down leadership. The previous principal made procedural and operational decisions, and high school department chairs dictated the curriculum. Students were divided into six academic tracks, which in 1990 the NAACP alleged discriminated against minority students by placing a disproportionate number in lower tracks. These charges were substantiated by a state investigation, and the district was required to make changes and establish a monitoring committee (Bradley, 2000). Cavalier was recruited to transition the school from a junior high (an organizational structure that resembles a "junior" version of high school) to a middle school (a high-performing school for young adolescents that is developmentally responsive and academically excellent). Prior to Mary's arrival the ninth grade was moved to the high school, which eased overcrowding and created a two-year middle school.

Getting to Know the School

Cavalier began her tenure focused on two objectives. The first was to get to know the faculty and community by gathering data about strengths and weaknesses, major issues, and individual goals and visions for the school. Her second "was to be a teacher" (Cavalier, personal communication, June 24, 2002) and to provide the school community with a fundamental understanding of the middle school philosophy and principles defined in *Turning Points* (The Carnegie Council on Adolescent Development, 1989) and in *This We Believe* (National Middle School Association, 1995).

My history prior to coming to Amherst plays a significant role in how I approached my new role in Amherst. I had worked successfully as a teacher and an administrator in a high functioning middle school in Connecticut. The principal of the school in Connecticut, my mentor, understood the importance of empowering teachers and embedding professional development into the daily life of the school. The school environment gave me a chance to work with a strong, creative faculty that was focused on encouraging students to stretch intellectually. Through this process I began to develop my mental image of what a model middle school should look, sound, and feel like.

In addition to my professional experience, my own personal life was going through major changes that caused me to look inward. It was my inward journey that prepared me to vocalize who "I" was as a person and what my core beliefs were. In turn this internal discovery facilitated my articulating my vision for leading a dynamic middle school that would engage all children in learning.

Personal Mastery: Change Begins With Ourselves

Laying the Foundation

In the first year, Mary realized that she could not make any changes without first helping the staff, students, and community to develop an understanding of the middle school concept. Although she was clear about the vision, she realized that others would need opportunities for learning about and observing other middle schools before they would be able to embrace change.

With the Staff. The core of an organization evolves from how its members think and interact; "thus, the primary leverage for any organizational learning effort lies not in policies, budgets, or organizational charts, but in ourselves" (Senge et al., 1994). This premise is the foundation on which Mary led the transition that took Amherst from a traditional junior high school that provided a solid education for the top 10 to 20% of the students to a model middle school that seeks to educate every student to a high standard.

Mary's first year had two major components. One role was as listener and learner; the other role was teacher, modeler, and cheerleader. She gathered evidence to help her understand the teachers, parents, students, support staff, and community that constituted Amherst Regional Middle School (ARMS). She met with large and small groups, individuals and teams, students, as well as parents and members of the larger community; and she listened to the history, the articulated core values, and the folklore.

With an abundance of data from a variety of perspectives, she identified what was best about the school and what were the challenges, the strengths and weaknesses, and the biggest issues and how those issues had developed at Amherst.

In her other role, she began the process of teaching:

> I began the first faculty meeting with James Garvin's book, *Learning How To Kiss a Frog* (1993). I asked faculty to bring in artifacts that were representative of them as early adolescents. We then shared our stories about those years. We laughed and cried together as we recounted our own youth and memories of "junior high," or for some of the younger teachers middle school. As teachers told their stories, we broke them into four categories of adolescent development: social, emotional, physical, and intellectual. We discovered that most of our own stories were in the areas of social, emotional, and physical. Only a small proportion were recollections about our intellectual development and most were negative recollections. At the end of this meeting, I told the faculty, "Perhaps now you know why the work you do is so challenging and just how terrific you are. Here you are, striving to help students grow intellectually and they are wondering if the person sitting next to them likes them and if their bad hair day really shows. You are wonderful teachers and clearly caring of each other and of your children."

With the Parents. Similarly, she took parents through the journey, back to their memories of early adolescence. With both the staff and the parents, her goal was to help them begin to understand why the culture and climate of the school needed to change. The change was not to diminish the high intellectual climate that already existed at ARMS, but to open it up for all students by increasing the attention paid to the social, emotional, and physical needs of young adolescents.

In addition to teaching middle school philosophy, Mary modeled elements of the philosophy throughout the day. She was out in the halls when students changed classes. She was in the lunchroom every day, talking and eating with students so that she came to know many by name. She was in the classrooms. She attended team meetings where she would use what she had seen in the classroom to help teachers think about their teaching and students' learning.

> Sometimes I would sit in on a team meeting when a parent was being disrespectful of the faculty and I would support the faculty in ending the meeting. Knowledge of this spread throughout the building. Other times I would say to teachers, "Let me be a seventh grader and tell you how what you did feels." Then I would brainstorm with teachers strategies for managing challenging situations in the classroom. I needed the teachers to trust that we were in this

together for the same core purpose. I was establishing a base in that first year around the vision, "It is our job to figure out how to make school work for every student."

Clarifying the Core Guiding Ideas

Margaret Wheatley in *A Simpler Way* (1996) refers to the schizophrenic nature of organizations and a lack of integrity with core guiding ideas. The core guiding ideas provide the creative approach in learning organization theory to conceptualize the ideal. With clear, core, guiding ideas, the organization's leaders are able to use systems thinking to design an organizational change that produces the vision naturally. Mary's clarity about her own core purpose, an effective middle level education that balanced the dual challenges of ensuring equity and excellence, provided the creative energy to conceptualize the ideal for the faculty. She realized, however, that the vision would thrive only if everyone shared and owned the same core purpose. She recognized that she would first need to let them know through conversation, recognition of their work, and her behavior toward all staff, students, and parents that she respected each of them individually.

In the spring of that first year I watched a strong and fine science teacher make a real shift in his thinking about his work with all of our kids. He had sent a particularly challenging eighth-grade girl to the office for clearly being disrespectful. As I met with her, she came to acknowledge that she was off base and having a very hard day. I suggested that we return to the classroom and she share with her teacher the insight she had had with me. She did so, apologizing in eighth-grade girl style, for being way out of line, and she was welcomed back into the classroom.

The next morning, the following note appeared in my mailbox from the science teacher: "I am beginning to understand that there are no longer throwaway children in our building, that it is our job to build relationships with all of our students and that you are here to help. Thank you." He then shared a quote with me from *A River Runs Through It:* "Sometimes it is wonderful to sit back and quietly watch yourself becoming the author of something beautiful."

I realized that my role was to teach by modeling and assisting as we made the shifts in our paradigms to a student-centered culture. In addition, my role was to facilitate problem finding by helping to gather and interpret data. If the faculty and I were defining the problems together, then I would be moving toward another core belief that we are in this together. The big problem that we surfaced, and which in turn shaped our shared vision, was that our job was to figure out how to make school work for every student.

Infrastructures Aligned With Guiding Ideas

Introducing Infrastructures to Support the Middle School Concept

By the end of the first year, Mary had laid the foundation. She had spent time getting to know the faculty and building their belief in her openness, integrity, and consistent commitment to honoring each individual. She also had invested the year in creating a shared understanding of a model middle school. This was done through faculty meetings, all of which were used for professional growth, never for administrative details; through site visits to exemplary middle schools by interested faculty; and by bringing external experts, such as Chris Stevenson, author of *Teaching Ten to Fourteen Year Olds* (2002), to the school for professional development. Chris, a passionate advocate for middle schools, painted a visual image for faculty about what happens for students when a true middle school structure is created; he then spoke specifically about how curriculum and instruction within that structure work to make schools a place of high achievement and success for every student.

Teaming and Heterogeneous Grouping. Teachers intellectually understood, and the majority of the faculty was supportive of the structural changes that would be implemented in the fall of Mary's second year. The teachers would be organized into newly configured teams that consisted of four core subject teachers who would all teach and support the same 100 students. Additionally, each team would work with one specialist such as a bilingual teacher or a special education teacher who worked with academically challenged students; this would support heterogeneous grouping and inclusive teams. An elective teacher—a teacher of subjects such as art, drama, health, shop, or computers—would be a member of the team for a quarter and attend all team meetings. All students on the team would take the same elective each quarter. The only faculty not included as members of a heterogeneous team were physical education and music teachers, who taught performance-based classes, and foreign language teachers. All students would be assigned to teams, including those with significant special needs. A few would have substantially separate programs, but they would still be included in the life of the teams. Some staff was shared between the high school and middle school, and this extra staffing component contributed to Mary's ability to create a true team structure with sufficient instructional and planning time for students and core teachers.

Block Scheduling. The other structural change was block scheduling. In the past the schedule had been 41-minute periods, seven periods a day. A bell would ring, and all 750 students would change classes. In the new schedule the day would be organized into blocks of time, which the entire team would follow. The team might start the day with two hours for instruction and then all students might go to foreign language instruction, during which time the interdisciplinary team has a common planning time. After lunch the team would have a second block of common teaching time. There would be a second time during the afternoon when each class attends music or physical education classes. During this time, teachers have time for individual preparation or can again meet as a team.

The Faculty Adopts the New Structural Changes. The faculty's trust in Mary and their growing understanding about middle school was evident in the spring of her first year when, at a full faculty meeting, they agreed to adopt all the changes suggested by the faculty Study Groups. These included changing the schedule, adopting an advisory program, and allowing for direction for curricular and instructional growth and improvement. Specifically, each grade level agreed to develop curriculum, both disciplinary and integrated, around several essential questions. The questions guiding the seventh grade curriculum are "Who am I? Who are they? Who are we?" The question guiding the eighth grade curriculum is "How do we know what we know?" This focus emphasizes the need to teach eighth graders to use the inquiry process effectively. When teachers returned in the fall, there was little heel dragging. Although some teams were able to function more smoothly than others from the beginning, everyone was willing to try. They all believed that Mary would continue to provide support, encouragement, and further recognition of growth when mistakes happened.

The District's Role in Implementing New Infrastructures. One way the district eventually supported a true middle school model was by providing sufficient numbers of teachers for teaming and for two common planning periods. However, this was not the case when Mary put together the first teams. The budget supported only three teams at each grade level and a split team. Because she knew that teams—two to four teachers that teach the same 100–125 students—with common planning time was an essential element of a middle school design, personnel became nonnegotiable in her third-year budget.

Beginning Year Two With Turning Points as a Partner

Before teachers left for the summer, they knew what their new schedules would be and the composition of their new teams. I had asked each staff member to provide me with the names of others with whom they would like to teach and the name of any person with whom they would find it difficult. This information was treated confidentially, and I would be the only person reading these requests. During the spring as I put teams together, I met first with the core group of teachers that had eagerly jumped on board. There is always that initial group, usually small, that grasps or holds the same vision. This is the first group that you nurture and enlist to help share the vision. I basically floated the trial balloons with this group. I watched for their reactions and listened to their advice.

When teachers returned in August, we were ready to make the first significant shift. The basic school structures would shift from a traditional junior high following the high school departmental design to a middle school model designed to build relationships with adults and students and to more effectively meet the physical, social, emotional, and academic needs of every child. The organizational structure of classes would no longer track students; students would be heterogeneously grouped, and the goal would be to educate all students to achieve at high academic standards. A support that came with the fall start was a three-year $50,000/year grant that we received from the State to work with the new school reform model, Turning Points.

I was pleased to have the additional funds to support additional professional development. The grant also benefited the district, which consequently provided me with additional credibility with the Superintendent and the School Committee. The grant provided four other elements, two of which I was not so sure I needed—a coach that would work with the school every other week and a network of like-minded schools, which we would meet with several times during the year. The other two elements I knew would be beneficial. All staff and students would participate in a comprehensive self-study that looked at issues of curriculum, instruction, climate, culture, and teacher-student interactions. The results would be analyzed by the Center for Prevention Research Development (CPRD) at the University of Illinois and returned to us in user-friendly graphs. The information would provide us with an overview of where we were as we began implementation of the middle school model and data over time, which would allow us to track progress. The fourth element was a three-day summer institute for a small team. Whether or not the training was useful was less important than the fact that I would have time to plan and debrief with a significant core group of teachers.

Our second year began with a relatively positive attitude considering all the changes. Teachers accepted the teams they were on, and the schedule worked well and significantly improved passing time and discipline problems that frequently occur when 750 students change classes every 41 minutes. However, in October, when the coach from Turning Points arrived, I began to worry about this element of the grant. The coaches typically work with teams, and the usual starting point for Turning Points coaches was looking at student work. I worried that this practice would be one innovation too many and would overwhelm a significant number of teachers. If I allowed the coach to proceed, would I fuel the resistance that was still present although minimal?

Using Systems Thinking to Analyze the Process

The Principal's Role in Balancing Innovations

A systems-thinking model provides a framework for exploring the value of Mary's resistance to additional innovations at this time. From a systems perspective, her resistance may have been a critical step in sustaining the early results from the structural changes and in continuing movement toward the larger vision. The larger vision was based on growth in practices that represent a middle school model as defined by the seven principles in Turning Points. These seven principles identified as essential elements for ensuring academic success for every child are:

- Create small, caring communities for learning
- Teach a core academic program
- Empower teachers and administrators to make decisions
- Prepare teachers for the middle grades
- Develop students' character, creativity, and health
- Re-engage families in the education of young adolescents
- Connect schools and communities (Jackson & Davis, 2000)

Within a year of her arrival, Mary had implemented small communities, or teams; begun the process of empowering teachers to make decisions about how to use time, block scheduling; implemented an advisory program to provide a caring adult for every child and a time for students to talk about issues important to them such as relationships, careers, conflicts, and independence; and extended the school's outreach to families and the community at large. These changes are labeled as "Structural Innovations" in the "Reinforcing Loop" in Figure 2.1, a simplified systems archetype (Kim, 1994). In the second year, teachers and students individually and as teams shared with the coach that the school had a more positive climate (coach's notes, November 1998). Data from a comprehensive self-study survey of all faculty and students also verified a more positive school climate (Center for Prevention Research Development Self-Study Survey, February 1999). By the spring semester of 1999, faculty also repeatedly talked about feeling

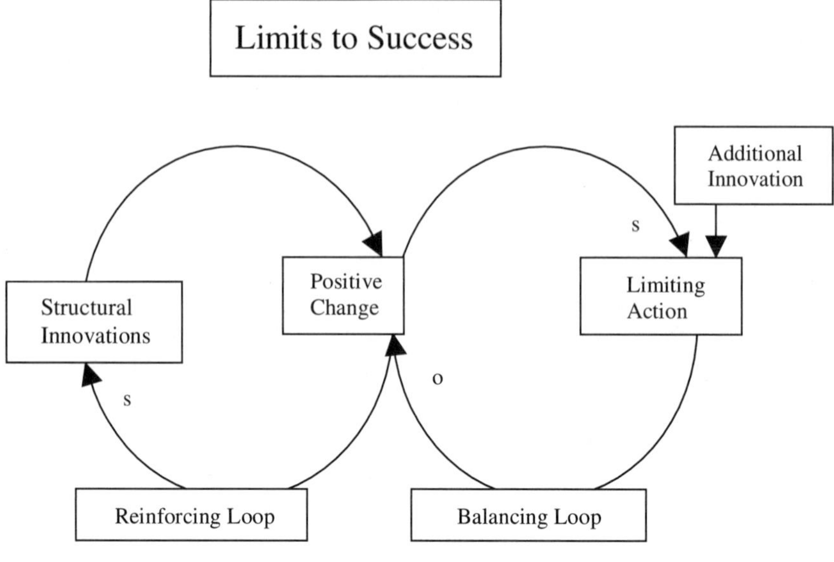

Figure 2.1 The Influence of Structural Innovations on the School System. This diagram is based on the Limits to Success Archetype (Pegasus Communications). In this archetype, (*s*) represents early efforts toward positive change in student achievement. If too many innovations are introduced, then the progress that is being made toward positive change (improved school climate, shared leadership, and ultimately increased student achievement) may slow down significantly or reverse direction. For example, if Mary had allowed the coach to introduce an additional innovation before the faculty was ready to absorb the impact of the previous innovations, then the positive progress might have stopped or even declined below previous levels of achievement.

SOURCE: Reprinted with permission from Pegasus Communication, Inc. *www.pegasuscom.com.*

exhausted. "This is such a different and better place to work than before Mary came, but I am overwhelmed with all the changes we have made" (personal communication, April, 1999).

Mary knew that the teachers were on the brink of overload. She was quite cognizant of the faculty's shifting attitudes. Teams were polite to the coach, but there was definite evidence of tacit resistance to any additional expectations from the teams (conversation between M. Cavalier and coach, spring 1999). Even the hint of additional innovations activated the "Balancing Loop" in the archetype, and the first "Limiting Actions" surfaced in faculty behavior.

Wisely, Mary and the coach agreed to nurture the faculty through the spring and allow time for the new structures to provide evidence of positive change.

> An important core value for me is respecting where each individual person is at the point where we began the process. I needed to recognize how enormous the change was for those teachers who had taught most of their career in a hierarchical, departmentalized, isolated model. I needed to allow adequate time for these teachers to change their mental images about what teaching practices were best for students. There was nothing familiar about the new structures, and there was an implication, although not intended, that the teaching they had practice in the past was bad teaching. For other faculty, sometimes but not always newer faculty, the changes felt comfortable or more accurately fit what they carried as a mental image of what a middle school should be and what they thought "good teaching" looked like. My role, based on my own personal belief system, was to acknowledge each teacher's current beliefs while at the same time providing opportunities for dialogue.

Initiating Shared Leadership

Implementing a Representative Leadership Team

One of the seven Turning Points principles is to "empower teachers and administrators to make decisions." The first step in this direction was to provide teams with common instructional time and give them the freedom to make decisions about how they used this time while still meeting state and district expectations for required instructional minutes. The second step was to implement a representative leadership team.

The National Turning Points Network provides the following description of the leadership team:

> The leadership team coordinates the school's efforts as its members gather information, guide the vision-making process, and communicate the school's progress to all members of the school community. . . . In a Turning Points school, the leadership team takes the central role of leading the change process that a school undergoes while ensuring that the faculty and staff are an integral part of all change. (National Turning Points, 1999, p. 11)

Although the representatives to the leadership team needed to be identified by the various teams within the school, Mary also knew key people that she needed to have involved.

> I personally encouraged official and unofficial school leaders to "volunteer" to be the team representative for the first leadership team. This included teachers who were enthusiastic about the core concepts of the middle school model and teachers who were skeptics or staunch supports of a departmentalized "junior high." Additionally, they all had influence on a segment of the faculty; they all were also excellent teachers committed to high achievement for students.
>
> I knew that if we were going to move the entire faculty, I needed to have all voices at the table. Our first leadership team was a strong, diverse, highly visible group of thoughtful educators. They all took the role seriously, and although some were more dubious about what "shared" leadership would look like in reality, they were all willing to allow it to unfold.

Conditions for Growing Effective School Leadership

The Turning Points coach helped Mary with organizing the agenda for the first meetings and modeled facilitating the meeting for approximately six months. The coach's facilitation helped to provide the team with space and time to reflect (what did each member really want to create by having shared decision making), to inquire (what did other members want to create by having shared decision making), and to become comfortable with her or his role in shared leadership (Argyris & Schön, 1996; Senge et al., 1994). It was not until the spring at the end of Mary's second year that the leadership team began to have in-depth dialogue (Bohm, 1990) about the role of the leadership team, the term of office, how decisions would be made, and what conversations and decisions should be on the leadership team's agenda. Three key elements were in place when these decisions needed to be made: (1) The majority of the leadership-team members were clearly invested in "inquiry and advocacy" (Senge et al., 1994, p. 256); (2) there was a sense of trust in each member's commitment to students; and (3) Mary understood and was willing to put issues on the table for decisions by the leadership team, even if the final decision differed from what she originally advocated.

Using Resources to Reinforce and Sustain Cultural Changes and Nurture Organizational Learning

Summer Funding for Professional Development. The fall of the third year followed a summer of intense curricular work by several of the teams. One of these teams decided that they would like to further integrate the content and that they would pilot an exhibition. This was another part of developing rigorous content that Mary understood well. Once again she provided opportunities for teachers to observe exemplars, and she provided the resources of time, money, and an environment that encouraged risk taking. The coach worked with this team in the summer, which also provided the coach with increased credibility with these teachers. The teachers on this team shared their positive experience with the coach with others, and by fall the majority of the faculty perceived the coach as a valuable resource. The coach's credibility was an important element in the continued growth and development of the leadership team.

> While I knew that I could help the team do the curriculum work, I recognized that the coach also understood integrating curriculum and exhibitions. Letting go of work that I thoroughly enjoy was at first difficult. It meant letting go of control. It also meant letting teachers have more independence and decision-making autonomy. However, I had come to trust the coach and believed that we shared a common vision about the dual importance of excellence and equity in an exemplary middle school.
>
> The team that the coach worked with in the summer had an outstanding first exhibition in late October. Everyone in the school saw all students engaged in the work. During the three intense days of preparation for the first exhibition, students were working in self-directed teams, peer editing the written part of the presentations, and peer coaching the oral presentations. Other teachers walking past the room were amazed to see the level of student engagement. Teachers also recognized that it was not just the traditional "A" students that were being successful; all students, including bilingual students, were reaching mastery.
>
> This success leveraged two critical elements in moving closer to the vision of a high-performing middle school. First, teachers now had a more concrete picture of what excellence and equity for all students looked like, and, second, the coach was now seen as a resource whose vision was aligned with mine.

Using an Outside Coach Effectively. The coach's credibility facilitated the development of shared leadership. At the first leadership team meeting in the fall, the coach reviewed the norms developed in the first year and the importance of consensus. She stressed the significance of one's right to ask that the group continue processing an issue until everyone felt that they could at least live with the decision.

She also used some additional tools for creating an environment that supported dialogue and collaborative problem solving. Dialogue is conversation that opens up the process of inquiry (Bohm, 1990; Senge et al., 1994). Participants share perspectives in an environment that reveals thought process and feelings. The goal is not to advocate but to develop an understanding of each person's point of view.

Introducing New Tools to Facilitate Organizational Learning

Two tools that help with this are "Ladder of Inference" (Argyris, 1990, p. 87) and the "Consultancy Protocol" (National Turning Points, 1999).

Ladder of Inference. The *ladder of inference,* shown in Figure 2.2, describes the mental pathway from observable data and experiences to decisions and actions. According to Argyris (1990), many conversations occur at the assumption stage after each participant has already selected data based on his or her underlying beliefs and added his or her own meaning to the data. When a group is carrying on a dialogue at the assumption level, frequently each party is using different data.

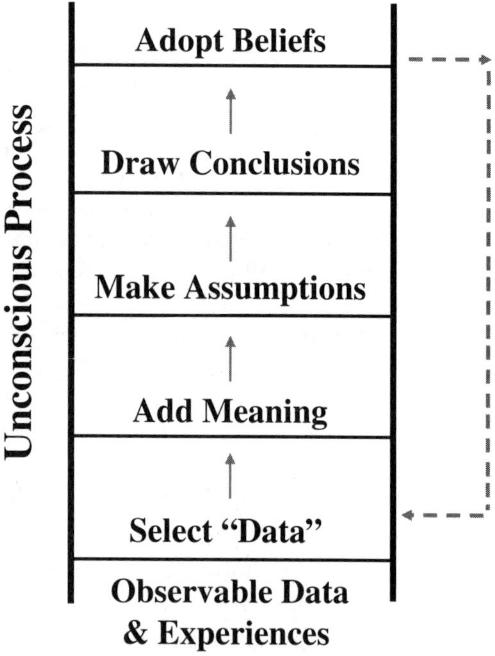

Figure 2.2 Ladder of Inference. The model explains how individual beliefs shape the data we observe or experience, select data for processing, add meaning to the data, draw conclusions from the data, and either confirm our current beliefs or change our beliefs so that we begin to see other data.

SOURCE: Adapted from *The Fifth Discipline Fieldbook* by Peter M. Senge, et al. Used with permission of Doubleday, a division of Random House, Inc.

In my third year at Amherst, it was clear that the faculty was well on the way to creating a model middle school. Teams were delivering more integrated curriculum, and teachers were taking risks in their teaching if they felt it would help students improve as critical thinkers. Teachers were exploring different models of assessment such as dramatic and portfolio exhibitions based on cross-curricular writing from the writers' workshop model.

The importance of shared leadership was more obvious to everyone as we began to delve into real issues around teaching and learning. This year the role of the coach, in helping the leadership team define its work and take the risk to do the work, was crucial. We had a chance to deepen our shared understanding of the team's purpose that fall.

As we continued to look for ways to continue to help all students reach high standards, we began to evaluate how we used time. We realized that as important as our music program was (approximately 65% of the students participate in band, chorus, or orchestra), it was difficult to justify having students participate in two music classes (one being band, orchestra, or chorus and the other an elective on classroom music that all eighth graders took) a day at least one quarter of the year when we had so many students who struggled with reading comprehension in the content areas and with being able to communicate effectively in writing and speaking. All three of these are standards that middle school students should be able to meet when they leave eighth grade.

Using the Consultancy Protocol to Promote Organizational Learning. The Coalition of Essential Schools and the Annenberg School Reform Networks have extensively used the consultancy protocol for looking at student work and solving problems. It represents a process for discussing problems in a structured format that promotes listening to each other as points of view are shared.

After a great deal of personal reflection and discussion with the coach and the administrative team, I brought to the leadership team a recommendation to implement a new teaching position in integrated studies. This teacher would work with each eighth grade team for one quarter to support reading comprehension and implementation of exhibitions, which exemplify critical thinking and effective communication skills. The coach helped us work through the process of making this decision. As demonstrated in the systems diagram [see Fig. 2.1], this was a new innovation, and that meant that there would be implications to other parts of the school system. The most obvious implication was that we would eliminate the second music elective.

Because of our shared communication structure, every team had time to discuss the issue prior to the leadership team meeting. I had been the leadership team member to put this on the agenda, so I described the proposal at the meeting. One of the first responses from a few teachers on the team was that this decision should not be made at the leadership team level; they believed this was a decision for the principal and superintendent. After a brief back-and-forth debate, the coach intervened in our discussion and, modeling the Ladder of Inference, refocused the discussion to data instead of assumptions and beliefs. One piece of information that surfaced was that several representatives and teams had assumed that this was a personnel decision. Our opening discussion was not occurring at the data level but at the assumption level of the ladder. I clarified that this was not a personnel decision and that no current staff member would lose his or her job if we decided to create the new position. Rather, we would be teaching classroom music in an alternative way.

The coach also reminded the leadership team that if they decided not to take the responsibility of making this decision, but to give it back to the principal and the superintendent, then they were abdicating their right to help make decisions about teaching and learning for Amherst.

This comment caused everyone on the leadership team to pause. It was clear that many had not thought through the many layers that create shared leadership. While I have to give away decisions that might be less time consuming to make on my own or with just a few teachers' input, faculty must also take on the responsibility of making difficult choices.

There were several faculty members that voted "no" on changing the elective, but they also asked for more information and an opportunity to go back and discuss it with their teams. The coach suggested that the music director and I, as representatives of both sides of the issue, use a Consultancy Protocol at the next meeting to help present all of the information. The Consultancy Protocol is a structured communication process for solving problems. While usually only one person presents the problem, the music director and I both presented the issue; the faculty then had an opportunity to ask questions for clarification and open-ended questions that might expand our thinking about the problem. After the questioning, the other members of the leadership team had a conversation about the issue while the music director and I listened. This structure took the two extremes out of the conversation and allowed the other faculty members to identify pros and cons. Meanwhile, the music director and I listened and took notes.

At the end of this meeting we still were not ready to reach consensus, but everyone was beginning to feel that they had a more comprehensive picture of the whole. We had begun to move the decision away from being personal to looking at long-term benefits for every student and to thinking systemically about the impact on the community as a whole.

It was the process of working through this issue that fully developed and clarified our understanding of shared leadership. It took approximately four months with give and take on both sides before we decided to add this additional exploratory teacher to the eighth-grade curriculum. Once the decision was made, the faculty was largely supportive of the decision, and I knew that the teacher in the position would be successful because no faculty would be trying to sabotage a decision they did not support.

Teaching and Learning Differently

Emerging Evidence of Sustainable Change

During Mary's fourth year as principal, the Amherst Regional Middle School was the first school to go through the National Turning Points Affirmation Process. This process is based on the belief that, if we are going to claim schools are exemplary models, then there needs to be a clear description of the criteria. Other Turning Points colleagues, principals, teachers, and coaches from other regions and schools need to be involved in evaluating the data the school collects and in observing the school in action.

Although teachers were nervous about a team of outside observers comprehensively evaluating all aspects of the school, they also felt confident that they were moving toward addressing issues of excellence and equity for all students. In addition to examining all aspects of the school life for evidence that the school was fulfilling its mission, the observing team looked for evidence that the school was implementing the seven Turning Points principles.

One area identified as outstanding was the criteria of shared leadership. The final report stated:

> In the area of leadership capacity and a professional collaborative culture, the school received a solid Phase III [Phase III is the highest rating]. The leadership team distributes an agenda a week prior to the meeting so that there is time for faculty input to representatives. Minutes also are distributed within days of the meeting to the entire faculty.
>
> The decision making process used in the leadership team demonstrates a commitment to a democratic school community. (Amherst Final Report, February 2001)

The school had embraced change and recognized that they were teaching, learning, and assessing in a very different way than when Mary had first come to Amherst Regional Middle School. They also had come to understand that, from a systems perspective, change is constant and that they always would need to gather, analyze, and use data to make informed decisions. The faculty also recognized that every student was now being asked to achieve at a high academic level and that structures to support reaching and maintaining the goal were in place.

Institutionalizing the Learning Cycle to Sustain Organizational Learning

> We also realized that as our external coach prepared to leave that we would need to have internal people who could facilitate in the same role. We would

> need someone who would support teams in looking at student work, help with problem solving, support the exhibitions, and continue to be an objective observer at the leadership team meeting. Although the National Turning Points' final report had given us a rating of excellent, we also knew that we would need to continue to monitor the process. There were going to be other difficult decisions to be made, and it would be helpful to have an outside voice that helped us to pursue dialogue prior to decision making.
>
> The leadership team agreed that this role would be more difficult for an internal person than it had been for the external coach. We decided to install three internal coaches. One coach would do most of the work with teams, one would support exhibitions, and one would work primarily with the leadership team.

The affirmation process was conducted in 2000, and the National Turning Points officially voted approval in February 2001. The Amherst Regional Middle School has continued to thrive and positively evolve. Leadership is at the individual level for students and teachers, at the interdisciplinary team level, in inquiry groups, and in the leadership team. Mary Cavalier continues to serve the critical role as the keeper of the vision. She never forgets that the school's focus must always be on the core purpose of the school: to ensure that every child is able to achieve at a high academic level in a caring, supportive community of learners. Through her thoughtful implementation of shared leadership, she, the faculty, the students, and the community at large have created a "learning organization."

Amherst as a Learning Organization

Together, the teachers have created a living, interrelated, self-renewing organism that understands the need for changing their approach for reforming and restructuring schools (Gardner, 1981; Wheatley & Kellner-Rogers 1996). Studies in business and in education identify organizations that support this kind of change as ones that are characterized by flexibility, adaptability, collaboration, creativity, and the ability to continuously learn and change (Darling-Hammond, 1990; Hargraves, 1995). They are referred to as "learning organizations." Learning organizations are inclined toward well-planned experimentation, are ready to rethink means and ends, are oriented toward inquiry, and recognize the human potential for learning on behalf of the organization (Argyris & Schön, 1996).

The Amherst faculty recognizes that teaching can no longer be viewed as a "routine job conducted with craft-like knowledge, in isolation from other adults, in a hierarchical status structure. The new perception of teaching, in contrast, views it as a non-routine activity drawing on a reliable body of technical knowledge and conducted in collaboration with other professional colleagues" (Leithwood, Begley, & Cousins, 1994, p. 126).

The professionalism of teaching supports the importance of an expanded foundation of pedagogical knowledge, content knowledge, and pedagogical-content knowledge (Clandinin, 1985; Elbaz, 1981; Shulman, 1987). "Thus the meaning of change for the future does not simply involve implementing single innovations effectively. It means a radical change in the culture of schools and the conception of teaching as a profession" (Fullan & Stiegelbauer, 1991, p. 142).

Although one cannot with absolute certainty predict the future of schools, what is evident at Amherst is that the vision is not Mary's alone. It has become embedded in the culture of the school and is shared by all. When Mary at some point leaves Amherst Regional Middle School, the vision will not go with her. Just as the school was able to sustain the role of the coach, they will also sustain their belief that teaching is a nonroutine activity that needs a collaborative, democratic environment.

Implications for the Future

Implications for Schools

The implications of this kind of democratic collaboration and professionalism are significant for students and teachers. The school has already seen statistically significant changes in standardized test data and expects the already noticeable trend toward higher academic achievement to continue to grow as teaching and learning continues to change. English Language Arts scores on the Massachusetts Comprehensive Assessment System test have risen steadily, both at the middle school and high school levels. Scores in mathematics have not seen as much improvement. Consequently, the school has an Inquiry Group studying this issue, which has identified some of the sources of the problem. The group intends to bring an action plan to the leadership team in the coming months. Suspension rates have dropped from more than 60 students during Mary's first year at the middle school to less than 20 this past year. There has been a corresponding increase in attendance rates. The list of students receiving D's and F's has declined significantly as well.

Teaching and learning are now the topics of dialogue at a majority of common planning time meetings, a noteworthy shift from the focus on student problems that was predominant in the beginning of Mary's tenure.

The dialogue among students is changing as well, with conversations about achievement and learning an important part of the school life of students. At the end of the third year, one team held exhibitions where each student was required to independently present individual research and be able to demonstrate several components of critical thinking, questioning, using prior knowledge, analyzing, synthesizing, and drawing inferences. At the end of the fourth year, several teams were involved in similar exhibitions, which asked students to publicly explain their work, both written and oral, and defend their conclusions. This year all eight teams at the school will ask their students to participate in exhibitions that demonstrate deep, connected understanding. There is a distinct atmosphere of shared, serious purpose in the school, with students and staff clearly committed to common goals of learning.

Implications for Preparing and Supporting Principals

Prior to coming to Amherst, Mary had taught in a magnet school based on the Coalition of Essential Schools whole school reform model, a model similar in its focus to the Turning Points model. She had a vivid mental model of an effective, democratic middle school, which expected high achievement for every student. She also received her administrative training at Bank Street College of Education. This college has been a leader in child-centered education for more than eighty years. Its mission "is to discover the environments in which children grow and learn to their full potential, and to educate teachers and others to create these environments" (*www.bnkst.edu;* accessed November 2001).

As long as we continue to educate teachers and principals in a hierarchical model, then that is the mental model they will teach and lead from. For future educators to be able to create environments in which middle school students can grow and learn to their full potential, teachers will need to experience such an environment in preparation programs and in their school systems. Through this type of experience they will begin to develop a clear conceptual model of shared leadership, equity, and excellence.

Implications for Districts

Implementing shared leadership at the school level also has implications for the district. The superintendent in Amherst was not a dynamic or visionary leader, but he was willing to provide Mary with the freedom and financial support to implement the new structures. This *laissez-faire* approach worked for the Amherst Middle School because it is in a small district with only one regional middle school and one high school. Shared leadership is more challenging when we look at urban schools (Burke, 2002). In an urban district, 20–40% of the students change schools within the district during the school year, which causes superintendents, striving to ensure that "no child is left behind," to mandate district curriculum, to develop more standardized district tests, and to impose specific expectations on schools, which in turn means that schools have little discretion over the budget.

This does not mean that urban principals and superintendents should abandon the principles of shared leadership, equity, and excellence. Instead, superintendents need to collaborate with district administrators, principals, and parents to clarify a broad shared vision. As with the leadership team at Amherst, when all members of the community are represented in setting the vision, then they will be more likely to implement the vision. Once a more global vision is set, principals need autonomy over their own budget, staffing, and curricular planning in order to work with their faculty and community to create a school-based vision that serves the unique culture of the school but aligns with the district vision. Urban schools can no longer simply accept that the size and complexity of their district allows them to step back in their leadership.

Implications for the Reform Models

Whole-school researched-based reform models also have an opportunity to provide support to districts and principals from multiple schools with common grade levels. Through network structures, reform models can provide the modeling, professional development, time, and space for like-minded schools to meet and formulate a common vision of teaching, learning, and assessment. With the commitment at the district level and external support from research-based reform models, each school community can develop a rigorous and relevant curriculum collectively. Each school can engage in creating a learning organization that is able to continuously learn and change to meet the ever-changing needs of young adolescents.

The Amherst model indicates that a democratic school with collaborative leadership and shared decision making is more likely to create a student-centered environment where students and teachers can grow and learn together. If we want other schools to achieve similar results, then large urban districts and small urban and rural districts will need to shift their mental construct of school and provide each school in the system with more autonomy. Amherst has been accountable. The state and the district were clear with Mary when she was hired that it was no longer acceptable to educate only some of the students. Every child needed to have an adult advocate in the school, to have an opportunity to experience a democratic environment, and to be supported in achieving at high academic levels. This is the dream that all schools must hold for every child.

References

Argyris, C. (1990). *Overcoming organizational defenses. Facilitating organizational learning*. Boston: Allyn & Bacon.

Argyris, C., & Schön, D. A. (1996). *Organizational learning II: Theory, method, and practice*. Reading, MA: Addison-Wesley.

Bohm, D. (1990). *On dialogue*. Cambridge, MA: Pegasus Communication.

Bradley, A. (2000, Oct. 4). A feast of offerings. *Education Week, 20*(5), 32–34.

Burke, P. H. (2001). *Amherst final report*. Boston, MA: The Center for Collaborative Education.

Burke, P. H. (2002). *Sustainable results in urban middle schools: How principals use systems thinking to lead effective change*. Unpublished doctoral dissertation, Lesley University, Cambridge, MA.

Carnegie Council on Adolescent Development. (1989). *Turning points: Preparing American youth for the 21st century*. Washington, D.C.: Author.

Center for Prevention Research and Development. (1999). *School improvement self-study*. Champaign, IL: University of Illinois.

Clandinin, D. J. (1985). Personal practical knowledge: A study of teachers' classroom images. *Curriculum Inquiry, 15*(4), 361–384.

Darling-Hammond, L. (1990, December). Achieving our goals: Superficial or structural reforms? *Phi Delta Kappan, 72*(4), 286–295.

Elbaz, F. (1981). The teacher's "practical knowledge": Report of a case study. *Curriculum Inquiry, 11*, 43–71.

Fullan, M. G., & Stiegelbauer, S. (1991). The new meaning of educational change. New York: Teachers College Press.

Gardner, J. (1981). *Self-renewal: The individual and the innovative society*. (Revised Ed.). New York: W.W. Norton.

Garvin, J. (1993). *Learning how to kiss a frog*. New York: Basic Books.

Hargraves, A. (1995). Changing teachers, changing times: Teachers' work and culture in the postmodern age. New York: Teachers College Press.

Jackson, A. W., & Davis, G. A. (2000). *Turning Points 2000: Educating adolescents in the 21st century*. New York: Teachers College Press.

Kim, D. H. (1994). *Systems archetypes I: Diagnosing system issues and designing high leverage interventions*. (Toolbox Reprint Series). Cambridge, MA: Pegasus Communications, Inc.

Leithwood, K., Begley, P. T., & Cousins, J. B. (1994). Developing expert leadership for future schools. Washington, D.C.: Falmer Press.

National Middle School Association. (1995). *This we believe.* Columbus, OH: Author.

National Turning Points. (1999). *Turning Points: Transforming middle schools: Guide to collaborative culture and shared leadership.* Boston: Center for Collaborative Education.

Senge, P., Kleiner, A. C., Roberts, C., Ross, R., & Smith, B. (1994). *The fifth discipline fieldbook: Strategies and tools for building a learning organization.* New York: Currency Doubleday.

Shulman, L. S. (1987). Those who understand: Knowledge growth in teaching. *Educational Research, 15*(2), 4–14.

Stevenson, C. (2002). *Teaching ten to fourteen year olds.* Boston: Allyn & Bacon.

Wheatley, M. J., & Kellner-Rogers, M. (1996). *A simpler way.* San Francisco: Berrett-Koehler Publishers.

3

Creating Meaningful Opportunities for Collaboration

Vishna A. Herrity

Pat Morales

Visioning is definitely one of Joanna's greatest strengths. She really does have vision, and the thing is that she has the short vision, the medium, and the long. She is really able to go through that and say, for the next year, the next month . . . whatever. But I think what is really her greatest strength is that she has the most positive attitude that things will happen, they will get better, and that she will be able to make a difference. . . . She has a sixth sense. Her desire to make the school environment better for the children, and therefore for us, is so powerful that I am so comfortable being around her because she just exudes it. I have been around principals that are very smart (she is very smart) but they don't have that power. I don't know how to call it. I guess that is visioning too. What I am saying is that she actually lets us be part of her aura.

—Connie Viera, Sixth-Grade Teacher
Learning Together Charter School

As schools have entered into the new millennium, they are facing complex and dynamic changes. Our educational system faces major demographic changes with tremendous increases in immigrant populations. Family structures have changed, with larger numbers of single-parent families, more mothers entering the work force, greater family mobility, and more children living in poverty. Furthermore, as a society, we have transitioned from a focus on industrialization to an emphasis on information technology and globalization. American schools must be willing to undertake major reforms to meet the challenge of creating a citizenry that will develop lifelong learning skills, competence in solving global problems, and cross-cultural communication skills. In order to accommodate these societal changes, some reformers have created "schools for the 21st century" and chosen administrators who can lead the schools effectively (Beck & Murphy, 1993). In an era of educational reform, Michael Fullan (1993) suggests that schools need "a leader who expresses but also extends what is valued enabling others to do the same, teamwork and shared purpose which accepts both individualism and collectivism as essential to organizational learning, and the organization which is dynamically connected to its environment" (p. viii).

The case study in this chapter describes the journey of an elementary school principal to institute a dynamic change process at Learning Together Charter School. Principal Joanna Santos serves as a model for transforming a school community using the charter school legislation to distribute leadership and carry out the school's commitment to biliteracy for all students—two ideas that are counter to the school district's norms and policies. Her ability to create meaningful opportunities for collaboration, empower teachers and parents to become leaders, promote creative problem solving, and institutionalize shared decision making enabled Principal Santos to transform the culture and climate of the school. Moreover, through shared leadership, she was instrumental in enhancing communication, increasing community support and school resources, and, most important, increasing the academic achievement of all students.

Context: Learning Together Charter School

Learning Together Charter School is a microcosm of the cultural, linguistic, and socioeconomic diversity reflected in the local city population. The central California elementary school was founded in 1926 and serves a bimodal K–6 student population of nearly 600 students. Of those, 52% are Hispanic or Latino and 43.6% are Caucasian, 2% African American, 1.6% Asian American, 0.5% American Indian or Alaska Native, and 0.3% Filipino American. The district boundaries were redrawn in the 1980s to achieve integration. As a result, approximately 50% of the student body is bussed from a lower socioeconomic neighborhood.

In 1993, the school was granted a "charter" from the state of California, forging a new partnership between the state, local district, and the school. Operating as a charter school gives it the authority, flexibility, and latitude to develop an innovative instructional program for its ethnically and socioeconomically diverse student population. The school has used this flexibility to hire a diverse staff and specialists. The school has 32 fulltime certificated classroom teachers, one resource specialist teacher, a special day class teacher, a librarian, a technology teacher, an assistant principal, and a principal. Parttime staff includes two speech and language specialists, a school psychologist, a counselor, and teachers of instrumental music, visual arts, ceramics arts, drama, and vocal music.

The school is autonomous in regard to its governance, including on-site administration, staff development, curriculum development, methodology, and delivery of instruction. It sets its own academic standards, instructional programs, assessment measures, and budgets without adhering to state and district policies.

The cornerstone of Learning Together Charter School is its commitment to provide a two-way bilingual program for Spanish and English speakers in grades K–6. Although maintenance programs are relatively rare in two-way models (Christian and Whitcher, 1995), the Learning Together Charter School program has evolved into a maintenance model with a two-way component. The program currently consists of primary language instruction for early and advanced literacy of Spanish speakers, basic English language development and Spanish language development for both language groups, primary language in the core curriculum, and a structured approach to the addition of English literacy in the intermediate grades. Moreover, the school offers an after-school advanced Spanish literature class for Spanish speakers who are achieving at high levels in the fifth and sixth grades, as well as an advanced Spanish class for English speakers starting in the third grade.

Learning Together Charter School offers a multitude of programs to meet the diverse needs of *all* of the students in an integrated, coherent manner that builds on state standards and reflects high expectations. According to Principal Joanna Santos, "It is like a puzzle that always fits. I think that we have designed it by matching the strengths of teachers, what they bring, to what the students need, what materials we would like to use, and what we have access to, and a bit of what our families want" (interview, 2002).

The climate of the school affirms the worth and diversity of all students through a comprehensive program that helps students to succeed and excel by engaging in rich and varied activities. The school's philosophy emphasizes creative and collaborative learning that combines academic instruction with firsthand experiences. Students learn to work cooperatively through such projects as the Sixth Grade Garden, which grows produce for the school's cafeteria; the Los Marineros Marine Biology Program sponsored by the Natural History Museum; performances and exhibitions such as Biography Night, Art Show, and Science Night; and musicals and dramatic productions such as the Bilingual Theatre Group.

An Early Intervention program is provided daily for 30 minutes to students in grades K–3 who are identified as having the greatest need in the area of English and Spanish literacy. An Artist in Residence program enables local artists to work in the classrooms to provide fine arts instruction. A total of six art specialists—three in the performing arts (e.g., drama, storytelling, and music) and three in the visual arts (e.g., fine arts, ceramics, and graphic arts through technology)—provide instruction in the arts. Having received a grant from the California Arts Council, an outdoor/indoor art studio, called the "Splash Zone," has been created. Opportunities for extended learning, including literacy classes, computer technology, Odyssey of the Mind, a program for divergent thinkers, Young Masters Art Class, and recreation programs, are offered after school. The after-school Homework Center (for grades 2–6) provides daily instructional support and study skill development to students, including English language learners. With the leadership of the school psychologist/counselor, upper grade students have been trained in conflict resolution through the "Learning Together Peacemakers" Program.

Study Approach

Although there seems to be some debate regarding the definition of a case study, Lancy (1993) describes it as "the method of choice for studying interventions or innovations" (p. 140). In order to obtain information related to the shared decision-making process in the natural setting of the participants, qualitative research methodology was employed. Throughout this case study, pseudonyms are used in reference to the school and all participants to ensure anonymity.

Data were gathered primarily through in-depth interviews with the principal, assistant principal, a primary grade teacher, and an upper grade teacher. The rationale for using in-depth interviews was to obtain valid information grounded in the daily experiences of the participants currently working at Learning Together Charter School. This study used a protocol of open-ended questions in formal interviews as a means of standardizing the topics under investigation. The open-ended nature of the interviews enabled participants to answer from their own point of reference. According to Marshall and Rossman (1989), the strength of this methodology includes obtaining large amounts of contextual data in the form of words that can later be used as quotations to substantiate the findings. Additional information was obtained through a review of school artifacts (e.g., newsletters, program descriptions, accountability reports, research articles on the school's achievement, and grant proposals).

Content analysis was based on Spradley's (1980) Developmental Research Sequence. Domain analysis yielded specific patterns in shared leadership practices by the principal. Taxonomic and componential analyses provided insights into the organization of the domains, established semantic relationships in practices, and revealed specific attributes of the distributive leadership process.

Perspectives on Leadership

The principal's leadership is one of the most distinguishing features of effective schools, especially those that serve ethnically and culturally diverse students (Sizemore, 1990). Today's leaders must have the capacity to deal with complex issues, collaborate with diverse constituencies, and remain informed about the best practices in education. They must infuse the school community with compelling ideas that serve as a vision for school reform and create a purpose for improvement initiatives. Effective leaders must also be responsive to the changing demographics of America's schools and the increasing needs of the students to attain high levels of academic achievement so that they can meet the demands of the Information Age and become contributing members of society. According to Greenfield (1995),

> Effective school administration is defined as a condition wherein successful and appropriate teaching and learning are occurring for all students and teachers in the school; the morale of students, teachers, and other school members is positive; and parents, other community members, and the school district's administration judge the school to be effectively fulfilling both the letter and the spirit of local, state, and federal laws and policies. (p. 61)

Hoy and Miskel (1991) view leadership as "cultural and symbolic, as well as instrumental and behavioral. Successful leaders infuse value into organizations, thereby creating institutional meaning and purpose that go beyond the technical requirements of the job" (p. 299). In undertaking major school reforms that transform schools, these leaders must be willing to take risks and build coalitions that will provide broad-based support for the change process over an extended period of time.

Research suggests that transformational leaders must identify the need for revitalization or change, establish a vision for the future, and institutionalize the change on a long-term basis (Tichy and Devanna, 1986). Burns (1978) further contends that such leaders are able to create followers, mobilize resources, and provide encouragement and support for staff members. They organize and facilitate the work of the system within the school to focus on the vision and shared goals; this in turn promotes a joint commitment for continual improvement. Moreover, these leaders develop incentives for the school staff to enhance their educational practices, which ultimately increases the capacity of the individuals and the school community to improve continually. In Senge's (1990) words, a transformational leader is systematically "building organizations where people continually expand their capabilities to understand complexity, clarify vision, and improve shared mental models—they are responsible for learning" (p. 340). Senge further states, "The rationale for any strategy for building a learning organization revolves around the premise that such organizations will produce dramatically improved results" (1996, p. 44).

This case study begins with the key educational events that shaped Joanna's ideas of leadership and provided models of how to share leadership. The data are then presented to illustrate the journey toward shared leadership; the importance of teamwork; the role of the principal as a catalyst for undertaking the change process; the specific strategies conducive to establishing shared leadership; the impact of shared leadership on teachers, families, and students; and the lessons learned from the process.

A Principal's Journey Toward Shared Leadership

Principal Joanna Santos came to the school in 1992, having previously served as a teacher and an assistant principal in a northern California school district. Inspired by a superintendent and assistant superintendent that embodied transformational leadership, she began to develop ideas of innovation and cutting-edge leadership. According to Joanna, the two visionary leaders "believed in nurturing the strengths of all staff. And that's why I got into administration, because they saw the leadership potential in me when I didn't."

Moving to the central California coastal region was purely for the "sense of community" that it offered, an enchanting place in which one would want to not only work but also eventually retire. The move came during a turbulent time in the new district, however. Warned by colleagues not to go there, she went anyway—determined to chart a course that would ultimately transform the school and receive the Distinguished California School status twice in five years.

Working in the new district proved to be extremely challenging. The spirit of collaboration that she had been accustomed to previously did not exist. Instead, there was tremendous central office bureaucracy and micromanagement by the school board. Moreover, she perceived the district to be at least 15 years behind the times in its curricular and instructional practices. This proved to be constraining for a principal with a mindset and desire for innovation. It was soon apparent that the school's administration, teachers, support staff, and parents were *all* ready for a change. Joanna recollected,

> I did have a vision and it has been surpassed. I wanted to change the culture and the climate of the school, the attitudes of the teachers, and the social and emotional atmosphere. I wanted to improve curriculum and assessment. I wanted teachers to serve as role models for the students. They can't problem-solve in class with students if they can't do it with their colleagues.

It was during that difficult time that the school charter law was passed. "I knew what we had to do, and we could only do it through the charter vehicle," Joanna said. She further explained,

> I think that watching the power of collaboration and the empowerment of teachers in that district and what can happen when you build on the strengths of the community, when you nurture leadership . . . nurture people's passion about something . . . that is *so powerful.*
>
> The other thing that I learned up there is the power of teaming. . . . There were about 45 people that met monthly in this district and . . . had the decision-making power in language arts. It wasn't the board. It wasn't the superintendent . . . That was *very powerful.* People were not paid to come. They came because they had a passion about it. They wanted to make a difference. They had the power. When people have the power to do something, the control over what happens with their passion, then they will do it.
>
> So when I came down to this district, I realized that none of that was happening. . . . The power of team; the locus of control being within the

> individual, . . . and for the school site meeting the needs. It was a major shift. The vehicle for that was the charter, because it could not have happened at that time because of the leadership in the district.

The Power of Teamwork

Although Joanna indicated that she had no formal training in the concept of teamwork during her administrator preparation program, she "had seen the power of it." She could pick out the pieces of it that worked. Through her participation in the Accelerated Schools Program (Levin, 1995) training in her previous district, as a facilitator, she learned essential group process activities. Joanna explained:

> The notion of taking stock of your situation, your school, and building on the strengths within your school, those two concepts are the key in what I do. . . . But also just watching how you can move a district forward if you have buy-in from people and they are really doing things that they know make a difference.

The change process requires people to think out of the box—to explore new paths that have not been taken before. It means creating both a vision and a dream of what the school *can* become. Block (1987) posits that, "Creating a vision forces us to take a stand for a preferred future" (p. 102). Reflecting on the pre-charter days, Joanna stated,

> Well, I think that sometimes the school culture has a restrictive feeling to it. That is that they say, "We can't." It's almost like not taking control of your own destiny . . . as a school and using excuses for not doing that. So that's kind of the culture I found here. "Well, they won't let us do it. We can't do that because . . . " What I realized was that even when those excuses were removed, we still didn't think outside the box because really, ultimately, it was they had never done it. *They didn't know the power of a team.* They did not know what it meant to think outside the box. . . . Then . . . they built their grade-level teams and we started realizing that yes, things can happen. The control shift changed but it took about . . . three years, once we had the permission—the charter—to really start making that ultimate shift.

Maintaining the vision of collaboration from her previous district in her mind, Joanna knew where she needed to go. Although she had experienced the power of teamwork and had a sense of direction in her mind, there was no predetermined agenda for creating change. She explained,

> I actually came here with two things going simultaneously. One was to find out what really worked—to find out how I could really support . . . the academic, social, and emotional growth of children and adults, . . . then looking from my perspective at what I know has worked from my past and seeing if I could bring my strength into the system and the organization. I think the two things for me were . . . *the power of teaming* and *the power of collaborative leadership.*

The Principal as a Catalyst for Shared Leadership and Change

Unlike the principal in a traditional school, who has as one of his or her primary functions that of enforcement of state and district mandates, policies, and compliance regulations, Joanna views her role quite differently. She sees her primary role as a "choreographer" who sets the stage—the "producer" who creates the play called "Education." The play is an improvisation that flows with the creativity of the participants. The team of teachers, parents, and support staff write the script. Thus, she provides the inspiration to build the momentum for innovation, facilitates and coordinates the activities of the shared decision-making bodies, and garners resources to enable them to carry out their plans.

John C. Maxwell (2001) refers to individuals such as Joanna Santos as *catalysts,* or "get-it-done-and-then-some people" (p. 74). He asserts that catalysts exhibit certain qualities that differentiate them from other individuals. These characteristics include:

1. Intuition: the innate ability to sense things that others cannot sense.
2. Communication: the verbal ability to get the team to take action.
3. Passion: a strong love for what they do that is shared with others.
4. Talent: the skill or ability to do the job and achieve results that gives them credibility.
5. Creativity: the ability to think innovatively or "outside the box."
6. Initiation: the strength to implement innovative ideas.
7. Responsibility: the personal accountability for making things happen.
8. Generosity: the willingness to use resources (e.g., time, money) to improve the team.
9. Influence: the ability to lead others in ways other individuals cannot.

Joanna Santos embodies all of these characteristics and is viewed as a catalyst for the change process, as is evidenced through the interviews conducted at the school. Paula Sanchez, a long-time teacher at the school and currently the assistant principal, recounts how the whole change process evolved when Joanna first learned about the new charter school legislation at a district Principals' Council Meeting:

> That was the first time that Joanna had heard about it and she started to do some research on it. . . . She talked to a couple of real critical parents—key players that sounded pretty excited about it. She got her information together and presented it to the staff with these parents with her. . . . Every time she would go to the staff with the idea, she would always ask them at the end, "Is this something we should continue or not?" She wanted complete honesty because she felt like she was not going to be able to do this by herself and did not want to do it unless she had the full support of the staff and parents. So, although the idea started with Joanna, my sense was that it never would have come to fruition without the support of both teachers and parents.

In his research on comprehensive school reform, Hutchins (1988) posits that the vision of the schools for the twenty-first century is "based on wide-scale participation of stakeholders in American education" (p. 49). In an effort to provide broad-based participation in the change process, Joanna held community and parent meetings in the evening where she conducted visioning activities. She asked, "If your child went to the ideal school, what would it look like?" Receiving support from the community, she also garnered support for the change process from teachers, classified staff, union representatives, and district officials. Interviews with support staff confirm that Joanna's inclusion of all stakeholders was critical to the change process:

> Joanna was very good about making sure that she had buy-in from all of the different stakeholders before they actually went forward. She met with the teachers' union representative. She met with . . . one of the school board representatives. . . . She had done all of the networking before writing the charter and then presenting it to the board for approval. . . . She said that if she did not feel that she had the support of everyone, she would not have gone through with it.

The process created numerous challenges, however. Paramount was the ability to make a major decision regarding school autonomy without alienating district officials. Joanna felt that it was critical to have a "political perspective"—to be "part of the team, but not wear the same uniform."

The charter was written by a team composed of the principal, an informal parent leader, and a teacher representative with "a vision and passion for change." Everyone associated with the school community had opportunities for input. As a result, a contract was negotiated to create a charter school as permitted under Senate Bill 1448 of the State of California. When the charter was taken to the school board for approval, Joanna invited the teachers, support staff, key parents, community representatives, local university faculty, California Teachers Association representatives, and classified staff representatives to attend the meeting. Being politically astute, she wanted to demonstrate that a broad-based school constituency supported the charter. The board voted unanimously to support the charter application.

Although the charter application was approved, questions still arose such as, "What does the charter really mean? What does it actually represent?" Joanna's perspective, given here, captures the essence of the charter's meaning:

> My values are embedded in this charter. They are. That's the value of each individual, the teaming idea, and the respect and nurturing of children and the adults in the community—bringing in the parents, opening the doors for parents and building on parents' strengths.

The sentiment expressed by Joanna Santos is also a reflection of what Newmann and Wehlage (1995) stress is needed for successful school restructuring: "If schools want to enhance their organizational capacity to boost student learning they should work on building a professional community that is characterized by shared purpose, collaborative activity, and collective responsibility among staff" (p. 37).

The Road to Shared Leadership

One view of leadership claims that leaders exist only because they have developed a relationship with their followers (Foster, 1989). In this notion, leadership may be considered as a shared, or communal, process in which followers can assume leadership roles and leaders can become followers. Thus, leaders can nurture and create other leaders. Joanna Santos also illustrates this view when she says, "Leadership is creating a setting where there are many leaders." As a result of personally experiencing the power of shared leadership, Joanna is comfortable with the notion of not always being in the forefront and empowering others to lead: "I want to walk with people and be part of the team, not out front."

Moreover, Joseph Murphy (1992) contends that in order to prepare students for a society based on complex knowledge, a shift is needed in the underlying principles of education and the way in which schools are organized, governed, and managed, which also includes a different form of school leadership. The change impacts social relationships and the fundamental conceptions of school management. It results in a shift from the principal as a manager to the principal as a facilitator, from the teacher as a worker to the teacher as a leader (Sergiovanni, 1991).

Although these shifts in school management and shared leadership are often difficult to undertake, this case study reveals that five key milestones were accomplished on the road to shared leadership: ownership of the charter, earning trust, creative use of time and resources, creation of a leadership team, and valuing teacher professionalism.

Ownership in the Charter

Taylor and Rosenbach (1989) posit that in entrepreneurial educational organizations, all of the team members ultimately provide both innovation and support to achieve a shared vision when there is a sense of ownership by the whole team. The path to shared decision making at Learning Together started with the process of *ownership in the charter itself.* Paula Sanchez explains the significance of creating ownership:

> I think it started with that because by getting those stakeholders' buy-in, it became not just her but everyone had ownership in the charter. That was the beginning of the whole shared leadership because she was not the sole decision maker as far as the charter went. It was a group decision. By participating in that decision, they were participating in the leadership. . . . The governing council gave opportunities for teachers to engage in some leadership activities—yes, both teachers and parents.

Collaboration was the key factor in fostering the school improvement and change process at Learning Together Charter School. With the formation of the 11-member Governing Council, consisting of three parents, four teachers, the principal, a classified representative, a community representative, and a school board appointee, the shared leadership process was solidified. The governing council has responsibility for meeting the accountability requirements established by Senate Bill 1448 and the school's charter. The council also sets the school calendar, develops and approves the budget, and makes revisions to the charter. According to Beck and Murphy (1996), "If an autonomous site takes seriously the challenge of reform, administrators, teachers, and parents must find ways to go beyond the maintenance of status quo to a state characterized by improved learning outcomes and organizational transformation" (p. 119). Although the council always promoted cooperation and consensus building to ensure the achievement of program goals, the process evolved gradually. According to Joanna, it took three years for the council to become a functioning decision-making organization.

Earning Trust

The change process was gradual, not only for the council but for teachers as well. The roles of teachers and administrator needed clarification. Before Joanna could get teachers to buy into the concept of shared leadership, she had to *earn their trust* as an "administrator":

> You know, it didn't happen overnight and I think there's still a mistrust of administration—administrators. It just exists. It took me a long time to come to terms with that because in my previous district maybe I already had built-in respect as a teacher. . . . When I came here, I was just an administrator. That was hard. My words had different meaning. When I'm just having a conversation with people, I think I am part of the group. They don't. They think I'm the administrator. . . . It has taken a while to build that.

Trust is an essential quality of leaders who inspire movements that create social change and successful organizations that achieve their vision (Bennis & Goldsmith, 1994). The authors note that leaders who can establish trust must possess four characteristics: vision, empathy, consistency, and integrity. These qualities in themselves are not enough to create trustworthiness unless the staff and community can see the principal actively practicing these behaviors on an ongoing basis, as is the case with Joanna. Connie Viera explains how a sense of trust in the belief system of the principal caused her to be more proactive.

> I guess what happens . . . is that when she . . . says that it is really going to work out, we really will get enough money, or there really will be enough kids . . . then I think what happens is, first, I relax because it is going to happen somehow. Then I participate more. I start asking kids for more help or I ask parents for more money. . . . I become active.
>
> Whereas, if you think that something is not going to happen, sometimes you just freeze or you just go back and say, "That is not going to be a reality, so I am not going to help with it." . . . But because I am trusting that it is going to happen, then I might be able to be a little bit more creative and come up with my own ideas to help the school. . . . I guess again that whenever you *trust* someone, then you are able to throw out some of your crazy ideas and go with it.

Creative Use of Time and Resources

Joanna Santos recalled that when she first came to Learning Together Charter School, teachers were already constrained by many of the factors that all elementary teachers face, including the number of different subjects they teach, adapting curricula to individual needs of students, and increased pressures for accountability. In order for teachers to begin to work together in grade-level teams and assume leadership roles in the decision-making process, Joanna realized that it was necessary to "create more time." As a first step, she eliminated yard duty for the teachers; other support staff instead provided the necessary supervision. This decision not only provided teachers with 30 minutes of additional time, but it also signaled that they were being considered as professionals—as instructional leaders—in the mind of the principal.

In an effort to further extend planning-time opportunities, Joanna hired a physical education teacher and three instructional assistants. While students engaged in physical education activities, teachers worked on committees or grade-level meetings. In addition, the school day was extended by 45 minutes, building in planning time and preparation periods during the school day rather than after school. Lastly, late-start Fridays were instituted for students, giving teachers yet more time to plan. One Friday a month, they were required to meet as a grade-level team.

Teacher interviews confirm that this *creative use of scheduling* and *providing fiscal resources* to create more time was instrumental in fostering an atmosphere of professionalism where teachers could begin to assume leadership roles in the decision-making process. According to Paula Sanchez,

> When we started the P.E. program and then started the late-start Friday, it gave the teachers the time to meet in these grade-level teams. The grade-level teams started to become a more formalized process as they had specific tasks to do, such as writing the year-long plan. . . . There were three of us, with three very different styles and opinions about 5th-grade curriculum, to sit down and actually come up with a year-long plan that fit everybody. We compared every month with the framework, specified what you were going to cover . . . and by when. The grade levels started to work as teams, and that gave them some leadership.

Creation of a Leadership Team

In addition to the governing council, which involved all stakeholders in decision making, Joanna wanted to create a setting where staff members could be empowered and nurtured in their leadership roles, with the ultimate goal of creating a cadre of leaders. She wanted her staff to experience the benefits of participating in a decision-making process that focused on critical areas such as curriculum and assessment, as she had experienced in her previous district. With this in mind, she established a leadership team with a teacher from every grade level.

> I do the leadership team, and that's where one representative from each grade level meets with me once a month. The grade level picks who they want to meet with me. . . . That's a communication between grade levels where I can get a sense of what's going on, what their issues are, and what their strengths are. That's where they can hear from each other what their struggles are at different grade levels, what their successes are. . . . If we have to do a new math adoption, then they take it back to their teams and they make a decision. They bring it back to leadership and we try to make a decision about it.

Assuming new leadership responsibilities can be challenging for some teachers, especially if they are not accustomed to working with adults. Most teachers enter the teaching profession because they have a strong desire to work with and help young children. Now they are faced with having to work with fellow teachers in roles that they may not have been prepared for. Connie Viera provides a teacher's perspective:

> It is difficult because people who might have come into the profession not necessarily wanting to work with adults. . . . They now need to present back to their team, or they need to present to a group, or they need to work with a group to solve a problem. . . . I think that what happens is that they recognize—well this is hard—it is hard to be part of a committee—it is hard to make change and to get your opinion across. I think that makes them more on the same wavelength as Joanna. . . . I think that if they get to work at Learning Together Charter School they know that they have really found the *ultimate* place to be. So, it has worked and I think that they actually enjoy it.

Valuing Teacher Professionalism

Teacher professionalism is valued and clearly stated in the philosophy of Learning Together Charter School. The Annual Report to the Community states, "Teacher professionalism will be supported with an appropriate budget, instructional materials, and staff development." The staff training is aligned with the instructional plan for English language learners (Milk, Mercado, & Sapiens, 1992). As part of the professional development of the Learning Together staff, a week-long Summer Institute is held at the end of the school year. It provides training, planning, evaluating, and development of goals and activities for the following school year. Teachers make a real commitment to participate in the institute and deliberate on such topics as curriculum alignment, staff development needs, parent education, student teacher preservice training, and multicultural education. They are dedicated to making the instructional program at the school work for *all* students, including English language learners. Connie Viera discusses the importance of the Summer Institute:

> The last week when school gets out, we spend a whole week creating, going over what works, what did not work, and then setting up for the next year. There is nothing better that she does than that! . . . My team just feels so connected. I feel so comfortable. I don't go away at the end of the year feeling—thank God the school year is over. I actually am motivated. I already have my class lists. We are already planning our home visits before the school starts. I am excited about what is going to go on the next year because we have gone through and we have planned it all out. . . . This sort of forces you to take the time to look at the big picture.

Through the staff development process incorporated into the Summer Institute, "there is a reorientation from bureaucratic to moral authority and to professional empowerment." Thus, the control is through "professional socialization, purposing, and shared values, and collegiality and natural interdependence" (Sergiovanni, 1991, p. 60).

A critical element of Learning Together Charter School's philosophy and strategies for school improvement is collaboration. The staff meets regularly to discuss student-centered learning and assessment. The K–3 and 4–6 grade-level teachers meet once a month to ensure consistency throughout all grade levels. For instance, teachers integrate the Mathland constructivist math strategies with Math Steps, a skill-based approach to provide a balanced program that meets state standards. The physical education specialist takes each grade level three times per week for 45 minutes of instruction, thereby enabling teacher study groups to focus on the comprehensive, year-long instructional plan, integrated curriculum content and assessment across the grade levels. All of these efforts enable teachers to gradually assume more leadership roles, do a better job of working and learning together as teams, and to make certain that all aspects of the curriculum are well balanced.

The collegial approach at Learning Together creates an environment that promotes mutual cooperation, emotional support, and personal growth as teachers work together to achieve what they could not accomplish alone and learn new ways to promote student success. According to Du Four and Eaker (1998), "The most promising strategy for sustained, substantive school improvement is developing the ability of school personnel to function as professional learning communities" (p. xi).

For some teachers, assuming leadership roles was a new skill that had to be developed. Just as students need practice learning new concepts, these teachers needed practice becoming teacher leaders. It was a slow and gradual process. This perspective was reflected in Paula Sanchez's comments:

> When we started doing more of the grade-level teams and doing more of the staff development type activities in the staff meetings, teacher leaders started to come forth because there would have to be one person on the grade-level team or one person during the staff meetings that would be the person that would report back. . . . I think that started to give people practice being teacher leaders. . . . The other part of that was during late start. We had committees, and teachers were leaders of those committees. Different teachers took on actual positions as part of those committees. So, it was kind of a gradual process of teachers taking on leadership roles that they had never taken on before.

Impact of Shared Leadership

Inclusive leadership recognizes that teachers and staff members play a critical role in the decision-making process and the success of the school. It provides opportunities for staff to contribute to the formation of important decisions that have lasting impact on the school. Once integrated into the leadership and shared decision-making process, many teachers do find it rewarding because they feel that they are making an important contribution to the educational process. Often they grow professionally as a result of having to work with other adults and making presentations to their team. They either learn a whole new set of skills or refine ones that were not being actively applied. Connie Viera adds, "I think it makes us better teachers."

The process of sharing leadership impacted three critical areas: the school culture, relations with families and the school community, and increased equity and student achievement.

Change in School Culture

Connie Viera has had the opportunity to teach students who have experienced the transformation at Learning Together after becoming a charter school and incorporating shared leadership into the management process of the school. The following account reveals the impact on the student body and the extended school community.

> Last year was my first class that started as kindergarten and had gone all the way through as a charter, so they were charter kids. They had signed up

> accordingly. I have noticed a real shift in the behavior, the parent involvement, the mix and how people interact with each other. Each year it gets better.

Providing teachers and support staff with the opportunity to assume greater leadership and decision-making roles had a clear impact on the culture of the school. Moreover, the personal support and increased resources that the staff members received from the principal made them feel that the work they did was considered valuable. Thus, there was a change in the overall school atmosphere, attitude, and morale of the teachers. Transformations occurred in the perceptions of individuals as to their importance in the school, resulting in enhanced communication levels of staff members, as reflected in the comments by Paula Sanchez:

> I think that it was a gradual process of people starting to feel more and more comfortable doing it because they would do things as simple as recording at a meeting or reporting back at a meeting. . . . But I think that as they become more and more accustomed to taking on that role, it was an *empowering* experience for them. I think that they really felt heard at this school, whereas before in the leadership that we had, . . . things were pretty much dictated to them. So, I think that teachers began to feel more *valued* and that they had a *voice* in what was happening at this school. . . . Now each grade level chooses a teacher for that year and they meet once a month with Joanna. That has become a real important communication tool.

Another teacher, Linda Aguilar, shares her perspectives on the transformation in the morale of the school staff as a result of shared leadership and teacher empowerment:

> The morale is really high, which is atypical of other schools in the district. Teachers in the district give input into such areas as text adoption and then the board decides otherwise. Here at Learning Together Charter School, teachers put their time in committees to make decisions, and those decisions are honored. The shared leadership is work that gives back. It is more fulfilling. You feel like you are making a difference.

Shifts in Teacher Interaction. Joanna also saw clear shifts in the conversations teachers were having in the staff lounge. She noted a more positive focus in general and particularly when talking about student achievement. She commented,

> Yes, they see the value for themselves and for their own teaching. . . . There was a shift in the staff lounge talk, which was a real sign to me. They used to go and they used to [complain] about stuff. Now they go and they talk about

> children. They talk about an idea they have or what they are doing in another grade level about this. There's been a total shift in the conversation. . . . It is not about the negativity.

Joanna also recounts the changes that began to occur among the staff members during their team meetings and staff meetings:

> In the team meetings, they have more of a trust among each other. I used to have this thing where they would bring their student work together, score it together on a rubric, talk about student work, and discuss how they got this from them. They were a little reticent. In fact, one teacher would always forget to bring her portfolio. She would forget that this was the day because they were not trusting of sharing.
>
> Now they really are a sharing staff amongst each other. If there is a teacher struggling in one of the areas, they have such a commitment that the grade level does well, that the students in that grade level do well, and that the teacher succeeds. It is really a focus on success. It is not competitive at all.
>
> This year, I moved one weaker teacher to a grade level with four really strong, strong teachers. They just shared materials, shared ideas, shared time so that this teacher is doing the best job she has ever done teaching because of the support of the teachers.
>
> Staff meetings have also changed. Before I came, staff meetings were very negative. Teachers would yell at each other. There was a lot of discord, a lot of discomfort. Over time they changed. There's celebration. There's good communication. One person doesn't take over. There really isn't any negativity at a staff meeting any more.

Paula Sanchez confirms the shift that took place in the staff meetings. Joanna had changed staff meetings from once a week to once a month. However, teachers had to agree to read the staff bulletins to remain current on school activities and programs. "We started doing . . . more staff development type things, like taking writing samples and sitting in grade levels and scoring writing samples and going through our curriculum. . . . So, from the staff meetings, I saw a shift from the principal dictating this is what is happening to more of a staff development focus."

Creating a Passion for Teaching and Learning. A school culture that considers administrators, staff members, and parents as team members who make valuable contributions to the educational enterprise also fosters a high degree of personal dedication to the work that evolves into a passion for teaching and learning. When Joanna was asked what makes her school a great place in which to work—to spend a great portion of her life—she responded:

> Well, I think that the positive focus on student achievement, but also student emotional, social, academic well-being—the whole thing about children is here. And the enthusiasm that the teachers have, the passion that they have for their job. . . . There is passion for planning for next year. The parents are excited and enthusiastic. The kids are too. I focus on the positive and if there is a problem it's more of an, "OK, how can we solve it? What creative solution? What practical solution?"
>
> It is very magical and I don't know if people really realize it. There is this one parent who came up to me and said, "I walk on this campus and there is something different here. I can't name it. . . . It's like I want to be here. My child is totally excited and well educated. It's a good place to be." . . . It's an environment that is rich and supportive of all aspects of human beings on this campus. . . . They start being the best that they can be.

Teachers who have internalized that passion for teaching, such as Linda Aguilar, see the impact on the achievement of academic goals and on teacher satisfaction. Linda adds her perceptions on creating a passion for learning at the charter school:

> The emphasis is on academic excellence. Working together in teams and bringing your passion together on a topic of discussion, you can't help but have excellence. Teachers are excited about learning. They love it here. Some teachers have been offered jobs in other places, but they won't leave.

Greater Family Outreach

Recognizing the important role that parents play in their children's education, family outreach and parent participation are ongoing goals of Learning Together Charter School.

Drawing on the principle that the students and the community are a valuable resource for undertaking educational improvement, home visits and interviews are conducted to determine the funds of knowledge that exist in the Hispanic households (Moll, Amanti, Neff, & Gonzalez, 1992). All kindergarten teachers visit the home of every new child, which establishes important home-school connections and yields an abundance of community knowledge. A parent leader, who has been cultivated and nurtured from the parent community, serves as a bilingual parent coordinator to promote ongoing home and school participation and to develop a directory of parent and school resources.

Parent Involvement. The involvement of parents in ensuring their children's academic achievement has been well researched (Epstein, 1986, 1992), particularly with immigrant and language-minority families. Positive effects of partnerships between families and schools have been found with both low- and middle-income populations and those of different racial and ethnic groups (Comer, 1986; Dauber and Epstein, 1993; Delgado-Gaitan, 1990; Epstein and Dauber, 1991; Hidalgo, Bright, Sui, Swap, & Epstein, 1995; Robledo Montecel, 1993.) Some of the long-term benefits include sustained gains in academic achievement, enhanced English-language skills, increased cognitive growth, improved behavior in school, better home-school relationships, higher self-concepts, and positive attitudes toward school.

Parent Empowerment. In studies conducted on effective schools, Carter and Chatfield (1986), Garcia (1990), and Moll (1988) posit that maintaining a systematic community/school process contributes significantly to the success of a school. Moreover, participation in the school's governance results in feelings of parent empowerment. At Learning Together Charter School, steps are taken to empower parents of English-language learners to participate in decision-making organizations, such as the Bilingual Advisory Committee, the District Bilingual Advisory Committee, Parent Teacher Organization, Governing Council, and School Site Council. Meetings and parent materials are always translated to facilitate this process. Families are invited to attend the open house during the Back-to-School Inservice Week for teachers so that families and students can connect with the school staff prior to the start of school. A parent/teacher retreat is held each spring to review the goals and achievements of the year, evaluate the charter, and plan for the following year.

The empowerment of parents has resulted in more control regarding school decisions.This has created a shift in the organizational structure from a "power over" to a "power to" approach (Sergiovanni, 1991, p. 57). According to Joanna, the role of the parents had changed dramatically since the inception of the charter school and the shared leadership model:

> I think that initially, when we started the charter, teachers were not used to opening the door up for parents. The parents could bake cookies for PTO, or whatever, but they weren't invited into the classrooms and they weren't welcome. The shift of that took a few years because they didn't know how to tap into the strength of parents. The parents ask hard questions sometimes. . . . It's really OK to ask hard questions because usually they are good questions to have an answer for. If you don't have an answer, then you have to rethink your practice.
>
> One of the things that I do sometimes is to facilitate the teacher/parent connection and model [the process]. . . . I focus them on what the charter is, what

is the path of the charter, and how do we want to move forward, rather than complaining about this or that. We have tapped into the wonderful richness of our parent population and the strengths of our parents. Much of what happens at our school is because of the parents. The teachers see that and know that—and now welcome and value parents. That's been a big shift.

And the parents feel like they are doing real things here. . . . I had a kindergarten parent come in yesterday. In fact, these flowers are from her. She said, "This is a *thank you* for honoring our ideas and helping us."

As part of the school charter, families are required to be involved at least three hours per month in school-related educational activities. The governing council organizes three town meetings for parents and community members. At these meetings, the governance structure of the school is discussed in English and Spanish, and families can decide to participate either directly on committees, teams, councils, in classrooms, and various grant activities, or indirectly at home with the family phone network or class-support activities. If childcare is a concern for parents, they may bring young children with them.

Parent Education. A major goal of Learning Together Charter School is parent education. The Family Literacy Project provides not only English language development and literacy instruction but also coordinates monthly trips for families to public community resources, including the library, art museum and the natural history museum. These weekend literacy field trips provide training, transportation, and school bonding for the two diverse linguistic communities. Parents have even gone on a whale-watching trip with the school. The project also provides bilingual books of instructional strategies for families to keep at home. Recently, a monthly family technology night has been organized to provide more opportunities for children and parents to develop computer literacy skills.

Impact on Student Equity and Success in School

Learning Together Charter School has a strong commitment to educational excellence and equal opportunity for *all* students. It manifests itself in the placement of students in integrated classes, the manner in which students play on the playground, and even in preferences in the cafeteria. According to Connie Viera, transformations have occurred in equity issues and integration during the past decade under the leadership of Joanna Santos:

There was also a division of ethnicity, the haves and the have-nots, and the language. All of those things played into having a divided school, which I have seen in our district and I have seen in other districts as well. The school might come off as a school that is really meeting the standards, . . . but when you take a closer look, you see that there are people on the side that are really not taking part. That is something that Joanna really worked hard on, which was to make the equity—the balance in the classrooms so you did not have the white room and the brown room, that teachers who were the most requested . . . if you give in to all of the requests you might end up with a population very out of balance with the other classrooms.

The other thing that happened was it used to be that the free lunch, cafeteria lunch, was just the standard lunch that was served to the rest of the district. Joanna and the teacher leadership team noticed that the kids who were on free and reduced lunch ate the cafeteria food and then the other kids ate their lunches from home. So they never sat together. We got rid of the district lunch program, and so now the food is homemade.

So, it was really brilliant to hire Laurel and do this whole wonderful café thing that everyone chooses. Most everyone now eats in the cafeteria. So then you are mixing the people, and you know sharing bread has got to be the greatest way to get people together.

Increased Student Achievement

The key to maintaining a well-balanced, integrated, innovative and enriching educational program for all students rests with the leadership of the school. A critical dimension of effective schooling for English language learners is school-level leadership. Carter and Chatfield (1986) and Lucas, Henze, and Donato (1990) identify the leadership of the school principal as a major factor contributing to a school's effectiveness. The principal plays a critical role in making the achievement of English language learners a priority, providing ongoing direction and monitoring of curriculum and instructional improvement, recruiting and maintaining dedicated staff, and promoting teacher leadership in the school improvement efforts.

According to Newmann and Wehlage (1995), student achievement tends to rise dramatically when schools create collaborative work cultures with teachers and parents that focus on instructional improvement based on student academic performance, align curriculum to external standards, and provide appropriate professional development. Such a collaborative work culture clearly exists at Learning Together Charter School. With its continued commitment to bilingual education, the school has achieved high levels of academic performance on California's standardized assessment instrument. In a study commissioned by a coalition named Californians Together, Colón-Muñiz (2000) reports that a preliminary review of the Stanford Achievement Test, Ninth Edition (SAT-9) data indicates that students in

10 school districts, with large enrollments of English Learners (ELs) offering bilingual instruction, *equaled* or *exceeded* those of three school districts showcased by proponents of California's Proposition 227, approved by voters in 1998, as successes of structured English immersion. The comparisons were done for most grades in mathematics and reading. Learning Together Charter School was cited as one of the 10 examples of bilingual schools reaching *high levels of academic performance* in English in the study. The school's charter maintains a strong commitment to biliteracy for all students.

Measurement of Success. While standardized tests are an important determinant of academic performance, Joanna indicates that she measures both teacher and student success in numerous other ways, some conventional and others quite unique.

> I measure success in weird ways like attendance, teacher attendance. Teachers aren't sick very often. Stress level is the way I measure, enthusiasm, feeling tone—the emotional state of people.
>
> We have portfolios for each student. That sort of documents, according to certain standards, the work that they are able to do to meet those standards. We have a whole database, which is really an exciting database to me. We use File Maker Pro, and we can put in any field we want. So, it's a way for me, as an administrator, to use data, and comprehensive data. It has everything on each student. . . . So, I can go and ask about Henry. How's Henry doing? What programs did he have? What's the parent involvement? What's the educational background of his parents? We have all these data and we do graphs, analysis, and all of this. We can use that as a measure of success and then also how I feel about it. What's going on? I just look around.
>
> You can walk into any classroom . . . and there's focused energy. The discipline is certainly not nonexistent, but just about. I can go for several weeks without talking to any child about discipline. The teachers have high expectations. The students know what those expectations are. They want to do well. They want to be successful. . . .
>
> The integration on the yard is another one to measure the success. I was out there this morning and I was looking at the basketball game. I was thinking that when I first came it would have been the Hispanics versus the whites or all Hispanic or all white. I looked and it wasn't about race, language, color—anything. It was about who likes basketball, who likes soccer, . . . or which groups were hanging out talking. It was more about interest and less about color and ethnicity.

When asked how shared leadership has contributed to the overall improvement in academic achievement, the assistant principal, Paula

Sanchez, indicated, "The grade-level teams have definitely contributed to academic achievement because there is more of a consistency in program. I think sometimes there is more communication too that leads to consistency throughout the school, which I think can help academic achievement."

Analysis of Assessment Results. Another strategy for improving academic achievement is a regular discussion of assessment results. In the beginning of the school year, the whole staff looks at test scores and seeks ways in which to strengthen them. Once a month, during committee meetings, the assistant principal meets with all of the kindergarten through third-grade teachers, and another leadership-team member meets with the fourth- through sixth-grade teachers to focus on assessment. They examine where the students are meeting established goals and where there are gaps. As a result, the teachers make revisions of what they are teaching and their instructional plan for the school year.

Acquisition of External Resources. Having an abundance of external resources, both financial and human, has also contributed to the improvement of academic achievement. Learning Together Charter School has obtained federal, state, and foundation grants to offer specialized programs for students and families. For example, it received funding from the U.S. Department of Education for Project Puente, a Bilingual Education Comprehensive School Grant to promote dual-language literacy, cultural literacy, and high academic achievement. It has also participated in several innovative supplemental education programs sponsored by a nationally recognized research center at one of the University of California institutions. Paula Sanchez further explains the resources for children and families:

> Through the years, we have always offered at least two to three parent workshops targeting mostly the primary parents, what they can do to help their children read at home, attain literacy skills at home, or how they can help them with homework. . . . We started the after-school homework clubs which have really been successful. . . . The [university-sponsored] Homework Project set up the standard. It was the seed from which those other homework centers grew. Now we have after-school tutorials and homework centers for all grade levels, kindergarten through sixth grade.

Lessons Learned Regarding Shared Leadership

Research on educational administration by Hoy and Miskel (1991) stresses that "the instructional leader is responsible for articulating the mission of the organization, shaping its culture and protecting and maintaining its integrity" (p. 299). It is evident from Learning Together Charter School that the personal philosophy, values, beliefs, willingness to take risks, and leadership style of the school principal play critical roles in articulating the mission, shaping the culture, and distributing leadership to teachers, support staff, and parents. Interviews with key participants reveal that the principal needs to possess certain traits to facilitate shared leadership successfully. Administrators thinking about embracing shared leadership might take these into consideration when planning their course of action. Although these qualities are not all inclusive, they do represent those that this case study found to be beneficial for building a school community's capacity to learn and work together, grow professionally, and turn visions for school improvement into a reality.

Philosophy of Working Together

One of the basic tenets of shared leadership is the underlying belief that by working together with teachers, support staff, parents, and students and empowering them to make decisions, one can create positive changes for the school. Principal Joanna Santos possesses this philosophy and has used it to guide her in employing the shared leadership process. According to Paula Sanchez, "I think that once you have that buy-in from the teachers and your philosophy is that everyone in the school works together, not that she is the sole decision maker, . . . that is the first step."

Achieving the goal of shared leadership is a complex process, however. It is contingent on the following additional characteristics: (1) Being inclusive, (2) creating a common set of values and beliefs, (3) setting ground rules, (4) establishing attainable goals, (5) implementing promising practices to achieve the vision, and (6) celebrating successes. Most important, there must be an extraordinary commitment and effort by all parties to *collectively* champion the cause.

Nurturing the Strength Within

A typical feeling that teachers possess in schools is that of being overworked and having too many responsibilities. In contrast, the teachers at Learning Together Charter School are the ones voluntarily taking charge of various committees and planning what takes place at the school. It did not happen by accident, however. The intuition for hiring quality teachers, proper placement in instructional settings, and the nurturing qualities that

Joanna possesses have all contributed to feelings of contentment among staff and a desire to participate in leadership roles.

All of the teachers interviewed indicated that Joanna Santos is very good at seeing what people's strengths are and where they would do well. She is astute about personnel issues and hires the most qualified and talented people. As an instructional leader, she uses good judgment about identifying those teachers who will work out well in the school environment and recruits those individuals. Paula Sanchez comments, "I think that she is good at seeing people's strengths and how they can be used . . . for everyone's benefit." A primary grade teacher, Linda Aguilar, further adds, "My dream has been to teach art classes. She recognizes my passion for art and finds a way to support it. She helps me write grant proposals to fund art programs."

Joanna reflects upon her own personal strengths in recognizing the potential for leadership and nurturing people as they participate in the shared leadership process. "I think one of my real talents . . . is nurturing people to find the strength within themselves, to be the best that they can be. . . . Someone was intuitive with me about my leadership skills and . . . nurtured that. I can see the potential in other people and nurture that."

Empowering the School Community

In order to maximize the educational success of the students and achieve the established goals, it is necessary to empower the school community, including administrators, teachers, classified staff, parents, and students to participate in the decision-making process. They must contribute to *important* decisions pertaining to such areas as budget, curriculum, instructional programs and materials, and assessment. The participants must feel that their voices are heard, valued, and included in the decisions that are made at the school. The administrator needs to enlist the talents of the stakeholders in the school community to make significant contributions to the decision-making activities that occur in the school. The connection between empowerment and leadership is best illustrated by the sentiments of Linda Aguilar:

> Teachers feel empowered as teachers, and that makes them feel like leaders. The principal must help people see themselves as being able to make decisions. Joanna Santos really respects teachers by making them involved in such things as the budget. She asks questions and lets them brainstorm solutions to problems. She guides them through the questions. As a staff, we love the idea of being empowered, and we feel we work harder than some other schools. There is extra intense thinking in the school—like a think tank.

Securing Resources

Another skill that is extremely beneficial to the whole school is giving the staff the resources to enable them to do their job to the best of their ability. These resources might be financial, human, programmatic, or technological. Joanna Santos has been able to bring into the school so many resources that teachers feel that they can accomplish great things with the students. She involves staff and parents in fundraising events and grant writing. As a result, the school has received Charter Dissemination Grants and Innovation Grants for high-functioning charter schools. One aspect behind the charter was to obtain fiscal autonomy so that the school would have control of its own money. In that manner, the school can use its resources creatively to support innovative programs. For instance, the school's federal Title 7 grant enabled them to promote the dual-language program, establish a computer lab, and implement the early intervention program.

Numerous opportunities exist for obtaining funding sources to support school programs at the federal, state, and local levels. Many community representatives support educational initiatives through philanthropic contributions directly to schools or by channeling their funds through foundations. Educational partnerships between schools, universities, and business are yet another vehicle for obtaining valuable resources. Administrators must be proactive in seeking out funding sources and engaging staff members in the grant-writing process to support innovative programs.

Establishing Grade-Level Teams

A powerful component of shared leadership is creating a system whereby staff members at all grade levels play an active role in the decisions that are made. Interviews with teachers in this case study indicate that the establishment of grade-level teams can be a very powerful tool for distributive leadership. Creating the *culture of grade-level teams*, however, needs to be a gradual process where individuals have numerous opportunities for assuming and practicing leadership roles.

Du Four and Eaker (1998) contend that through collaborative teams there is a focus on organizational renewal and the willingness to work together in a continuous improvement process. This form of distributive leadership leads to greater buy-in on the part of the members of grade-level teams, fosters articulation between the grades, and promotes the accomplishment of the established instructional goals.

Creating Meaningful Opportunities for Training and Communication. Professional development is another essential component of shared leadership. Some individuals assume leadership roles very readily, but others may find it difficult to initiate discussions on critical issues, use problem–solving strategies, take notes during team meetings, summarize ideas, bring a group to consensus, or report back to a larger group. As Connie Viera notes,

> A lot of what you do in your daily job—whether it is with children, parents, or teachers—is communication and rapport development. Resolving conflicts and discussing issues requires some communication skills. . . . The more proactive that you can be, the better—meeting individually with people and then gradually building those stakeholders and building that support.

Effective communication is critical to the shared-leadership process. It manifests itself in cultural, written, verbal, and nonverbal forms. The content and style of communication can impact the way an individual perceives critical issues. Research suggests that greater success occurs as a result of frequent communication, working together, and sharing new ideas and possibilities for accomplishment (Little, 1986). Members of both grade-level and leadership teams would benefit from training in areas such as open communication, problem-solving strategies, group dynamics, and conflict resolution.

Staying Current: Knowing Best Practices

Interviews with teachers reveal that it is important for the principal to have a firm grasp of curriculum and knowledge of best practices in teaching. Although having a strong teaching background and knowledge of what needs to take place in a classroom is beneficial, it is not sufficient. Principals must be able to exercise their influence as instructional leaders. They should serve as "coaches and facilitators who help students, teachers, and other staff understand the mental models and basic assumptions about teaching and learning in particular school communities" (Hart & Bredeson, 1996, p. 137).

As both teachers and learners, principals must model behaviors of active learners. They should read current professional journals and attend conferences and other professional development opportunities in order to better understand the latest research and translate it into practice. Connie Viera comments on the powerful impact of these behaviors as exhibited by Joanna Santos: "She reads and she goes to conferences. She learns and she comes up with new ideas. . . . And so when she reads something and shares it with us, that makes me feel like a colleague of hers, . . . like I am working *with* her, not for her."

Reflecting on Practice

Effective leaders use the principles that emerge from theory and research to determine their practice (Brandt, 1992; Schön, 1983; Sergiovanni, 1992a, 1992b, 2001). The information derived enhances judgment and decision making. Reflective practice means remaining current with the research on best practices and analyzing one's own approaches for shared decision making and school improvement. Principals must provide optimal opportunities for staff members to reflect on their own practice and on new strategies that have been used to meet school goals. They need to share successes and brainstorm new strategies for continual improvement. Teachers like Linda Aguilar and Connie Viera believe that it is important to reflect on the progress of the school year. They believe that the optimal time for reflection is at the end of the year. In June the accomplishments are still fresh in one's mind and it is an opportune time to examine what worked and what didn't and to determine why.

Conclusion

In order to make the greatest impact on academic excellence and student success, schools must be responsive to the demographic, family, and technological changes that have emerged throughout our society. Educational leaders must change their paradigms and mental models to meet the needs of students, parents, teachers, and staff in a perpetually changing school community. Critical to this process is having a collective vision for improving the school environment and enhancing the academic achievement of students.

Although this case study demonstrates that many benefits are associated with undertaking change for the sake of school improvement, the school administrator also takes risks when initiating a change process. Pressures may come from individuals representing the political spectrum within the district, teacher associations, parent groups, or community leaders to maintain the status quo. Thus, the administrator is faced with multiple challenges and opposing views that may lead to his or her personal introspection and clarification of beliefs, as is evidenced by the recollections of Joanna Santos on the risk taking involved in establishing a charter school and incorporating elements of shared leadership:

> There were risks. I think the whole charter concept was a risk. All of the time in the initial stages of my job, especially when the charter went in a different direction from the rest of the district, all the time, my own job was at

> risk. . . . But to me, more of a risk is not doing what you totally believe in and know is right. . . . If what I do and what I value, related to the educational environment of the school, is in conflict with the district, then I have to do what I think is needed at the school site. . . . So, I always knew my job was on the line. I was threatened, all of that. A school board member called me the day after we got our charter and basically threatened me. Some of the things we have done along the way have been risk points, but we just had to move forward on that.

Challenges also exist in making certain that teachers have an equitable role in shared leadership, even though teachers may not necessarily have developed the leadership skills necessary for the task. Sometimes the teacher that is selected as the representative for the leadership position may not be the best person for that role due to a lack of expertise at that particular grade level or an inability to communicate effectively with team members. Providing the necessary training, nurturing, and support will elevate diverse individuals to more productive levels of leadership.

Moreover, going through a shared leadership process takes a great deal of time. Teachers may feel fearful initially about the amount of time and work required to participate actively in shared decision making. It may necessitate changing the organizational structure of the school day to enable teachers to have more frequent meetings, extended time to reach consensus on major decisions, and opportunities for reporting back to other staff members.

Although some administrators believe that shared leadership makes it easier to be an administrator due to its distributive nature of sharing responsibility, Paula Sanchez puts it into perspective: "It can backfire if you don't have the right people taking on those leadership positions. . . . Once in a while you can get an individual teacher who can kind of undermine the whole process." In undertaking a change process, it is important for the administrator to be able to determine people's strengths and guide them in directions where those strengths can be maximized. However, as Joanna discovered, "Sometimes people had to leave."

While establishing a charter school was the vehicle for school reform that Joanna Santos used, it is not the only model for restructuring a school and distributing leadership to diverse stakeholders. By examining the journey taken by Joanna at Learning Together Charter School and the application of the key concepts that emerged from the data in this case study, administrators can begin to gain the knowledge and skills necessary to facilitate shared leadership—to create a trusting and nurturing environment within any system where school members are considered as professionals and given meaningful opportunities and resources to assume leadership roles and participate in shared decision making with colleagues and parents. Enabling staff members to see their own values as being closely connected to those of the school administrator, so that they *are aligned* and *have the same interests for children,* makes it more motivational for them to assume leadership roles at their school. Furthermore, by creating a community of learners who continually strive to construct new understandings, work collectively for a shared purpose, gradually assume meaningful leadership roles, and reflect on their practice, school administrators can have a major impact on the transformation of a school community.

References

Beck, L. G., & Murphy, J. (1993). *Understanding the principalship: Metaphorical themes 1920s-1990s.* New York: Teachers College Press.

Beck, L. G., & Murphy, J. (1996). *The four imperatives to a successful school.* Thousand Oaks, CA: Corwin Press.

Bennis, W., & Goldsmith, J. (1994). *Learning to lead.* Reading, MA: Addison Wesley.

Block, P. (1987). *The empowered manager.* San Francisco: Jossey-Bass.

Brandt, R. (1992, February). On rethinking leadership: A conversation with Tom Sergiovanni. *Educational Leadership, 49*(5), 46–49.

Burns, J. M. (1978). *Leadership.* New York: Harper and Row.

Carter, T., & Chatfield, M. (1986). Effective bilingual schools: Implications for policy and practice. *American Journal of Education, 95,* 200–232.

Christian, D. & Whitcher, A. (1995). *Directory of two-way bilingual programs in the United States.* Revised Ed. Santa Cruz, CA and Washington, D.C.: National Center for Research on Cultural Diversity and Second Language Learning.

Colón-Muñiz, A. (2000, September-October). Parents given the choice for bilingual education have reason to celebrate. *Multilingual News,* 6–9.

Comer, J. P. (1986). Parent participation in the schools. *Phi Delta Kappan, 67*(6), 442–446.

Dauber, S. L., & Epstein, J. L. (1993). Parents' attitudes and practices of involvement in inner-city elementary and middle schools. In N. Chavkin (Ed.), *Families and schools in a pluralistic society* (pp. 53–71). Albany: SUNY Press.

Delgado-Gaitan, C. (1990). *The role of parents in children's education.* New York: Falmer Press.

Du Four, R., & Eaker, R. (1998). *Professional learning communities at work: Best practices for enhancing student achievement.* Bloomington, IN: National Educational Service.

Epstein, J. (1986). Parent's reactions to teacher practices of parent involvement. *The Elementary School Journal, 86*(3), 277–294.

Epstein, J. (1992). School and family partnerships. In M. Alkin (Ed.), *Encyclopedia of educational research,* 6th ed. (pp. 1139–1152). New York: Macmillan.

Epstein, J., & Dauber, S. (1991). School programs and teacher practices of parental involvement in inner-city elementary and middle schools. *Elementary School Journal, 91*(3), 289–303.

Foster, W. (1989). Toward a critical practice of leadership. In L. Orozco (Ed.), *Educational leadership perspectives* (pp. 3–15). Madison, WI: Coursewise Publishing.

Fullan, M. (1993). *Change forces: Probing the depths of educational reform.* London: Falmer Press.

Garcia, E. E. (1990). *Education of linguistically and culturally diverse students: Effective instructional practices.* The National Center for Research on Cultural Diversity and Second Language Learning. Educational Practice Report, No. 1. Washington, D.C.: Center for Applied Linguistics.

Greenfield, W. D., Jr. (1995, February). Toward a theory of school administration: The centrality of leadership. *Educational Administration Quarterly, 31*(1), 61–85.

Hart, A. W., & Bredeson, P. V. (1996). *The principalship: A theory of professional learning and practice.* New York: McGraw-Hill.

Hidalgo, N. M., Bright, J., Sui, S. F., Swap, S., & Epstein, J. (1995). Research on families, schools, and communities: A multicultural perspective. In J. A. Banks & C. A. Banks (Eds.), *Handbook of research on multicultural education* (pp. 498–524). New York: Macmillan.

Hoy, W. K., & Miskel, C. G. (1991). *Educational administration: Theory, research, and practice.* New York: McGraw-Hill.

Hutchins, C. L. (1988). Design as the missing piece in education. In *The design of education: A collection of papers concerned with comprehensive educational reform,* Vol. 1 (pp. 47–49). Far West Laboratory for Educational Research and Development.

Lancy, D. F. (1993). *Qualitative research in education: An introduction to the major traditions.* White Plains, NY: Longman Publishing Group.

Levin, H. M. (1995). Learning from Accelerated Schools. In J. H. Block, S. T. Everson, & T. R. Guskey (Eds.), *School improvement programs.* New York: Scholastic.

Little, J. W. (1986, September). The effective principal. *American Education, 73*, 3.

Lucas, T., Henze, R., & Donato, R. (1990). Promoting the success of Latino language-minority students: An exploratory study of six high schools. *Harvard Educational Review, 60,* 315–340.

Marshall, C., & Rossman, G. B. (1989). *Designing qualitative research.* Newbury Park, CA: Sage.

Maxwell, J. C. (2001). *The 17 indisputable laws of teamwork: Embrace them and empower your team.* Nashville, TN: Thomas Nelson.

Milk, R., Mercado, C., & Sapiens, A. (1992). Re-thinking the education of teachers of language minority children: Developing reflective teachers for changing schools. *Occasional Papers in Bilingual Education, Number* 6. Washington, D.C.: National Clearinghouse for Bilingual Education.

Moll, L. C. (1988). Some key issues in teaching Latino students. *Language Arts, 65*(5), 465–472.

Moll, L. C., Amanti, C., Neff, D., & Gonzalez, N. (1992). Funds of knowledge for teaching: Using a qualitative approach to connect homes and classrooms. *Theory Into Practice, 31*(2), 132–141.

Murphy, J. (1992). *The landscape of leadership preparation: Reframing the education of school administrators.* Newbury Park, CA: Corwin.

Newmann, F., & Wehlage, G. (1995). *Successful school restructuring: A report to the public and educators by the Center for Restructuring Schools.* Madison: University of Wisconsin.

Robledo Montecel, M. (1993). *Hispanic families as valued partners: An educator's guide.* San Antonio, TX: Intercultural Development Research Association.

Schön, D. (1983). *The reflective practitioner: How professionals think in action.* New York: Basic Books.

Senge, P. (1990). *The fifth discipline: The art and practice of learning organizations.* New York: Doubleday.

Senge, P. (1996). Leading learning organizations. In F. Hesselbein, M. Goldsmith, & R. Beckhard (Eds.), *The leader of the future* (pp. 41–58). San Francisco: Jossey-Bass.

Sergiovanni, T. J. (1991). *The principalship: A reflective practice perspective.* (2nd ed.). Boston: Allyn & Bacon.

Sergiovanni, T. J. (1992a, February). Why we should seek substitutes for leadership. *Educational Leadership, 49*(5), 41–45.

Sergiovanni, T. J. (1992b). *Moral leadership: Getting to the heart of school reform.* San Francisco: Jossey-Bass.

Sergiovanni, T. J. (2001). *The principalship: A reflective practice perspective.* Boston: Allyn & Bacon.

Sizemore, B. A. (1990). The Madison elementary school: A turnaround case. In K. Lomotey (Ed.), *The African American experience* (pp. 155–180). Albany: SUNY Press.

Spradley, J. P. (1980). *Participant observation.* Orlando, FL: Holt, Rinehart and Winston, Inc.

Taylor, R. L., & Rosenbach, W. E. (Eds.) (1989). *Leadership: Challenges for today's manager.* New York: McGraw-Hill.

Tichy, N. M., & Devanna, M. A. (1986). *The transformational leader.* New York: Wiley.

4

Reflections on Practice

An Administrator's 16-Year Journey to Promote Teacher Leadership and Learning

David Burke

Ian Mitchell

What factors are key in realizing the ideals of teaching and learning in sustainable, ongoing professional learning teams? The thoughts in this chapter are based on the reflections of an administrator who led and supported programs that have had a consistent and coherent emphasis over a 16-year period. The length of time is important to this story; across the world, schools are littered with defunct programs or "two-year wonders." This story offers insights and strategies and raises important questions and challenges for principals and academic collaborators. There are no simple answers that keep on working; like teaching and learning, the ever-changing contextual aspects of a school require leadership to also be constantly analytical, reflective, and reactive.

AUTHORS' NOTE: Quotations used in this chapter were reprinted with permission from their anonymous sources.

This chapter, written primarily by David, a member of a secondary school administrative team, is a "self-study" covering some 16 years in guiding change in teaching and learning. The school is in Portland, Australia, a country town in the state of Victoria. It describes David's efforts in building a culture of reflective practice, focusing on how students learn by inviting teachers to meet in what we label *professional learning teams*. Institutionalizing changes such as these across an entire faculty is not easy (Curry, 1997; Fullan, 1994, 2001), and David's journey has involved many cycles of innovation, reflection on outcomes, and reframing and redesign of (his) practice in the light of new wisdom. For this reason, although "self study" was not a term in his lexicon, we regard the work as a self-study. The second author, Ian, who works at Monash University in the state capital, Melbourne, is a founder of the Project for the Enhancement of Effective Learning (PEEL; Loughran, 1999). This project has involved volunteer groups of teachers in many schools, engaging them in collaborative action-research aimed at developing teaching strategies that support more metacognitive learning (Baird & Northfield, 1995). Thus, the chapter serves three purposes. First, it helps to illustrate the vicissitudes and challenges for administrators and teachers who dare to engage in the process of continuous improvement. Second, it offers insights into the complexities of achieving long-term whole-school change and the implications of these for principals. Third, it demonstrates the value of a university partnership to support the process.

The chapter is structured around eight "episodes." Each episode is described in terms of the situation, problems and strategies, and outcomes and lessons. These "lessons" were insights that emerged from the episode and that provided advice about school leadership and facilitating teacher change. They are framed in terms of how they were seen by the authors at the time, and several of them are developed and refined through the eight episodes. In most cases, the advice was not clear until after the episode and hence constitutes a record of what was an ongoing reframing of leadership practice.

Context

The professional learning teams that were central to David's strategy were voluntary; their viability was entirely dependent on the teachers' ongoing participation, having perceived the teams as relevant, useful, and important. This means that the most important and obvious source of data was whether teams were meeting, with high attendance rates, and whether their focus and output remained on the issues of learning and teaching that were associated with David's long-term goals.

The setting is a rural high school that had about 500 students annually from 1975 to 1991, when it amalgamated with the local technical school to form a larger college of about 800 students with approximately 60 teaching staff. The material that follows begins with a description of David's early teaching career, during which time he began to take on significant teacher leadership roles in his department and then the school. In the episodes that follow, he explores the role his principals played in supporting his growth as a leader. In 1991 he became an assistant principal, which gave him a different platform from which to exercise leadership with colleagues. As the episodes unfold, David reflects on his own role as a leader committed to involving teachers. Finally, in 2002, he stepped into the role of principal.

The material up to here has been written in the voice of both authors. David writes what follows in the first person as a self-study. The final section reverts to the voice of both authors.

David

In the early 1980s, because of my interest in curriculum, I undertook subject department (hereafter just called department) coordination roles, first in science and then in mathematics, continuing until 1989. From 1986, my role broadened beyond this subject-based work to include coordinating faculty development—initially addressing cross-age tutoring and cooperative learning, and then "learning about learning" through the PEEL project learning with Ian Mitchell. During these years, I pursued personal growth as a teacher as well as promoted the leadership growth of colleagues. My appointment as an assistant principal in 1991 involved responsibilities in leadership in both curriculum and professional development. I am now principal.

From 1986, my goal has been to work continually on developing reflective teachers, expert in a broad range of learning strategies, who effectively engage students in student-centered classrooms and who regularly collaborate to examine their current practice and to develop, share, and refine new practice.

Episode 1: 1975 to 1985

Typical Teacher Years

Typical of other young and enthusiastic teachers, I adopted a range of teaching and learning activities intended to motivate students and develop subject knowledge and skills. Excellent student performance outcomes, rather than my later focus on the ways that students went about their learning, were my reward. As time passed, I realized that "doing all the right things" was only part of what teaching was all about and I became interested in questions such as "Why were these particular activities good? What is learning? How do we learn?" My school, however, similar to many others, did not have a culture that promoted and supported teacher reflection, collaboration, and innovation. Learning how to build such a culture is the focus of this chapter. The second principal of the school during this period was very supportive of innovation and encouraged the faculty to try new approaches. Like virtually every other principal of that time, however, it did not occur to him to establish structures that would stimulate and support such teacher behaviors. With hindsight (a phrase that recurs in this chapter), I have realized that the school culture over these 10 years was not one that set out specifically to develop risk taking or reflective practice as a means of improving classroom teaching and learning.

Lessons

1. When the time is right, principals[1] should start inviting faculty to consider certain aspects of learning more explicitly, such as the move from teaching only content and skills to also facilitating learning about learning. Note that often we need to allow new teachers time to adjust to classroom management and consolidation of the teaching of subject-based knowledge and skills.
2. An important role for principals is to be analytical and reflective about the faculty and to know how to help them grow professionally, a lesson which emerges from Lesson 1.

Episode 2: 1986 to 1988

Beginning Action Research and Cooperative Learning

In this period, I began to pursue teaching and learning issues. A conference I attended as curriculum coordinator on cooperative learning (by an American, Carol Cooper) inspired me to try her strategies and also to interest a group of twelve other faculty to become involved. In forming this group, I had two objectives in mind: first, to develop cooperative learning skills; and second, to encourage faculty of all levels of experience to share their problems and experiences. The weekly lunchtime meetings that evolved included open sharing, where perceived "very good teachers" put their classroom problems on the table for discussion. Less experienced teachers soon followed suit. The most important outcome turned out not to be cooperative learning but rather the birth an action-research based group (not that we knew this term at the time), with the (voluntary) participants pursuing issues of mutual interest and becoming empowered to learn with each other.

I have tried to build several features of that first group into all my subsequent initiatives in what I call professional learning teams. This first group became effective because the teachers involved brought in their experiences and their problems for reflection. The importance of celebrating successes and freely discussing concerns and failures was paramount. The mutual support achieved through these regular meetings was essential in promoting sustainability. We also found that, for the meetings to be valuable to the participants, it was important that they work on classroom aspects that they saw as interesting or important. I could not have imposed, and did not impose, my concerns on the group.

Over time, I realized that individuals progress through three stages: initially trying the ideas of other faculty, then building the confidence and methodologies to devise and test their own ideas, and finally becoming truly reflective practitioners. After a year or so most are established "risk takers," with a "rucksack" or "knapsack" of strategies, allowing them to become more reflective about learning situations within their classes. An important part of the journey is to engage students in discussion on learning about learning; a process that leads to new understandings of what is going on as teachers teach. We found that the interest we took in the students' learning and views enhanced our teacher-student relationships, which further motivated teachers. We also discovered that by demonstrating risk taking, we were publicly valuing a trait that we wished to develop in our students. Our classrooms became more open, with team teaching and peer mentoring occurring naturally.

My experiences, in moving from experimenting and risk taking in my own classes and then involving others in investigating their practice, helped me identify essential skills and strategies needed by teacher leaders and principals who want to guide colleagues effectively. As most of this type of development work is undertaken in a group setting, I learned about the power of effective meetings and what makes a good meeting culture. Over the succeeding years, I always remained a member of the groups we established; this helped to create a culture of "power with", not "power over", my colleagues.

Lessons

1. Principals need to create and support a sharing culture that develops reflective teachers—create the meeting time, support the group leaders, and celebrate the successes!
2. Principals should promote good meeting and group dynamics.

3. Principals should be involved in these groups.
4. Groups should be structured so as to facilitate teachers becoming risk takers and to be open about their experiences.
5. Principals can provide and develop the structure and the overall direction, but the participants need to work on ideas and concerns that matter to them and that pertain to their classrooms.

Episode 3: 1989 to 1991

Beginning PEEL: Learning About Learning

Our professional learning team (a label I had not yet coined) grew in size, and the members developed in their thinking. They expressed a desire to learn more about learning. In 1989, to meet this need, I attended, as curriculum coordinator, a conference on metacognition. The presenters, including Ian Mitchell, from the Project for the Enhancement of Effective Learning (PEEL) project, were inspiring. This conference was the single most important of my career. Its content addressed the interests of my colleagues and myself, and it provided concrete ideas for initiating a pathway for me to lead and manage professional development across the school. A third benefit was that the strong link created between my school and Ian's university would prove valuable for many years to come. After the conference, Ian and I organized and led a professional development day for all faculty; this became the beginning of our efforts to build a teaching and learning ethos that still endures today. At the end of that day, 35 out of 45 teachers indicated some interest in pursuing the PEEL ideas. This pleasing response was more than we could accommodate initially. The original PEEL group had met during the school day, and we decided to follow that example. We also decided to begin with just one group. The school schedule allowed no more than about 18 teachers to be timetabled off (released) at the same time for meetings.[2] Operating within this constraint, I selected 12 teachers who had expressed very strong interest and whom I felt were likely to be valuable members for our initial group. Eight became our regular "PEELers." A good start to an initiative is a factor in sustainability. We decided to start small and set easily attainable goals such as bring one idea back when one is ready (not one per week). The scheduling and setting of achievable goals led to a viable and effective team during 1990 with well attended meetings. During this first year, our members mostly were trying out and adapting strategies previously documented by other PEEL teachers. They typically worked through three stages: trying the ideas of others, devising and testing their own ideas, and becoming truly reflective practitioners.

As stated earlier, our meetings were timetabled during the school day in common spare periods, an arrangement that resulted in very productive meetings. This scheduling became difficult to sustain by mid-1991, and meetings were moved to after-school hours. A second reason to move to after-school meetings was the need to allow more faculty to participate. Labels of elitism were being applied to the restricted membership of the timetabled PEEL group; a degree of negativity grew among those who wanted to be involved and felt locked out. Unfortunately, we found that the after-school meetings were less effective, even when we provided some beverages and snacks. At the time, I felt that it was because teachers found the meetings difficult at the end of a school day, but in retrospect another significant factor was that too many people may have been attending on a drop-in basis, expecting someone else to develop them. With hindsight, we can see an issue that we did not recognize at the time and hence did not manage as well as we would now: a successful group depends on people both bringing ideas to the group and contributing to the development of ideas that others bring. Another factor is that, with a more fluid membership, ideas and issues did not carry over as well from one meeting to another. I was thus confronted with the dilemma of allowing all who wished to participate to do so at the expense of some meeting effectiveness and vitality.

We found groups of 8 to 10 resulted in the best meetings, large enough if one or two were unavailable, but small enough to promote and allow contributions from all members. At this time, it became clear to me that what and how we learn are based on our need to learn; quality change can occur only with the consent of the learner, and empowerment is vital. For the teacher to be truly committed, he or she must have the desire to move from one who transmits knowledge and skills to one who both facilitates and teaches the learning process.

The PEEL connection showed us the importance of school-university partnerships in promoting teacher growth and development. Links between schools and universities provide channels along which ideas flow; the academics are a source of ideas, research support, and inspiration, and the school provides a rich context for data generation and the development of knowledge that only practicing teachers can generate (Loughran, Mitchell, & Mitchell, 2002). Within a year, we moved from being dependent on the initial resource documents on strategies of metacognition to developing and sharing strategies through *PEEL SEEDS*, the PEEL journal[3]—the second of the three stages listed earlier, devising and testing their own ideas. Seeing our ideas in print for a wider audience was rewarding and a source of confidence. Our school is some four and a half hours from Melbourne, the site of Monash University, a fact that has limited the frequency of the interaction between the two institutions and between our school and other PEEL groups. However, some strengths have resulted from our geographical separation from our university colleagues. We have used their experiences, expertise, insights, inspiration, and energy to build our culture more independently than might otherwise have been the case. I think this is a significant factor in the long-term sustainability of our program. Yet we felt close in that we were valued by our academic colleagues; they published our strategies, invited us to write sections of three books, supported specific research projects, provided opportunities for us to conduct workshops for other schools, and promoted the success of our work. This recognition beyond the school was vital for the in-school leaders in particular.

In June 1991, Ian asked me to facilitate a workshop for the entire faculty of another school—it was to be a pivotal experience for me. Although I had experience in conducting in-service work with faculty in my own school, this was a leap outside my comfort zone. It was a positive experience that helped me clarify my future in terms of leading change in teaching and learning. Facilitating this and other workshops and presentations was enjoyable and affirming; I realized how far I had come, how much I now had to share. Whenever possible, to spread this benefit, I now involve colleagues by inviting them to assist in conducting the smaller group workshops.

Toward the end of 1991, my role became that of assistant principal with responsibilities in staffing, curriculum, and professional development. As this phase of my career drew to a close and I moved from teacher leader to a more formal administrative position, several lessons again emerged that would be useful for future practice in initiating and guiding teacher development and encouraging teacher leadership.

Lessons

1. Use outside facilitators for initial input, and develop both need and consent for taking on the role of learners.
2. Build the first phase with the most enthusiastic faculty on a voluntary basis, establishing a working structure that can be extended to include others later.
3. Endeavor to include all interested faculty as soon as possible once structures/meetings/procedures have been established.
4. Personally facilitate and encourage others to lead in-service work.
5. Establish and maintain links with critical friends in universities for support but not direction.
6. Build ways for new ideas to regularly enter the school and for teachers to share their ideas with others outside the school. Assist transmission of ideas outside and into school.

Episode 4: 1992

Government Change Impacts: Huge Staff Reductions

During 1992, two external factors prevented teaching and learning groups from functioning. First, a system-wide cut of nearly 20% in the numbers of teachers drastically affected the staff and staff morale. Second, our two local secondary schools were forcibly amalgamated into one school of about 800 students. This further affected staffing and school culture and required a shift in time, energy, and resources.

The urgencies of school reorganization under amalgamation and coping with collapsing staff morale served to completely distract everyone from teaching and learning, and myself from educational leadership in this area. This was an emotionally draining time with more than 40 faculty leaving the school. The rhetoric of our new conservative government left faculty feeling like workers rather than professionals. I personally found this year very frustrating in terms of growth in teaching and learning; however, I felt that I could not and should not continue to push these issues at the time.

Lessons

1. Be patient! Sometimes a period of "time out" may be necessary to allow staff to cope with difficult developments.
2. Remember that schools are never completely in charge, but must respond to the larger political and educational system context in which they are embedded.

Episode 5: 1993 to 1995

Rebirth of PEEL and Other Teaching and Learning Groups

Once the school reorganization was complete, I felt that faculty had a growing desire to (re)build an ethos that focused on teaching and learning in our new college. They indicated that they were ready to take on what we decided to call "professional learning team" commitments. Out of 65 faculty, 45 volunteered to form into groups focusing on PEEL and co-operative learning. We were able to schedule one period per (10-day) cycle for teachers to meet. The Mixed-Ability Curriculum Coordinator and I (assistant principal/professional development coordinator) guided and coordinated these meetings.

In employing new staff after 1993, we consciously and explicitly set the culture on entry to this college: a teaching and learning focus and the need for all staff to share experiences and problems were key criteria for selection and discussions. These new, and mostly young, staff became important sources of energy in our professional learning teams. A key aspect of my role over this period was to empower these individuals by inviting them to be team leaders. I was now thinking in terms of several years, setting out to develop teachers who would engage in ongoing teacher research/reflective practice and who would take ownership of and develop new ideas rather than seeing a book of solutions as holding the answers. Faculty attending teaching and learning conferences invariably went on to become more involved as leaders of professional learning teams and in research projects like PAVOT (the Perspectives and Voice of the Teacher project, Loughran, Mitchell, & Mitchell, 2002). PAVOT was set up to provide an opportunity for PEEL teachers to engage in more formal research. Research-grant funding allowed for more support than PEEL teachers had received previously, but most of the time and energy still came from the teacher.

In 1995, we introduced an internal fortnightly, or bi-weekly, PEEL newsletter (or journal), as staff had progressed from using published ideas to developing their own solutions to problems in their classrooms. Part of celebration and recognition includes the process of writing. We encouraged faculty to write up their experiences for our local internal PEEL newsletter and for *PEEL SEEDS*. Clerical support was useful in producing a monthly newsletter to celebrate and share locally developed strategies. We used articles from *PEEL SEEDS* in our internal newsletter to supplement editions when our teachers had written too few articles.

The year 1995 was to be our most outstanding for some time. PEEL was operating the way it was intended (as good action research focusing on promoting metacognitive learning), but other interests were also being pursued. These included meeting mixed-ability needs, Benjamin Bloom's taxonomy of the cognitive domain, multiple intelligences, as well as cooperative learning, all of which were being incorporated into subject-based units. We had six professional learning teams, totaling 50 faculty. Realizing that group leaders needed some extra support, I scheduled focus-group-leader meetings with the curriculum coordinator and myself with the aim of developing a new level of leadership.

These groups formed under various labels (PEEL groups, teaching and learning groups, and focus groups). Faculty involvement was voluntary, and attendance levels ranged from moderate to 100%. It was important to me that faculty perceived this long-term development as coherent and consistent: that we were not seen to be jumping around always trying new ideas, but using and adapting these as needed to a stable set of long-term goals that focused on student and teacher learning. My role was to provide the structure and direction. I found that leaders emerged from the faculty. The nurturing of these leaders was important not only for supporting the reflective culture with faculty but in terms of succession planning: I did not want innovation collapsing because an important source of energy moved to another school. I became more conscious of the importance of encouraging leadership in others and the fact that sustaining change requires more than one or two leaders.

I also learned that long-term improvement in teaching and learning also requires that this work is regarded by faculty and principals as our core function and not just work we do if we get time when the "day-to-day" work is done—otherwise, the time doesn't often come!

I believe a necessary prerequisite for leadership, in order to "talk the talk," is for one to have "walked the talk" by being actively involved at the classroom teacher level; demonstrating knowledge of and commitment to improved learning approaches. One must be aware of just where faculty are operating and their needs at that time, when to encourage them to progress to a higher level, when to empower them with more leadership responsibilities. Trust is an essential component if teachers are to become risk takers. Principals must be seen to be supportive and not judgmental of efforts and experiences. I did not assume that the faculty knew what I valued; I was openly clear about supporting those who were taking risks, particularly when they had classes that were actively involved as colearners and researchers. As a teaching principal, I involved other teachers in my classes and regularly worked in their classes.

In stimulating individual faculty to reflect on their practice, the need to change must be nurtured. (This may take years.) Teachers need a secure environment to share both failures and new ideas (just as students do). Over the years, it has become evident that different teachers have developed in different ways in the professional learning teams. I find it useful to think of teachers in four groups. The first group attended meetings to find solutions to problems they had not defined and did not own. These teachers invariably did not find the time valuable; eventually they lost interest and became non-attendees. A second group comprised teachers who, year after year, were happy to try out or test the strategies of others, but did not move beyond this stage. This group needs a lot of support as they need constant exposure to new ideas. A third group developed their own strategies, while a fourth moved to engaging in more formal research projects and presented their results at both internal and outside forums. I have learned that one cannot expect all teachers to make the journey of the last two groups, but these teachers tend to be self-motivated and do assist in motivating others—a level of leadership. The overall impact of the professional learning teams was substantial. In at least a broad sense, it was reasonable to claim that the whole school was focused on the classroom and on improvement of teaching and learning. It was noticeable that, even when classroom PEEL activities were not formally planned, many strategies happened naturally for experienced staff. Once teachers are generally more reflective about the learning as a result of being more aware of good learning behaviors, they are more likely to identify problems and work on improvements.

Lessons

1. Support internal in-service work for new faculty as part of their orientation into the school; that is, promote and support professional learning teams so that experiences are shared and celebrated across all faculty.
2. Find ways to promote teaching and learning development work over daily administration by initiating research and providing resources.
3. Provide administrative support for the production of internal newsletters (sharing ideas within the school) and encourage publication outside the school, for example, in *PEEL SEEDS*.
4. Spread the coordinating load by encouraging young teachers to lead groups and have facilitator meetings scheduled. Avoid allowing the group to become dependent on the leader to come up with ideas; the group leader's role is more like one of a director.
5. Actively share leadership as a succession planning approach.
6. Ensure that new faculty attend external teaching and learning conferences.
7. Reward group leaders with a responsibility allowance or with time where possible.
8. You may change your focus, but keep a consistent overall direction within the constant theme of improving teaching and learning through reflection and sharing in professional learning teams (but under various names). This means building coherence between subsequent developments and initiatives.
9. Incorporate teaching and learning goals into the teacher selection process.
10. Where possible, administrative leaders should teach!
11. Be explicit about what you value; for example, noisy classes are fine if they are on task.

So far, with the exception of the external factors behind Episode 4, our story is one of continued progress in building a culture of collaborative action research focused on learning and teaching. The next two episodes involve serious reversals and apparent loss of many of the gains of the previous decade. The final episode describes what I did in response. Two very different reasons existed for the setbacks: the first was a wrong decision that I made; this was followed by a new principal's change in emphasis in what was valued.

Episode 6: 1996 to 1997

A Wrong Turn

In 1996, with about 80% of the faculty involved in voluntary professional learning teams, I moved to have the time spent in these teams counted in the teachers' workload in the same way as other duties. The Staff Development Coordinator, with my support and that of the group leaders (who were again mostly young faculty), coordinated the whole process. This structure was intended to be the pinnacle in terms of involvement. Teachers could opt to not join a team and not "do" this work; if so, I would replace it with two extra yard duties[4]—something that involved the same length of time as a meeting. This seemed reasonable to me; when I put it to the faculty, they all agreed, but all of them chose to join a team! One reason for this was the tedious nature of yard duty, but I believe that another was the peer pressure inadvertently created by our success. The result was a very valuable lesson for both authors. My school had achieved the highest level of participation in PEEL of any of the schools in the project, and this seemed only a small extra step. With hindsight, I underestimated the consequences of pressuring the last 20% of teachers to become involved.

The focus of the groups in 1996 was intended to be the incorporation of more teaching and learning ideas in written units of work. As the year progressed, however, other issues began to take over the agendas, such as bullying and harassment-policy development and complaint sessions about managing particular students. Many groups became discontented and seemed to lose their way. With the wisdom of hindsight, we have realized that PEEL meetings depend on teachers being willing to problematize their practice—to raise perceived weaknesses in what is occurring in their classrooms. The last 20% included many teachers who did not want to do this—and it cannot be forced. These teachers were vocal that the meetings were a waste of time. It was too hard for the others to sustain a good meeting dynamic in the face of these sorts of comments.

There was also a commonly held view that we had begun to over-document the meetings and that it became too closely related to our (new) teacher review and performance processes. The state government imposed these review changes and required faculty to develop personal professional development plans and then discuss their practice against these plans in a review meeting with a senior member of staff. We had believed that the professional learning team experiences would give teachers plenty of positive things to report in their annual reviews. In fact they have; in subsequent years, many teachers have made rich use of ideas from PEEL, Bloom's taxonomy, Howard Gardner's multiple intelligences, and cooperative learning, and they have described in their reviews what they have done with them in this process. They have become much more confident in defending their practice as a result. In 1996, however, all of this was new and viewed with cynicism by many faculty. In addition, we made what turned out to be a mistake in rushing in with a detailed documentation and accountability structure for what had been very relaxed and informal meetings. Interestingly, at the end of the year, in spite of all these problems, faculty voted to continue with the groups into 1997.

Apart from the problems of pushing for 100% involvement, I realized that a well-defined teaching and learning focus is needed for professional teams to work. Without this, they get lost attempting to solve other non-core issues. The issues just listed did not make for stimulating meetings. Moreover, this work should be related to professional development rather than performance measurement. After all, will teachers exercise risk taking in a performance review environment?

The "getting lost" experiences of that year meant that, in 1997, the groups voluntarily focused back on PEEL, motivation in the 15 and 16 year olds, cooperative learning/table groups, and our first funded research group (PAVOT). The PAVOT group investigated links between PEEL and cooperative learning. The PAVOT teams were valuable for the participants (including me). With hindsight (again), they kept a number of key faculty involved in initiatives that were extending and rewarding and were hence a source of reserve energy that I could draw on in subsequent years. To help maintain a school-wide focus on teaching and learning, department coordinators were asked to encourage more teaching and learning discussions in the existing regular department meetings. Only limited success was evident in this initiative, with the administrative issues continuing to dominate. It worked best in the English department, which consisted mainly of PEELers who had developed the skills of reflective thinkers, whereas other groups had bigger proportions of blockers. The idea here was probably a reasonable one, but my timing was wrong. I needed a bigger proportion of staff members who could see value in this change from long-established practice.

Lessons

1. Do not pressure teachers who do not have concerns about their practice into situations where they are expected to identify and admit to such concerns.
2. Maintain a focus for professional learning teams on issues of teaching and learning; issues of management and discipline are very likely to lead to unproductive meeting dynamics.
3. Principals must be publicly supportive of teacher development work: provide resources (e.g., cater for meetings), encourage risk taking, value such use of time, recognize efforts and outcomes, trust teachers to determine the agendas, and set goals.
4. A strategic rationale and framework for action should be incorporated into the school's charter priorities and policies.
5. Ensure that timetabled meetings aren't affected by "extras" (where teachers have to cover for an absent colleague). As a means of recognition, include or acknowledge the time as part of teachers' workload (like any other duty), but beware of the downside of forcing teachers into participation.
6. Be sensitive to where faculty are in their development and risk-taking ability, and provide appropriate support.
7. Work toward the goal of discussion about learning and the sharing of teaching strategies becoming an accepted part of department meetings.

Episode 7: 1998 to 2000

Some Declining Years

Over the years 1998–2000, professional learning teams gradually collapsed. In 1998, there was no doubt that staff were feeling an increase in work pressure and the intensity of school life and resorted to survival strategies and "making do." As a faculty we identified some 30 aspects of workloads to reduce, with the discussion itself being as important for morale as the workload reductions. This was a real "time out—let's re-energize" year.

With the 1999 appointment of a new principal, who assumed control of curriculum, priorities changed. From my perspective, it seemed that more emphasis was placed on how good our classes looked compared with the teaching and learning focus of how good our classes were. I was surprised by just how much power a principal seemed to have in this area to define what was important. It was a difficult period for me, and I chose to take personal "time out" from leadership of improvement in teaching and learning across the school. The principal and a few other faculty regarded teaching and learning developments as the soft work compared to the "real hard work done by coordinators in student management." There is no doubt in my mind which work is the harder and more demanding, and it is not the work related to day-to-day tasks, even though this must be done. The biggest single obstacle to improving teaching and learning is that we all tend to do our "task related, day-to-day" work first and then that "nice teaching and learning stuff" when time allows us.

With no general professional learning teams operating, only eight teachers continued with their work in the externally funded research projects (PAVOT), which involved three different projects over the next three years. I remained heavily involved with these teachers. These projects were funded through Ian at Monash University and were extremely valuable experiences for those involved. The outcomes and reports were impressive, with the teachers receiving acknowledgment from faculty within the school, and externally in published articles. Engaging teachers in funded research with critical friends at the university empowers them in the study of the learning process by structuring their reflections on a particular aspect of learning. It is important to celebrate outcomes by encouraging teachers to share their projects and findings with the entire faculty.

Even at this low point, we found the insights of our university colleagues and other visiting academics brought vitality by adding perspectives of what we had achieved. Occasions when they commented on this, or when our faculty engaged in discussions with other schools, helped us value and be better able to see what progress had occurred. Although learning teams were not meeting and teachers tended not to be developing new practices, they had not gone backwards. Because their previous innovative ideas for promoting quality learning had arisen from concerns held by the teachers and had been developed or adapted by them (not just imported from outside), they had become engrained parts of their teaching. These changes resulted in a faculty that was proud of what they do (and perhaps have taken for granted) and was invaluable in terms of providing the energy to keep going. I remember the comments of several Belgian academics after they visited classrooms. They said that the learning activities they observed were the best they had seen: "the school was a paradise." These sorts of comments have an uplifting effect on faculty.

My response, as assistant principal, to this decline in what mattered to me was to initiate a review of the school leadership structure with a somewhat hidden goal of refocusing the whole school back onto teaching and learning, even given the lack of support of the principal. Our school charter, which is a required document in all schools in Victoria, has staff development/improving teaching and learning as one of its two main priorities. I set out to ask hard questions about what we meant by this. The process was conducted consensually and involved most of the school's leadership team. One outcome was the revelation that the gains of 1986–96 in support for learning teams had not actually been lost. Once teachers had experienced a loss of emphasis in these areas, they missed the stimulation of the meetings and became supportive of reinstating them. The structure that emerged from this review included two new senior positions called managers of effective teaching and learning. The principal was not in favor of this significant change to the school leadership structure. He wanted no such positions, but the strong support from the staff, who had voted for three such positions, and from all other members of the leadership team, meant that we agreed on a compromise of two.

As I mentioned earlier, department meetings at our school, like most schools, have been largely administrative and hence not empowering. We had tried to reverse the emphasis and not been successful, so our solution was to reduce their frequency and replace them with meetings set up around learning and teaching agendas.

Lessons

1. Allow timeout for faculty to freely discuss stress/workload concerns. Then refocus faculty energy by reminding them of past achievements and successes with students.
2. When teachers genuinely control their own professional development, the changes become permanent parts of the practice.
3. Leadership by assistant principals and other members of the administrative team is important, as is overtly clear support for a teaching and learning focus. The school charter should have teaching and learning as the key priority.
4. Develop a focused teaching and learning leadership structure.
5. Facilitate funded research/links with critical friends and university or other partners.
6. Encourage faculty to take on higher levels of leadership by facilitating workshops for colleagues or other school members or undertaking extended research projects for publishing.
7. Ensure that meetings are an empowering experience for faculty.

Episode 8: 2001

Restructure and Rebirth

In response to the events of 1996–2000 and to the faculty responses to the review of the school leadership structure, we addressed "meeting empowerment" by changing the emphasis in meetings. In a 10-week term we now have two weeks of department meetings, five weeks of teaching and learning focus group (cross department) meetings, and two weeks of department meetings. This has meant that *cross-department* professional learning teams that focus on teaching and learning replaced some of the more administrative department meetings. "Take something out of the backpack before putting something else in," and be mindful of widespread workload concerns. Our two managers of effective teaching and learning, along with myself, coordinated and supported these focus groups covering PEEL, independent learning, middle years of schooling issues, assessment strategies, and information technologies. Groups are well administrated, with outcomes posted on our local intranet. Involvement is voluntary; it began at pleasingly high levels and has increased to close to 100%. Staff from these teams presents findings at full staff meetings. One art teacher, for example, who became interested in and proficient in the use of the PEEL CD (a database of more than 1000 articles written by PEEL teachers; Mitchell, Mitchell, McKinnon, & Scheele, 2003) to develop good learning behaviors, initiated a focus group to examine its use and in doing so inspired others. I was then able to acknowledge her excellent work in her review process.

Teachers seem most responsive when they choose whether to participate and which group they are involved in. Each semester we now ask for teaching and learning suggestions that faculty would like to investigate, select the seven or so most popular, and then allow teachers to select their group.

We have learned to emphasize the word *learning* in the label professional learning teams. The members prod each other to regularly step out of their comfort zones. "How will this be *new* for you?" is a common question.

With varying levels of commitment and some blocking influences at work, I instigated some "core value" discussions at faculty meetings for four weeks. Another consideration was that new faculty commented that they were receiving mixed messages from their colleagues about what the school's goals were. On reflection, this could be explained by the fact that about half of the faculty had joined the team since the initial work on establishing the amalgamated college in 1992–93. These sessions provided opportunities for the "blockers" to have their say. For me, however, the most reassuring aspect was to hear many faculty so strongly defending the importance of our professional learning teams in supporting and developing our sharing/teaching and learning ethos.

Faculty meetings now also place teaching and learning issues as the highest priority on the agenda, with a wide range of staff presenting and facilitating sessions. These sharing sessions often involve using or demonstrating a particular strategy in addition to raising an issue or outcome. For example, recently a "speak easy panel" of faculty was used to conduct a discussion on the values associated with the use of cooperative learning. Faculty attendance (voluntary) at learning team meetings has increased to close to 100%.

Teachers attending external activities invariably report back to faculty on just how well we compare to other schools; "We seem so far ahead with all the classroom strategies we are using. We are years ahead; they don't even talk about those things." In reflection, we seem to be back on track as a learning community. The principal also began to publicly celebrate these success stories and began to list teaching and learning as a strength of the school. These issues did not become his top priority, but he did come to recognize their importance for many faculty. Helping a new principal understand our culture proved a challenging but not insurmountable task.

Lessons

1. Do not assume that because a previously well supported initiative has died that support for it has dried up. Let teachers experience its absence and then decide what to do.

2. Plan and implement workshops to build the initiative into school policy and clarify common values. With faculty changes, it is necessary to revisit the core values of the school in terms of teaching and learning, in a collaborative process, every three to four years.

3. Use external professional development activities to provide new ideas and stimulate learning. When possible, send a team to these and assist them to plan, implement, and follow up where they see it as appropriate.

4. As principals, openly place importance on the central role of reflection and sharing of ideas by faculty in all meetings (not position it, as I've heard it described, as "coffee talk"). Endorse staff development and curriculum work as vital, not peripheral.

5. The administrative team, in particular the principal, must be seen to be supportive, knowledgeable, and an active leader in the area of faculty development. Too often, too much is delegated to rather than shared with other coordinators, like the professional development coordinator.

6. Principals should feature and celebrate activities that highlight achievements and ensure that feedback from visitors to the school is used to affirm what we all "take for granted."

7. Be prepared to make major changes to school structures, but remember that experience precedes understanding and support.

8. Be mindful of workloads and practice the notion of creating space before asking for more.
9. Effective educational leadership will ensure that teaching and learning has the highest priority, but do not expect major changes in school culture to occur in one or two years; think instead in terms of five years.

Postscript

In 2002, the principal took a position in another school, and I was appointed to take his place. Ian believes that it is important to report that this was met with a long standing ovation at the faculty meeting where it was announced. This was a good moment that gave powerful feedback on the perceived value of what I had been trying to achieve.

Conclusions and Discussion Questions

David's experiences provide valuable insights into the roles that teacher leaders, assistant principals, and principals can have in promoting and supporting sustainable professional learning teams that lead to and result in improved classroom learning and staff development. As we reflected on the 16-year journey, it was clear that the result has been a profound change in the culture of the school and in how teachers operate in and out of classrooms. These changes occurred gradually and sometimes were not noticeable until well after they had occurred, but they are real.

Owen, Johnson, Clark, Lovitt, and Morony (1988) identified nine principles underpinning the design of effective professional development (p. 16). This professional development does the following:

1. It addresses issues of concern recognized by teachers themselves.
2. It takes place as close as possible to the teachers' own learning environment.
3. It takes place over an extended period of time.
4. It has the support of both colleagues and the school administration.
5. It provides opportunities for reflection and feedback.
6. It enables participating teachers to feel a substantial degree of ownership.
7. It involves a conscious commitment on the part of the teacher.
8. It involves groups of teachers rather than individuals from a school.
9. It uses the services of a consultant and/or critical friend.

This list resonates with some important aspects of this story. Several other features, however, emerge from this 16-year story and its emphasis on schoolwide change.

Persistence

Institutional change can be a gradual process only, one that is mediated by the constant changes in faculty as teachers retire and new ones are hired. It is essential that the school leadership have a clear vision of what they want and are prepared to invest years in achieving this.

Consistency

Very early, David developed a vision of what he wanted in and outside of classrooms. This vision became more informed over time, but all initiatives and responses to external pressures were consistent with both his long-term goals and his beliefs about how to achieve them. This is the antithesis of moving every year or so to a new fad or program and illustrates what is required to implement complex research-based instructional strategies such as cooperative learning.

Coherence

Schools are not islands, and there were regular pressures from outside as well as new ideas from within the faculty and external critical friends. It is very easy for these to appear to faculty as the new flavor of the month. Building an explicit coherence between these was crucial to the long-term success of the program. New pressures such as the need to incorporate information and communication technologies into schools or new assessment procedures at high-stake years such as year 12 need to be filtered through an overall strategic vision.

Focus on Learning and Teaching

This focus has been essential; other issues such as management and student interest have been shown to flow from the core issue of how the students are learning and interacting with teachers about what they are learning.

Time

All changes need time, and systems in particular are notoriously impatient in their timelines. This story highlights the time needed for staff to build a shared vision of what changes are possible, both inside and outside classrooms as well as how and why these might be valuable. These changes in conceptions and perceptions require years to develop.

Structural Changes

It is very easy, and common, for principals to ask for changes such as those that are the focus of this story as add-on extras to existing structures in the school. David engaged in systematic efforts to reduce the perceived importance of administration and student management issues in comparison with issues associated with how students were learning and interacting with teachers. This required structural changes in the leadership positions in the school as well as the grouping and meeting structures in the school. These were profound changes that could not have been introduced at the outset—he had to engage faculty with him, and once again this required time.

Treat Staff as Professionals

Changes that matter in how teachers work cannot be mandated, however much one would like to do so. All initiatives need to begin from the premise that change can occur only with the consent and support of the teacher. This does not mean that all teachers have to consent to a change; rather, that change needs to be structured in ways that allow teachers to change, or not change, in their own time frames and from entry points that matter to them.

Devolve Leadership

Create a range of leadership roles that reduce the load on the primary source of energy, broaden what can be done, provide new career opportunities, and ensure a succession if the source of energy leaves the school.

Expectations of Difference

Different staff will change both at different rates and to different degrees. One should expect this variability and capitalize on it by nurturing and supporting teachers who react quickly to take on leadership roles.

Questions the Administrative Team Could Ask Themselves

Faculty Engagement/Recognition. How many of the faculty would like to pursue improvements in teaching and learning, and how can we find out?

Do they trust us enough to engage in risk taking action-research activities? How do we know? What recognition do we currently give for innovation in this area? How do we ensure empowerment and independence in individuals and groups? Do faculty regularly share teaching and learning ideas? How? Have they debated core values/developed goal congruence on teaching and learning? What are the current levels of in-school and ongoing teacher development? What activities are involved?

Structures/Resources. Does the leadership structure have teaching and learning as its main priority? Are teaching and learning professional learning team meetings given priority and valued as a core function of teachers? How often do meetings focus on teaching and learning over and above subject type aspects? Is this done in cross-curricula groups as well as departments or grade levels? Do we work with critical/university colleagues? How? Do we encourage and support action research work?

Administrative Leadership Role. Are we personally knowledgeable of teaching and learning issues/strategies? Do we openly show support? How? Do we facilitate and encourage others in facilitation of in-service work? What does educational leadership really mean? Do we analyze and encourage staff (at the right level/time)? How do we analyze, define, and document the teaching and learning culture in our school? How have we rallied others to help build a teaching and learning culture in our school?

Notes

1. For ease of reading, we use the word *principals* to refer to both principals and assistant principals.
2. Australian schools "timetable" their classes so that, within each 5-day or in some cases 10-day period, every student has their assigned number of classes in each of their subjects (most subjects are taught three times in five days). Within each 5- or 10-day period, every day has a different timetable. This system gives "Timetablers" some ability to give a group of teachers a common nonteaching period where they could meet.
3. Information about any of the publications of the PEEL project can be obtained from the authors or from *ross.mackinnon@education.monash.edu.au.*
4. Australian students do not stay inside during recess and lunch breaks; they play outside. Yard duty involves ensuring that school rules are not broken.

References

Baird, J. R., & Northfield, J. R. (Eds.). (1995). *Learning from the PEEL experience.* Melbourne, Australia: PEEL Publishing.

Curry, B. K. (Ed.). (1997). Continuity and reform: A new discourse for discussion of change in schools. *Education Planning, 11*(1), pp. 21–30.

Fullan, M. (1994). *Change forces: Probing the depths of educational reform.* School Development of Change Series 10. London: Falmer Press.

Fullan, M. (2001). *The new meaning of educational change.* New York: Teachers College Press.

Loughran, J. J. (1999). Professional development for teachers: A growing concern. *The Journal of In-Service Education, 25*(2), pp. 261–72.

Loughran, J. J., Mitchell, I. J., & Mitchell, J. A. (2002). *Learning from teacher research.* New York: Teachers College Press.

Mitchell, I., Mitchell, J., McKinnon, R., & Scheele, S. (2003). PEEL in practice:1000 ideas for quality teaching (CD). Melbourne, Australia: PEEL Publishing.

Owen, J., Johnson, N., Clark, D., Lovitt, C., & Morony, W. (1988). *Models of professional development.* Canberra, Australia: Mathematics Curriculum and Teaching Program.

5

A Middle School Strives to Achieve Team Leadership Through Opposition and Uncertainty

Kathleen J. Martin

Janet H. Chrispeels

From the beginning of her tenure as Paramount Middle School principal, Chris Morris wanted to involve teachers in the decision-making process of the school.[1–3] She wanted an "advisory team sharing their knowledge" to help make important decisions and to gather information that would inform those decisions. Toward this goal, she created the School Leadership Council (SLC), and from this council emerged the School Leadership Team (SLT). Under her leadership, Chris envisioned the faculty and staff working together as a team in which "everyone would have equal weight in their decisions." This was to be the beginning of a new form of leadership at Paramount Middle School, unlike what teachers and staff had seen in previous years. Sharing leadership responsibilities is something that "I believe in. . . . I really feel the more teachers and staff members are empowered in decisions, the more you get buy-in," she said. As Peter Senge (1990) indicates, however, making "changes in infrastructure, like reorganizations and changes in reward systems, often have far less impact than expected" (p. 40) and can be difficult to achieve when environmental, organizational, and intergroup factors conspire to thwart the process.

This chapter focuses on the actions Chris Morris took as principal of a middle school to fulfill her goal of shared decision making. It also presents the personal uncertainty she wrestled with as she attempted to achieve her vision for Paramount Middle School and the opposition she encountered from district administration, leadership team members, and staff. We examine how relationships among the superintendent, principal, and SLT contributed to ambiguity and conflict for the principal as she endeavored to clarify her own role and achieve an empowered school leadership team. Often attempts at shared leadership are not as straightforward as implied, and the concept of "team" suggests that together the team "can accomplish more than the sum total of the individuals involved" (Professional Development Seminar, 1996). We highlight the many complex interactions that emerge as the teachers and principal work to implement bottom-up reforms that challenge traditional patterns of interaction and leadership at the school and in the district.

Wrestling With Shared Leadership

Schools throughout the United States and many other countries are implementing various forms of shared decision making and establishing site-based management (SBM) teams or committees (Clune & White, 1988; Hargreaves & Evans, 1997; Johnson & Pajares, 1996; Malen & Ogawa, 1988; Wallace & Hall, 1994; Wohlstetter, Smyer, & Mohrman, 1994). Although the desire to incorporate effective shared decision making is widespread and has been presented as the optimum form of leadership for more than ten years, school systems continue to wrestle with defining and implementing SBM to ensure that school self-governance influences teaching and learning practices. Boards of education want self-governance that improves student learning, but the link between SBM and student achievement has been shown to be tenuous and often indirect (Malen & Ogawa, 1988; Marks & Louis, 1997; Smylie, Lazarus, & Brownlee-Conyers, 1994). The establishment of teacher leadership teams creates new roles and relationships for teachers and principals within schools and between the school and the district. Leadership teams also must cope with multiple reforms, rapid changes in district or site leadership, shifting policies, and environmental factors that affect their schools often in ways beyond their immediate control. They are expected to change established patterns of behavior while simultaneously running the school and succeeding with students. Such changes in social position can often contribute to role ambiguity and role conflict (Bertrand, 1972; Biddle, 1979; Kahn, Wolfe, Quinn, Snoek, & Rosenthal, 1964). Furthermore, if district policies or practices are unclear or contradictory, the conflict can undermine team effectiveness, lead to open hostility or withdrawal, and diminish the potential of the team to bring about student learning. If teachers and administrators display ambivalence about decision-making opportunities or feel frustrated with the lack of needed skills and information, the sense of empowerment essential to effective decision making may be undermined (Fuhrman, 1993; Hart, 1994; Johnson & Boles, 1994; Weiss, Cambone, & Wyeth, 1991).

Efforts to empower teachers and establish shared decision making demands new knowledge and skills and clarification of rights, obligations, and expectations of who should be involved. Few studies have investigated the relationships among team, principal, and superintendent as they each assume new roles and shift their responsibilities. In addition, although training is seen as important, research has not explored how training may enhance role clarity and understanding or contribute to role ambiguity and conflict. In this chapter, we explore the principal's, superintendent's, and team members' perceptions about shared decision making and the ways these perceptions impact their work and their roles at the school. We examine the ways the principal and School Leadership Team (SLT) cope with issues of conflict and ambiguity as they attempt to implement school reforms and participate in a three-year team training program. Most important, we examine a history of district and school events and the ways these events impact relationships and the potential for the school to establish shared decision making (Chrispeels, 1997).

Getting Acquainted With School Leadership

Paramount Middle School and the School Leadership Team Program

Paramount Middle School is located in a small suburban, semi-rural district in Southern California. The district serves 3,100 students in one high school, one middle school, and four elementary schools. During the late 1990s, the district experienced rapid growth in the student population and was beset by a lack of adequate school facilities. When class-size reductions were introduced, more classrooms were needed in the lower elementary grades, which further impacted the existing K–8 facilities. With the recent passage of a school bond measure, the district began construction of a new elementary school, remodeling an existing elementary site, and repairing the aging middle school facilities. Paramount Middle School serves 700 sixth through eighth-grade students, 54% of whom are Latino and 45% of whom are white. Of the 35 fulltime teachers, 26 are female and 9 male. Four of the teachers are of Latino background, one Asian, and the remainder are white. The 9 sixth-grade teachers work in interdisciplinary teams, but the 26 seventh- and eighth-grade teachers remain in a more traditional departmental structure.

The School Leadership Team Program was initiated in 1993 by the California School Leadership Academy (CSLA) as a statewide capacity-building effort to develop a team of teacher leaders who are able to lead their schools in ways that will result in "powerful student learning" (CSLA, 1996). Each of the 12 CSLA regions in the state recruit schools to participate in this voluntary program. Schools agree to send a team, usually composed of teachers, staff, and administrators, to the regional training sessions five times a year. Team-member selection is left to the discretion of the school, and teams vary in size from 6 to 15 members. Although most teams remain relatively stable for the duration of the seminars, new team members are integrated and welcomed at the training. The teams attend five sessions each year for two (or an optional three) years and pay a small fee each year to cover materials and refreshment costs. Teams are clustered at the training sessions into groups of 5–10 teams within regions to foster collaboration across schools. During the all-day sessions, SLT teams explore themes such as the change process, shaping school culture to support collaboration and continuous improvement, creating a vision of powerful teaching and learning, and designing curriculum and assessment in the service of powerful learning. They learn about group facilitation skills, including problem solving, decision making, conflict resolution, and establishing roles for team members. Active learning approaches engage team members in data collection and analysis, collaborative action research, and curricular and instructional restructuring efforts (CSLA, 1998).

Understanding the Work of the Team and the Role of the Principal

To understand the roles of the Paramount team and the principal, CSLA professional development, and the school and district factors that shaped these roles, we began attending and videotaping SLT training seminars with the team between January 1995 and May 1997. The purpose of the videotaping was to observe the team's development in the seminars over time and to capture the issues the team chose to address. We also conducted audiotaped interviews with Paramount Middle School team members, teachers who were not team members, the principal, the vice principal, and the superintendent during the spring and fall of 1997 and winter of 1998. The purpose of the interviews was to understand the impact of the SLT program on school actions to meet student needs from the perceptions of the team members as well as others at the school. Interviews were semi-structured so that similar data were collected from each person being interviewed, but they provided ample opportunities for interviewees to talk freely about their experiences and perceptions. In addition to the focused data collection at Paramount in 1995 and 1996, 148 teams participating in the statewide SLT program completed two surveys for each year of training: a 32-item Team Assessment instrument and a 25-item SLT Implementation Continuum. The surveys provided perceptual data about the Paramount team's progress regarding team functioning and accomplishment of the program objectives (Chrispeels, Castillo, & Brown, 2000).

Collection and analysis of the videotapes and interviews took place in cycles, with each round of collection and analysis leading to additional data collection and analysis as new questions emerged. The videotapes were transcribed and analyzed using a computer program called C-video, and the tapes were searched for themes that were common across seminar meetings. These included themes such as role definition; topics most frequently discussed; the impact of training on the team's functioning; and the nature of communication and interaction within the team and with the staff and district administrators.

History of Events, Episodes, and Perspectives at Paramount Middle School

In videotapes of SLT training seminars, team members appeared frustrated about what they perceived to be their ambiguous leadership role and their inability to accomplish the goals they had set for their school. Key events or decision points repeatedly emerged as defining moments for the team, principal, and superintendent. A review of documents associated with the school such as the district's Tentative Agreement with teachers, SLT training materials, and minutes from team meetings surfaced potential contradictions in language about teachers' decision-making roles. Through the use of textual analysis and the key events from the videos, we developed a timeline to purposefully examine events occurring in the district and school between 1992 and 1998 that were recognized, acknowledged, and considered socially significant by the participants (Bloome & Egan-Robertson, 1993; Chrispeels, 1997).[4] Table 5.1 presents and summarizes a brief chronological history of significant school events that influenced the SLT.

Table 5.1 Chronological History of Significant School Events That Influenced the Paramount School Leadership Team's (SLT) Capacity

	School Year 1992–1993	*School Year 1993–1994*	*School Year 1994–1995*	*School Year 1995–1996*	*School Year 1996–1997*	*Summer 1997*
SLT Training and School Awards	Distinguished School Award	Paramount invited to attend SLT training, fall 1994	SLT training: Year 1	SLT training: Year 2	SLT training: Year 3	
School Structure Changes	Paramount becomes a Middle School	Six-period day proposed and accepted		SLT proposes 7th period; rejected superintendent	District changes Middle School designation; moves sixth grades	Principal initiates one lunch period*
Administrative Changes	Jan. '93, new co-principal designated	April '93, new sole principal designated		New district superintendent		New assistant principal
Scheduling Changes	Two lunch periods for 700 students initiated			After school tutorial proposed and accepted	Superintendent changes school start time; SLT proposes later start time	Superintendent and principal change school start time. One lunch period initiated*
Leadership and Tentative Agreements	School Leadership Council initiated	Initial Tentative Agreement signed		New Tentative Agreement signed		

NOTE: * The move to a one-period lunch was perceived by the principal as a structural change that would promote teacher interaction and collaborative time. Teachers perceived it as a scheduling change.

The table is an event map that provides a broad context for examining the history of events at Paramount. Through this history, we present four specific episodes that transpired as a result of proposals initiated by the SLT and that reflect the team's effort to define and carry out its assumed role as decision makers. Fast-paced changes and multiple transitions often complicate existing relationships at schools and contribute to a sense of unease for participants.[5] Therefore, we also examine the individual perspectives of the superintendent, principal, and team.

History of Events

In 1992, Paramount Junior High School received a California Distinguished School Award, and at the same time the superintendent announced that Paramount would become a middle school the following school year. This meant that the sixth graders would move to Paramount and the ninth graders to the high school. (See Table 5.1 for more on the history of events.) According to interviews with teachers, this announcement about the move came without prior notice or preliminary discussion and was driven by the lack of space to accommodate the sixth graders at the elementary schools as opposed to pedagogy. Over the next several years, this change in configuration had several implications for discipline, student achievement, and communication at the school. When interviewed in 1997 about the change to a middle school, SLT members reported, "there was huge antagonism. It was really a hard change for the school . . . [and] we had many discipline problems."

Chris Morris became co-principal of Paramount in January 1993 and became sole principal in April. She introduced to the faculty the concept of a School Leadership Council (SLC) to advise her on a wide range of school issues. The teachers accepted the SLC concept and selected representatives from each department. One of the council's actions was to develop a proposal for a six-period schedule (five instructional periods plus one prep period). The teachers viewed this as a major accomplishment for their new SLC. The six-period plan was accepted by the district and implemented in the 1993–94 school year.

In January 1994, the district and the teachers' union signed a Tentative Agreement to "affirm their commitment to shared decision making" in schools throughout the district. The agreement language did not specify the domains of decision making, nor was it clear regarding the nature and extent of the decisions to be made by the school and/or the district. The agreement stated:

> Leadership Councils shall be immediately implemented . . . to endorse the concept of continuous improvement for the instructional programs of the District by including teachers in those decisions impacting instruction. . . . A Site-Based Governance Committee . . . shall determine which decisions may be reserved entirely to the sites, which decisions are shared, and which decisions are reserved to the traditional decision-making structures of the District.

The agreement recognized the importance of training in decision making for both administrators and teachers, yet the district provided neither training nor clarifying information. In reflecting back on this period, the teachers reported that the areas of decision making included personnel, budget, and curriculum and represented a shift in their role from advisors to the principal to one of apparent shared decision makers. They reported feeling uncertain of their responsibilities and confused about how to handle these new areas.

In the spring of 1994, the California School Leadership Academy (CSLA) initiated the School Leadership Team Professional Development Program and invited Paramount Middle School to participate. Chris, a graduate of the CSLA Principal's Academy, welcomed the idea and proposed it to the SLC. They agreed and anticipated that training would help them to develop decision-making and problem-solving skills. In the fall of 1994, they began participating in the School Leadership Team (SLT) program, regularly sending a team of five SLC members and the principal to the training sessions. The SLC consisted of four core members who attended each session and a fifth position filled on a rotating basis by a member of the larger school council. This approach gave all team members an opportunity to attend and participate in SLT trainings. Team members attended 15 training seminars over a three-year period. At the school site, this core group played the lead role in introducing the major episodes (to be discussed below) to the larger SLC.

The 1995–96 school year opened with a new superintendent, Norm Green, who was uneasy with the ambiguous language of the 1994 Tentative Agreement. He negotiated a new contract with the teachers' union that emphasized the principals' responsibilities and authority and decreased the decision-making power of the school site management teams. The contract affirmed the following:

> The administration is responsible for certain issues on any site and that the principal cannot relinquish those responsibilities to other individuals or committees. . . . [Teachers] must be included in decisions related to educational programs, budgets, staffing, and instruction . . . [and] teachers may desire to participate in certain areas and not in others.

The ways in which teachers were to be involved, however, was not clearly specified. The new contract solidified the role of teachers as advisors "included on various committees" and "encouraged to participate," but with little or no decision-making authority, including whether or not the school was to maintain the SLC. The Paramount team continued with a second and third year of training and maintained its leadership role in defining much of the work of the SLC.

In the 1996–97 school year, the district again proposed reconfiguring Paramount Middle School and moving all the sixth graders to a new site due to lack of space. In the following year, the school board approved the change and initiated site remodeling.

Episodes

We turn now to four specific episodes confronting Paramount Middle School from 1992 through 1998 as a way of highlighting core SLT-trained team leadership and problem-solving actions. The episodes represent two main concerns faced by the school and addressed by the SLT team: student achievement in Episodes 1 and 2; and scheduling in Episodes 3 and 4. In each episode, the team presents a proposal designed to change or modify existing school patterns: (1) a seventh period, (2) a study hall program, (3) the number of lunch periods, and (4) the school start time. Together, these episodes provide insight into the interactions among the superintendent, the principal, and the team.

Student Achievement (Episodes 1 and 2)

The SLT initiated two projects to help students who were not achieving success at school. Interviews with team members indicated that the issue of lack of student achievement and low grades were a concern. In the first episode, Superintendent Norm Green rejected the team's proposal due to legal implications. In the second episode, the team was able to accomplish its goal by focusing on a more limited solution designed within school and district parameters.

Episode 1. In the fall of 1995, during Paramount's second year of SLT training, the team proposed a seventh period to provide instructional assistance for students who were receiving D's and F's. Team members and other school staff volunteered to teach the seventh period "because we were so anxious to see if it makes any difference with these kids." The principal, as a team member, was involved in the development of this proposal, and she submitted it to Superintendent Green. He rejected it on the grounds that it violated the California Education Code to require some students to stay at school longer than others.

They perceived the rejection as a lack of district support. Team members indicated they did not meet with the superintendent to discuss the proposal rejection, nor did they look for workable solutions. As indicated by one team member, "We never did really bring him over here and say why not. . . . When [we] hit the wall . . . we stomped off in frustration." Team members felt the proposal rejection from the district was inconsistent with the Tentative Agreement to promote school-based leadership, and they interpreted this as a message from the superintendent that they did not have decision-making authority.

Episode 2. The concern over the increasing number of students receiving D's and F's and their lack of success at school persisted. With encouragement from the SLT training seminars, the team continued to seek solutions. According to team members, the staff made repeated efforts to communicate with parents during parent-teacher conferences, but they saw no improvement in students' performance. As one teacher indicated, "Nothing is happening and . . . it doesn't seem to be working." As evidenced in the video data during a SLT training seminar, the team discussed the issue and decided that poor grades may be due to students' failure to complete homework. They decided to interview and survey students to try to discover if this was the case.

In the interviews, teachers stated "many of these kids [reported they] were on the D and F lists because they didn't do their homework. . . . There were huge homework lapses from these particular kids." Students indicated that the primary reason why they did not complete their homework was that "no one was home to assist and support them." Based on these findings, the team recommended the homeroom period be shifted to the afternoon so that students could get tutoring assistance from teachers during school hours. Additional tutorial assistance was provided to any student until 4:00 P.M. every day on a voluntary basis. Although all students were welcomed, students on the D and F lists were encouraged to attend the tutorial sessions. By using the homerooms as a tutorial program, the school was not required to get the district's approval, thus overcoming the challenges the team encountered in trying to establish a seventh period.

Scheduling Issues (Episodes 3 and 4)

Episodes 3 and 4 are reflective of scheduling issues that were a major component of the team's work and focus: first, the number of lunch periods, and second, the school start time. In both episodes, Principal Chris Morris made the final decisions during the summers when most of the teachers were on vacation and unavailable, and team members felt excluded from the decision-making process.

Episode 3. In 1992, with the transition from a junior high to a middle school, the former principal at Paramount structured two lunch periods into the schedule to minimize supervision concerns. Chris Morris preferred one lunch period so that she had more time to talk to all of the teachers and ease scheduling difficulties. She reported, "Every year there was an outcry for communication, that staff could never meet together, even as simple as having lunch together." However, due to the vice principal's insistence, they decided not to change to one lunch period. The team discussed the issue at one of the SLT training seminars when the principal was absent, and they agreed (contrary to the principal's perception) that two lunch periods were beneficial. One member reported, "It used to be a nightmare around the lunch room, and now it's calm and you get your space. . . . If you start talking to people you may find out that some people disagree with [one lunch period]."

In the summer of 1997, the principal hired a new vice principal who was familiar with one lunch period of 700 students. Chris said during an interview, "I was really excited, and I said we've got to do this! This is fantastic—the teachers have wanted one lunch for so long. This is going to go over great!" Chris made the decision to have one lunch period without involving the SLC or teachers in the decision because, according to her, "they were not involved in supervision." In fact, "I think if every teacher would have voted, I mean if they were going to vote, which we usually don't vote, [they would have wanted one lunch period]."

Episode 4. The superintendent said that parents in the community were complaining that all the schools in the district started at the same time. In fact, "We had a number of complaints from parents . . . who had to drop off their kids at three different schools. They all start at 8:00 A.M. . . . so someone is too early and someone is too late." In the spring of 1997, the district agreed to stagger the start time for the following school year, with Paramount to start at 7:45 A.M., fifteen minutes earlier than previous schedules. Team members were concerned for two reasons. First, from their experience, they knew how difficult it was for most of their students to start as early as 8:00 A.M. Second, they were upset that the superintendent did not consult with them as the SLT before making this decision.

During the SLT training seminars, with the focus on research and data collection to make decisions, team members began collecting research on adolescent students that supported what they observed in their school. The research indicated that adolescent students who start their school day later in the morning tend to have better performance than those who start earlier. Based on their findings, team members asked the principal to discuss the time-change issue again with the superintendent. The principal reported that she approached the superintendent, and he said it was impossible to change the schedule for the coming year. SLC members and teachers felt frustrated and complained to the principal for not having the opportunity to influence the district's decision. The principal stated, "There were teachers who just kind of threw up their hands and said is the district listening to us? . . . Why are we doing this work if they are not listening to us?" In addition, the principal and the superintendent also received complaints from several parents who were "just up in arms" about the district's decision to start the school day at 7:45 A.M.

Principal Morris continued discussing the school start-time issue with Superintendent Green during the summer of 1997. In her interview she reported that the current time decision "is really against everything we [the SLC] have been working for. I know it may seem like a minor thing but [it's an indication of how much] the district listens to us, and what we do as professionals." The superintendent decided to have a meeting that summer with district staff, Paramount administrators, and team members and teachers to study the feasibility of changing the start time from 7:45 A.M. to 8:30 A.M. During her interview, Principal Morris stated,

> I tried to get a hold of every leadership team member [and] I couldn't get hold of hardly anyone. I had to make the decision and I made it. . . . I couldn't help that it happened during the middle of the summer. I based the decision on things that we had talked about that I felt were important to the whole staff.

According to Superintendent Green, it was decided that a change to 8:30 A.M. would be feasible. Principal Morris was excited about the decision. When the new school year began, however, some team members as well as other teachers were upset over the start-time change. They complained that, again, the principal did not involve them in the decision. As the superintendent noted, "She was [excited] . . . it was just wonderful. Then some of the teachers got all [upset] about that [because] it wasn't [their] decision." Team members and teachers believed there was nothing wrong with the principal's summer decisions; it was the fact that they were not involved in the decision-making process that upset them.

Summary

In the four episodes, the team's interactions and attempts to implement change to improve student learning can be understood as a sequence of events that built into an overall perception of its decision-making capabilities. In the first episode, team members were thwarted in their efforts. In the second episode, with the help of the SLT training, they regrouped and persisted with the issue of concern. Their high sense of efficacy and commitment to the good of the students as revealed in an SLT evaluation survey is an indicator of why they were able to persist. The third episode appeared to have less importance for the team than the episodes that revolved around student learning. It did have an influence on communication difficulties between the teacher team members and the principal, and it represented an instance when the team felt inadequately involved in the decision-making process. In the fourth episode, team members' frustrations were exacerbated by their lack of involvement in the decision, particularly when they had completed research on the issue and their professional judgment was involved.

The following perspectives focus on the superintendent's, principal's, and team members' perceptions about their relationships, roles, and responsibilities.

Perspectives

The Superintendent

Superintendent Norm Green's philosophy of management is to be supportive of principals and to help them meet the needs of their schools. He does not believe in managing schools from his office, but rather allowing principals the autonomy to operate their sites. He used Paramount as an example of his philosophy by saying that the principal "happens to like the CSLA training . . . [and] I don't want to go over there and muck it up, because that's kind of micromanaging the school." He visits a school when "invited to come in and talk about district policy or . . . once or twice a year on a major issue. [Otherwise] I think it is better for me to keep my hands out of it."

In 1995, when Superintendent Green assumed his position, he believed the Tentative Agreement, signed by the former superintendent and the Teachers' Federation, "wasn't really clear [about] how things were supposed to work." It "was interpreted as any decision dealing with personnel, budget, and curriculum" and was open for discussion. According to Green, this lack of clarity in the language of the contract regarding the decision-making authority of the leadership councils at district schools led to different interpretations. In some schools, the staff attempted to have committees manage areas of routine administrative decision-making procedures such as "what kind of paper to order for the [copy] machine." The superintendent believed this limited the authority of principals to perform their jobs effectively, and principals "felt handcuffed by the [Tentative Agreement]." He also reported that some teachers in the district felt they should not be making decisions about the daily management of schools, and they were "coming to these meetings upset, [saying] why are we wasting our time." Therefore, one of his first goals as superintendent was to clarify the ambiguity through negotiations between the district and the Teachers' Federation.

According to Norm Green, the new contract clarified the responsibilities and authority of teachers and administrators. It defined the concept of shared decision making as "having people who are going to be affected by decisions be involved to the degree that they would like to and the degree that it is helpful in the process." Under this contract, teachers were included in decisions related to educational programs, budget, personnel, and instruction. The ultimate decision, power, and responsibility, however, remained with principals who "cannot relinquish those responsibilities to other individuals or committees." The superintendent felt that establishing clear parameters of decision making was necessary and that the previous contract led to a great deal of frustration and mistrust. He cautioned, "The worst thing to do is [delegate responsibility for] decisions and then after the decision is made say that's not the right decision." He believed it's the principal's responsibility "to define and make it clear what decisions are being made . . . [and] figuring out how you're going to make [a decision], what information you need, and who is going to be involved."

The Principal

Initially, Paramount's principal, Chris Morris, wanted to involve teachers in the decision-making process of the school. She said, "[I wanted] information before I made decisions, you know . . . an advisory kind of situation. . . . I believe in that kind of style. I really feel the more teachers and staff members are empowered in decisions, the more you get buy-in." Furthermore, under the former superintendent she was encouraged to involve teachers in a wide range of decisions as part of the "union contract that there will be a leadership council." She created the SLC. Chris stated, "I had this grand vision that teachers and everybody on the team would have an equal weight in their decisions, and I have come to find this is not realistic." Chris learned from Superintendent

Green that her role as principal was to have a district perspective instead of a school perspective and that she would make the "ultimate decisions" for the school. In her interview Chris said, "I was a little bit nervous when that kind of proclamation, if you will, came down, but actually it seemed to be a relief to some of the teachers. . . . [It was] finally clear that when an ultimate decision needs to be made the principal does it." She believed she had "to take the front in decisions," and that Superintendent Green's primary goal "in the last three years has been consistency and the reason is all based on [student performance]."

Chris Morris felt that the teachers were not always familiar with the district's perspective on issues such as scheduling and personnel, and she found herself in the middle of the teachers and the district. She believed that "oftentimes that has been a problem with the leadership team, it's not like they are anti-district, but maybe [without] a clear understanding." Yet, she believed that the district approved the team's proposal to start the day at a later time because she had considered the district's perspective, and they worked together toward finding a solution. Chris now recognized the challenge to implementing her initial goals for the leadership team in decision making.

School Leadership Team

At the beginning of the Paramount SLT training seminars, the interview and video data suggest confusion and uncertainty among team members regarding their responsibilities as a decision-making team. The team considers lack of communication the primary source of misunderstanding between administrators and themselves, and members hope "to be perceived as a body that will promote communication." Through the training, they hope to gain new insights into their role as leaders in school restructuring, and the importance of "taking the responsibility to be an active participant in [their] work." One team member noted, "I see the development of a strong team as changing who . . . get[s] access to . . . the information by having a larger group of people that make decisions." During the training, the team addressed questions of purpose such as: "What brings [us] together as a team? What is [our] purpose for working together as a team [at the school]?" Another activity provided them with the opportunity to complete a "school systems graph" that encourages team members to look at roles and responsibilities.

During the SLT seminars, teams were provided with process and educational content knowledge, and they gained facilitation, communication, and problem-solving skills. They used their developing skills to research and identify problems and develop new programs for their school. Similar to other teams that received three years of SLT training, the team reported improvements (significant at the 95% confidence level on a yearly evaluation survey) in their use of data and focus on issues of teaching and learning. The training seminars provided the team with multiple opportunities to engage in a dialogue about significant educational issues away from the pressures of their school in an atmosphere of support and encouragement—conditions of professional development identified by Little (1993) as essential if a school staff is to be able to implement meaningful school reform. This focused time enhanced their skills in identifying problems, collecting data, and using research to propose solutions. Through the training, the team actively defined its role as problem solvers, addressing issues they perceived would enhance student learning. Team members reported that when the superintendent made decisions without consulting them, "a lot of people got really frustrated . . . [and asked], why are we going to all these committee [meetings]?"

Inconsistent and conflicting messages and expectations from the two superintendents and the principal contributed to team members' confusion about their new role as school leaders. As one member noted, "I think the role of the team right now is vague . . . my attendance at these meetings just confuses me. . . . You go to a meeting and you think that the issue has come to some conclusion when it [hasn't]." Another team member said, "Maybe things were already decided somewhere else by the time we got there . . . so some people weren't sure why [we] were there." Team members believe that at this time it is difficult to say what the actual role of the leadership team is at the school. One team member explained part of the difficulty "seems to be a lot of newness. We have a new super, new budget person, and the principal is new and she is not used to junior high school."

In the next section, through the multiple lenses of history, episodes, and frameworks, we examine the roles of the principal and the team from an integrated conceptual perspective as a way of looking at the social phenomena of schools.

Integrating Perspectives to Explore Principal-Team Dynamics

Many authors have attempted to describe the inherent complexity of organizations and systems in which individuals participate. These descriptions have tended to present organizations as somewhat static, more or less impervious to interpersonal relations, and with discreet boundaries between the inside and outside of the organization. These traditional theories of organizations are important for furthering our understanding. Yet, as changes occur in the dynamics of organizations and the roles individuals are expected to play, the patterns of behavior have not always followed the same course. Often individuals within schools continue to perceive the working of schools and the role they are to play in a hierarchical way with top-down decision making and direct instructions from superintendents and principals. With the advent of SBM and SLTs, individuals in schools (e.g., superintendent, principal, teachers, and staff) must readjust their behavior patterns and assumptions of the role they are to play in governing the school. Both SBM and SLTs call for a bottom-up decision-making process that asks teachers, staff, and others to make decisions important for their school.

By integrating perspectives, we see this as a "systemic-structural perspective" (Altrichter & Elliott, 2000), not as "orthodoxy," but in combination with micropolitical analysis (Mawhinney, 1999; Wallace, 2000). For achieving these ends, we draw on concepts from a systems and structural perspective of organizations (Hanna, 1997; Hardy & Clegg, 1996; Scott, 1992; Senge, 1990) and micropolitics (Blase & Anderson, 1995; Mawhinney, 1999; Wallace, 2000). Core concepts from these theories allow us to view the work of the principal and SLT from the macro-organizational level of school structures, environmental influences, and role theory that shape and define the actions of the team. The micro-perspective, which encompasses intergroup factors and micropolitics, helps us to understand the implicit cultural prescriptive that guide participants' actions. Integrating these perspectives offers insights into ways that school leadership teams lead their schools in the reform process because reforms tend to politicize schools and threaten existing roles, relationships, power, and resources. These dynamic relationships are portrayed in Figure 5.1, an Integrated Perspectives Model, which encompasses systems theory (Hanna, 1997; Scott, 1992; Senge, 1990) and a micropolitical perspective (Blase, 1991; Datnow, 1998; Mawhinney, 1999). Systems theory includes three components and indicates the relationships among (1) environmental factors, (2) organizational factors, and (3) intergroup relations.

Environmental factors, by definition, are everything outside the system's boundary. In this study, we perceived demographic changes in the school district as an objective environmental factor influencing and challenging the school and the leadership team to think in new ways about its students and the issues they faced. The SLT training was also viewed as a environmental

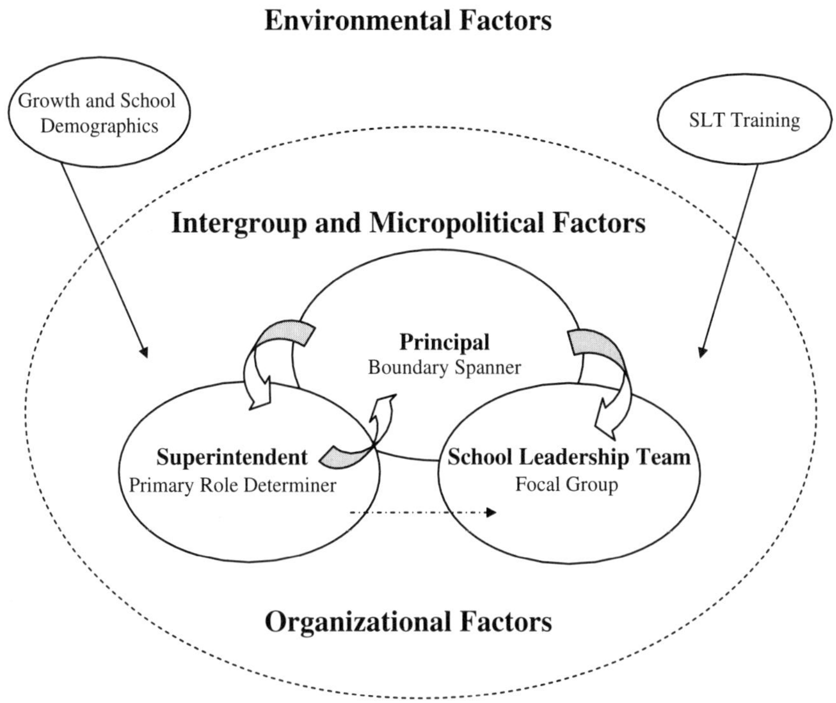

Figure 5.1 An integrative perspective model of environmental, organizational, and micropolitical factors that influence school leadership team decision making, power, and authority.

factor because it provided the team with an expanded perspective of its potential to lead the school and to learn needed knowledge and skills to assume its new role.

Organizational factors include structure, policies and procedures, timeline and deadlines, role requirements of position, purposes and goals, and leadership transitions that influenced the team and the team's functioning. Team members had to further their understanding of the structure of leadership at their school, learn the policies and procedures that would affect what they were able to do and how they could do it, gain new responsibilities, and adopt new roles.

Research using intergroup and interpersonal factors includes elements of climate and structure that surround the focal group (the team) in an organization. For this case, critical intergroup factors are the mode of communication, the frequency of interaction, physical location, feedback, and participation (Van Sell, Brief, & Schuler, 1981) among the superintendent, the principal, and the school leadership team. We found that infrequent interaction, indirect mode of communication, and perceived negative feedback from the superintendent adversely affected the team and its sense of accomplishment. The focus on the team as a whole is supported by the work of Hackman (1991), who argues "the way a group relates to other groups sometimes [is] more important to its effectiveness than the way members relate to each other" (p. 2).

Systems and Role Theory

Through a systemic perspective incorporated with role theory, we gained insights into the issues faced by the Paramount SLT as they assumed new roles and responsibilities at the school. A common understanding of systems (Hanna, 1997; Scott, 1992) is that there is interdependency between organizations and their environments. An open systems approach seeks to identify components, understand the nature of interaction between them, and examine the influence of the external environment on internal organizational functioning (Hanna, 1997). Although this separation of components is possible in theory, as we see in the Paramount case, the boundaries among components and participants are not so clearly defined in actuality. As Clegg and Hardy (1996) suggest, boundaries break down and issues merge and blur as actions occur in a complex system. In attempting to understand this complexity, role theory can provide insights into existing organizational structures and systems.

Importance of Role Theory in Understanding Organizational Conflicts. Role theory seeks to describe "patterned forms of behavior, social positions, specializations, and divisions of labor" (Thomas & Biddle, 1966, p. 3) as well as the processes by which members communicate, learn, and are socialized. The roles that individuals play include a set of prescriptions that define the behavior of participants within the social system. Furthermore, roles are not limited to "one person's behavior, but must include the behaviors of others which provides the rights enabling those actions" (Lopata, 1995, p. 1). For instance, members of the Paramount team assumed the role of leadership with the definitions of that role as presented by the first Tentative Agreement, the SLT training seminars, and the principal. Each individual team member defined and integrated their role as a teacher, member of the team, and school leader. With changes in superintendents, uncertainty and ambiguity was introduced into the relationships. When roles are in transition or new roles are introduced, individuals' past behaviors and patterns of interaction may not be appropriate, and new behaviors and patterns need to be learned. This learning occurs through communications and repeated interactions of different members within the system and with outside forces such as the leadership team training (Kahn et al., 1964). As these new roles are being learned, there is a strong likelihood of both role ambiguity and role conflict.

Challenges When Roles Are Ambiguous and Conflictual. Role ambiguity and conflict have been widely researched as a way to understand the stresses associated with membership in organizations (Miles & Perreault, 1976; Netemeyer, Johnston, & Burton, 1990; Van Sell, Brief, & Schuler, 1981). Role ambiguity and role conflict "have been established in organizational literature as important, influential factors in the work setting" (Olk & Friedlander, 1992, p. 389). Role ambiguity is defined as "a lack of clarity regarding the expectations for one's role, the methods for fulfilling those expectations, and the consequences for effective or ineffective performance" (Olk & Friedlander, 1992, p. 390). Although the sources of role ambiguity vary, they can occur out of three general conditions: "organizational complexity, rapid organizational change, and managerial philosophies" (Kahn et al., 1964, p. 75). Individuals at Paramount Middle School were confronted with multiple aspects of ambiguous and new circumstances that demanded a change in their roles and behaviors. They worked to redefine the way the school functions with a leadership team; however, their attempts were in direct opposition to the hierarchical nature of the district.

Role conflict typically "arises when a person is faced with expectations requiring behaviors that are mutually competing or opposing" (Olk & Friedlander, 1992, p. 389). Van Sell and colleagues (1981) indicate that some consequences of role conflict are unsatisfactory work group relationships, inadequate perceived leader behavior, and unfavorable attitudes (p. 49) toward those in positions of power and who are initiating new roles. In organizations, this person generally plays a central role in intergroup relations as a "boundary spanner," someone who helps facilitate communication between groups (Friedman & Podolny, 1992). As can be seen in Figure 5.1, the principal was in the role of boundary spanner and was most likely to encounter role conflict as a result of membership in multiple groups (Van Sell et al., 1981).

Types of Role Conflict. Five major types of role conflict are relevant to this study (Kahn et al., 1964; Miles & Perreault, 1976; Van Sell et al., 1981): (1) *intrasender conflict:* the extent to which two or more role expectations from a single role sender are mutually incompatible (e.g., the superintendent's understanding of the principal's role as one of management, in contrast to her belief in shared decision making as a responsibility of all members at the school); (2) *intersender conflict:* the extent to which two or more role expectations from one role sender oppose those from one or more other role senders (e.g., the superintendent and leadership team both communicated opposing expectations to the principal); (3) *interrole conflict:* pressures associated with membership in one organization that are in conflict with membership in other groups (e.g., the principal experienced conflict in her role on the SLT and in her role as principal as defined by the superintendent; these roles had opposing perspectives and associated behaviors); (4) *person-role conflict:* the extent to which role expectations are incongruent with the orientations or values of the role occupant (e.g., the principal whose value orientation supported shared decision making, but whose formal role was defined as authoritarian); (5) *overload:* the extent to which the various role expectations exceed the amount of time and resources available for them to be fulfilled (e.g., as exhibited by the principal and the team members regarding the time frame for their decisions).

Useful for understanding the Paramount case is the Kahn and colleagues' (1964) role theory model that depicts the interpersonal process between the person being sent role expectations and those sending the expectations. (See also Van Sell et al., 1981.) The district superintendent plays the most important role in defining the team's role and sets expectations for the team. According to this model, the principal is an important boundary spanner receiving messages from the superintendent and communicating them to the team.

Micropolitical Perspectives

Micropolitical perspectives of organizations offer the potential for insights into the relational and power issues faced by school leadership teams as they assume new roles and responsibilities and negotiate their place in the system. According to Blase (1991), "Micropolitics refers to the use of formal and informal power by individuals and groups to achieve their goals in organizations" (p. 357). This perspective emphasizes that "school reform is rarely a politically neutral event . . . teachers often have one overriding concern—the preservation of a stable sense of personal and professional identities" (Datnow, 1998, p. 21). Unlike organizations in which environmental and external forces may be reduced by strategies designed to minimize influence, schools are more open to relational factors from multiple constituents who have the ability to influence or change them. Micropolitics turns our attention to the sources and use of power "to determine which issues and questions are seen as relevant and critical and which will be viewed as irrelevant and illogical" (Mawhinney, 1999, p. 164).

In this study, two sources of power are particularly significant: (1) power derived from legitimate authority to make decisions as a leadership team, and (2) power acquired through expert knowledge gained through the SLT seminars. The political dynamics of team members encompasses the actions of the team, the norm of equitable relationship among colleagues, as well as the interactions of the team within the hierarchical district structure. Thus, a micropolitical perspective can help to investigate how power is used by the team in conflictual situations as well as how power is used to "build support to achieve their ends" (Mawhinney, 1999, p. 168).

In a study of teacher leadership roles, Hart (1994) found that "during periods of change, roles and social systems may exert a powerful influence, particularly as coalitions are being formed and a new interpretation of reality is emerging" (p. 494). As Paramount developed new role configurations as a leadership team for decision making, adjustments in behavior and expectations affected organizational functioning. As the team engaged in leadership training, new perceptions and interpretations of their role at the school emerged, contributing to frustration and even conflict. Thus, attempts to make structural changes—such as implementing a new school leadership team, reconfiguring an organization, and shifting role relationships—need to be viewed as significant undertakings and as political events.

What We Learned From an Integrated Perspective

By adopting the lens of an Integrative Perspective Model (Figure 5.1), we identify critical factors contributing to role ambiguity and role conflict for Paramount's principal and leadership team. Through a historical perspective of environmental and organizational factors, we surfaced conditions contributing to role ambiguity and role conflict and identified key micropolitical dynamics. The analysis of intertextual relationships among written policies, interviews, and SLT training seminars created a basis for assessing the congruence among texts and examining how the team recognized, acknowledged, and found the texts socially significant (Bloome & Egan-Robertson, 1993; Chrispeels, 1997). As Bloome and Egan-Robertson (1993) argue, "intertextuality is socially constructed by members of a group and thus involves more than juxtaposition of texts by a researcher" (p. 332). By examining a series of episodes, we explored how elements of intertextuality as understood by the team and principal defined their role *vis-à-vis* the district policies and the SLT training. The model helps to highlight the complex and embedded nature of school systems that must continually respond to environmental pressures.

This chapter illustrates the ways role theory provided insights into the frustrations experienced by the principal and team as they attempted to carry out their work. Role theory drew attention to the critical role of the principal as a boundary spanner in sending, receiving, and responding to messages. Use of the Episode Model with organizational history and individual perspectives was useful in examining the work of the team over time as it struggled to implement shared decision making. A chain of episodes illustrated and documented the development of patterned responses. They portrayed participants' perceptions, future interactions, and their sense of power, control, and relationships to others in the organization. However, the episodes took on their full meaning only when they were placed in the larger historical context. In addition, our analysis suggests the value of combining multiple perspectives and frameworks to analyze complex phenomena. Systems theory, with its greater attention to organizational and environmental factors, contributed to our understanding of why there was evidence of role conflict and role ambiguity. Examining organizational factors highlighted the clash between a new order of teacher empowerment and the "old order" (Chion-Kenney & Hymes, 1994) of hierarchical decision-making structures and thinking. This district operated with the best of intentions to empower teachers and gave them greater say in a wide range of decision-making areas. It is not enough, however, to implement shared decision making at the site without taking into account its consequences and implications for other levels of the organization. Combining systems theory with event mapping helped to illuminate the turbulent environment over time and provided "a longitudinal examination of historical contexts for interpreting the actions and responses of particular groups" (Chrispeels, 1997, p. 457). In essence, event mapping made visible the historical context and political variables that contributed to role conflict and ambiguity.

Implications For School Leadership

A number of implications for policymakers and practitioners who are implementing site-based management and establishing school leadership teams emerge from this study. First, systems thinking is critical when implementing a major innovation such as site-based management. Schools are complex systems that need to encompass environmental, organizational, and intergroup factors, and teachers cannot be empowered without concomitant changes in the district administration. Relationships with the district are a key factor in a team's ability to assume new responsibilities, implement change, and successfully accomplish goals (Chrispeels, 1996; Senge, 1990). The superintendent negotiated, with the teachers' union, language to clarify the concepts of teacher empowerment and roles and responsibilities of leadership teams. He did not, however, examine other aspects of the system, such as training, relationships with principals, and interaction with the team. Without knowledge of the training and direct dialogue with the leadership team, the superintendent was not able to facilitate and support the work of the team. This lack of interaction and understanding helped the superintendent to maintain the traditional hierarchical model, and at the same time, stymied his efforts to promote shared decision making. His management style empowered the principal but undermined her efforts to empower the leadership team, leading to role conflict for the principal and role ambiguity for the team.

Second, enacting a policy to empower teachers and include them in decision making does not predetermine how teachers will interpret and take up the new roles. This chapter indicates the need for specificity and clarity in defining how and in what ways teachers and others are to be involved in decision making. Furthermore, the experiences of Paramount's team suggest negotiations must be ongoing as district administrators, principals, and team members gain confidence and knowledge in how to lead. It also confirms the value of training for enabling team members to suggest innovations for their school, use research to guide their decisions, and pursue solutions. However, the district and leadership team were unable to capitalize fully on these new abilities and help the district accomplish its mission of improved student learning. This finding implies the need for the district and team to coordinate and integrate the training to meet district and site goals.

Finally, relationships, roles, and responsibilities need to be specific and coupled with opportunities for ongoing negotiation and refinement to overcome inconsistencies between beliefs and practices in ways that can impact student learning. Relationships with the district remained a key factor in the team's ability to assume new responsibilities, to implement change, and to successfully accomplish goals for the school. Paramount's SLT, after three years of training, was poised to address important issues of teaching and learning. Yet neither the team nor the superintendent, with all communications being filtered through the principal, were able to sufficiently align policies and practices and give the team a sense of accomplishment and effectiveness. This points to the need for congruence between policy and practice when implementing structural changes or shared decision making (Chrispeels, 1996, 1997; Fuhrman, 1993). In conclusion, the good intentions of the superintendent, principal, and school leadership team were not sufficient to overcome the incongruence between beliefs and practices. This minimized the school's and the district's ability to capitalize on the SLT training so as to enhance the team's ability to lead its school in the process of reform in ways that could dramatically impact student learning.

Notes

1. Research presented in this article was supported by a grant from the Spencer T. and Ann W. Olin Foundation. A portion of this paper was presented at the 1998 annual meeting of the American Educational Research Association, San Diego, California.

2. This chapter is a revised version of an article originally published in the *Journal of School Leadership,* Vol. 9, September 1999, entitled "Role Conflict and Role Ambiguity: The Challenges of Team Leadership at a Middle School." Permission to reprint obtained October 28, 2002, Rowman & Littlefield Publishers.

3. Pseudonyms are used for the school and all participants in this study. The authors would like to thank the superintendent, the principal, and the School Leadership Council and School Leadership Team members who allowed us to follow their work. We hope that the ideas presented assist them and others in the challenging tasks they are undertaking to improve their schools. The authors also wish to thank Itamar Harari, Cheryl C. Strait, and Marisol A. Rodarte who provided research assistance useful in clarifying issues and ideas for this chapter and the original article in the *Journal of School Leadership.*

4. See Bloome & Egan-Robertson, 1993, p. 311, and Chrispeels, 1997, for a detailed description of this method of intertextual analysis and of historical analysis. The concepts from systems theory (Hanna, 1997; Scott, 1992), role theory (Kahn et al., 1964; Van Sell et al., 1981), and intertextual analysis (Bloome & Egan-Robertson, 1993) provided a framework for reanalyzing and interpreting the data presented in the research.

5. For more detailed information on conflict and ambiguity arising from norm conflict, see Bertrand, 1972; for typical antecedents leading to role conflict and role ambiguity, see Kahn et al., 1964; and Van Sell et al., 1981.

References

Altrichter, H., & Elliott, J. (2000). *Images of educational change.* Buckingham, UK: Open University.

Bertrand, A. L. (1972). *Social organization: A general systems and role theory perspective.* Philadelphia: F. A. Davis Company.

Biddle, B. J. (1979). *Role theory: Expectations, identities & behaviors.* New York: Academic Press.

Blase, J. (1991). The micropolitical orientation of teachers toward closed school principals. *Education and Urban Society, 23*(4), 356–378.

Blase, J., & Anderson, G. (1995). *The micropolitics of educational leadership: from control to empowerment.* New York: Cassell.

Bloome, D., & Egan-Robertson, A. (1993). The social construction of intertextuality in classroom reading and writing lessons. *Reading Research Quarterly, 28*(4), 304–333.

California School Leadership Academy (CSLA). (1996, 1998). *School Leadership Team Development Series.* Hayward, CA: Author.

Chion-Kenney, L., & Hymes, D. L. (Eds.). (1994). *Site-based management and decision-making: problems and solutions.* Arlington, VA: American Association of School Administrators.

Chrispeels, J. H. (1996). Evaluating teachers' relationships with families: A case study of one district. *The Elementary School Journal, 97*(2), 179–200.

Chrispeels, J. H. (1997). Educational policy implementation in a shifting political climate: The California experience. *American Educational Research Journal, 34*(3), 453–481.

Chrispeels, J. H., Castillo, S., & Brown, J. (2000). School leadership teams: A process model. *Journal of School Effectiveness and School Improvement, 11*(1), 22–56.

Chrispeels, J. H., Martin, K. J., Harari, I., Strait, C. & Rodarte, M. (1999). Role conflict and role ambiguity: The challenges of team leadership at a middle school. *Journal of School Leadership, 9*(5), 422–553.

Clegg, S. R., & Hardy, C. (1996). Introduction: Organizations, organization and organizing. In S. R. Clegg, C. Hardy, & W. R. Nord, (Eds.), *Handbook of organizational studies* (pp. 1–28). Thousand Oaks, CA: Sage.

Clune, W. H., & White, P. A. (1988). *School-based management: Institutional variation, implementation, and issues for further research.* New Brunswick, NJ: Rutgers University. Eagleton Institute of Politics, Center for Policy Research in Education.

Datnow, (1998). *The gender politics of educational reform.* London: Falmer Press.

Friedman, R. A., & Podolny, J. (1992). Differentiation of boundary spanning roles: Labor negotiations and implications for role conflict. *Administrative Science Quarterly, 37*, 28–47.

Fuhrman, S. H. (1993). The politics of coherence. In S. H. Fuhrman (Ed.), *Designing coherent education policy: Improving the system* (1–34). San Francisco: Jossey-Bass.

Hackman, J. R. (1991). *Groups that work (and those that don't).* San Francisco: Jossey-Bass.

Hanna, D. (1997). The organization as an open system. In A. Harris, N. Bennett, & M. Preedy (Eds.), *Organizational effectiveness and improvement in education* (pp. 13–21). Philadelphia: Open University.

Hardy, C., & Clegg, S. R. (1996). Some dare call it power. In S. R. Clegg, C. Hardy & W. R. Nord (Eds.), *Handbook of organizational studies* (pp. 622–641). Thousand Oaks, CA: Sage.

Hargreaves, A., & Evans, R. (1997). *Beyond educational reform: Bringing teachers back in.* Philadelphia: Open University Press.

Hart, A. W. (1994). Creating teacher leadership roles. *Educational Administrative Quarterly, 30*(4), 472–497.

Johnson, M. J., & Pajares, F. (1996). When shared decision-making works: A 3-year longitudinal study. *American Educational Research Journal, 33*(3), 599–627.

Johnson, S. M., & Boles, K. C. (1994). The role of teachers in school reform. In S. A. Mohrman & P. Wohlstetter and Associates (Eds.), *School-based management: Organizing for high performance* (pp. 109–137). San Francisco: Jossey-Bass.

Kahn, R. L., Wolfe, D. M., Quinn, R. P., & Snoek, J. D., in collaboration with Rosenthal, R. A. (1964). *Organizational stress: studies of role conflict and ambiguity.* New York: Wiley.

Leithwood, K., & Menzies, T. (1998). Forms and effects of school-based management: A review. *Educational Policy, 12*(3), 324–346.

Little, J. W. (1993). Teachers' professional development in a climate of educational reform. *Educational evaluation and policy analysis, 15*(2), 129–151.

Lopata, H. Z. (1995). Role theory. In J. R. Blau & N. Goodman (Eds.), *Social roles and social institutions* (pp. 1–12). New Brunswick, NJ: Westview Press.

Malen, B. & Ogawa, R. (1988). Professional-patron influence on site-based governance councils: A confounding case. *Educational Evaluation and Policy Analysis,* 10, 251–270.

Marks, H. M., & Louis, K. S. (1997). Does teacher empowerment affect the classroom? The implications of teacher empowerment for instructional practice and student academic performance. *Educational Evaluation and Policy Analysis, 19*(3), 245–275.

Mawhinney, H. B. (1999). Reappraisal: The problems and prospects of studying the micropolitics of leadership in reforming schools. *School Leadership & Management, 19*(2), 159–170.

Miles, R. H., & Perreault, Jr., W. D. (1976). Organizational role conflict: Its antecedents and consequences. *Organizational Behavior and Human Performance, 17,* 19–44.

Netemeyer, R. G., Johnston, M. W., & Burton, S. (1990). Analysis of role conflict and role ambiguity in a structural equations framework. *Journal of Applied Psychology, 75*(2), 148–157.

Olk, M. E., & Friedlander, M. L. (1992). Trainees' experiences of role conflict and role ambiguity in supervisory relationships. *Journal of Counseling Psychology, 39*(3), 389–397.

Professional Development Seminar. (August, 1996). *Creating a school of the future: Key leadership and management skills for the principal in a three-day residential program.* Melbourne, Australia: Brian Caldwell and Max Swatzki Consultants.

Scott, W. R. (1992). *Organizations: Rational, natural and open systems.* (3rd Ed.). Englewood Cliffs, NJ: Prentice Hall.

Senge, P. M. (1990). *The fifth discipline: The art and practice of the learning organization.* New York: Doubleday.

Smylie, M. A., Lazarus, V., & Brownlee-Conyers, J. (1994). Instructional outcomes of school-based participative decision-making. *Educational Evaluation and Policy Analysis, 16*(3), 181–198.

Thomas, E. J., & Biddle, B. J. (1966). The nature and history of role theory. In B. J. Biddle & E. J. Thomas (Eds.), *Role theory: Concepts and research* (pp. 3–63). New York: Wiley.

Van Sell, M., Brief, A. P., & Schuler, R. S. (1981). Role conflict and role ambiguity: Integration of the literature and directions for future research. *Human Relations, 34*(1), 43–71.

Wallace, M. (October, 2000). Integrating cultural and political perspectives: The case of school restructuring in England. *Educational Administration Quarterly, 36*(4), 608–632.

Wallace, M., & Hall, V. (1994). *Inside the SMT: Teamwork in secondary school management.* London: Paul Chapman Publishing.

Weiss, C. H., Cambone, J., & Wyeth, A. (1991). *Trouble in paradise: Teacher conflicts in shared decision making.* NCEL occasional paper no. 8, Cambridge, MA: National Center for Educational Leadership, Harvard Graduate School of Education. ED332 346.

Wohlstetter P., Smyer, R., & Mohrman, S. (1994). New boundaries for school-based management: The high involvement model. *Educational Evaluation and Policy Analysis, 16*(3), 268–286.

6

Evolving Roles and Sharing Leadership

The Path of One Leadership Team

Shiou-Ping Shiu

Janet H. Chrispeels

Robin Endacott Doerr

> *It is as foolish to think that only principals provide leadership for school improvement as to believe that principals do not influence school effectiveness.*
>
> —Hallinger and Heck (1999, p. 186)

The role of the principal is recognized as a critical factor in building an effective school leadership team (Chrispeels, Brown, & Castillo, 2000; Chrispeels, Strait, & Brown, 1999; Waters, Marzano, & McNulty, 2003). Principal leadership is also essential for creating an empowered school culture where teachers are actively involved in the improvement process (Behar-Horenstein & Gonzales, 2002; Lieberman & Miller, 1984). "Without principal support there is little scope for others to make a contribution" (Wallace, 2002, p. 166). The challenge, however, is finding the right balance of principal leadership and direction, on the one hand, and opportunities for others to shape, guide, and lead school change and development on the other. This kind of dilemma can create internal conflict for the principal about what it means to be a leader and external conflict between principal and teachers over who has authority and what issues are open for shared decision making.

One notable dilemma in shared leadership is the control/dominance issue. Many principals, given their training and predisposition toward taking charge, struggle with how to share their knowledge without dominating the work of a teacher leadership team (Berlak & Berlak, 1981; Chrispeels et al., 1999). Yet little research has been undertaken to understand how the principal and the leadership team learn to share leadership and resolve dilemmas that face them.

The research in this study explores how a single school leadership team works together to redefine their respective roles and learns how to share power and authority. Their story illustrates the types and sources of issues that can derail the process of sharing leadership and the pivotal role that training in collaborative processes plays when undertaking shared leadership. This chapter identifies three types of leadership observed to be operating at the school. They are: (1) teacher leadership based on expert knowledge, (2) principal leadership based on position and expert power, and (3) shared leadership emerging from a common knowledge base and shared sense of purpose. This study makes visible the interplay of actors on the team as they assume different leadership roles. It also shows how the team wrestles with two major challenges to sharing leadership: (1) how, what, and with whom to share leadership when the school principal is ultimately held accountable for decisions and outcomes; and (2) how mental models support and constrain the development of shared leadership.

Methods

Context

This study represents a "telling case" (Van Maanen, 1988) whose story may help to inform others working in schools that are struggling, under pressure, to raise achievement scores of predominantly low-income English Learners (EL). The setting is one of 10 participating elementary schools in a low-performing school district in California engaged in a partnership with a local university to implement an Effective Schools Initiative (ESI), a research-based, data-driven education reform process. Like many schools in the district, this school operates on a four-track, year-round schedule to accommodate approximately 700 students, of which more than 80% are EL and 85% receive free or reduced lunch. The principal has been at this school since its opening in 1995.

As part of the reform process, all 10 elementary schools are involved in aligning their curriculum to the California curriculum content standards. They are guided in this process by a site-based leadership team composed of the school principal and eight teacher leaders selected by the principal to represent grade levels and tracks. The leadership teams receive seven days of training each year focused on building skills, knowledge, and capacity for leadership; engaging in professional discourse; and supporting collaborative practice centered on teaching and learning to use as a leadership team and to share with colleagues. Each team guides the school community in setting improvement targets and developing a school action plan designed to move the school toward raising and sustaining academic achievement for all students.

High-stakes testing and accountability measures from federal and state laws put school principals and the district administration in a vulnerable position if their schools do not achieve state-specified growth targets within a given timeframe. As a result of changing job responsibilities, definitions, and expectations of leadership, principals face paradoxes and dilemmas as they try to fit concepts of shared leadership required by state reform agendas within existing bureaucratic, hierarchically organized school systems (Chrispeels et al., 1999; Dimmock, 1996; MacBeath, 1999; Yep & Chrispeels, see Chapter 7, this volume).

Data Collection and Analysis

We used ethnographic methods to access the research setting and to collect and analyze data between August 2000 and June 2002. Bimonthly leadership team trainings held off site and weekly leadership team meetings held at the school were videotaped and transcribed (approximately 200 hours of observations). All the leadership team members, including the principal and eight teachers, were interviewed using an open-ended interview schedule to explore their issues of interest. Interviews lasted about 45 minutes and were tape recorded and transcribed, if permission was given. Through an open-coding review (Strauss & Corbin, 1990) of field notes, meeting minutes, interviews, and transcribed videotapes, the researchers discussed their observations of the progress of leadership team meetings and team learning. A constant comparative method was used to identify emergent themes and contrast data with theoretical constructs. The comparisons between data units from transcripts, field notes, and meeting minutes provided a variety of sources for triangulation.

Logs of key events (see Table 6.1) of the content of team training sessions were created and compared with an event log of issues that the leadership team discussed at weekly team meetings. The logs enabled us to trace the impact of team training sessions on weekly school site grade-level and leadership team meetings as well as observe the influence of other district issues on the leadership team's work and discussions. As the logs show, the process was not a linear one. Themes introduced in the leadership team trainings were sometimes addressed or emerged in the next leadership team meeting at the site. In other instances, the theme emerged much later. Themes were also often recycled or reemerged as the year progressed.

Table 6.1 First Year Log of Key Events Showing the Influence of the Leadership Team Training on the Leadership Team Meetings at the School

First Year Timeline	ES Leadership Team (LT) Training	Key Events of Leadership Team Meetings
August 2000	Introduced to Effective Schools research Team building, learn to use student data and implement ES Process Introduce Language Arts content standards and curriculum maps	1. Planned how to implement Effective School process in the school 2. Planned team presentation and presented to staff Standards and curriculum maps 3. Defined the roles and goals of leadership team 4. Defined the role of the facilitator
September 2000	Introduced unit planning	
October 2000	Building a team: facilitating roles, characteristics of effective teams. Setting priorities for team's work: home-school relations	1. Principal urged and team agreed to focus on parental involvement 2. Principal asked teachers to share grade level work in LT 3. Resolved guest teachers' problems 4. In and out track communication issue 5. Defining the role of the facilitator
November 2000		
December 2000	Building a team: Gnatt Chart and goal setting. An approach for reaching consensus on tough issues. Roles of successful teams	1. Meeting run by principal: presented test books 2. Teachers planned parents' workshops 3. LT discussed starting unit plans in grade level meetings (GLM) 4. Planned to have GLM file storage 5. Discussed the focus of the LT 6. Discussed using time more effectively in LT
February 2001		
April 2001	1. Building a team: tools for communication 2. Leadership roles: planners, communicators, decision making and staff development 3. Learn a process for analysis 4. Introduced book "Strategies that Work"	1. **Principal presented Test Prep.** * 2. Teachers decided to send Test Package to parents twice in March and May 3. LT discussed how to make other staff volunteer with parents nights
June 2001	1. Building a team: discussing the undiscussables 2. Leadership: time use in school 3. Developed plans for the coming year	1. Leadership newsletter to inform and update the staff in regards to leadership team meetings 2. **Test Prep: assess materials** * 3. **Selecting graphic organizers** * 4. Scheduling next year's calendar

(Continued)

Table 6.1 (Continued)

Second Year Timeline	ES Leadership Team Training	Key Events of Leadership Team Meetings
August 2001 September 2001	1. Building a team: problem meeting behaviors chart, searching for clues about team building 2. Instructional practice: "Strategies that Work" overview 3. Analysis: unpacking the standards, curriculum calibration 4. Standards: standards-based classroom practices 5. Effective Schools process: guiding principles	1. Norms building 2. Facilitator presented the Effective Schools' goal for the year 3. Began student achievement data analysis 4. Follow-up e-mail problem 5. **Explore Test Prep***
October 2001	Analysis: analyzing correlate data and identifying priority areas of their school action plan Reviewed school organization chart & committee structure	1. Principal stated that all first-grade teachers have to do Test Prep 2. Showed how AL room is organized 3. Principal wanted each teacher to figure out the API for their class and set an objective for raising API 4. **Science planetarium*** 5. **Government reading program*** 6 **Test Prep continued***
December 2001	1. Analysis: using data to align school improvement, worksheets to summarize Effective Schools correlate data 2. Effective Schools Planning Process: strategies, assessment data, action plans, and school portfolio	1. Final decision on graphic organizers 2. Worked on job descriptions for committees 3. Created handouts of SAT 9 booklets 4. **Test Prep continued*** 5. **Government reading program***
January 2002	1. Instructional practices: "Strategies that Work" presentation 2. Analysis: using data to align school improvement	1. Started committees issue 2. **Presented results of graphic organizers to staff*** 3. **Government writing program*** 4. Technology concerns regarding to computers 5. Revised site based calendar
March 2002	Instructional practices: resilience education	1. Committees: planned to discuss at staff meeting 2. Team made a list of technology concerns for principal and conferred with school technology person 3. **Planned literacy nights*** 4. Vertical teaming 5. Planned retreat for leadership team
June 2002	Celebrate progress and accomplishments, share instructional resources and develop plans for the coming school year	1. Committees: presented to staff and had them signed up 2. Vertical teaming 3. **ESL teaming*** 4. Budget for next year reviewed 5.Talent show plan developed

NOTE: * (Asterisk) indicates a district-driven issue.

Changing Nature of Leadership Roles

Traditional Principal's Role and Job Description

As school size increased and schools were centralized into districts, especially in large cities in the 1920s, the job of principal evolved into one of middle manager within a larger district organization. At the same time, principals still retained ultimate responsibility for their individual school. With the emergence of a bureaucratic form of organization, as Smylie and Brownlee-Conyers (1992) point out, principals' work became more general and managerial in nature. They assumed responsibility for the everyday functioning of the physical plant, site fiscal resources, employee performance and evaluation, public relations, and students' safety and learning. The principal now must frequently select among personnel whom the district hires, work to integrate them into the existing culture, and manage resources across classrooms—looking beyond the school walls to the school's relationship to district administration, parents, and other community constituencies. Furthermore, the principal has the critical task of ensuring the school implements district, state, and federal mandates, which often puts the principal in the middle—pulled by the desire and beliefs of faculty and the demands of the central office. This tension exacerbates the challenge of sharing leadership (Chrispeels, Martin, Harari, Strait, & Rodarte, 1999). In fulfilling these tasks, principals develop knowledge and expertise of the whole organization, which combines with their position power to place them in a strong leadership role (Chrispeels, Strait, & Brown, 1999). This hierarchical organizational model, however, frequently distances principals from the essence and processes of classroom instruction (Meier, 1985; Sykes & Elmore, 1989). The lack of opportunity for principals and teachers to interact substantively about issues of classroom instruction reinforces this distance. Infrequent classroom visits and observation of teachers at work with students reinforces this distance further (Dornbusch & Scott, 1975; Natriello & Dornbusch, 1980–1981).

Traditional Teacher's Role and Job Description

In contrast to the principal, teachers, through job definition and school organizational structures, are isolated in classrooms, with specific knowledge and limited perspective of system-wide issues. "Typically, teachers see their primary function as working with children and draw their primary professional rewards from such work" (Smylie & Brownlee-Conyers, 1992, p. 152; see also Mitchell, Ortiz, & Mitchell, 1987). This exclusive focus on students and the classroom distinguishes teachers from principals (Barth, 1990; Johnson, 1990). This persistent structure of school and the norm of equal collegial relations among teachers have meant that teachers usually do not see themselves as leaders. On the one hand, teachers are often reluctant to take leadership positions because they reject the traditional definition of leadership as having *power over* their colleagues, which they frequently perceive principals exercising (Chrispeels, Brown, & Castillo, 2000). On the other hand, they also feel and experience a sense of powerlessness and pessimism about the power and opportunities to influence school policy (Johnson, 1990).

Effective School Leadership Team's Role and Job Description

From the brief synopsis of the principals' and teachers' jobs, training, and predisposition to their roles, we see that neither is well equipped to share leadership. Both principals and teachers generally operate within a classical leadership frame defined by a bureaucratic hierarchy and have little experience in working with alternative models. The classical leadership model and a model of shared leadership are presented and compared in Table 6.2.

The establishment of the Effective Schools leadership teams offers both structure and space for the principal and teachers to come together for discussion, dialogue, and the practice of shared leadership. Teams also help teachers begin to develop a larger perspective as they work to resolve issues at their school. Through the Effective Schools team training seminars, teams have the opportunity in a safe setting to practice many of the dimensions of shared leadership outlined in Table 6.2. The challenge for teachers and principals as they practice these new ways of leading is to evolve new concepts of leadership that can guide the team's work in ways that optimize the potential of a leadership team as a force for change (Chrispeels, Castillo & Brown, 2000; Chrispeels et al., 2000).

Constructive Leadership

The concept of constructivist leadership, developed by Lambert and associates (1995), provides an overarching construct for considering the specifics of shared leadership. According to Lambert (1995), "Constructivist leadership involves *the reciprocal processes that enable* participants in an educational community to construct meanings that lead to a common purpose of schooling" (p. 33, italics in original).

Leadership teams can become important situated sites for learning as well as provide opportunities to develop social capital as norms of isolation are broken down and the team works toward accomplishing group tasks that lead to improvements in student outcomes. "When actively engaged in reflective dialogue, adults become more complex in their thinking about the world, more tolerant of diverse perspectives, more flexible and open toward new experiences" (Lambert, 1995, p. 28). The capacity for reciprocity is the result of long-term meaning making with others (Kegan, 1982). Thus both

Table 6.2 Comparison of Classical and Shared Leadership Models

Classical Leadership	*Shared Leadership*
Displayed by a person's position in a group or hierarchy.	Identified by the quality of people's interactions rather than their position.
Leadership evaluated by whether the leader solves problems.	Leadership evaluated by how people are working together.
Leaders provide solutions and answers.	All work to enhance the process and to make it more fulfilling.
Distinct differences between leaders and followers: character, skill, and so forth.	People are interdependent. All are active participants in the process of leadership.
Communication is often formal.	Communication is crucial, with a stress on conversation.
Usually relies on transactional honesty exchanges. May involve secrecy, deception, and payoffs.	Values democratic processes and shared ethics. Seeks a common good.

SOURCE: Adapted from material in G. Nemerowicz and E. Rosi (1997). *Education for leadership and social responsibility*. London: Falmer Press, p. 16.

individual and group learning are important for team members in order to effectively share leadership and enhance organizational learning. Creating an educational community that serves as a setting for meaning making and human development requires members to work interdependently. Creating interdependence requires new forms of leadership, especially a shift from the classical/hierarchical model to a shared model. Highlights of what this shift will require are suggested in Table 6.2.

Mental Model

Senge's (1990) concept of *mental models* is also instrumental in framing this research. According to Senge, mental models are "deeply ingrained assumptions, generalizations, or even pictures or images that influence how we understand the world and how we take action" (1990, p. 8). Senge argues that "new insights fail to get put into practice because they conflict with deeply held images of how the world works, images that limit us to familiar ways of thinking and acting" (p. 174). Our research applies the concept of mental models to explore the process whereby the principal and teachers were constrained and supported by their mental models to move from classical/hierarchical leadership toward shared leadership in the face of top-down accountability pressures for performance. To transform a school from a hierarchical model to shared leadership requires challenging preconceived notions of leadership. Mental models need to be reconstructed. Leadership needs to be seen as more than role and position (Lambert, 1995). The Effective Schools leadership team trainings were designed to provide an opportunity for principal and teachers to explore new relations, develop collaborative skills, and gain knowledge needed to build trust and understand the challenges of change. The interactive relationship of the principal and teachers' mental models with the training as an intervening variable between the individuals and the leadership team is shown in Figure 6.1. This study provided the opportunity to test this conceptual framework of how a team might move from a classical model of leadership to a constructivist shared model.

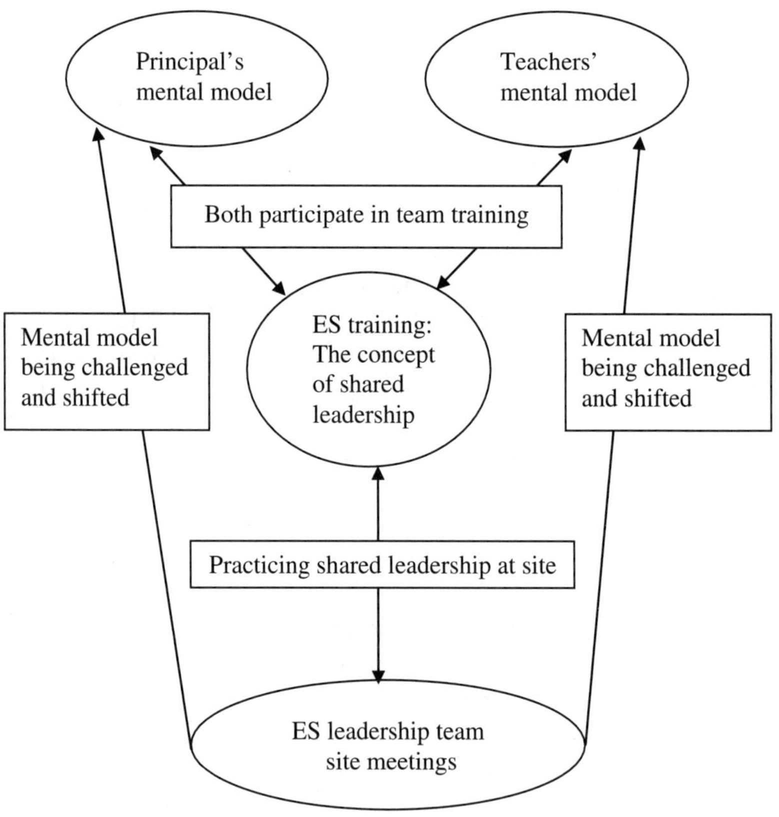

Figure 6.1 Concept Map of How Principal and Teachers Learn and Practice Shared Leadership

Three Types of Leadership

Observations and interviews at this school revealed a staff that is committed to school reform and that is beginning to experience some success in their efforts to raise student achievement. After reviewing more than 200 hours of observations, we found leadership expressed in three ways at the school site: (1) teacher leadership based on expert knowledge; (2) principal leadership based on position and expert power; and (3) shared leadership.

Teacher Leadership Based on Expert Knowledge

At the beginning of the reform initiative, some leadership team members from each school in the district attended a week-long Curriculum Redesign Workshop where they worked with other teacher colleagues to align the district's curriculum to the state curriculum content standards, create performance indicators, and develop curriculum maps to guide implementation. In addition, the entire case-study leadership team also attended a three-day leadership team retreat with the other participating schools. These professional development opportunities equipped the leadership team with knowledge of the California content standards and curriculum maps, knowledge about ES correlates and process, and team-building skills. During the retreat, they discussed how to implement the Effective Schools (ES) process in their school and planned what information was to be shared with the staff. When they went back to their school, they became the *experts of the ES process and the curriculum redesign work*. These teacher leaders planned a presentation for the entire staff (see Table 6.1, which shows that this occurred soon after the Leadership Team Retreat in 2000). In one staff meeting, they explained the ES process and gave a mini-workshop to help their colleagues understand the content of curriculum redesign, including performance indicators, standards, and curriculum maps. At this staff meeting, the principal opened the meeting and then turned control of it over to the teacher leaders who shared their recently acquired expertise and guided their colleagues in a collaborative learning process similar to what they had experienced at the team training.

At subsequent training sessions, the team learned how to analyze both achievement data and Effective Schools' perception data. Based on this work, the teacher leaders decided to organize a parents' workshop on the Stanford-9 testing system and what parents could do to help their children. Teacher leaders' expert knowledge in these areas enabled them to assume leadership at the beginning of the first year. The principal played a supportive role in this ES process and let the teachers take the lead. In carrying out this activity, the leadership team experienced two feelings. On the one hand, they were elated at the positive response of their colleagues at the first staff presentation and of parents to the workshops (more than 350 parents attended). On the other hand, they were frustrated by how hard it was to get their colleagues to participate in the evening parent workshops. When they initially asked their colleagues to volunteer to help, there was limited response. As the event drew near, the teacher team members turned to the principal for help in pressing teachers to take part. These examples show that when teachers have expert knowledge, they can assume important leadership roles with their colleagues. These events also suggest that tacit as well as active support from the principal is crucial.

Principal Leadership Based on Position and Expert Power

A second type of leadership revealed during data analysis was the principal's assertion of leadership through position and expert power, which occasionally resulted in his dominating meetings. We especially observed this reassertion of authority when the principal received requests for action from the district (e.g., implementing test prep, selecting graphic organizers to be used schoolwide, and allowing a planetarium presentation). These district issues usually took priority over and usurped any existing agenda and led to principal-dominated leadership team meetings.

One unscheduled presentation represents an example of the paradox of district pressures and the principal's response to them. An example occurred in October 2001, the beginning of the second year. The meeting began with one teacher reading the agenda: "Okay, so our agenda today, we have explored other test-prep materials, graphic organizers, and government reading programs, for clarification of this program." The principal did not pick up on what the teacher was saying and jumped in with an unrelated topic, "Who's sitting here?" After sitting down, the principal asked, "Who has the agenda?" The teachers started to review items on the agenda. The principal at this point took charge of the meeting and announced his agenda, which would be a presentation that the team members did not know about. As the following transcript shows, the teachers had a number of issues (raised by fellow teachers through the "concerns" box the team had established in the teachers' lounge) that they wanted to discuss, but the principal said all he wanted to do was list the issues.

Principal: *oh*

I just wanted to know the issue

Teacher 1: that's it

Principal: *anything else?*

Teacher 2: assemblies

if we can keep assemblies off

from

happening on Tuesdays

Teacher 3: also

assemblies

um

if we could have 'em shorter and after twelve o'clock

because there's been so many

and it's ah really hard to stay on target

and teaching our units

and PIs [that we're]

Principal: *I didn't want to get into it*

I just wanted to

get it down

everybody give me the information

anything else

Teacher 4: Ah, just one more

It makes it a little hard when you're doing kindergarten

and it's a [collapsed stage] with special assembly

on a Tuesday

Principal: *that's still assemblies*

okay, let's move on

	that's it
	those are all the issues
	okay, um
	I needed to modify the uh
	agenda
	in order to provide time for both presenters
	to come in and do a presentation
	um
	I wanted them to bring it in to you guys
	to make a decision
	about a year or two ago,
	we bought a science
Teacher 5:	planetarium
Principal:	*planetarium*
	and so

Whenever a request comes from the district, the principal tends to give it priority, overriding the team's agenda. These impromptu changes stem from the definitions of the job of principal that are embedded within the culture of the district as well as his personal perception of the job. The lack of dialogue and open exchange between the principal and teachers in the transcript suggest that the principal fails to perceive the need of bringing to the group the issue of changing the agenda. There is no discussion about the change in plans. The principal runs the meeting according to previous practices and behavior patterns, as he would have in the past before the formation of a leadership team. In subsequent teacher interviews, teachers recalled this incident and felt the principal was still dominating and unwilling to communicate so that others hear and understand the need for a change in agenda. Furthermore, the principal, although supporting teacher leadership and consciously developing his own ability to work with the leadership team, indicated in an interview, "I'm not ready at this point to give up total control. So we do discuss it, but the final decision actually resides with me."

Based on a review of meeting agenda and minutes, two additional incidents indicate that at other times the principal did not necessarily override the agenda but was in charge and ran the meeting. Again, both of these meetings had to do with district demands. One was to select a graphic organizer that all teachers would agree to teach their students and use throughout the year. The other was the presentation of the test-prep materials. In both cases, the principal was the expert and had the information as well as position power to take charge, and he did.

Shared Leadership

The third type of leadership observed was shared leadership in which neither principal nor teachers dominated. Many of the topics discussed and acted upon in a shared fashion were those that came from the leadership team trainings. In these discussions, we often observed the team applying and practicing some of the group-process skills they had learned. Both principal and teacher leaders practiced the roles of facilitator, recorder, and timekeeper at team meetings. For example, they discussed the role and function of the university Effective Schools consultant assigned to guide grade-level meetings, reported what was happening in grade-level meetings, the problems and concerns of the guest teacher program (regular substitutes to release teachers to meet weekly with their grade levels). In the first year, these issues were crucial to the implementation of the Effective Schools Initiative.

The role of the principal in these meetings was as an expert informant and mentor as he shared his knowledge and vision of the whole school with the team members and dealt with important issues as a school leader but not the sole decision maker. Data analysis revealed that, upon learning new ways, the leadership team members would share their new knowledge (e.g., the ES process) with others through words and behavior.

For instance, the teacher leaders in the second year took up the issue of examining the function of school committees. This action was stimulated by a presentation and activity at the leadership team training, which urged teams to examine how all parts of the school organization supported school goals. Teacher team members raised the topic of too many committees in two subsequent team meetings soon after the team training. By the February meeting, the teachers were leading the meeting and preparing a presentation for the whole staff, describing areas of responsibility for each of the existing 30 committees. At this meeting, the principal acted as a member of the team, listening and following the discussion.

At a midpoint in the meeting, as the following dialogue shows, the principal eased into the discussion with an "mm" and "well," as opposed to seizing the floor as he had done in the October meeting:

2/18/02 Leadership Team Meeting

Principal: *mm*

Teacher 1: or what?

Principal: *well*

Teacher 1: what's the problem?

Principal: *my original understanding was that*
this issue was being brought up
because it was a concern about, ah
who was doing what on the committees and
that some committees weren't active . . .
so that kinda needs
I'm assuming to be

Teacher 1: addressed?

Principal: *addressed because*
that was the original approach to
that was set up at the table when
Janet and her sister were here
and that whole issue came up
and so um, you know
we've been talking a lot
and so I've been waiting to hear that issue come up again
and I haven't.
And so my question in my mind
so I'm questioning the validity of that
that complaint and in this exercise
because we went through this whole exercise and that
is not

	being addressed
	so if you just give this to the staff without addressing the issue
	I would not be in the right frame of mind to hear
	about this issue again.
	You know what I'm saying?
Teacher 2:	And [I like to] determine if we should delete something maybe
Principal:	*Yeah, well*
	that was part [of the]
Teacher 2:	[we've got so many]
	parts of the discussion
Teacher 1:	I think we have too many [committees] myself
Principal:	*But you got to lay that out for the teacher 'cause if [you don't]*
Teacher 1:	yeah definitely
Teacher 2:	and I think that's one of the things that
	we wanted to give them this [one of the team members] suggested that maybe we need to ask them
	and let them know
	so that they themselves
Principal:	*right*
Teacher 2:	'cause she suggested that
	we don't want to tell them
	we want them to . . .

The principal and teachers had a shared concern on the topic of the need to reorganize their committee structure to increase staff involvement and focus the committee work on achieving school goals. The way the principal entered the conversation helped the teachers to think through the issue. He moved from his old mental model of taking charge to guiding the teachers to be leaders with their colleagues, reminding them of their original purpose in pursuing this topic. The team and principal are dealing with a classic team problem: getting "buy-in." In addressing the question "How do you represent your work to the whole faculty and staff to get their 'buy-in'?", the principal was helping the teachers to think from a leader's perspective along with some of the ramifications of taking leadership.

The dialogue reflects the shift in the relationship between the principal and the teachers on the leadership team and is further confirmed in the principal's interview at the end of the second year. In response to the question: "Has the process of decision making changed in any way?", the principal responded:

> Oh yes. It has changed I think dramatically. One, is that—and I don't know whether we've really reached a crucial issue that would test me—but more or less it's been an activity of me letting go, and not really taking on the leadership or pushing a decision, but letting it evolve, which is something totally different. . . . Another way that it's changed, it has slowed down significantly. The process of making a decision—I think individuals who are involved at this point in time are truly cognizant of trying not to step on toes. And they'd rather try to get input from each and every individual on the staff, where I might have thought well, we don't need everybody.

Throughout the principal's interview are phrases such as "I think it evolved . . . as we read research," "We're moving in that direction, but I don't think we're there yet. I still have things I need to work through myself, and I believe that's true with the teachers who are on that leadership team," "They are taking on the whole picture rather than just an individual concern." These statements suggest the development of new mental models about leadership and the principal's role.

The teachers also realize that shared leadership is a learning process. As one commented:

> I have found I have a clearer picture, but then, I also see how the staff still has a fuzzy picture . . . being on the leadership [team] is like, oh yeah, I have a very clear picture of the goal and what we're supposed to do, but then, when I talk to my people in upper grade, they are clueless as to that picture. So being on, seeing both sides, now I am on the leadership, I am saying, 'Wow' maybe at the grade level, as leadership person, I am not communicating the goals.

Another teacher continued, "I think the reason why that might happen is because the leadership team received certain training in certain areas. . . . We are informed ahead of time."

After participating in the ESI for two years, both principal and team members have learned about shared leadership and developed a clearer picture of schoolwide goals. They constructed meaning and knowledge together that was leading toward a common purpose of schooling (Lambert, 1995). They also recognize that they are still in a learning process, learning to share decision making and exploring the boundaries and potentials of shared leadership. When both the principal and teacher leaders develop greater understanding of shared leadership through peer discussion and dialogue about critical issues affecting teaching and learning, joint planning, self-reflection, and participation in regular team trainings that support their work, they are more likely to move toward genuine shared leadership.

Challenges to Sharing Leadership

The data suggest that external demands from the district, internal control and accountability needs, and existing mental models make it difficult for a principal to change from a classical leadership model to a shared leadership model. This study surfaced two major challenges for the teachers and principal:

- Determining how, what, and with whom should leadership be shared when the principal is ultimately held accountable for all decisions
- Recognizing the power of existing and predominant models of hierarchical leadership

Determining How, What and With Whom Should Leadership Be Shared When the Principal Is Ultimately Held Accountable For All Decisions

This challenge surfaced when decisions that the leadership team assumed it would make were in fact made by the principal outside of team meetings. An example of this was a request by the leadership team to discuss how teachers could have more time to set up their classrooms in preparation for the first day of school, which also included an orientation and open house for parents. From the minutes of the team meeting in June 2001, it was clear that the team had agreed to move the open house to the first day of school, an idea they had learned from the team trainings. "This issue must be decided upon by consensus. All grade levels have agreed to have it before school starts except the upper grades. At grade level meetings today we will get the final consensus" (Teacher, Team Minutes, June 19, 2001). As a result of this consensus decision to move the open house, the team requested that teachers be allowed to come to school on Friday and have access to the school Saturday and Sunday to prepare their rooms. Instead of discussing and deciding this issue as a team, the principal announced to the teachers that he would open the school on Friday, but not on the weekend. This was frustrating to the leadership team members, as one reported:

> Last year, we said [to the principal], it would be very nice to have an open house at the beginning of the year. . . . We can come in ahead of time and prepare the rooms, we don't want to have [one] day to prepare and then parents. It will be exhausting, and normally, teachers have the weekend. . . . So this year, yeah, he let us come in on Friday, and then, he said, no one may come in on Saturday and Sunday, because he wanted to do the work by himself. So everybody was totally out of crick, nobody was prepared, the room wasn't ready yet, . . . We had to come in on Monday and have pupils and parents come in our room. Everyone was very upset about that. And then we said to him, "Why couldn't you let teachers come in on the weekend?" He said, "Because I say so." And so, is that leadership we have? Yeah, we have leadership, yeah, let's do it, give us Friday and then he took away two days.

Although the principal and team members have a mutual desire to implement shared decision making, these roles are still new for both. There is a lack of clarity about which decisions will be shared, the boundaries necessary to frame shared decisions, and which decisions the principal will make and be solely responsible for. Clear decision rules have not been established (e.g., will decisions be made by vote, majority vote, or consensus?). Both the principal and team members had the same observation about this confusion. One teacher said, "There are confusions . . . because we are confused . . . if he is not present at that meeting, can we go ahead with this decision. Can we make the decision?" Similarly, the principal observed of the leadership team at the end of the second year:

> The process was all new to us, the meeting at grade level, sharing those ideas at a leadership [meeting] and guiding the school through this Effective School process through the leadership team, was all new, something that the staff was not used to, and didn't know how to measure . . . for lack of a better word . . . the power of the leadership team. . . . They are not quite sure what to make of the leadership team. The leadership team themselves has another picture, and they're at a point where they're using my words, my phrases, to make the point that this should be a leadership decision.

As the principal pointed out, the ES process is new to the school. Both the principal and teacher leaders were still learning it. The "lack of a better word" indicates that there is a lack of knowledge and skills. It suggests the need for both the principal and team members to learn a new language to both describe their emerging roles and relationships and to develop a common understanding about the purpose, functions, and decision-making authority of the leadership team. The principal reflected on the dilemmas confronting teachers serving on the team:

> And that's always being looked at and examined [by the teachers], you know—how far can we go, what decisions can we actually make, before the principal will step in, or before the district will step in, and say no you can't do that. . . . And the questions always asked: Can we do this? And that's where it falls back onto me, that's where sometimes I have to say, or I have to let go of my own personal needs I guess in terms of being a school principal and letting that go, letting the leadership team make those decisions.

The principal recognized that his personal needs, in terms of being a school principal, contribute significantly to the leadership team's confused feelings about the decision-making process. The principal is strongly influenced by the pressure of the district and state accountability (Yep & Chrispeels, Chapter 7 in this volume). One teacher confirmed that the principal is in the key position to draw a line in who decides. The leadership team recognizes that shared leadership is an evolving process and that they cannot draw the fine line between team decisions and principal decisions. They need the principal to clarify the process.

Recognizing the Power of Existing Mental Models of Hierarchical Leadership

Both principals and teachers enter and participate in new structures such as leadership teams with existing mental models of leadership. Traditionally the dominant model of teaching in the United States is isolated and individualistic. New teachers are expected to go it alone and not display weaknesses or ask for help (Johnson, 1990; Lortie, 1975). Lortie found that this isolation reinforces a culture of "presentism, individualism, and conservatism." Teachers rarely discuss each other's work, almost never observe their colleagues teaching, and have few opportunities to work together collaboratively as a team. The principal in this case was inculcated with these beliefs of being in charge and making the decisions:

> I think it's the self-satisfaction that . . . when I went into teaching, I went into teaching because I thought I could do a better job of teaching than some of the

> teachers I had [when I was a student]. . . . And so that was a sense of strong satisfaction in myself as an individual, as a teacher, someone who was capable of having an impact on children.

These ideas learned early in the principal's career as a teacher were transferred to his concept of the principalship:

> The idea of principalship to me was one where I could expand that concept. Not only was I affecting my classroom, but I would be able to affect a school. And so that was the perspective that generally guided me as I was making these decisions, and doing these things, and when they worked out, I had the self satisfaction that I helped create that, that was the guiding force behind me. And so that is the hardest thing I think to let go and allow a consensus to direct us in that direction, allowing that to grow.

One paradox seems at play: the principal indicates wanting to share leadership and responsibility but finds it hard to "give up" power and to trust the capacity of others; he wants to reserve the right to make the final decision or override decisions made by the leadership team.

When asked about the relationship of the principal and the leadership team at the end of the first year, one teacher responded:

> Oh, at the beginning, it wasn't good at all because I thought he [the principal] is too dictatorial. I don't like people like that. So the first year, I stayed because teachers who were working with him said he changes and helps in other ways.

This concern for lack of willingness to share power is echoed by other team members. One member said:

> We don't have real power, you know. We can come up with these ideas and talk about everything and then they don't get carried out. Or the principal decides to change something, he just says no because I say so. And this is the end of that, so we don't have final leadership, either.

Another member described the same problem, but felt the principal was trying to change behavior and share decision making and leadership with the team:

> He *does* look to the leadership [team], [we] discuss and make our decisions. At the same time, he sometimes overrides our decisions. We'll decide something at the meetings, and then next week *he has decided!* And, What! We were working on that. So he is working on that, it's a process [emphasis in the original].

Others also recognized the principal was changing, but change is a slow process. One team member (Teacher L) was somewhat discouraged when the second year began and she saw the principal once again "telling what to do instead of sharing and delegating to other people." However, through her participation on the team, she gained her own voice and now reported talking directly to the principal to express her concerns. "We have to talk about it. . . . He accepts it, he accepts it, but he didn't say anything. That is okay, but at least I tell him." Fortunately, at a leadership team meeting later in the year, she realized that the principal really had been listening. "He acknowledged to me that 'I know, Teacher L, you have told me that I have to give positive words to the teachers, but I don't know how to do it.' That tells me that he thinks when I tell him, he thinks. So that's good."

Evolution of Shared Leadership

Creating an educational community that serves as a setting for meaning making and human development requires members to work interdependently with each other. The observations and interviews from this study revealed a shared commitment by teachers and principal to develop the leadership team. In the first year, however, the members operated mostly as individuals representing their grade level; they accepted responsibility for carrying out individual tasks but usually did not reflect that they were operating with a schoolwide shared goal or vision. For example, in presenting to the staff some of the information from the first leadership team retreat, members willingly agreed to assume responsibility for a particular task, but the presentation did not reflect joint work. We can also see that the tasks they undertook were primarily concrete ones such as organizing a parent night and sharing information from their respective grade levels. Although this team had not developed a common purpose or engaged in joint work in the first year, they had started creating and engaging in common experiences that involved reciprocal relationships; they were climbing the learning curve of shared leadership.

Toward the end of the first year and throughout the second year, this team began to develop common goals. Over this two-year period, they invested time and energy in defining their roles and learning to work together. They set goals, developed an improvement plan, and addressed the need to communicate more effectively with the staff about the leadership team's work. They prepared and distributed their meeting minutes to all the staff. The team welcomed anonymous input from the staff by establishing a "concerns" box in the teachers' lounge and creating a bulletin board to display team news.

In the second year, the team tackled the sensitive issue of the school's committee structure based on ideas presented in the leadership team trainings. They began to wonder and explore why they had so many committees and what function the committees actually served. They saw dysfunction in the wide array of committees. Some teachers were in several (six or seven) committees, and at the same time some of the committees met only once a year. They took the initiative to develop a more effective structure that would significantly engage teachers in the process of improvement. These discussions energized the team, and specific actions emerged from their conversations. The meaning-making process of team meetings enabled members to clarify their school goals, to begin developing a common purpose of schooling, and to make team decisions that led to purposeful actions. These ongoing and spiraling processes of team trainings and team meetings, as displayed in Table 6.1, developed synergy as an educational community within the leadership team. Sustained over time, these processes gave participating members opportunities to learn new roles, relationships, and ways of acting that influenced their mental models about leadership.

As a result of leadership team trainings and site meetings, team members began to develop a whole-school perspective. In this case study, the principal expressed appreciation that teachers were gaining a broader perspective of the school as they participated in the trainings and worked collaboratively to resolve issues at their school. Among the themes, which surfaced during data analysis, were factors that influenced the group dynamics and created challenges for both the principal and teacher leaders in implementing a shared leadership model in their school, represented as a concept map in Figure 6.2. This revised concept map takes into account the influence of external factors, such as district mandates that push the principal and teachers to revert to their old mental models. Teacher concerns and issues, such as having extra time to prepare for the open house, show that teachers themselves revert to subservient positions when the principal asserts his authority in an autocratic way.

The case-study data suggest that this school might be considered at a midpoint in learning and practicing shared leadership. At this stage of development, we would conclude that their mental model of shared leadership is fragile and unstable. As shown in Figure 6.2, however, the team is able to apply the concept of shared leadership to the issues that emerged through the Effective Schools training. This is illustrated as the main path of decisions made by the team. Figure 6.2 suggests that the process of shared leadership can be disrupted either by district mandates or by the

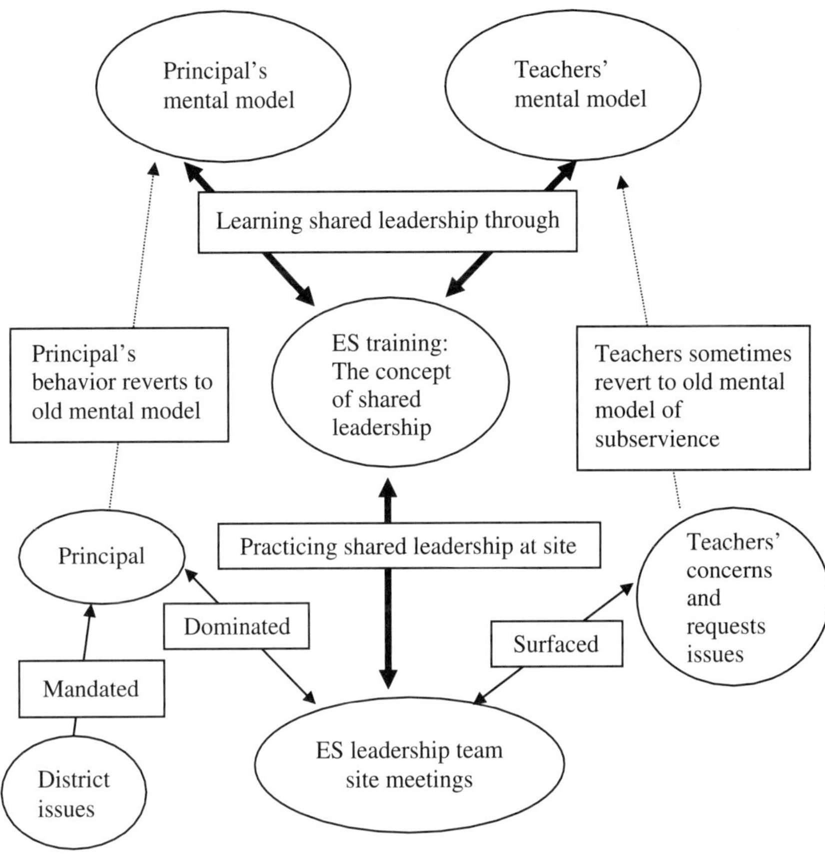

Figure 6.2 Revised Concept Map of How Leadership Teams Learn and Practice Shared Leadership

principal overriding or altering decisions made by the team, which reverses the developing shared-leadership process and resurfaces a hierarchical model. The failure to create room for discussion before changing an agenda or making a decision became a cause for frustration. Both the principal and teachers found it difficult to use their new knowledge of shared leadership when dealing with old issues in the school. These insights led us to revise our concept map of the process of learning shared leadership to suggest that shared leadership, at least in the early stages of development, is influenced by the content and sources of the issue being decided. The revised concept map also suggests the need for teams to be helped in understanding the diversity of decisions made at different levels of the system and in clarifying which issues can be most productively taken up by the leadership team and which ones are better left to the discretion of the principal.

Conclusion

This longitudinal study examined the interactive relationship of the principal's and teachers' mental models with the Effective Schools team training content as the leadership team navigated the unchartered waters of shared leadership. As participants expressed in the interviews, learning to share leadership is a slow and sometimes painful process. It is difficult for a principal to relinquish control, given the accountability pressures of the position in a classical leadership frame in a bureaucratically and hierarchically organized district. Teachers question their authority to make decisions, too, because this is new territory outside their traditional job description, experiences, and training.

A recent synthesis of the leadership literature by Waters, Marzano, and McNulty (2003) indicates that ensuring that schools develop effective ways of sharing leadership can have significant payoffs in improving student learning. They found that "the extent to which the principal involves teachers in the design and implementation of important decisions and polices" had an effect size on student achievement of 0.30, which represents a moderate effect (Waters et al., 2003, p. 11). This significant effect size suggests that establishing ways for teachers to be involved in teams where decision making and leadership are shared, as was done in the Effective Schools Initiative described in this chapter, needs to be considered as a critical variable in district and school efforts to improve student achievement. Our study surfaced several significant findings that will be useful to educational leaders interested in building strong models for shared leadership that can increase the potential of a team's impact on student learning The study also has implications for those involved in designing leadership team training and development.

First, our study indicates that norms for decision making need to be clearly specified and understood to minimize confusion about decision-making authority at the site level. In addition, systemic clarity is needed in order to understand accountability issues of decisions made by a leadership team. School leadership teams, as this study so clearly illustrates, do not operate in a vacuum. District goals, mandates, and directives must be clearly articulated to the team to help lessen potential conflicts and tensions between the principal and the team. In establishing leadership teams, the district administration and board of education also have a responsibility to respect the needs of teams to make decisions that meet the unique cultural and programmatic needs of the school within a general framework of district goals and expectations.

Second, our research indicates that attention needs to be given to surfacing preexisting mental models and the assumptions that may underlie them. These models may need to be reexamined and reshaped in light of the desire to share leadership. This study confirms that providing team training can be one means to help principals and teachers explore new relationships and develop collaborative skills and knowledge, which in turn build trust and understanding within the team. Through participation in the trainings and weekly leadership team meetings at the school, team members created and engaged in common experiences that involved reciprocal relationships, a building block of constructivist leadership. Gradually their mental models of leadership began to change. This research demonstrates that training must be provided, practiced, sustained, and reiterated in order to move along the continuum of shared leadership. One important implication for those involved in preparing teachers and principals is that preservice teachers and future principals during their preparation need to begin understanding the value of collaboration and the mental images they hold that may support or constrain collaboration. The study also suggests that institutionalizing processes that foster and nurture new mental models of shared leadership will not be easy and may require second order, fundamental changes by all those involved in the system.

Third, our findings indicate that in addition to building trust and a reciprocal relationship, shared leadership demands collaboration, which in turn requires time. Establishing leadership teams through the ESI provided structure, space, and time for the principal and teachers to come together to discuss, dialogue, and practice shared leadership. Providing time to talk and a safe space in which to practice new skills and ways of being were fundamental for this leadership team to move toward shared leadership. As Kegan (1982) points out, the capacity for reciprocity is the result of long-term meaning making with others. We believe that school leadership teams can develop mature shared leadership relationships as long as they continue to engage in reflective dialogue and meaning making with each other and with other teams. Through this process, team members become more complex in their thinking, more tolerant of diverse perspectives, and more flexible and open toward new models of shared leadership.

Fourth, this study illustrates the fragility of shared leadership in systems that remain basically bureaucratic and hierarchical in structure. Team members reverted to their previously held mental model of autocratic-subservient behavior patterns when external demands intruded. These external demands usually originated from the district and required immediate response. This change to old behavior patterns suggest ideas for further research. For example, research is needed to better understand the pressures that lead team members and the principals to revert to previous practices. Do leadership team members revert to their old mental models because the district (hence, "the boss") continues to operate in a classical/hierarchical leadership model? Or is it because the basic tenet of constructivist leadership (allowing time for dialogue and processing) is insufficient? What kinds of training and development are needed that can more quickly help teams identify and clarify appropriate decision-making models needed in varying contexts?

Finally our findings can help central office staff, boards of education, principals, teachers, and community members recognize that learning new skills and ways of operating is a process that takes time and evolves over time. In the beginning stages, team members are likely to continue to operate as individuals. Over time—as the team moves into joint productive activities, interdependency becomes a norm, significant goals are pursued, and results begin to emerge—sharing leadership can become a reality. The time line of this evolutionary path is not certain, but it is clear that unless the team is nurtured and encouraged to evolve, the benefits of shared leadership for student learning will not be realized.

References

Barth, R. (1990). *Improving schools from within.* San Francisco: Jossey-Bass.

Behar-Horenstein, L. S., & Gonzales, L. D. (2002, April). *Sustaining teacher leadership beyond an enabling culture.* Paper presented at the American Educational Research Association, New Orleans, LA.

Berlak, H., & Berlak, C. (1981). *Dilemmas of schooling, teaching and special change.* London: Methuen.

Chrispeels, J. H., Brown, J. H., & Castillo, S. (2000). School leadership teams: Factors that influence their development and effectiveness. In K. Leithwood, (Ed.). *Understanding schools as intelligent systems* (pp. 39–74). Stamford, CT: JAI Press.

Chrispeels, J. H., Castillo, S., & Brown, J. H. (2000). School leadership teams: A process model of team development. *School Effectiveness and School Improvement, 11*(1), 20–56.

Chrispeels, J. H., Martin, K. J., Harari, I, Strait, C. C., & Rodarte, M. A. (1999). Role conflict and role ambiguity: The challenges of team leadership at a middle school. *Journal of School Leadership, 9,* 422–453.

Chrispeels, J. H., Strait, C. C., & Brown, J. H. (1999). The paradoxes of collaboration. *Thrust for Educational Leadership, 29*(2), 16–19.

Dimmock, C. (1996). Dilemmas for school leaders and administrators in restructuring. In K. Leithwood, J. Chapman, D. Corson, P. Hallinger, A. Hart (Eds.), *International handbook of educational leadership and administration* (pp. 135–170). Dordrecht, the Netherlands: Kluwer Academic Publishers.

Dornbusch, S. M., & Scott, W. R. (1975). *Evaluation and the exercise of authority.* San Francisco: Jossey-Bass.

Hallinger, P., & Heck, R. (1999). Can leadership enhance school effectiveness? In T. Bush, L. Bell, R. Bolam, R. Glatter, & P. Ribbins (Eds). *Educational management: Redefining theory, policy and practice* (pp. 178–190). London: Paul Chapman.

Johnson, S. M. (1990). *Teachers at work: Achieving success in our schools.* New York: Basic Books.

Kegan, R. (1982). *The evolving self: Problem and process in human development.* Cambridge, MA: Harvard University Press.

Lambert, L. (1995). Toward a theory of constructivist leadership. In L. Lambert et al. (Eds.), *The constructivist leader* (pp. 28–51). New York: Teachers College Press.

Lieberman, A., & Miller, L. (1984). School leadership: There is no magic. In A. Lieberman & L. Miller (Eds.) *Teachers, their world, and their work: Implications for school improvement* (pp. 61–80). Alexandra, VA: Association for Supervision and Curriculum Development.

Lortie, D. C. (1975). *Schoolteacher: A sociological study.* Chicago: University of Chicago Press.

MacBeath, J. (1999). *Schools must speak for themselves: The case for school self-evaluation.* London: Routledge.

Meier, D. (1985). Retaining the teacher's perspective in the principalship. *Education and Urban Society, 17,* 302–310.

Mitchell, D. E., Ortiz, F. I., & Mitchell, T. K. (1987). *Work oriented and job performance: The cultural basis of teaching rewards and incentives.* Albany: SUNY Press.

Natriello, G., & Dornbusch, S. M. (1980–1981). Pitfalls in the evaluation of teachers by principals. *Administrators' Notebook, 29*(6), 1–4.

Nemerowicz, G., & Rosi, E. (1997). *Education for leadership and social responsibility.* London: Falmer Press.

Senge, P. (1990). *The fifth discipline: The art and practice of the learning organization.* London: Doubleday.

Smylie, M. A., & Brownlee-Conyers, J. (1992). Teacher leaders and their principals: Exploring the development of new working relationships. *Educational Administration Quarterly, 28*(2), 150–184.

Strauss, A., & Corbin, J. (1990). *Basics of qualitative research: Grounded theory procedures and techniques.* Newbury Park, CA: Sage.

Sykes, G., & Elmore, R. F. (1989). Making schools manageable: Policy and administration for tomorrow's schools. In J. Hannaway & R. Crowson (Eds.), *The politics of reforming school administration* (pp. 77–94). New York: Falmer Press.

Van Maanen, J. (1988). *Tales of field: On writing ethnography*. Chicago, IL: University of Chicago Press.

Van Maanen, J. (1995). *Representation in ethnography*. Thousand Oaks, CA: Sage.

Wallace, M. (2002). Modeling distributed leadership and management effectiveness: Primary school senior management teams in England and Wales. *School Effectiveness and School Improvement, 13*(2), 163–186.

Waters, T., Marzano, R. J., & McNulty, B. (2003). *Balanced leadership: What 30 years of research tells us about the effect of leadership on student achievement*. Boulder, CO: Mid-continent Regional Educational Laboratory (McREL).

PART III

Cross-Case Studies of Shared Leadership

7

Sharing Leadership

Principals' Perceptions

Maureen Yep

Janet H. Chrispeels

> *Leadership in high-performing learning organizations is decentralized, facilitative and exercised fully at all levels of the organization.*
>
> —Marks & Seashore Louis (1999, p. 714)

The quote at the beginning of this chapter encompasses an ideal. In shared leadership, as in most things, the path between belief and implementation can be both confronting and rewarding, as the study described in this chapter affirms. It tells the story of principals on their journey from belief to realization of shared leadership, and the issues that support and impede their path. What do principals think about shared leadership? What do they want to achieve? Principals talked about their beliefs and aspirations and the things they find help them move forward toward achievement of their goals.

What gets in the way? Principals identified components that make achievement or even implementation of beliefs problematic. The most important finding in this study, however, is that although obvious blockers were identified, the data revealed many paradoxes subtly embedded in personal, school, and systemic practice. These paradoxes emerged as powerful blockers that serve to dynamically obstruct implementation of change. These blockers are sustained, unchallenged, and unaddressed because they are hidden within the norms of everyday occurrence. The study identifies those paradoxes and their impact.

A great deal has been written about the concept and practice of shared leadership in schools, but only a few studies (i.e., Blase & Blase, 2000; Hsieh & Shen, 1998) have given consideration to the principals' perspectives about sharing leadership and the personal and professional challenges involved in its implementation. In research literature, the principal is acknowledged as critical to the process of change (Fullan, 2001; Waters, Marzano, & McNulty, 2003), and so it is important to ascertain principals' understandings and attitudes regarding shared leadership and what they believe affects its implementation in their schools. This chapter addresses these issues.

Shared leadership is often implemented within a context of wider change and generates further change as principals and teachers move to a collaborative, democratically based model. In underperforming schools, such as many of those in the study, the environment is one of strong political pressure for accountability and increased application of prescriptive solutions. An inherent duality of values and practice emerged from the research as a particularly significant factor. In this chapter we examine the changing nature of leadership; outline the study, together with its demographic and district context; report the research findings; discuss key issues and implications arising from the findings; and close with conclusions and suggestions for future action.

The Changing Nature of School Leadership

Leadership in many countries, traditionally and historically, has been positional, the prerogative of the principal at the school site or of senior administrators at district and state levels within a hierarchically tiered system. Administrators held the power, made the decisions, and took responsibility, acting in accordance with the prevailing structure, duties, and responsibilities of the position. As the role of principal evolved, their tasks were increasingly seen as managerial, especially in large schools; being strong, decisive, and "in charge" were considered as desirable operational qualities. The role of staff was to comply with district demands and principal requests and to be effective professionals in their classrooms. Data suggest that the district in the study operated within similar traditional forms of leadership structures, organization, and roles but is now in transition, broadly as part of a global process of change in leadership models, and specifically in accordance with the design principles of a district/university reform partnership.

Pressures on Leaders for Increased Accountability

Many influences are leading to worldwide change. There is concern regarding educational standards and pressure to improve the academic performance of *all* students. For most, this is based in concepts of equity and equal access; for some, it is also based on being internationally competitive. Most states have established professional standards for teachers and administrators that form part of their accountability. Academic standards for students are also the norm. In some states, including California, which is the context for this chapter, the state mandates (often as a condition for funding) specific curriculum, texts, programs, and training for districts that have many underperforming schools. State testing provides information on student performance and is used as a primary measure and arbiter of accountability. Testing has become high-stakes, with district and principal accountability linked to standardized test outcomes and performance standards. The schools in the research district are under enormous pressure to effect improved student achievement and lift their school ranking within the state.

Critical Role of Principals as Instructional Leaders

Nationally and internationally, a renewed focus on learning and teaching has brought a change in role and focus for principals from site managers to instructional leaders. This shift in role has been congruent with collaborative leadership and increased involvement of teachers and community in decision making through devolution of authority to individual schools (Caldwell & Spinks, 1992, 1998; Telford, 1996), which has been extensively implemented in countries such as New Zealand and Australia. In the United States, implementation of shared leadership and decision making through school councils has been common in many communities (Donaldson, 2001; Pounder, 1998; Reed, 2000; Smylie & Brownlee-Coyners, 1992). More recent research has focused on shared leadership that is dispersed, integrative, and democratic as a means of cultivating teacher empowerment and enhancing teachers as leaders (Bennett, Wise, Woods, & Harvey, 2003; Crowther, Kaagan, Ferguson, & Hann, 2002; Ekholm, 2002; Gronn, 2000; Harris 2002; Riley, 2002; Seashore Louis, 2002). The move to strengthen the role of the principal as an instructional leader and to expand the leadership role to others in the school community, especially leadership teams, places new demands on principals. They need to know both how and when to share leadership. Waters,

Marzano, and McNulty (2003) have recently completed a meta-analysis of leadership studies conducted in the past 30 years. They have identified 21 leadership responsibilities most closely associated with improved student learning, two of which are relevant to the findings presented in this chapter: (1) the willingness of the principal to challenge the status quo; and (2) the extent to which principals involve teachers in shared decision making. They assert that the task of being an effective instructional leader requires not only undertaking the right work but also understanding the magnitude of the change that may be required.

Transitioning from Hierarchical to Collaborative Systems

The principals in this study are in transition from the traditional system in which they grew up and in which they have spent most of their professional lives to the changing attitudes, requirements, and roles of current times. The district plays a dual and ambiguous role that fluctuates between espousing and supporting site-based management and collaborative processes, and implementing and enforcing state and district mandates and accountability measures. Marks and Seashore Louis (1999) found:

> Paradoxically, organizational learning also requires strong and sometimes directive leadership. . . . Studying school implementation over time, Huberman and Miles (1984) note that "pressure and support" from the district office are critical to maintaining the scope of the effort, whereas Bryk et al. (1996) found that effective organizational leadership in developing professional community was supportive as well as authoritative. (p. 714)

This study suggests that this duality can also be a powerful negative force to effectively sharing leadership if it is not acknowledged and addressed.

The Study

Context

This study was conducted within a single elementary school district in southern California, which, in partnership with a local university, is implementing a comprehensive reform initiative based on the Effective Schools process (referred throughout as the Effective Schools Initiative, or ESI). Fifteen schools participated in the district-wide components of ESI, and 10 of the 15 engaged in more intensive site-based work. In the past 10 years the school district has experienced rapid growth, particularly of its low-income and Latino student population. This growth continues, but over the past two years pockets of greater affluence are emerging as white and Latino middle-class families move into newer housing estates that are replacing farming tracts. In this still predominantly Latino school district, where two-thirds of the schools have 80 to 99% Latino students, approximately half of the district's students need special English language instruction. A bilingual program operates in the first four years of schooling with a transition to English-only instruction by the end of fourth grade. The parents often have limited English language facility, education, or comfort with school interaction, and student mobility exists with itinerant working families. Academic expectations tend to be low, and few students continue their education beyond high school. Although academic gains are evident in the schools intensively involved in the ESI—those receiving regular training of their leadership team as well as bimonthly facilitated grade level meetings—Chrispeels (2002) comments on the district's achievement in 2000 as follows:

> On the Stanford-9 Achievement Test, most schools are ranked in the bottom achievement range for the state. Even when they are compared with schools that serve students of similar socio-economic status, students received among the lowest scores in the region. (p. 23)

School organization is made quite complex by a shortage of sufficient buildings to accommodate all students. Most schools are large, with 700–1,100 students, and all operate on a multitrack year-round schedule. This means all staff or students are never at school at the same time. Although K–3 classes are generally staffed at 20–1 as a result of class-size reduction legislation, grades 4–6 are large as a consequence. As a high-growth and high-needs district, with bilingual instruction and year-round multitrack schooling, attracting and holding suitably qualified teachers is a challenge, resulting in significant numbers of new and uncredentialed teachers working in the district's schools each year. Although the district is active in redressing this, no school at the time of the study had all credentialed teachers. The already challenging process of change and reform is thus additionally pressured by these contextual factors that are frequently linked to lower student achievement.

Participants and Data Collection

The primary participants in the study are principals of 13 of the 15 elementary schools. The principals were interviewed to explore their views on shared leadership. Individual hour-long interviews were conducted in

December 2001, with eight of the 10 principals participating in the intensive implementation of the university-district reform partnership. The five principals whose schools were less intensively involved in ESI were interviewed in March 2002. These interviews were 45 minutes in length and focused only on shared leadership. The data from the two groups of principals were not analyzed separately because of considerable movement of principals within the district and because they had all participated in district-level ESI work.

Three Domains of Shared Leadership

Analysis of the principals' interview data draws on Spradley's (1979, 1980) technique of domain analysis that seeks patterns within the data that reveal the inherent categories of meaning. The analysis revealed three broad domains: principals' perceptions of shared leadership; factors identified as assisting its implementation; and factors that obstruct, either directly or inherently, effective implementation of shared leadership.

Domain 1: Principals' Perceptions of Shared Leadership

From the data analysis, four major categories were identified within Domain 1: (1) what "shared leadership" means, (2) who is included, (3) what is shared, and (4) how principals feel about sharing leadership.

What "Shared Leadership" Means

Some principals gave actual definitions of shared leadership, such as "administration . . . sharing leadership with staff" and "most fundamentally the empowerment of teachers to have a share in the direction the school is going," but most defined shared leadership through its attributes, processes, and practice. All principals see shared leadership as working with their teachers, and that involving teachers in the life of the school outside their classroom is essential to their buy-in and commitment to educational change. Through data analysis, we found sharing leadership encompassed the following:

1. *beliefs* (values, philosophy)
2. *direction* (focus, vision, mission, goals, objectives)
3. *governance* (consultation, decision making, equity, equality, democratic processes such as collaboration and consensus, empowerment, responsibility)
4. *knowledge* (expertise)

5. *operations and practices* (workload, dialogue, planning, implementation, problem solving)
6. *relationships* (support, collegiality, trust, confidentiality)

The three areas of greatest commonality in the principals' responses were having a unified vision, direction, and goals; participating in making, implementing, and being responsible for decisions; and effecting staff buy-in, commitment, and ownership. Typical comments included:

> I see shared leadership as a collective of people at a school site or wherever, who have the unifying vision, goal, objective, and we use that vision, that goal, to make sound decisions and judgments about what we're supposed to do in order to move closer to that goal. . . . So that's how I see it. It's just a collective and I'm part of that collective, but the decisions and the allocation of resources and the direction of the school is all being decided by that group. Everyone in that group shares in that mission, that vision—so much so that the decisions are no longer made on a personal basis but for the benefit of achieving that goal.

> . . . it's something that needs to have a high trust level, one in which you have teachers feeling comfortable about making suggestions and taking risks in the process. This is what I feel is shared leadership—opportunities for everybody to be collaborative and collegial in working with the process [that] we should all strive for, I think, in the democratic society in which we live.

The interviews revealed variance in how principals interpreted terms such as "shared leadership," "involvement," "participation," "collaboration," and "empowerment," and the practices that ensued, and also revealed some incongruence between principals' positive endorsement of shared leadership and their actual practice. Shared decision making ranged from teachers having referent, consultative roles to teachers being empowered to make and implement schoolwide decisions, yet each principal believed that they were engaged in shared leadership.

One principal, despite gains, recognized the distance between his concept and implementation and was committed to putting his beliefs into practice:

> I think the biggest way [my leadership role has changed] is just sharing the responsibility of making decisions and trying to move forward with them and make an impact on the lives of children. I've always thought that I did some kind of shared management. Well I was probably fooling myself, you know, because through the process I really found out that even though I may have called it site-based management and shared decision, it really wasn't shared decision as it has evolved to this point. . . . Your eyes do open up.

Three principals indicated that their perceptions were undergoing change over time: "It's evolving," and "It's changed over the years."

The most developed implementers of shared leadership seem to be principals who are committed to the concept, are highly reflective about its implementation, and are serious and active in seeking ways to improve learning in the school; who constantly question and honestly acknowledge the specific issues that support and hinder the process, including their own attitudes and actions; and who consciously and consistently struggle to address and change those things.

Who Is Included in the "Sharing"?

Principals varied only slightly in their concept of who "shares" leadership. Essentially they see leadership shared with their professional staff—the teachers and, in applicable schools, their assistant principals. Three mentioned classified staff. In their evaluation of 77 empirical and case studies on school-based management, Leithwood and Menzies (1998) noted at least three different forms distinguished by the locus of decision-making power and control: (1) administrators, (2) professional staff, or (3) community. This is consistent with other research such as Kagan's four-stage Continuum of Leadership cited in Court (2002). Within these frames, the increased collaborative and shared decision-making practices evidenced in this study appear consistent with early to mid stages in the transition process from traditional, hierarchical leadership to shared leadership.

Most principals, although seeing shared leadership as ideally being a schoolwide collaborative effort to effect change and improve student outcomes, predominantly work with the formal structures—leadership teams, lateral and vertical grade-level teams, and site committees, as these provide a ready forum. Several principals expressed the importance of schoolwide representation on leadership teams. Two principals added direct personal interaction, dialogue, expectation, and support of individuals as expressed in the following quote: "I would hope I can establish a relationship with each of them on a one-to-one basis, where I understand what they are doing in their classroom and as a person."

The perception that leadership is shared with professional staff draws attention to the omissions. Parent involvement is a correlate of Effective Schools and other reform programs, and so greater awareness by schools participating in the study might be expected. The data indicate, however, that parent/community involvement is predominantly initiated by the principal or leadership team and is initiated in ways they perceive as desirable or necessary (such as supporting school test preparation). Principals indicated minimal inclusion of students, parents, or the wider school community in collaborative leadership roles, and they provided little evidence of committed attempts to develop high levels of engagement in school decisions or to actively build parent leadership roles or capacity. Involvement of students in democratic processes, decision making, and leadership was not expressed by any of the principals, although one principal indicated that he was reflecting on his and the school's practice in regard to parents and students. Even where principals acknowledged involvement of community members, inclusion was not commonly verified in their language or examples that focused on teachers. It is also of note that, although the principals clearly involve teachers in their concept of shared leadership, their interview language remains predominantly "I" statements rather than "we" statements.

Also absent in the principals' concepts of shared leadership was inclusion of others beyond the school, either "sharing up" with the district or "sharing out" with the unions or the wider community. Tensions exist in the study schools that may limit such an expanded concept of shared leadership. Several principals view the teachers' union as difficult and confronting, as espousing but actually resistant to collaborative practices, as expressed in the following:

> I think the thing that was the most significant for me . . . coming in from another district [is the] rigid perspective I perceive coming from the teachers' union. Even though they articulated to me that they wanted shared leadership, they wanted participatory decision making, etc., when I first attempted to do those things they backed off immediately.

What Is Shared

All principals saw curriculum as an area where leadership could, and should, be shared with teachers, and they gave examples of teacher leadership in their schools based on curriculum expertise. Three principals declared instruction as an intentional focus. One expressed the view that, although wider teacher involvement is encouraged, the teachers' key responsibility was to the children in the classroom.

Four principals saw shared leadership, especially through the leadership team, as without area limits—"I am farming it *all* out"—with teachers empowered, increasingly informed, and proactive on all schoolwide issues. One also saw it as shared responsibility for handling needs and resources and dealing with the most difficult issues and decisions to make real improvement in every aspect of the school environment. Individual principals articulated sharing work, concerns, solutions, values, culture, beliefs, ideas, knowledge, planning, professional dialogue, different perspectives, camaraderie, and social activities; addressing organizational, procedural, and practical issues; having ethics such as respect and confidentiality; and recognizing the importance of shared humor.

What is not shared is the final decision. All interviewed principals placed limits at some point on decision making by others, reserving the right to make a final decision because they see themselves as ultimately responsible, especially for ensuring that safety, legal, district, or state requirements are met. They therefore have to be convinced that others' decisions are in the best interests of the school, and are acceptable to their personal and professional parameters, before acceding to their ideas or approving implementation.

How Principals Feel About Sharing Leadership

The principals confirmed that a hierarchy previously operated within the district and that they now perceive a change taking place, as the following comment shows:

> I was here in the old days when we had dictatorial principals . . . they had their own little kingdoms and they ruled with an iron hand. . . . I think that's where it starts, to empower others, because the structure that existed, at least in my school, was one where the principal was basically the head and everyone else fell underneath the principal. Moving to shared leadership teams, people will sit at the table with you.

The data revealed that all 13 principals positively endorsed the change from hierarchical to shared leadership, though the strength of endorsement varied. Comments ranged from "I'm comfortable with it" to "I think that shared leadership is imperative if you want to make change in your school." For several principals, endorsement has moved to commitment, as expressed in the following comment: "I am hoping to reach that model of shared leadership. That's something that I've committed myself to see . . . and to practice . . . it's my preferred mode of operation."

Domain 2: Principals' Perceptions of Factors Assisting Shared Leadership

In the study, principals identified many things that assist the development of shared leadership in schools. Five interconnected categories emerged from the study, each encompassing a range of assisting factors, and each contributing to the development and implementation of shared leadership as shown in Figure 7.1.

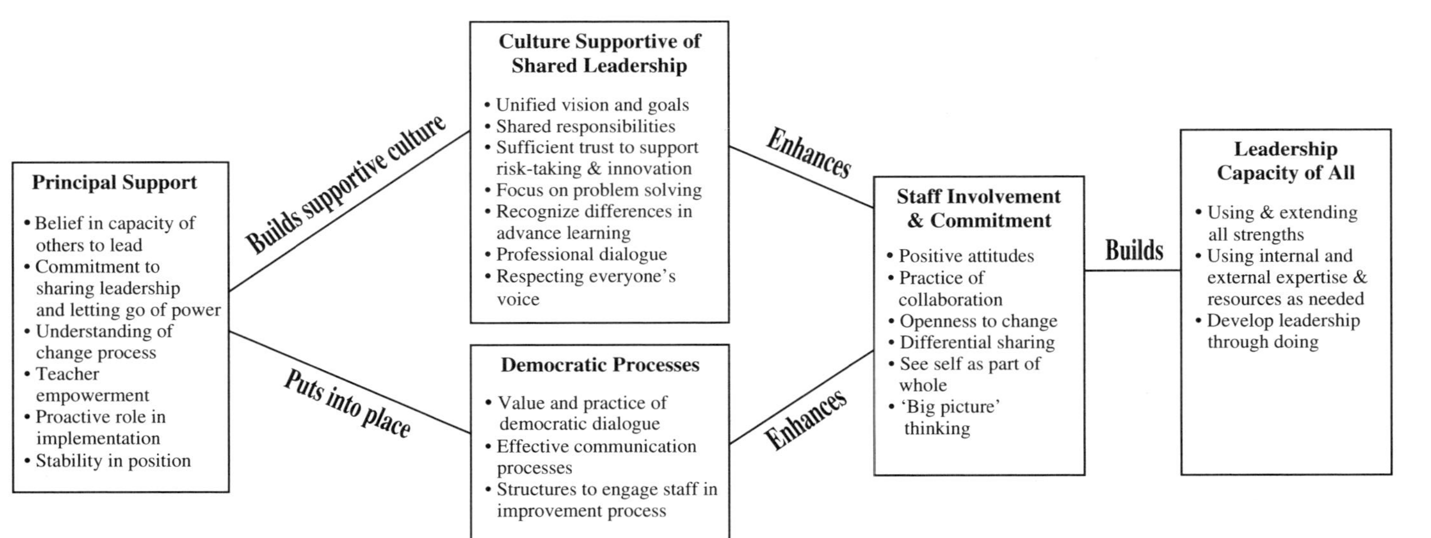

Figure 7.1 Summary of Actions By Principals That Enhance Distributed Leadership

A number of these findings are expected, in that they are consistent with what is already known from research on the importance of a positive and learning-focused school culture (Deal & Peterson, 1998); developing learning communities (Senge, 1990; Sergiovanni, 1994); empowering teachers through participation in decision making and problem solving (Blase & Kirby, 2000); listening to and respecting everyone's voice, (Lambert, 1998); building the leadership capacity and effectively using the resources of all (Stoll, 1999; Stoll, Fink, Earl & Earl, 2002); and sharing a vision, having clear goals, and acknowledging the importance of openness to and skills in the change process (Fullan, 2001). Figure 7.1 demonstrates that these factors occur as mutually supportive and interconnected actions. As principals create conditions for involvement and implement democratic practices, teacher support and participation are likely to increase, which in turn feeds back and potentially reinforces principal behaviors. The optimal outcome is increased leadership capacity throughout the system.

Principals' Support

Principals' belief in, commitment to, and consistent support of shared leadership were the assisting factors most strongly expressed in the study. One principal expressed it succinctly: "It all has to do with the principal, because if the principal doesn't want to do it, it's not going to happen."

Espousing shared leadership is not doing it, and two principals raised concern that it not be mere rhetoric: "Sometimes you wonder if it's . . . verbiage . . . that we're giving out [about] participatory management. I know that it's not always possible." Another stressed that shared leadership should be evident in practice, not just be the ideal: "To me it's . . . down and dirty you know. It's not just idealistic. It's how we run the school." One expressed that a principal needs to clearly stand for something, and their staff needs to know that the principal will stand up for their beliefs and stand up for them.

An important change for principals is to let go of the control, to believe and trust in the capacity of others to actively participate and lead. This means new ways of operating for principals. They identified proactive roles for themselves to replace control such as facilitating, supporting, and finessing. The role of the principal thus changes from control to support, mentoring, and coaching; from positional status to knowledge status; from being head of a hierarchy to being one member of a team. Encompassing, actively practicing, and seeing positive outcomes of dispersed leadership all further assist the change. Several, however, commented that continuity of principal leadership is needed if they are to have the time needed to guide school development and sustain the initiatives toward shared leadership. As an evolving process, it takes time to implement; there are no simple, fast solutions. They understood that it requires preparedness to change personally, to redesign their practice, and restructure their schools to support dispersed leadership.

Establishing a Supportive Culture

Many principals identified a culture conducive to sharing leadership as highly important. In such a culture trust was most commonly expressed as the key variable because it assists shared leadership and underpins the nature and structure of relationships in a school. Principals are historically patterned in directing others, checking up on them, or doing the job themselves. Building trust, therefore, was viewed as essential to openness, innovation, and a collaborative culture.

Principals recognized that developing shared leadership means engaging the school in a change process. Understanding the complexity and variety of school and systemic factors operating in the process and having the ability to read and act appropriately on those factors was an important skill for principals. They saw that they needed to help staff deal with change. They recognized the need to model, value, and expect differential ideas, strategies, and personalities; to keep the focus on shared leadership; to assist alignment of goals, action, and resources; and to provide staff with the structures and resources to effectively share leadership.

Democratic Processes

Education is a "caring" profession, and this can assist collaboration. Some principals, however, demonstrate caring by being very protective of their staff. One principal saw the potential for *overcaring* to be a barrier to their empowerment: "As an administrator, the more you [do by yourself], the less your staff knows about what's going on, and that's the problem." Most principals recognized that collaborative engagement of all staff expands the base for solving problems and implementing solutions, builds schoolwide capacity where everyone is a resource of some kind, and increases respect and understanding for working cooperatively and democratically. Apart from valuing shared leadership as a concept, principals pragmatically realize that the workload is too big for one person and acknowledge that they can't do it all. They recognized the necessity of aligning leadership and school practices to team effort with real benefits for all. They also identified increased consistency of focus, processes, and practice as important, and realized that establishing the leadership teams had created an important structure to assist them.

Principals saw effective communication of the information and knowledge that teachers need to actively participate in shared leadership, contribute to professional discussion, and make informed decisions as crucial. It enables "big-picture" thinking and responsibility. Usually effective communication was seen as a two-way process, but one principal extended this concept further:

> Well, it actually shouldn't be up and down, it should be crossing, or even an oval. . . . I agree somebody at some time has to make a decision, but perhaps it should be an internal one where a person is in the middle and [communicating] ideas from everywhere.

Staff Involvement and Commitment

All principals acknowledged that shared leadership operates only when staff are highly engaged and committed to the change. Many struggled between the *ideal* of shared leadership involving everyone and the *reality* of differential contribution and commitment. They commented that teacher contributions ranged from nonparticipation to those who do it all and overextend. Several principals valued differing opinions, especially in opening up thinking and discussion and moving ideas and actions in new directions through challenging the status quo. However, differences and questioning made other principals uncomfortable, for they viewed it as conflictual and potentially disruptive to harmonious staff relations.

Several principals commented that teachers who participated on the leadership teams were changing and shifting from a classroom perspective to a whole-school perspective, and they realized that this broader view was particularly significant in fostering shared leadership. The shift assists staff to be proactive and involved, particularly in schoolwide issues and in complex or difficult decisions. It supported the idea of teachers accepting shared responsibility for actions and outcomes across the school.

Building the Leadership Capacity of All

The model presented in Figure 7.1 suggests that with principal support to develop a culture conducive to shared leadership and the democratic processes to enact it, staff commitment and involvement in shared leadership will build the leadership capacity of all. Most principals in this study saw the support and intervention of outside organizations, such as the university in the ESI project, as valuable in setting this process in motion and developing leadership capacity in their staff. The work done with leadership teams and grade-level teams within the ESI was particularly acknowledged.

Domain 3: Principals' Perceptions of What Obstructs Shared Leadership

In spite of wanting shared leadership in their schools, principals identified many blocking factors at personal, school, and systemic levels that make development and implementation of shared leadership in schools difficult. They are shown in Table 7.1. Many are simply a deficit of the assisting factors presented above, but new factors were also evidenced.

Table 7.1 Factors Obstructing Shared Leadership

Personal Blockers

- Historical influence and patterning
- Issues of control: "letting go"
- Accountability

Blockers Within the School

- Genuine constraints (e.g., year-round schools, overcrowding)
- Time and workload (principals and teachers)
- Competing demands such as loyalty to union and sense of professionalism
- Teacher buy-in/motivation/ownership/responsibility
- Negative teacher attitudes toward district, principal, colleagues, or students
- Staff lacking the necessary skills/support/models for their new role
- Staff passive or resistant to change
- Conflicts between new teachers and veterans

Blockers From "the System"

- Lack of real choice
- Imposed decisions/mandates
- Politicization of education
- Pressure of focus on test scores and Academic Performance Index (API) ranking
- Lack of recognition of schools' other achievements
- Accountability pressures—fear of job loss or failure
- Compliance, not risk taking or innovation. "Play it safe" attitude
- Labeling of children/schools as "failing" is counterproductive
- "Blame" mentality rather than support and solutions

Studies of change most commonly focus on factors operating within the specific organization—in this instance the school—that support or constrain innovation. The "within school" blockers identified in this study contain few surprises. The issues of time and workload for principals and teachers, the influence of demographic features, and the importance of teacher attitudes and school culture are factors one would expect to be raised by principals as blockers (Fullan & Hargreaves, 1996). One within-school factor that did not commonly surface in the literature, but that was discussed by several principals, was the tension between enthusiastic new teachers who were excited about the opportunities for collaboration and shared leadership and experienced veteran teachers who were antagonistic to the change. Perhaps more important, this study reveals that the principals also identified personal and systemic blockers that significantly influence what happens within the school.

Personal Blockers

Historical Influence and Patterning

Patterning has led principals to see their role in traditional ways within hierarchical constructs. Their experience as students, teachers, and principals has been in a positional leadership context where the principal had power, status, and control; made decisions; acted in isolation; and didn't commonly delegate, interact with, or rely on others. They "did it all themselves" and still often see that as "easiest." Even in a climate of different expectations and a commitment to sharing leadership, changing one's patterning can still be quite difficult or fearful. Leithwood and Menzies (1998) also showed that "adherence to traditional roles" was by far the most frequently cited obstacle by principals.

Issues of Control

Many principals in the study identified the problem of "letting go" as the key personal and professional obstructor, and they feared accountability retribution if they did. Many principals, even though they want to move to shared leadership, find it hard to let go of the control they have always had, especially over budgets, as typified in the following:

> And if shared leadership means sharing the purse strings, and I think by definition it has to be because most things you want to do cost money . . . that's the biggest inhibition, the principal letting go of all the money.

> And the pithy statement: Give them the money, give them the power.

Letting go of curriculum decisions seemed acceptable, perhaps because principals know the expertise of their teachers and often rely on it. Conversely, several principals regretted letting go of curriculum. They see themselves still as teachers with valuable experience, knowledge, and expertise to share. "I was a curriculum person. I worked in a district office for eight years, so it was hard for me to let go . . . playing expert in certain areas of curriculum."

Some principals found it hard not to influence and "push" for a particular decision, manipulate people to get the result they wanted, take over the leadership to achieve a quick or specific outcome, or rush in and cut across the process with "the answer." Some had difficulty trusting the capacity and professionalism of others, accepting that they could do it "properly." Others feared failure in unfamiliar territory, especially coupled with a lack of systemic support—no clear guidelines and procedures to sharing leadership, no training, nor models as to "what it looks like" nor how they were to achieve it. No principal was prepared to relinquish the power of being the final arbiter should they "need" to exercise it, nor does the system support that action.

The data clearly indicated gradual change in control issues. One long-term principal felt that trust had built slowly and was now high enough for him to let go of everything, but added: "If you had asked me that question three years ago [before the ESI leadership team and its training], I wouldn't have felt the same way." Another principal found that although sharing leadership brought many positives, it also diminished his sense of personal satisfaction and achievement in the school's successes, requiring new ways of being affirmed. For another, it meant new leadership approaches:

> I try to approach it [the leadership role] differently than I have in the past. I try to sit at the table and be a member of the group. Usually I like being up there, writing stuff up and doing. . . . I think it's a control thing. You know, you've got to be the guy with the pen, you've got to be the guy that talks, you've got to be the guy that reports. . . . I changed that. I've really been working on it.

Several principals spoke about learning to "button their lips" or "hold their tongue" and allow others to emerge and develop as leaders. One principal expressed it thus: "So it's been a process for myself to *allow* the momentum to move in that direction [of shared vision and leadership] without trying to control it and maintain the 'power.'"

Accountability

The principals' perceptions are that, although teachers may be fully participatory in decisions, there is reluctance to accept the accompanying responsibility. Principals clearly felt that *only* the principal is held accountable for what happens in the school—accountable for implementation of standards-based instruction and accountable to the district and the state for levels of student achievement, safety, and legal concerns. Currently the demands for accountability are high, and principals perceive that narrow measurement tools are applied. Principals, therefore, feel torn between wanting shared leadership and the pressures of systemic accountability. Insecurity regarding being moved or losing their job emerged as a genuine fear for a number of the principals. Many expressed a strong sense of personal accountability to their students, schools, and profession, but they felt that aligning their personal integrity with systemic dimensions of accountability presented difficulties.

Systemic Blockers

Blockers from outside the school seem particularly influential. Work load; lack of resources, especially time; the nature, volume, and disruption of change; and the perceived negativity and rigid attitudes of the union were all cited as factors that obstructed the development of shared leadership in the school. The main blocker, however, which was expressed by every principal, was the lack of real choice. They feel that, even though they allegedly have site-based management, and even though the district supports the concept and practice of shared leadership, *the majority of decisions are made outside the school* through imposed mandates and decisions and external measures of achievement. These include state student-performance standards and curricula, professional standards, state-required professional development, and mandated improvement programs for underperforming schools. Choice is limited to selecting a state-approved program-improvement provider and one of two texts from a state-supplied list.

The principals also indicated that site-based choice is limited by requirements that are formally negotiated between the district and the union and embodied in the union contact. The contract specifies many governing and operational conditions in the school and the district, and it constrains site-based flexibility. Choices may also be influenced by an informal union position and pressures from union leaders on members at the building level to comply. Principals feel disempowered by the plethora of imposed decisions, and this limits their ability to offer further distribution of power to others. According to several principals, these imposed controls also create a "them-and-us" mentality and reaction. Principals commented:

> I would say seventy percent outbound in everything, it's been decided for us. . . . There were certain things they [the district] want to see carried out instead of taking the longer route of working within the school, addressing the issues, then going from that perspective. If it's already been determined that this is the road we're going to go on, then there isn't shared leadership.

Some principals, in observing the dominant position held by the state and, to a lesser degree, the district in controlling what happens in schools, commented on the current politicization of education where political agendas, not pedagogy, drive educational decisions. As one principal commented: "The problem with education today is that is has become so politicized we can't remember what the ideal was."

Student Test Scores and School Scores as Blockers

Principals feel incredible external pressure on schools to improve performance as measured by student test scores, the school's Academic Performance Index (API). As one principal expressed it: "Right now . . . the state's sole target for improvement is the API scores. It doesn't matter whatever else is happening, the scores, if they don't reach a certain level . . . the principal is gone." More recently the Annual Yearly Progress (AYP) scores, part of No Child Left Behind legislation, is adding to that pressure. Although not opposing either standards or accountability, principals do question, particularly in a bilingual context, the measurement's accuracy, appropriateness, and its validity as sole judge of a school's achievements. One principal made the observation that educational and decision outcomes are hard to measure: "What I see in education . . . is that we're working with the abstract. It's not a physical, concrete thing most of it. . . . How do we impart knowledge? What is knowledge?"

Another principal commented that it is tough to support teachers to take risks, to make decisions and deal with the outcomes:

> As a principal I don't think we are allowed to fail, to take those risks and fail. . . . And so it's almost in a way system-wide that we need to play it safe, to ensure that we don't fail, which means that we're not going to dare greatly either—because if you dare greatly, you're going to fail and make mistakes along the way.

One principal expressed the sentiments of many of the principals when he said:

> My accountability [to the state/district] is only through student achievement. You know, I have legal accountability there. . . . I don't know, the whole accountability issue is, you know, more of a political discussion than an educational one. I have a professional accountability . . . my accountability is to myself and why I am here, and why I do this for a living. And that has to do with kids and achievement and breaking down some of the barriers that we see for them, and that is a far greater accountability I think . . . because the other accountability is . . . that's politically defined by the politicians. Whether that is real or imagined, whether that is rhetoric or reality, it still remains to be seen.

Key Issues and Their Implications

The data indicate that, although there is common support for the concept and goal of shared leadership, principals hold differing understandings of what shared leadership is, and they vary in level of implementation and operational practices. Their concept of sharing leadership is largely limited to their assistant principals and professional staff. Inclusion of classified staff was minimal, and the data suggest that inclusion of parents, students, and the wider community in leadership is rare. Principals identified various factors that assist implementation of shared leadership. These factors provide strong positives to work within school sites. They also raised a number of overt personal, school, and systemic-level blockers that make implementation of shared leadership difficult. The most significant finding from the study is that the data revealed key conflicts underpinning the stated concerns. These arise from implicit, and often tacit, systemic incongruencies, ambiguities, and inconsistencies, which we have termed *paradoxes.*

The study shows that many inherent paradoxes operate at all three levels, and these are potentially the most powerful blockers because they are not easily surfaced. The unstated conflict creates mixed messages and resultant tensions and dilemmas for principals. Principals are thus constantly working with conflicting values, rules, and requirements as they try to effect change and implement shared leadership in their schools. In spite of positive and encouraging change within the schools, principals' comments revealed considerable distance between rhetoric and reality, between what is espoused and what is either practiced or possible at personal, school, and systemic levels. The study is important because it surfaces the paradoxes that occur in three linked areas—power, accountability, and coherence.

The systemic levels of state and district exercise the greatest power and political decision making; they are consequently the major source of directives and their enforcement. Their directives constitute the major source of ambiguities and conflicting demands for principals. It is the sphere of least principal influence. Principals indicated that the school is the arena of influence for them, but only within the parameters set by state and district. Principals feel this seriously limits what is possible and what can be shared. Principals, while rarely part of systemic decision making, are placed in a representational role to ensure implementation of the mandate. This chief implementer role constrains principals' collaboration with staff, especially if other supportive factors are not in place and principals have not developed flexible approaches for living with the ambiguities. The tensions between autonomy and accountability and between line management and school leadership in collaborative forms are most apparent.

The volume of "work" perceived as coming from external sources is identified as adding to principals' (and teachers') work load and stress as well as to their sense of disempowerment, their feeling that so many things are outside their control and out of control. Principals perceive many changes as fragmented. Disjointed requirements come through so rapidly that principals can react only in a continuum of isolated actions. These actions and reactions are often unrelated to current practice, and they may even run counter to previous requirements or the school's wishes. Proactive, interactive, and interrelated actions, actions that are reflective or coherent with other policies and practices, seem to be either difficult or do not happen. Principals recognize the lack of internal and systemic alignment and coherence of vision, power, ideals, and action. The opening of new schools as well as the district's policy to frequently move principals add to the fragmentation and to subsequent lack of continuity of ideas, focus, relationships, and programs. A key issue is: How can researchers and practitioners better understand the root causes of these tensions?

A Theoretical Perspective

One may look at research findings within a range of theoretical and conceptual frameworks, and each gives its focus and emphasis to the interpretation of the data. Easterby-Smith, Burgoyne, and Araujo (1999) describe organizational learning theories as providing "lenses" and not "tools" for interpretation. Although open to the many possible "lenses," we sought one that would assist understanding the key research finding of inherent paradoxes. Argyris and Schön (Argyris, 1999) developed the theoretical construct of espoused theories and theories-in-use. They propose that all individuals have two programs, or theories of action, in their heads on how to act effectively in any interaction. "There is one that they espouse. It is usually expressed in the form of stated beliefs and values. Then there is the theory that they actually use" (Argyris, 1999, p. 56).

Argyris and Schön craft a theory-in-use where paradox has a primary role. They believe paradoxes, and subsequent dilemmas, arise from the difference between what you say and what you do, resulting in mixed messages. Argyris (1999) gives as an example the dilemma of autonomy versus control:

> The subordinates push for autonomy, asserting that leaving them alone is the best sign that they are trusted by top management. They push for a solution that combines trust with distancing. The superiors, on the other hand, push for no surprises by using information systems as controls. The subordinates see the control feature as confirming mistrust. (p. 93)

He advances the belief that paradoxes are endemic to organizations and their managers; they exist tacitly in the defensive routines individuals develop to deal with the mixed messages. These mixed messages can become embedded in organizational beliefs and assumptions that evolve into norms. Argyris, furthermore, identifies two types of organizational learning: single-loop and double-loop. He finds that most organizations engage in only single-loop learning because it is designed to identify and correct errors within stated policy and largely leaves underlying beliefs, norms, and assumptions undisturbed. In contrast, double-loop learning requires questioning the underlying issues and assumptions. By accommodating or ignoring the conflicting messages and tensions, the person is protected from the dilemma, but it becomes deeply embedded within individuals and systems as an "undiscussable," preventing anyone correcting or even acknowledging the underlaying cause.

Framing this study within the above theory, principals' beliefs about what shared leadership is and how it should be practiced is their espoused theory. The operational context and actual practice is their theory-in-use. Principals identified factors that obstructed implementation of shared leadership at multiple, interconnected levels. The paradoxes also occur at these levels and obstruct implementation of shared leadership, but they appear to be tacit. Choo (1998) concludes that dealing with ambiguities and balancing tensions is part of how organizations construct meaning. Principals in this study rarely defined or articulated the many opposing concepts, demands, and practices inherent at all levels. The paradoxes emerged, instead, from the data analysis, which showed that implementation of shared leadership abounds in issues based in contradictions and inconsistencies. This would seem to support Argyris's assertion that paradoxes move to being undiscussed and unaddressed. Both tacit and explicit blockers appear substantial, but the paradoxes particularly act to confuse, disempower, constrain, support negativity, and act as disincentives to involvement.

The two key areas for principals seem to be the gaps between what the *system* espouses and what it practices, expects, or supports, and between what *principals* want to achieve and what they perceive as possible given external intervention. Tables 7.2 through 7.4 present the paradoxes identified in data analysis for each of the three levels. Some occur across levels but are listed at the level of greatest significance.

Table 7.2 Systemic Paradoxes

What Is Espoused	*The Dilemmas*
Shared leadership and decision making wanted by principals and system	Imposed decisions, mandates, directives
Site-based management	State/district control of many areas
Autonomy	Accountability issues
Choices	Limited choices because many key school decisions are already made by the system
Empowerment	Disempowerment through external control
Questioning, risk taking	Compliance required and enforced through rules, contracts, and state programs
Creative solutions to problems Collaborative processes	Frequently few collaborative processes demonstrated by state, district, union, or principals' associations or preparation programs
Consensus decision making	Time, pressures, and current structures do not support consensus building
Coherence, alignment of goals, funds, practice, and programs	Fragmentation through multiple programs, laws, and lack of coherence through competing goals
Focus on students, instruction, and learning	Focus on management, test prep, and test scores
Strong district support	Given in many ways, but also role of enforcer of own and state directives

Table 7.3 School-Based Paradoxes

What Is Espoused	*The Dilemmas*
Shared leadership wanted by teachers	Some do not. Resist work and time commitments; assert it is not their responsibility
Teacher empowerment desired	Empowering processes such as leadership teams exist side by side with disempowerment. External limitations on sharing power but not responsibility/ accountability
Teacher involvement in shared leadership	Lack of buy-in, commitment, and responsibility. Burn out
Whole-school view and commitment	Culture of individual autonomy. Own classroom focus
Focus on students—their needs and achievements	Much of the focus is teacher-centric—teacher needs, convenience, patterns in union contract
Student, parent, and community involvement and partnerships	Not highly evident in practice or intent. Shared leadership remains with professionals
Professional dialogue valuable	Teacher isolation, no time for predialogue
Assumption that people want to/can work effectively together	Often problematic through lack of skills and tradition of historic isolation
Strong communication, staff cohesion	Year-round school and multiple-track schedule make cohesion and collaboration difficult
Coherence, alignment of goals, funds, practice, and programs	Fragmentation through multiple programs; lack of coherence
Teachers committed to focus on instruction and learning, valuing learning	Required focus on test scores and also on externally imposed tasks in competition with the school's focus

Table 7.4 Personal Paradoxes

What Is Espoused	*The Dilemmas*
Shared leadership and shared responsibility wanted by principals	Difficult to "let go" of the power Difficult to trust the capacity of others Retain right of final decision or veto
Autonomy and belief in own efficacy	Accountability is externally driven with single public measure
Believe they can make a difference	Serious lack of time, work overload, feeling powerless
Believe they can effect change	Principal turnover creates unstable context for continuity Insufficient time given to allow success before the next change comes along Pressures for the quick fix
District policy of five-year appointments for principals, then enforced rotation	Higher frequency of change; tenure in one site varied from two to seven years. Change is district directed

Conclusions

The study provides information on principals' views of shared leadership and the many factors that assist and impede implementation of the concept in practice. These factors arise within individual principals, their schools, and the systemic context. Many principals and teachers are seeking ways to overcome the blockers within their schools and themselves and move further along the shared leadership continuum in practice. The difficulties in implementing shared leadership, however, are greatly exacerbated by powerful paradoxes. Although evident at all levels, the systemic paradoxes are particularly influential and seemed to constrain principals' movement toward shared leadership. In part this is because of the decision-making power and political influence operating at that level, but also because principals perceive that they have limited influence in the district and state policy-making spheres.

We draw several implications from this study. First, at the larger state and national levels, powerful pressures for achievement appear to operate that undermine principals' and teachers' options for collaborative action. As Wagner (2003) has asserted, instead of a culture of encouragement that acknowledges and builds on successes and collaboratively finds long-term solutions, often the public, media, and a politicized system function on a deficit mode—playing a *blame game* and wanting *quick-fix* answers. When solutions do not produce immediate results, the system apportions blame and rapidly moves onto the next, and often more prescriptive, *right answer*. Wagner suggests, and this study confirms, that such actions are counterproductive to deep and sustained change. In such a climate, districts, schools, principals, and teachers all become targets of blame. They are held responsible not only for complex educational issues but often for wider societal problems for which politically agreed solutions have not yet been found. Principals in this study reported that they and the teachers work extremely hard under difficult conditions. When test scores do not reflect that effort, and pejorative labeling of the district, schools, teachers, and students is the result, it is difficult to maintain the positive attitudes and incentives needed to continue trying to make a difference.

Second, at the district level, systemic paradoxes appear to be particularly powerful because they are largely *undiscussables* and remain unvoiced, unchallenged, and unaddressed. Our findings indicate it may be critical for system leaders to ensure that the paradoxes are more openly acknowledged, discussed, and resolved. Coherence and alignment of belief, vision, purpose, and actions are critical, as is developing a culture of collaborative practice and mutual support within the broader system. The current tensions and fragmentation are exhausting and counterproductive for all involved.

Fink (1999) found in his long-term study of school change that,

> Many of the factors [influencing the school] . . . were conditions over which the school had very little if any control. . . . There is no question that contextual factors were powerful and pervasive. For schools of the future the unpredictability of these forces will increase. (p. 286)

Fink further makes an important observation that although the literature on change has grown significantly in recent years, most of it attends to the strategies required to effect change in operations or to create learning organizations that can respond to the vicissitudes of a rapidly changing context. Little is written about school and district work in maintenance, continuity, and sustainability. For example, the high level of principal mobility within the district in this study could be a significant blocker, and to some degree is an underlying undiscussable, to shared leadership and increased programmatic coherence. High principal mobility negatively impacts those elements identified by the principals as supporting shared leadership—building morale, trust, and relationships; sustaining shared vision and goals; sustaining coherence in focus, action, programs, and process; having sufficient time to successfully implement change; and developing a sense of personal and site efficacy.

Third, at a school level, the findings from this study suggest that personal and school paradoxes seem more within the control of principals. These paradoxes need to be actively surfaced and addressed if principals are to move forward in creatively collaborating with their staff and community to find possible solutions to pressing problems of underachievement. One of the principals understood the power of sharing leadership; however, he also recognized that making such a change is much easier when other schools in the system are moving in that direction and receiving support from the district:

> You know, times have changed, and all my colleagues . . . they're all good people, they're all my friends, they're all interested, they all have kids at heart, and they all want to share. So it's good being part of that. I'm glad that we're not isolated, [that] we're not the only school that's doing it. Shared leadership! Everybody is striving to do that and that's a good feeling.

Nevertheless, there is also a need for principals, singly and collectively, to actively address system blockers by finding ways to communicate their concerns *up* and *out*. They need to become politically astute, actively voice their concerns instead of sublimating them, become influential in what and how educational decisions are made, and ensure that decisions are made in the interests of children and effective learning. It is incumbent on principals to draw on collective wisdom and experience to propose alternative ideas and credible options, give feedback, or take a stance when an imposed directive is unsuitable or undesirable. Yet given the hierarchical systems in which they are embedded, this is obviously very difficult.

Fourth, the study findings demonstrate that we must look beyond the obvious and identify the underlying factors that cohere or fragment thoughts and actions. The paradoxes revealed in this study, and the dilemmas they create, appear to be the most powerful of the blockers to shared leadership and serve to impede the assisting factors as well. It is also our contention that the paradoxes, particularly at the systemic level, negatively impact schools, learning, and change on a broad palette of issues with implications far beyond sharing of leadership.

Finally, this study informs the practice of sharing leadership by identifying effective ideas and practices and clarifying issues and paradoxes confronting principals, personally and within complex contexts. If shared leadership is to become a reality, principals need support, personally and systemically, to understand what it is and how and when to achieve it. They also need to experience, practice, and see shared leadership modeled by district level administrators. Coherence and consistency between what is espoused and what is practiced at personal, school, and systemic levels are essential. Democracy is not just an ideal or a system we teach about. It needs to be what we believe and live in all our actions, how we organize our schools, what we model in relationships, and how we learn. Moving the sharing of leadership from rhetoric to reality requires a systemic culture that consistently and coherently engenders, expects, and values collaborative and democratic practice.

References

Argyris, C. (1999). *On organizational learning* (2d ed.). Malden, MA: Blackwell Business.

Bennett, N., Wise, C.,Woods, P., & Harvey, J. (2003). *Distributed leadership.* Nottingham, UK: National College of School Leadership.

Blase, J., & Blase, J. (2000, January). Principals' perspectives on shared leadership. *Journal of School Leadership, 10,* 9–39.

Blase, J., & Kirby, P. (2000). *Bringing out the best in teachers: What effective principals do* (2nd ed.). Thousand Oaks, CA: Corwin Press.

Bryk, A., Camburn, E., & Louis, K. S. (1996, April). *Promoting school improvement through professional communities: An analysis of Chicago elementary school.* Paper presented at the Annual Meeting of the American Educational Research Association, New York.

Caldwell, B., & Spinks, J. (1992). *Leading the self-managing school.* London: Falmer.

Caldwell, B., & Spinks, J. (1998). *Beyond the self-managing school.* London: Falmer.

Choo, C. W. (1998). *The knowing organization: How organizations use information to construct meaning, create knowledge, and make decisions.* New York: Oxford University Press.

Chrispeels, J. (2002). An emerging conceptual and practical framework for implementing districtwide effective schools reform. *Journal for Effective Schools, 1*(1), 17–30.

Court, M. (2002). *Delegated, devolved, dispersed or democratic? Co-principalships and teacher leadership teams as examples of distributed leadership.* A paper presented at the British Educational Leadership, Management and Administration Society Annual Conference, September 20–22, 2002, Birmingham, England.

Crowther, F., Kaagan, S., Ferguson, M., & Hann, L. (2002). *Developing teacher leaders: How teacher leadership enhances school success.* Thousand Oaks, CA: Corwin Press.

Deal, T., & Peterson, K. (1998). *Shaping school culture: The heart of leadership.* San Francisco: Jossey-Bass.

Donaldson, G. (2001). *Cultivating leadership in schools: Connecting people, purpose, and practice.* New York: Teachers College Press.

Easterby-Smith, M., Burgoyne, J., & Araujo, L. (1999). *Organizational learning and the learning organization: Developments in theory and practice.* London: Sage.

Ekholm, M. (2002). *To make schools democratic—a long term commitment.* A paper presented at the Commonwealth Conference on Educational Administration and Management, September 22–25, 2002, Umeå, Sweden.

Fink, D. (1999). The attrition of change: A study of change and continuity. *School Effectiveness and School Improvement, 10*(3), 269–295.

Fullan, M. (2001). *Leading in a culture of change.* San Francisco: Jossey-Bass.

Fullan, M., & Hargreaves, A. (1996). *What's worth fighting for in your school.* New York: Teachers College Press.

Gronn, P. (2000). Distributed properties: A new architecture for leadership. *Educational Management and Administration, 28*(3), 317–338.

Harris, A. (2002). *Distributed leadership in schools: Leading or misleading?* A paper presented at the British Educational Leadership, Management and Administration Society Annual Conference, September 20–22, 2002, Birmingham, England.

Hsieh, C., & Shen, J. (1998). Teachers', principals', and superintendents' conceptions of leadership. *School Leadership & Management, 10*(1), 107–121.

Huberman, A. M., & Miles, M. B. (1984). *Innovation up close: How school improvement works.* New York: Plenum Press.

Lambert, L. (1998). *Building leadership capacity in schools.* Alexandria, VA: Association for Supervision and Curriculum Development.

Leithwood, K., & Menzies, T. (1998). A review of research concerning the implementation of site-based management. *School Effectiveness and School Improvement, 9*(3), 233–285.

Marks, H., & Seashore Louis, K. (1999). Teacher empowerment and the capacity for organizational learning. *Educational Administration Quarterly, 35,* 707–750.

Pounder, D. (1998). *Restructuring schools for collaboration: Promises and pitfalls.* Albany: State University of New York Press.

Reed, C. (2000). *Teaching with power: Shared decision-making and classroom practice.* New York: Teachers College Press.

Riley, K. (2002). *"Democratic leadership"—A contradiction in terms?* A paper presented at the Commonwealth Conference on Educational Administration and Management, September 22–25, 2002, Umeå, Sweden.

Seashore Louis, K. (2002). *Democratic schools and leade*rship. A paper presented at the Commonwealth Conference on Educational Administration and Management, September 22–25, 2002, Umeå, Sweden.

Senge, P. (1990). *The fifth discipline: The art and practice of the learning organization.* New York: Currency Doubleday.

Sergiovanni, T. J. (1994). *Building community in schools.* San Francisco: Jossey-Bass.

Smylie, M., & Brownlee-Coyners (1992). Teacher leaders and their principals: Exploring the development of new working relationships. *Educational Administration Quarterly 28*(2), 150–184.

Spradley, J. (1979). *The ethnographic interview.* Fort Worth, TX: Harcourt Brace Jovanovich.

Spradley, J. (1980). *Participant observation.* Fort Worth, TX: Harcourt College Publishers.

Stoll, L. (1999). Realising our potential: Understanding and developing capacity for lasting improvement. *School Effectiveness and School Improvement, 10*(4), 503–532.

Stoll, L., Fink, D., Earl, L. & Earl, K. (2002). *It's about learning (and it's about time)*. London: RoutledgeFalmer.

Telford, H. (1996). *Transforming schools through collaborative leadership.* London: Falmer Press.

Wagner, T. (2003). *Making the grade: Reinventing America's schools.* New York: RoutledgeFalmer.

Waters, J. T., Marzano, R. J., & McNulty, B. A. (2003). *Balanced leadership: What 30 years of research tells us about the effects of leadership on student achievement.* Aurora, CO: Mid-continent Research for Education and Learning.

8

Lessons Learned About Sustainable Results in Urban Middle Schools

Four Principals and Their Reflection on the Process of Change

Peggy H. Burke

Using portraiture (Lawrence-Lightfoot, 1983; Lawrence-Lightfoot & Hoffman Davis, 1997), this chapter looks at four principals in the vortex of educational reform. The four principals included in this portraiture are women of color working in one urban district. Each was chosen because she is committed to grappling with the ambiguity and confusion that is integral to reform and is amplified in the context of urban communities and young adolescent lives. These four stories elucidate the challenge of implementing school-based reform within a large, complex urban system that is also engaged in systemic reform. Through the process of voting to implement Turning Points, a New American Schools Model for Reform, the principal and faculty in each school began the process collaboratively of conceptualizing the big picture of where they were going, or their shared vision. Simultaneously the district's central office and the primary outside funding agency also began clarifying a vision for improving schools on a district-wide basis. The chapter demonstrates that, although all the participants in the system held a vision, the perception was that the visions were not aligned. Burke (2002), in a previous study of these schools, argued that how principals conceptualize the big picture, create aspiration in the school, and engage in reflection about the process are critical elements in actualizing the vision and developing shared or distributed leadership. However, she also found that when the district did not involve principals in developing a shared purpose for the district or in shared leadership, it was difficult to sustain the changes at the building level. Through an examination of these schools within the district context, this chapter explores the issues that sustain and constrain school reform in complex, interrelated systems.

Middle School Reform

The American public has been engaged in a period of school reform of unprecedented tenure (Bell, 1993; Berliner, 1993; Stringfield, 1995; Tyack and Cuban, 1995). Although a review of America's educational history confirms that every generation has experienced at least one period of national debate over the quality of schooling (Dewey, 1900, 1990; George, 1990; Gruhn & Douglass, 1971; National Commission on Excellence in Education, 1983; Ravitch, 1983), the current reform period began in 1983 with the publication of *A Nation at Risk* (National Commission on Excellence in Education, 1983). Reasons for such a lengthy period of reform may be attributed to issues such as the shifting power of political parties, the increasing diversity of our society, the increasing social expectations placed on schools, and a dramatically changing economy based on a growing need for a highly skilled, articulate work force, a decline in the number of unskilled factory jobs, and an excess of poorly educated employees from a global market (Stringfield, 1995).

Although the initial response to the National Commission on Excellence in Education's report focused on high schools, the Carnegie Council on Adolescent Development, sponsored by the Carnegie Corporation of New York, drew attention to young adolescents (10–15 year olds) by publishing *Turning Points: Preparing American Youth for the 21st Century* (1989). The report raised the nation's awareness that, if school reform was to improve adolescents' ability to "meet adequately the requirements of the workplace, the commitments of relationships in families and with friends, and the responsibilities of participation in a democratic society" (p. 8), then it would need to address social, emotional, and academic issues in middle schools. The council concluded that for many young adolescents, "Middle grade schools—junior high, intermediate, and middle schools—are potentially society's most powerful force to recapture millions of youth adrift" (p. 8).

After the publication of the report, the Carnegie Corporation funded extensive reform projects in 15 states and research of these projects by the University of Illinois Center for Prevention Research Development. In the past two decades, structural changes (how students and teachers are organized for teaching and learning) became common in many middle schools. Although it produced benefits for students in the sense of greater emotional well-being (Jackson & Davis, 2000; Midgley & Edelin, 1998), there was no significant change in academic performance, especially in urban middle schools. (More discussion of this reform takes place in Chapter 2.)

Many middle schools have not gone beyond the structural changes. They put teachers in teams, but they failed to create time, space, or an environment that encouraged dialogue, risk taking, or collaboration in which real reform might take place. They have not "taken the critical next step to develop students who perform well academically, with the intellectual wherewithal to improve their life conditions" (Lipsitz, Mizell, Jackson, & Austin, 1997, p. 539). Brown, Roney, and Anfara (2003) would argue that missing from the Turning Points structures are elements of "organizational health" (p. 5). The lack of "organizational health" is even more evident in urban middle schools that serve high-poverty and racially and ethnically diverse populations.

Early and Limited Findings of Successful Implementation

Although reform started slowly, findings by the Lilly Foundation, the Edna McConnell Clark Foundation, the Carnegie Corporation, and the W. K. Kellogg Foundation indicated that it was possible to achieve sustainable middle grades school reform (Lipsitz et al., 1997). Brown and colleagues (2003) argued, however, that the reform model was not sufficient in low-economic urban schools, and more attention needed to be given to improving school culture and climate before reform models were implemented.

It might be further argued that a healthy culture will develop if schools are first clear about their core purpose and are given sufficient time and intensity to bring about the desired results (Burke, 2002; Lipsitz et al., 1997; Senge, 1990). Too often in school reform, districts "purchase" or support a packaged model; the core purpose for the reform model is not clear at the building level, especially among teachers. Implementation is a checklist. A frequent comment from faculty in such cases is, "Oh, this is Monday, it's Turning Points Day" (personal communication from faculty, 1998). The faculty is not clear about the purpose of the work. The reform is further complicated by districts implementing myriad fragmented initiatives with the hope of a rapid turnaround in student achievement. There is a significant difference between implementing the Turning Points structures and developing a shared vision and leadership around the core belief that every student can achieve at high academic levels.

The longitudinal research by Felner, Jackson, Kasak, Mulhall, Brand, and Flowers (1997) and sponsored by the Carnegie Corporation to look at Turning Points schools provided the first early evidence of a growing consensus on what middle grades schools should look like. They found in their study of Illinois's Turning Points schools engaged in comprehensive school transformation that "implementation must be comprehensive and integrative, with careful attention to sequencing and the establishment of some Turning Points building blocks on which other elements can be mounted" (p. 547). They also noted that the most significant changes in student achievement occurred when the structural changes were "idea-driven" by the Turning Points recommendations rather than "checklist based" (Felner et al., 1997, p. 547).

The wave of middle schools established in the mid 1960s and then again in the early 1980s reflected the structures that had been identified as essential, but too few were "idea-driven" (Epstein & Mac Iver, 1990; George, 1990; Hill & Bonan, 1991; Lipsitz, 1994; Merenbloom, 1991). Many were established because of overcrowding at the elementary or high school level; others because the district was able to sidestep court-ordered desegregation rulings. All too often the shift was economically or physically driven rather than idea-driven. Neither at the district level nor at the building level was the "core purpose" of the middle school embraced.

The research of Felner and colleagues (1997), and, more recently, of Brown, Roney, and Anfran (2003), Burke (2002), and Senge, Roberts, Ross, Smith, and Kleiner (1994), demonstrated that effective school reform needs to be "idea-driven" around a common core purpose. In a study of six high-performing suburban schools and six low-performing urban schools, Brown, Roney, and Anfran (2003) reported that "findings concur and reinforce the importance of returning to the meaning and purpose of middle level schooling" (p. 14).

In an earlier report of the study of four urban principals in the Park Public School System (names in this study are pseudonyms), Burke (2002) argued that how principals conceptualize the big picture, create aspiration in the school, and engage in reflection about the process are all critical elements in actualizing the vision and developing shared, or distributed, leadership. She also found, however, that when the district did not involve principals in developing a shared purpose for the district or in participating in shared leadership, it was difficult to sustain the changes at the building level.

Burke found that there is a demonstrated lack of skill with conceptualizing the whole system. The structural changes, often attempted in reform efforts such as teaming and block scheduling, are a small part of the whole change and are frequently not tied to the broader vision of ensuring opportunities for academic success for every student. Earlier research by Mac Iver and Epstein (1993) also indicated that the focus was on organization and structure rather than the broad core purpose of high academic achievement for every student.

> Most middle grade classes emphasize passive learning and a drill focus in language arts basic skills, math computation, science facts, and facts of history. Most middle schools infrequently use active and interactive instructional approaches, including writing and editing, small groups, and other cooperative learning methods, and technology in science and math. (p. 520)

Lipsitz and colleagues (1997) also found that many middle schools engaged in transitioning from a junior high to a middle school had not "taken the critical next step to develop students who perform well academically, with the intellectual wherewithal to improve their life conditions" (p. 535).

The Special Challenge of Urban Middle Schools

These findings are even more evident in urban middle schools that serve high-poverty and racially and ethnically diverse populations. "The poor quality of middle grades education in America's cities means that up to half the students in our nation's largest cities are unable to make a successful transition to high school (Balfanz & Mac Iver, 2000, as cited in Jackson & Davis, 2000, p.6). The National Assessment of Educational Progress (Weissglass, 2001) further substantiated this point when it reported that the achievement gap between white students and black or Latino students at the eighth-grade level has not changed in any state in the last 10 years.

These statistics sadly reflect little change since Sarason's (1996) reflection in the mid 1990s that inner-city schools provide a very turbulent backdrop for implementing change. Inner-city schools face significant challenges of shifting student demographics, underprepared teachers coupled with high teacher turnover, conflicting political beliefs about what content standards should be included in the curriculum, pressure for using standardized tests as the only source of assessment, students ill-prepared to score well on such tests, and an exponentially expanding knowledge base about best approaches to teaching and learning. Policymakers, the community, the parents, the school board, the administrators, the teachers, and the students influence what choices are made and what actually occurs in schools. In turn, each of these groups represents different cultures, racial and ethnic backgrounds, special interests, and beliefs and values. No wonder that members of the same school district frequently believe that there is no coherent plan of action about what reform to implement, what the process should be, or who should pay for the reform.

Context of This Study: Implementing Turning Points in Urban Middle Schools

This study, taken from a series of portraits of middle school principals, looks at four principals in the vortex of educational reform. As stated earlier, these four women share their commitment to working with the uncertainty of reform in urban middle schools because of the young adolescents they encounter daily. The four principals selected for this particular portraiture are women of color working in one urban district. Each was chosen because she is committed to grappling with the ambiguity and confusion that is integral to reform and is amplified in the context of urban communities and young adolescent lives.

The four principals in this study—Ms. Tucker of the Cotton Middle School, Ms. Luce of the Lee Middle School, Ms. Bagé of the Brown Middle School, and Ms. Clemette of the Highlander Middle School (all pseudonyms)—chose Turning Points as the overarching model for their vision. Through their choice to join, and their early actions after joining the Turning Points Network, they indicated their own understanding about the purpose of middle school as defined by the seven principles of Turning Points. These principles are:

- Create small, caring communities for learning
- Teach a core academic program
- Empower teachers and administrators to make decisions
- Prepare teachers for the middle grades
- Develop students' character, creativity, and health
- Reengage families in the education of young adolescents
- Connect schools and communities

Although the funding amounts for implementation of the Turning Points practices varied depending on the year the school became involved in the reform process, the schools joined through a similar process, which included:

- A letter of invitation to the principals with a brief written description of the initiative
- An overview session about the model and the process involved with all interested principals
- A presentation and question-and-answer period at a full-faculty meeting
- A day of meetings with grade-level clusters to answer further questions and to address concerns
- A faculty vote. In order to join the Turning Points Network, 80% of the faculty had to vote in favor of the initiative

Joining the network was voluntary and was not mandated by the district. When schools decided to join the network, they received significant support toward implementation of the model. The primary benefits in the first year and for at least two subsequent years included the following:

- A $7000 grant for teacher stipends and substitutes
- A coach one day per week to meet with teachers and to help the school implement the Turning Points design model
- A comprehensive Self-Study Survey and subsequent analyzed data
- Opportunities for a five-person team to participate with other like-minded schools in three all-day network meetings and a four-day summer institute
- A national opportunity for principals to network with other Turning Points principals

This chapter specifically addresses the Turning Points principle of empowering teachers and administrators to make decisions. Before joining Turning Points, each of these schools had only nominal leadership teams and either no interdisciplinary teams or ineffective teams. The primary role of the Turning Points coach was to work with schools in implementing leadership teams that exemplify shared leadership and the development of effective interdisciplinary teams.

The paradox that these four principals exemplify is that they were being asked to change their mental models of school organization, structure, and leadership while the traditional, bureaucratic hierarchy of the central office remained substantially unchanged. Although lip service was given to site-based management, the system-wide decision making and fiscal control remained in the hands of the school committee and the central office.

The Theoretical Framework

Looking at Process Through a Systems-Thinking Framework

Senge and colleagues (1994) define the central concept of learning organization theory as systems thinking. This is a framework and set of tools for "seeing wholes, recognizing patterns and relationships, and learning how to structure our organizations in more effective ways" (Lannon, 1995, p. 18). An organization that engages in systems thinking develops a new mindset for thinking and interacting; it recognizes that because a system is complex and dynamic, all parts are connected to the whole; a change at one point may influence the immediate connected relationships as well as influence relationships more distant in time and space.

> The essence of the discipline of systems thinking lies in a shift of mind:
> - Seeing interrelationships rather than linear cause-effect chains
> - Seeing processes of change rather than snapshots (Senge, 1990, p. 73)

Such organizations need leaders that are "adept at handling situations of uncertainty, uniqueness, and conflict" (Schön, 1987, p. 16).

The principals in this study faced formidable challenges in creating schools that were focused on meeting the needs of urban adolescents so that the students were able to perform well academically and have the ability to improve their life conditions. The principals had to lead a slowly changing faculty in meeting the needs of a rapidly changing student population in a continuously evolving society, while still educating students to meet specific standards and ensure that they become "successful" adults.

From past experience in implementing whole-school change, the "*manner* or *means* by which decisions are made, announced, and implemented" (Sarason, 1995, p. 79; emphasis in original) is critical to their success. Implementation and adoption of "successful models" depends on predominant attitudes, interrelationships within the school culture, and sufficient time for dialogue among all the members of the school community (Sarason, 1995). In this case, the principals were juggling multiple models with little time to examine attitudes or create time and space for dialogue among the school members. They were asked to deliver steady improvement in student achievement, without time to develop a shared vision of where they were going.

Single-Loop Learning: A Traditional Method for Innovation

Reform is further complicated by the traditional method of change implementation: a problem is identified and an immediate solution is pursued without examining underlying issues, beliefs, or attitudes (Argyris & Schön, 1996). To address both the perception of failure and the real problems in teaching every student to read and write, calculate, think critically, and create, schools and districts continue to add single and multiple innovations, all under the name of reform. This process of change does not lead to sustainable school reform.

For example, in the Park Public School District (Burke, 2002), in year one of the district reform, the central office mandated that schools implement five-paragraph essays in language arts classes. The essays had to follow a specific format and were evaluated by district-identified criteria such as, "introduces paper with a strong thesis statement, conclusion summarizes the three main ideas, and interprets and uses quotes to support main ideas" (district rubric for assessment). Schools were required to administer the essays, under test-like conditions, three times per year. The goal was to improve writing in the district and student performance on the state's mandated standardized test.

Two years later, the district mandated that schools implement Writer's Workshop, a cyclical writing process of drafting, editing, and revising. Both initiatives have value, but the compatibility of the two initiatives, or the reason for implementing another process, was not clear at the school level (Burke, 2002). One reason that might have caused the district to seek another strategy was that student scores on the standardized language arts tests did not improve significantly or as rapidly as the district expected. Another factor was that new administrators had joined the central office and found the second initiative more effective. These central office administrators, unlike the principals and teachers, had ready access to the superintendent. The knowledge or beliefs at the central office level is what Argyris (1993) contends was necessary data but not sufficient to be acted upon by practitioners at the school level. There was little two-way communication between central office and the schools. Principals complained at their monthly meetings that they were being asked to provide instructional leadership for the writing process at the building level without first having an opportunity to understand the process. Teachers also complained at their school leadership team meetings and at weekly common planning meetings with Turning Points coaches that they were never included in the decision to change how they taught writing (Burke, 2002). The central office administrators, the principals (individually and as an association without a union), and the teachers (with divided loyalties to their content area, the school, and the teachers' union) represent multiple entities within a large district system; they are all competing for power and resources. The lack of two-way communication and shared reflection about the data and core beliefs was symptomatic of problems that arise when there are limited resources, competing forces and visions, and no shared understanding about the core purpose of the organization.

Double-Loop Learning: A Process for Enhancing Metacognitive Awareness

In contrast, an organization that conceptualizes the whole and recognizes the circular nature of innovations on systems and the importance of feedback implements innovations through a process of double-loop learning. In double-loop learning, the focus is on both the problem and the metacognitive process of examining beliefs, actions, and outcomes. The double loop "refers to the two feedback loops that connect the observed effects of action with strategies and values served by strategies. Strategies and assumptions may change concurrently with or as a consequence of change in values" (Argyris and Schön, 1996, p. 21).

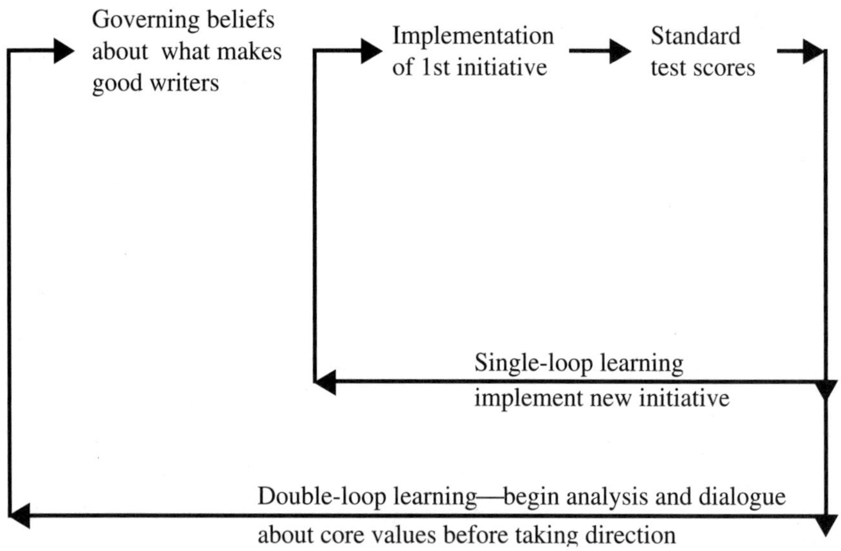

Figure 8.1 Single-Loop and Double-Loop Learning Model for Writing Initiatives

In a double-loop learning process, data is collected from the first initiative and shared across the district to document the outcome and value of that initiative. At the same time, background information on the second initiative and a comparative chart showing both initiatives are shared with teachers and administrators. Within the schools and across the district through dialogue, or "thinking together" (Senge, 1990, p. 10), teachers, administrators, and students identify where the initiatives are compatible and where they are in conflict. Then, there is dialogue about beliefs and assumptions, such as what contributes to being good writers and what expectations teachers hold about the extent and the number of revisions (Weissglass, 2001). By basing decisions for changing practices on data, a comprehensive understanding of shared beliefs, and dialogue, the district and individual schools develop a shared ownership in the decision (Schön, 1987; Senge, 1990). When all constituents share ownership in the decision and recognize the connectedness of decisions, then innovations shift from being single events to long-term patterns that support the school and district's vision.

In the case of the writing initiatives in this district, when the first innovation was introduced many teachers did not believe that most of their students had the ability to write five paragraphs. Three years after the initiative was introduced, significant evidence suggested that most students had the ability to write five paragraphs but that the paragraphs lacked content (data from looking at student writing samples with teachers at all four school sites, Burke, 2002). In schools that initiated conversations about implementing the writing process, teachers began to recognize the value of transitioning their writing program to the second initiative, the Writer's Workshop. In schools where there was no conversation, teachers continued to struggle with implementing either writing process. The district-wide implementation process did not recognize different points of view, failed to foster conversation, and appeared oblivious to how multiple initiatives impacted the whole system.

Methods

Portraiture

Because of a long-standing and collegial relationship with the principals and the joint roles of researcher and Turning Points coach, portraiture seemed to offer the best methodology to capture and negotiate an authentic and significant narrative of each principal's vision and the process of change. Portraiture provided a collaborative method of inquiry between the researcher and the subject that blended "aesthetics and empiricism in an effort to capture the complexity, dynamics, and subtlety of human experience and organizational life" (Lawrence-Lightfoot & Davis, 1997, p. xv). Although there was no collaboration on the interpretation of the data, there was a five-year relationship created through working together regularly on the implementation of the Turning Points model and facilitating development of a shared vision among the teachers and the administration.

Portraiture provided an opportunity to paint a multilayered perspective of four principals engaged in the process of implementing reform in urban middle schools. The smallness of the sample size and the single geographical region restrict the generalizations that can be drawn from this study. However, the depth of the data and the variety of data sources should provide those interested in shared leadership in learning organizations and middle school reform to draw their own conclusions and identify questions for future research.

Data Collection

Data for this study were gathered over time through a variety methods and sources: a formal interview with each principal, observations and informal conversations with staff in the schools, several informal phone conversations with staff members, follow-up conversations with the principals, data from the school's self-study, and other documents.

Other data sources include the following:

- Formal coaching reports (my own and those of other Turning Points coaches)
- Personal notes taken during meetings and journals written after meetings
- District evaluation reports
- School improvement plans
- State reports
- Newspaper accounts
- School and district Web sites
- Conversations with district personnel and Turning Points staff

A Snapshot of Four Urban Middle School Grappling With the Ambiguity of Reform Between 1997 and 2002

One of the early distinguishing qualities about the four principals included in the study was how they talked about the process of change. The four women frequently talked about the big picture in four distinct ways:

(1) how they were sharing power—"I felt they [the teachers] didn't have a say before and I have encouraged them to make decisions themselves. I have given them ownership and responsibility, and they are accountable" (conversation with Ms. Bagé); (2) the broad barriers—"Until as a district we can quit pretending that certain things are happening that aren't, then it's kind of hard to say how much of this stuff is systemic, problems created by our system versus what might be an individual's shortcomings in terms of not having some aspect of your life or the job together" (conversation with Ms. Luce); (3) what change they wanted from the teachers—"I want teachers to truly embrace the six essentials of reform—to naturally put the essentials into practice. I want the teachers to see the value of moving the kids along" (conversation with Ms. Clemette); and (4) what they wanted from the school for students—"I want my school to have a good reputation, and not just fluff either: substantive stuff, where kids are actually learning and it is just a wonderful place physically, mentally, and educationally" (conversation with Ms. Tucker). Based on their core beliefs about the purpose of middle schools and the potential that these principals saw in Turning Points, they encouraged, invited, and lobbied the faculty at each school to vote to join the Turning Points Network. The extent of their involvement varied, but all have advocated for using the principles of Turning Points to guide middle school reform. The Cotton Middle School, the first school to be a member of the network, joined in 1994, and the Lee was one of the last. The Lee Middle School joined in 1999 when the principal, Ms. Luce, moved from her previous position as a principal in another Turning Points School to the Lee School.

Other characteristics, unique to these four women, included their (1) willingness to talk openly about their work; (2) engagement in critical analysis of themselves, their faculties, and the district; and (3) conceptualization of the process of change around the research on middle schools. There was also slight but growing evidence of change in student achievement and in faculty engagement in the process of change at each school. Finally, these women, among the 24 middle and K–8 principals in the district, most consistently attended network meetings and supported the implementation of Turning Points in their schools and in the district.

Shared Leadership at the School Level Collectively Modeled by Principals

Another unique aspect for these schools was a growing unification in the district of the middle school principals. Two of the four women played a significant role in shifting the focus of the Middle School Principals' Association (MSPA) from a social, support network for principals to that of advocate for the needs of young adolescents and the needs of middle schools. One of the achievements of MSPA was the development of a middle school mission statement and a shared vision of where they were going. The MSPA mission statement was based on district expectations for principals and the Turning Points principles.

The mission statement and the vision, after multiple revisions and presentations to the superintendent, were taken to the Park School Committee. The school committee did not adopt the mission statement as policy, but it endorsed the articulation of the vision. At the time, the MSPA felt that the endorsement was a partial victory. The association had at least provided a public platform for discussion about the specific needs of the young adolescent. The mission stated:

> The Park Middle Grade mission is to create small, caring communities of learners who are engaged intellectually in rigorous academic work, literate, socially committed, and morally responsible. Under the principal's instructional leadership, each school will encourage academic excellence around a core body of knowledge and promote healthy lifestyles and socially responsible citizenship. The schools are committed to forming partnerships with families and the community to support this mission and achieve their goals.

Within a year, however, it was clear that the mission statement and the shared vision had little or no impact at the district level. The district continued to underfund the staffing needs for effective middle schools and to calculate the student-teacher ratio based on elementary self-contained classes rather than interdisciplinary teams. Schools were also given mandated time blocks for writing and mathematics, which created barriers in meeting the exploratory nature of middle schools and addressing social, emotional, and health issues for young adolescents (Burke, 2002).

For the members of the Park MSPA, the value of creating the shared vision was the dialogue that occurred about current research on middle schools, school reform initiatives and the impact on student achievement, and about their values and beliefs about young adolescents and every student's ability to achieve at high academic standards. Through the dialogue, these four women in particular became more clearly focused on their core purpose, which helped them balance the Turning Points and district initiatives, which were occurring simultaneously and sometimes competitively.

Turning Points Role and Interrelationship With the Schools

What the Turning Points model offered to these four principals and their leadership teams was the framework for their vision and a clear purpose for the middle school. The Turning Points Network meetings provided time, space, and professional development focused on a common purpose for members of each school's leadership team to work with other likeminded schools. At the school, Turning Points coaches provided structured time for conversation and professional development during teachers' common planning time, and coaches assisted in the development of a leadership team that was representative of all members of the school community and that met consistently.

All four of these principals had a vision and a comprehensive picture of their current reality in juxtaposition to their long-term vision. When asked to give a portrait of their school, they all began with statistics: "eighty-five percent are on free or reduced lunch, 52% of the students are African-American, 33% Latino, 9% Caucasian, 2% Asian" (Ms. Bagé, principal at Brown). Although the percentages vary some, the majority of students in the four schools were students of color, and more than three-fourths of the students were on free or reduced lunch, an indicator of high poverty. When pushed to describe beyond the numbers, however, there was also a common thread about purpose. They recognized that for many students middle school was their last opportunity to see themselves as learners and to recognize their ability to achieve.

Ms. Tucker: The Cotton Middle School

When asked to give a portrait of her school, Ms. Tucker at the Cotton Middle School said:

> I feel that Cotton Middle School represents an environment of caring adults with an intentional purpose. They understand that kids are not the same emotionally, physically, and so forth where kids used to be five or ten years ago. So you don't hear, "Well the kids are not the way they used to be" anymore. I mean teachers have the expectation that these kids that are sitting in front of them come with baggage. (Interview, 2000)

Although she believed it was a strong staff, she was also aware of those that were not yet on board in regard to changing their instructional practices or meeting the needs of all students. "If I have to generalize, I would say that there is a good percentage, a solid 85–90% of the staff is doing what it is they are supposed to do, but then the challenge is for that other 10–15%."

Toward the end of Ms. Tucker's third year, one of her teachers commented in a phone interview:

> I see a Bernadette [Ms. Tucker] I didn't see two years ago. She knows where she is going—stays on us like a taskmaster. People are taskmasters when they have a vision down the road. Our former principal, if you told her the sky was falling, she would say, "Yes, the sky is falling but look at the pretty colors." Ms. Tucker, if you tell her the sky is falling, she says, 'Well this is what we have to do." She moves on things. (Phone conversation, February 2000)

Ms. Luce: The Lee Middle School

When Ms. Luce arrived at the Lee Middle School, she was amazed to discover that the school still had tracking. The most significant change Ms. Luce made in her first year was to eliminate the 10 levels of tracking and the practice of using tracking to reward and punish students.

> The high scores were in the A Sections and then it went down in some cases to Section J. In addition to ability grouping, there was also a carrot that was held out in front of students so that if you had a student that was very able but messed up behaviorally they would threaten [him or her] with being kicked down the alphabet, moving from Section A to Section B to Section C and so on. To that end, there were a number of teachers who only had advanced classes. The tendency was that those that had the best management of student behavior ended up with lower sections.
>
> So that when I came in August, there were mixed reviews [regarding detracking]. Those who had had lower-level students were appreciative of the fact that they had the opportunity now to teach a more diverse group of students. And, of course those who had had only the crème de la crème were sort of out of sorts in terms being faced with having to teach a more diverse student population. (Interview, 2000)

Ms. Luce viewed her faculty from a different perspective than Ms. Tucker. Ms. Tucker had been a member of the Cotton faculty for a long time, first as teacher, then as curriculum director, and finally as principal. She helped "create the Turning Points legacy" (Ms. Tucker, personal communication). Ms. Luce was a senior member in the district but was in only her second year at Lee. She knew that she hired a few good teachers when she arrived, and that there were a few strong teachers already at Lee, but she described Lee as having been in a time warp from the rest of the district.

> It is interesting that this school kind of functioned as an island unto itself and that it was probably the very last of the middle schools that really operated strictly as a junior high model, with a horrendous amount of ability grouping characterizing the way the school was structured. (Interview, 2000)

She also felt that the faculty was very didactic and still wedded to whole-class instruction. "There is very little individual grouping or instructional practices such as shared reading, guided reading, or project-based work that happens with a degree of regularity." Based on the school's professional development plan, she saw instructional practices changing. She also recognized the need to continue to make alterations in the schedule so that teachers had longer instructional blocks, longer common planning time for professional development, and more cohesive teams, including two-person teams.

She hoped in the next three to five years to create a student body that understood that "school is a place that one comes to, to learn." She modeled this practice in the spring of her first year by inviting small groups of eighth-grade students to talk with her about their academic performance and what they needed to do to graduate. She also required students to always have a book with them and expected teachers to model and clearly set this expectation with all students.

Ms. Luce was direct with the faculty; although she advocated dramatic changes, she was, for the most part, respected by the faculty. At meetings teachers would speak positively about Ms. Luce. "She demands a great deal, but it is clear she cares about the students and her expectations are based on helping every child succeed" (comment made to another teacher in a team meeting, December 1999). She was skilled at making it uncomfortable for teachers to stay at Lee if they were not committed to ensuring that all students have the opportunity and tools to meet high academic standards. She set clear expectations, rewarded teachers who performed to her standards, and encouraged teachers whose basic beliefs about teaching and learning differed from hers to look for other positions (based on personal observation and conversation). One teacher said, "You know who her favorites are, and while it is based on how they interact with kids and teach, it does not build a collaborative culture among the teachers" (personal conversation, 2000).

Ms. Bagé: The Brown Middle School

The third principal in the study, Ms. Bagé, was in a unique school. It had been reorganized in 1990 under the guidelines of the first Turning Points report (Carnegie Council on Adolescent Development, 1989) to serve as a pilot project for future reforms. The school day was extended and class sizes were smaller. School was from 7:30 A.M. to 3:30 P.M., four days a week, and on Friday students left at 12:30 and faculty had time for professional development. Although there were dramatic improvements in student performance when the pilot was first established, and the school won two blue ribbons from the federal Department of Education for demonstrated excellence and significant academic improvement, the financial costs made this model too expensive to be adopted district-wide. This school was considered a "plum" assignment for administrators and teachers (personal comments from other administrators). It also was one of the few schools in the district that had autonomy over decisions about who was hired to teach at Brown.

As one might expect with a longer day and select teachers, the students at Brown, in comparison to other middle schools in the district, scored the highest on the state standardized tests. However, Ms. Bagé recognized that they were still allowing too many to fail.

> With this school, and the resources they have, we shouldn't have any students at level one [failing]. To ensure this, I need to help us focus—"how do we make sure that every single child at Brown is at or just above grade level?" We really, really [voice shakes a little with emphasis] should not have any students at level one.

Brown's implementation of Turning Points was modified more than in the other three schools, as faculty felt they had already been involved with Turning Points in the past. Instead, Ms. Bagé used Turning Points and the district initiative to create space for dialogue on what success for every child looked like and what teachers were doing to ensure that success.

> The staff is predominately white, but we have a good percentage of African Americans and Latinos. There is a difference in the staff at Brown than the staff at Penn [former school]. They are a younger staff at Brown; I don't know whether that may be the difference. They ask questions. The staff wants to do well and wants to know they are doing well. They ask hard questions and speak freely, sharing their opinions. (Interview, summer of 2000)

She also talked about giving the staff the freedom to make their own decisions, but then she let them know that they were accountable.

> Some people on the staff have said that I have given the staff too much freedom, too many choices. I listen to that and wonder about it. Have I not focused it properly? And I'm not sure that I gave them too much freedom. I felt

> they didn't have a say before and I have encouraged them to make decisions themselves. I have given them ownership, responsibility, and they are accountable. I don't want to do all the work myself. (Interview, summer of 2000)

Ms. Clemette: The Highlander Middle School

Ms. Clemette at Highlander was the fourth principal in this study. She was extremely clear about her core beliefs, and after two years of working with the faculty, she had a core of teachers who were committed to the same vision.

> Renee [Ms. Clemette] is very focused on her vision. She wants to give students an opportunity to have a base of academic knowledge so that they will be able to compete in any place. . . . An active one-fourth [of the teachers] has the same vision . . . others are pulled along, one-third or even one-half just have a job—a paycheck for a period of time of showing up. (Telephone interview with teacher, summer of 2000)

Ms. Clemette, similar to Ms. Luce at Lee, is not afraid to identify and address the barriers that will prevent the school from moving toward the vision. She talked about three different types of resistors: skeptics about her, teachers opposed to heterogeneous grouping, and those who do not expect much from "these kids."

She gave the skeptics time as she felt that, given the revolving door of administrators during the past six years, their attitude was justifiable. She had actively courted the lead resistor in this group. She asked this teacher to participate on the leadership team and involved her in the process of thinking about change, but after two years she still was not clear about this teacher's commitment to the same vision. Ms. Clemette decided that she had wooed this teacher long enough and that to continue would not benefit the school or the students. "While I value her teaching I am not going to court her anymore; she needs to decide whether she wants a role in this school or to move on to another school" (personal communication, April 2001).

The second group, teachers opposed to heterogeneous grouping (including students of different ability levels in the same class), were vocal in expressing their belief that some students were preventing others from soaring. Ms. Clemette hoped to address this group through literature, research, and professional development on instructional strategies that meet the needs of diverse learners. The 2001 School Improvement Plan (SIP) called for "the literacy coach and specialist to model and demonstrate lessons in class, focusing on strategies such as Reciprocal Teaching, Read Aloud, and

Modeled Writing." She assumed that the resistance of this group of teachers was because they felt unsure about how to meet the diverse needs of a heterogeneously grouped class, not because they believed that some students, students who are poor, from single-parent homes, or students of color, "can't learn."

The third group of resistors worried Ms. Clemette the most. They did not believe that their students were going anywhere. "It is as if they want to protect students from knowledge. It comes across in a caring way, but is more dangerous thinking" (personal communication, April 2001).

Ms. Clemette approached the change process in a scholarly, thoughtful, and deliberate manner. She stressed the importance of data and wanted teachers to look at what the research suggested about changing schools and moving kids along. "I think it makes us more professional when we look at what the research says. When we look at our data and examine our work, we need to ask, "Why did this work? Or why did it not work?" (interview with Ms. Clemette). However, she also recognized that many staff members were resistant to using data and studying current research and that, if she wanted to bring the majority of the staff on board with a shared vision, she had to move slowly and purposely.

The vision, which the principals were passionate about, focused on graduating *every* student equipped to achieve at a high intellectual level; unfortunately, by the end of the study, commitment to the core purpose was still limited in each school. At times it seemed that the number of teachers committed to the same vision was growing, but for a variety of reasons, such as retirements or promotions of key people, new district mandates, and/or budget cuts, it was not clear that the growth of the vision across the school community was sustainable.

Barriers to the Collaborative Learning That Builds a Shared Vision

Although it was each principal's expressed intent to negotiate the vision collaboratively, her own past experience in leadership, the district's intense monitoring and directing, and the pressure to rapidly improve student performance caused full implementation of a shared vision to be an elusive goal. These four women were, professionally, products of a traditional hierarchy that in the past had been a bastion of white, male, dictatorial leadership. In contrast, they also brought to the position what Sonia Nieto describes as a multicultural perspective: "Learning to work with colleagues in collaborative and mutually supportive ways; it means challenging conventional school policies and practices so that they are more equitable and just; and it means working for changes beyond the four walls of the school" (1999, p. xviii). These two conflicting aspects of each woman's own understanding of leadership were evidenced multiple times during the process of change. The most common evidence of this occurred in decisions made by the leadership team that were not aligned with the principal's opinion. For example, at one leadership team meeting the principal was absent but had asked that the team discuss and plan the upcoming school open house. She had shared with the assistant principal her views on how she wanted the event organized, but the assistant principal did not convey this information to the teachers. The teachers had been unhappy with the previous open house when the principal had passed out the report cards at the door. The teachers felt that they should have the report cards to pass out—a decision the principal had already told her assistant was off the table. Both sides had valid concerns, but the principal's arguments were not surfaced at the meeting. When she came in the next morning and read the revised plan, she abruptly notified the staff that they would not be following the plan approved by the leadership team. This was a major setback to the team. Many of the younger faculty, who had been supportive of the new vision, lost confidence in the principal's willingness and commitment to shared leadership; they began to listen to the veteran faculty who constantly complained that they had no say in critical decisions.

Within any school building, there are so many demands on everyone's time and so many issues seeming to require immediate decisions that taking time to gather evidence or develop a shared understanding of the issues is skipped. Urban schools feel even more pushed for quick action in the current climate of accountability when there is no evidence that the district, the state, or those who fund the reform initiatives subscribe to the belief that "it can be extremely efficient to 'waste a lot of time' building a shared vision" (Leithwood, Begley, & Cousins, 1994, p. 73). Unless school leaders take and are given time to develop a shared vision, then misunderstandings based on assumptions are going to continue to erode the process of creating shared leadership. Well-meaning principals will revert to old behavioral models of running a school when they feel there is too much at stake for students.

Conclusions

School principals, superintendents, and central office personnel need time to develop a shared vision based on a discussion about core beliefs. There is a stark incompatibility within the system if a single building system is operating from a place of coherence, shared vision, and feedback loops, while the larger district system is operating from a hierarchical frame of reference using linear thinking to solve the same problems.

The Park Public School System discussed here is typical of many large urban systems. When Turning Points first began working with schools, the district's vision was not as well defined as it was toward the end of this study. The district and Turning Points both refined their models because of new data, experience, dialogue among the leaders, clarity of purpose, and external pressures for resources from state, federal, and nonprofit funds. Although there was collaboration between the Park Public School District and Turning Points at the beginning of the work, when resources became tighter several fundamental differences in beliefs such as building-based autonomy over resources and hiring, shared leadership, and assessment of student achievement caused a significant rift in the relationship. Although Turning Points coaches continued to work in many of the schools in the district, the ability of the organization to advocate for middle schools significantly declined.

Evidence suggested, however, that the members of the Middle Schools Principals' Association did find their own voice, and they were being heard. To some extent Turning Points helped carve out space for a few years while the principals gathered their own voice and clarified their own purpose for being. Because they were more aware of what they wanted, when the resources provided by the district were not appropriate they seemed more inclined to collectively push back. For example, as a group they resisted the professional development designed at the central office because it was not what they needed to assist teachers in implementing a writing model that was feasible in middle schools. They explained their reasoning to the superintendent and advocated for what they felt they needed. Because they were able to articulate their needs and what was driving their vision of professional development, the district listened and delivered what they wanted.

In these four schools, the shared and distributed leadership that was in place because of the affiliation with Turning Points significantly enhanced their ability to implement the second writing initiative. The principal had structures—the leadership team and the interdisciplinary teams—that provided teachers with space and time to dialogue about the advantages and disadvantages of both writing initiatives. The teachers also felt they had some voice in the implementation process, and they could examine data, which supported the shift to the second initiative.

Perhaps Turning Points as an outside organization served its purpose. It helped a significant number of principals in one district become clearer about what they as an organization truly wanted; it had helped them as a group develop a shared vision, which gave them the leverage to facilitate the changes they needed. At the same time, the district also took a significant step in recognizing that this was not idle grumbling but the protest of a group of leaders who shared a common core purpose.

This study and the research by Felner and colleagues (1997) and Brown and collaborators (2003) demonstrate that it is not sufficient to implement a set of new structures and expect that they will significantly impact student improvement over time. However, in contrast to the work of Brown and colleagues, this research would suggest that the healthy climate based on double-loop learning (see Figure 8.1) is an outcome of a clear purpose and not an essential element to establishing purpose.

Five years after all four schools had adopted Turning Points, there was evidence of consistent gains in student achievement as measured by standardized tests. In comments by the principals and several staff members since the study was completed, however, it is clear that the schools are still struggling to meet the needs of all students. The results of this research concur with the finding by Hargraves (1995): "The collective wisdom of contemporary literature on corporate management and organizational change is that conventional, bureaucratic organizations (and here we would include most secondary schools and their departments) do not fare well in the volatile conditions of postmodernity" (p. 62).

Sustaining continuous learning and shared vision in schools is a multilayered process. The process first calls for principals who are able to conceptualize the whole, see patterns of change, and clearly articulate the organization's core purpose. Concurrently, the principal must engage the faculty through the leadership team and interdisciplinary teams in dialogue that will lead to a shared vision of what the organization truly wants to create. Finally, the principal must assist the faculty in maintaining the image of the current reality in juxtaposition with the vision they have collectively created. However, this process is extremely difficult when the principal and school organization are also embedded in a large, complex district that does not practice the same process of shared leadership.

The analysis shows that all four principals in this study had the ability to conceptualize, aspire to, and reflect as defined through systems thinking. The data also suggest that the principals did become clear about the purpose of the Turning Points reform initiative and committed to ensuring success for all children. Although these two components had a significant impact on each woman's ability to stay focused on moving the school in a shared coherent direction, they were not sufficient when embedded in an urban bureaucratic system, which was not also committed to shared leadership with representatives of all the differing voices. The district also failed to provide sufficient time for shared reflection and to recognize that the introduction of innovations must be coupled with public analysis of the data and dialogue around assumptions, beliefs, and common purpose.

As previous research on organizational change has recognized (Argyris & Schön, 1996; Hargraves, 1995; Kanter, Stein, & Jick, 1992; Leithwood & Seashore Louis, 1998; Marsh, 1997; Mink, 1992), the types of organizations, including schools, most likely to achieve their core purpose are those with autonomy, collaboration around a common purpose, flexibility, and continuous commitment to problem solving and learning about their environment and themselves. In urban districts with such diverse voices and beliefs about the purpose of school, it may mean that individual schools will either need to have an equal voice in the decision making and the vision setting or be given more autonomy to chart their own course.

References

Argyris, C. (1993). *Knowledge for action: A guide to overcoming barriers to organizational change*. San Francisco: Jossey-Bass.

Argyris, C., & Schön, D. A. (1996). *Organizational learning II: Theory, method, and practice*. Reading, MA: Addison-Wesley.

Bell, T. H. (1993, April). Reflections one decade after *A Nation at Risk*. *Phi Delta Kappan, 74*(8), 592–597.

Berliner, D. C. (1993, April). Mythology and the American system of education. *Phi Delta Kappan, 74*(8), 632–640.

Brown, K. M., Roney, K., Anfara, Jr., V. A. (2003, May). Organizational health directly influences student performance at the middle level. *Middle School Journal, 34*(5), 5–15.

Burke, P. H. (2002). *Sustainable results in urban middle schools: How principals use systems thinking to lead effective change* (dissertation in print). Cambridge, MA: Lesley University.

Carnegie Council on Adolescent Development. (1989). *Turning Points: Preparing American youth for the 21st century*. Washington D.C.: Author.

Center for Collaborative Education. (1990). *Design overview. Turning Points: Transforming middle school*. Boston, MA: Author.

Dewey, J. (1900; reprinted 1990). *The school and society & The child and the curriculum* (A centennial ed.). Chicago:The University of Chicago Press.

Epstein, J., & Mac Iver, D. J. (1990). *Education in the middle grades: Overview of national practices and trends*. Columbus, OH: National Middle School Association.

Felner, R., Jackson, A. W., Kasak, D., Mulhall, P., Brand, S., & Flowers, N. (1997, March). The impact of school reform for the middle years. *Phi Delta Kappan, 78*(7), 528–532, 541–550.

George, P. S. (1990). From junior high to middle school—Principals' perspectives. *National Association of Secondary School Principals Bulletin, 73*(521), 86–94.

Gruhn, W. T., & Douglass, H. R. (1971). *The modern junior high school* (3rd ed.). New York: Ronald Press.

Hargreaves, A. (1995). *Changing teachers, changing times: Teachers' work and culture in the postmodern age.* New York: Teachers College Press.

Hill, P., & Bonan, J. (1991). *Decentralization and accountability in public education.* Santa Monica, CA: RAND Corporation.

Jackson, A. W., & Davis, G. A. (2000). *Turning Points 2000: Educating adolescents in the 21st century.* New York: Teachers College Press.

Kanter, R., Stein, B., & Jick, T. (1992). *The challenge of organizational change.* New York: The Free Press.

Lannon, C. P. (1995, Summer). Creating organizations that learn. *New England Nonprofit Quarterly,* 18–23.

Lawrence-Lightfoot, S. (1983). *The good high school: Portrait of character and culture.* New York: Basic Books.

Lawrence-Lightfoot, S., & Hoffman Davis, J. (1997). *The art and science of portraiture.* San Francisco: Jossey-Bass.

Leithwood, K., Begley, P. T., Cousins, J. B. (1994). *Developing expert leadership for future schools.* Washington, D.C.: Falmer Press.

Leithwood, K., & Seashore Louis, K. (Eds.). (1998). *Organizational learning in schools.* Exton, PA: Swets & Zeitlinger.

Lipsitz, J. (1994). *Successful school for young adolescents.* New Brunswick, NJ: Transaction Books.

Lipsitz, J., Jackson, A. W., & Austin, L. M. (1997, March). What works in middle grade reform. *Phi Delta Kappan, 78*(7), 517–519.

Lipsitz, J., Mizell, M. H., Jackson, A. W., & Austin, L. M. (1997, March). Speaking with one voice: A manifesto for middle-grades reform. *Phi Delta Kappan, 78*(7), 533–540.

Mac Iver, D. J., & Epstein, J. L. (1993). Middle grades research: Not yet mature, but no longer a child. *The Elementary School Journal, 93,* 519–533.

Marsh, D. D. (1997, March). *Educational leadership for the 21st century: Integrating three emerging perspectives.* Paper presented at the American Educational Research Association, Chicago, IL.

Merenbloom, E. Y. (1991). *The team process.* Columbus, OH: National Middle School Association.

Midgley, C., & Edelin, K. C. (1998). Middle school reform and early adolescent well-being: The good news and the bad. *Educational Psychologist, 33*(4), 195–206.

Mink, O. G. (1992). Creating new organizational paradigms for change. *International Journal of Quality and Reliability Management, 9*(3): 21–35.

National Commission On Excellence in Education (Ed.). (1983). *A nation at risk.* Cambridge, MA: U.S.A. Research.

National Middle School Association. (1995). *This we believe.* Columbus, OH: Author.

Nieto, S. (1999). *The light in their eyes: Creating multicultural learning communities.* New York: Teachers College Press.

Ravitch, D. (1983). *The troubled crusade: American educations 1945–1980.* New York: Basic Books.

Sarason, S. B. (1995). School change: The personal development of a point of view. In P. A. Wasley, A. Lieberman, & J. P. McDonald (Eds.). *School reform.* New York: Teachers College Press.

Sarason, S. B. (1996). *Barometers of change: Individual, educational, and social transformation.* San Francisco: Jossey-Bass.

Schön, D. A. (1987). *Educating the reflective practitioner: Toward a new design for teaching and learning in the professions.* San Francisco: Jossey-Bass.

Senge, P. M. (1990). *The fifth discipline: The art and practice of the learning organization.* New York: Currency Doubleday.

Senge, P., Roberts, C., Ross, R. B., Smith, B. J., & Kleiner, A. (1994). *The fifth discipline fieldbook: Strategies and tools for building a learning organization.* New York: Currency Doubleday.

Stringfield, S. (1995). Attempting to enhance students' learning through innovative programs: The case for schools evolving into high reliability organizations. *School Effectiveness and School Improvement,* 6(1), 67–96.

Tyack, D., & Cuban, L. (1995). *Tinkering toward utopia: A century of public school reform.* Cambridge, MA: Harvard University Press.

Weissglass, J. (2001, August 8). Racism and the achievement gap. *Education Week,* pp. 49–72.

9

Principals Conceptualize the Development of Teacher Leaders

A Cross-Case Study of Shared Leadership in High-Poverty Kentucky Schools

Deborah H. McDonald

John L. Keedy

This chapter presents a study of how three elementary school principals conceptualized the sharing of leadership and then developed teacher leaders within the policy framework of the Kentucky Education Reform Act of 1990 (KERA). In this cross-case analysis, we found that these three principals understood the conceptual framework of KERA soundly enough to incorporate its tenets in enlisting teacher support, collaboration, and decision making. The implicit intent of KERA was to restructure school practices in ways that would result in higher levels of total school success, which meant that even poor students would learn. These principals accomplished both KERA goals and shared leadership in ways that focused on holding administrators and teachers alike accountable for continually improving student learning—the ultimate goal of KERA. To achieve the KERA goal, these principals purposefully set out to share the enigmas of instructional leadership with teachers who were the classroom leaders and who were most directly responsible for student learning. Principals shared this leadership in three ways: that is, by (1) setting the norm that shared leadership was a "core value" of the schools' culture; (2) using the Consolidated Plan as a tool for managing partnerships, collective accountability, and shared decision making; and (3) playing the role of "analytical guides" providing appropriate internal and external resources and supporting teachers as leaders. The authors speculate that mandated policies, contrary to rebuttals by their critics, can have positive effects on schools as organizations: Kentucky legislators implemented significant changes in curriculum, instruction, and assessment through both accountability and decentralizing measures within a coherent framework. We conclude this chapter with suggestions for policymakers, practitioners, and researchers.

The concept of principals sharing leadership with teachers matters immensely. The hypothesis of this study was that principals themselves could not through unilateral practices improve instructional outcomes for low-income students through administrative prerogative. The complexities and demands of the principal's position have become overwhelming (Hurley, 2001), and the principal's direct influence on the "technical core" of classroom instruction is marginal when it comes to making curriculum engaging and thoughtful for all students (Rallis & Highsmith, 1986). The most prescient principals now understand that they need to develop teacher leadership to accomplish genuine reform and change within the current accountability environment (Holmes Group, 1986; Rosenholtz, 1989). Principals are becoming dependent on teacher leaders. Improving student outcomes on a continuous and sustained basis requires partnerships with the school personnel who are closest to students—the teachers themselves—and who are directly responsible for student learning; as a result, principals must share school-level leadership decisions.

Drawing on a two-year study of how principals shared leadership and helped develop teacher leaders in three Kentucky schools, this chapter discusses how three principals used the Kentucky Education Reform Act of 1990 (KERA) to lead their schools in a process of continuous improvement. KERA formed the backdrop and stage on which these principals embraced accountability and acted to distribute leadership among their staff in ways that shared responsibilities so that all could be accountable in improving the achievement of the largely low-income student populations.

In explaining how principals shared leadership and helped develop teacher leaders within the framework of KERA, we have two objectives in this chapter. First, we illustrate how these principals explicate the basic tenets of KERA. Second, we use both individual cases and cross-case analysis to demonstrate how these three principals went about deliberately sharing the leadership with teacher leaders and accomplishing distributed accountability. Before proceeding to the KERA framework, we briefly explain the research method.

Method

In this research we used the case-study design because the school context allowed us to identify and examine attributes that have become commonplace to principals and teachers. Observing the three principals within the context of their schools allowed for individual analysis of each case as well as for a cross-case analysis, as pointed out by Merriam (1998): "Qualitative case studies rely heavily upon qualitative data obtained from interviews, observations, and documents" (p. 68).

Selection of Research Participants

A purposeful selection method (Hunter, 1953; Whitaker, 1997) was used to determine school selection. The selected schools demonstrated continuously increased student achievement for three consecutive biennia (i.e., six years) and earned rewards status on the Kentucky assessment despite high levels of student poverty indexed to free and reduced lunch data. The graduated elevation of assessment scores every two years is referred to as the *biennial bar,* and schools that exceed their goal by specified amounts earn rewards status (see Appendix A at the end of this chapter). Principals had at least six years' tenure at the school and during these six years had established reputations for shared leadership, according to interviews with state, intermediate, and local agency personnel. Each selected principal and school was provided a pseudonym: Principal Adams at Arno School, Barnes at Bentley, and Calatri at Cannon.

Data Collection

We used three data collection methods: (1) interviews (both individual and focus group), (2) observations, and (3) document analysis. Interviews were semi-structured (Merriam, 1998). Original interview questions were structured, and appropriate follow-up probing provided participants the opportunities to expand on their responses and allowed the researcher to solicit additional facts and opinions (Merriam, 1998; Yin, 1994).

Interview. Two types of interviews were used: individual and focus group. Principals were interviewed a minimum of six times over the course of each case (see Appendix C). The principals then selected their teacher leaders for interview (Appendix D). All teacher leaders who were recommended participated. The possibility for additional teacher interviews or follow-up questions at a later time also remained open until adequate patterns had been identified. Follow-up interviews were conducted with the principal and selected teacher leaders.

A purposeful selection process was used to identify teacher leader participants for "focused interviews" (Yin, 1994, p. 84). The principal was first given a description of teacher leadership (see Appendix B) and asked to identify interview participants. Each teacher selected by the principal was then asked to identify other colleagues they perceived to be teacher leaders using the same description. This method was preferred to random participant selection because those individuals who were most likely to provide the desired information could be targeted as participants (Creswell, 1994). Focus group interviews incorporated open-ended questions that were designed to confirm or deny tentative findings from preliminary data such as interviews, observations, and document mining. Assertions that developed from other data sources were confirmed or denied by the teacher leader focus-group responses.

Observation. Principal-teacher and teacher-teacher interactions were the focus of observations throughout each site visit. The researcher first "shadowed" and observed the principal. Emerging categories generated from the principal observation and initial interviews with teachers formed preliminary data patterns and categories and determined a more precise approach for later observations. Observations also included faculty meetings, parent/teacher meetings, and school-based decision-making team meetings. Site visits were scheduled to maximize data-gathering opportunities.

Document Mining. The Kentucky Department of Education required schools to have some documents on file, such as the improvement plan (i.e., Consolidated Plan [CP]) and school-based decision-making (SBDM) policies. Most schools also maintained meeting agendas, school handbooks, and faculty correspondence including memos, meeting notes, and notes for announcements. These documents were included as sources for document mining. The researcher looked for evidence of focus on student achievement, wide teacher involvement, and responsibilities that were shared by teachers and the principal.

Data Analysis

Data from both the individual and focus-group interviews were tape recorded and later transcribed into computer files for coding purposes (Coffee & Atkinson, 1996). Codings were standardized by source of data across the three schools to facilitate the cross-case analysis. This triangulation, or combination of methods, was chosen because it allowed an in-depth analysis without being obtrusive to the operation of the school while simultaneously minimizing researcher error or site bias (Creswell, 1994). Data were analyzed by the constant comparative method (i.e., iteration between data collection and analysis), as categories both emerged and were modified as fresh data were collected (Coffee & Atkinson, 1996). Matrix displays (Miles & Huberman, 1994) were used to illustrate themes and categories within each case. Cross-case analysis (Hart, 1990) consolidated the multiple case findings as commonalities developed among the cases.

We now turn to the first objective of this chapter: describing Kentucky's reform framework to illustrate how these principals explicate the basic tenets of KERA.

The Framework of Shared Leadership in the Kentucky Reform Era

Perhaps nowhere is the need for teacher leadership as acute as in the state of Kentucky, whose landmark reform act of 1990 specified both accountability for student learning *and* decentralization through the school council. This omnibus bill clearly executed the best practices for increasing student learning as identified by education researchers (e.g., accountability, autonomy, and resources) and included the importance of principal and teacher relationships in the shared leadership of Kentucky schools (e.g., school-based decision making). The bill focused on classrooms in a way that requires the cooperative efforts of principals and teachers. KERA, likewise, moved educators from a need for distributed leadership to the necessity of distributed accountability by forcing measures of student achievement to the school level. The finely tuned blending of autonomy and accountability balanced the equality fulcrum at the heart of Kentucky's reform. KERA further incorporated the conceptual framework of both school and principal effectiveness research. According to the Legislative Research Commission (1994, pp. 14–15), twelve components comprise this reform framework:

1. High educational goals set by Kentuckians to clearly state what graduates were expected to know and be able to do.
2. An assessment system to measure whether all students were reaching the goals.
3. An accountability system to reward those schools improving their success with students and to intervene in those schools failing to make progress.
4. School councils made up of educators and parents to make decisions on curriculum, instruction, and school management, and to create an environment for student achievement and school success.
5. Increased funding for professional-development activities for educators to learn new ways to more effectively achieve success with all students.
6. Early childhood education programs to better prepare children who were at risk of educational failure.
7. Funding for a longer school day, school week, and school year to assist students who needed more time to achieve academic success.
8. A major commitment to technology as an instructional and administrative resource.
9. Funding for family resource and youth service centers to assist students and families in need, by providing resources and referrals to service agencies in the community, so that students can focus on learning.
10. Changes in the governance structure, to reduce the politics involved in the operation of many of Kentucky's school districts and to improve the leadership capability at the state and local levels.
11. A new funding system, to correct the financial disparity between wealthy and poor school districts.
12. A major funding commitment to support the new education initiatives in the state.

A corresponding standards-based accountability package articulated the educational goals as Kentucky academic expectations, which every Kentucky student would accomplish. These broad goals and supporting academic expectations responded to earlier calls for specific identification of what students would know and be able to do when they exited schools (Goodlad, 1984; Holmes Group, 1986). Also, KERA validated the importance of local decision making by providing site autonomy to offset the accountability but held every school responsible for continuous improvement each biennium (every two years). The framework, moreover, dictated a unique approach for achieving those goals through the inclusiveness of the accountability formula. Every Kentucky school was given a state-directed, continuous improvement goal, and every Kentucky student was included, even those in special ed. Accountability for all students, including students who had never achieved success in the past, became a reality (see Appendix A).

A baseline was provided for each school, and success was outlined as reaching a predetermined improvement goal each biennium. Success in the individual classroom was insufficient because accountability was measured at the school level. New teacher roles outside the classroom became a reality. Teachers had to work together and with principals to accomplish alignment of curriculum, instruction, and assessment in a schoolwide manner.

Bottom-up restructuring that assured accomplishment of world-class standards by 80% of Kentucky students was "something no state has ever accomplished before" (David, 1994, p. 710). The importance of teachers and teacher leadership were visibly validated in the KERA reform legislation (McDonald & Keedy, 2002). David identified the classroom teacher as most responsible for school-level accountability. Other researchers established principal leadership on student learning as indirect (Blase, 1989; Hallinger & Heck, 1996; Keedy & Achilles, 1997). Implications for the school principal's role were amassed throughout the legislation, as principals were challenged to become the "coordinator of teachers in instructional leadership" (Glickman, 1991, p. 7).

KERA provided statutory support to functionally advance teacher leadership in Kentucky schools by negating the concept of principal as the only school instructional leader. Kentucky school-level decision making included all curricular decisions and textbook selections. Schools were also expected to develop a state-mandated annual school plan based on analysis of student work and test results (i.e., Consolidated Plan). Schools were treated as independent units in KERA legislation. Although districts provided assistance, school-based decisions took precedence over district decisions. Schools were, therefore, charged with decision making that was of critical importance to success with accountability (e.g., curriculum, assessment, and instruction). Together, principals and teachers were to maximize school improvement by sharing leadership. KERA responded to Blase's (1989) request to "find ways in which administrators and teachers together can effectively share responsibility and power in the governance of public schools" (p. 404).

The KERA framework, in effect, grounded this study's hypothesis: that the strong accountability mechanism that held the individual school accountable for improved student academic success; the decentralization provided through school councils; and the overwhelming managerial responsibilities of the principal combined to provide unparalleled incentives for a new type of leadership—a hybrid of principal and teacher leadership. Success with all students depends on the involvement of many individuals—namely, principals and teachers—and they must all share the leadership role to maximize achievement. Principals cannot through instructional leadership make the instructional changes in classrooms that result in enriching curricula and students' thoughtful engagement in meaningful tasks. Only teachers ultimately can engender these changes in their own classrooms; no magical wands here. Without shared leadership, classrooms may never change, as has been demonstrated by various accounts of reform efforts (e.g., Murphy, 1991).

Yet the task of shared leadership is filled with pitfalls because teacher leadership is not a naturally occurring phenomenon. Teacher leadership cannot be accomplished by "simply forming a leadership team. . . . [It requires] principals' signals that they are willing to listen, respect teacher decisions, and support following through on teacher-led initiatives [to] reduce ambiguity and promote consensus" (Clift, Johnson, Holland, & Veal, 1992, p. 905).

We now turn to the second objective of the chapter: explicating how these three principals went about deliberately sharing the leadership with teachers and accomplishing distributed accountability.

Three Case Studies of Principal-Shared Leadership

Generally, these principals used KERA as a professional philosophical platform to pressure teachers to move forward into leadership positions. They presented accountability as a school-level issue to be distributed among all teachers. As principals and teachers institutionalized KERA, teacher conceptualization of schoolwide shared leadership, in turn, was enhanced. These principals were "Lone Rangers" who used school-level autonomy and shared leadership with teachers to consistently accomplish reward status for three biennia (i.e., six years). These schools were exemplary because, although they received the same resources as other schools in their district and region, they consistently outperformed other schools despite high-poverty circumstances.

Principal Adams and Arno Elementary School

Ninety-five percent of the student population at Arno, one of ten schools in an eastern Kentucky district, qualified for either free or reduced lunches. Arno School is located on a two-lane paved, crooked road lined with private residences and is eleven miles from the closest town. The school was created in 1990 when two rival schools were consolidated. Student enrollment for kindergarten through sixth grade in 1999–2000 was 287, and transience ranged from 2 to 3%. Average daily attendance was 95%. A total of 29 certified staff, 10 aides, 5 food-service employees, 4 custodians, 2 nurses, 2 family-resource-center employees, and 11 bus drivers serviced the school.

Principal Adams was in his thirty-first year as an educator and had been a principal for 27 years. Adams was sole principal at Arno in the 11 years the school had existed. He grew up in the area and indicated an interest in educating the "whole child" in both the local and global cultures. Adams's soft-spoken yet straightforward, no-nonsense demeanor immediately announced the seriousness he perceived in his duties as principal of Arno.

Principal Adams was quick to point out that he was only one member of the Arno team and that it was the classroom teachers who deserved most of the recognition that might come to the school. "I accept their strengths," he declared. "I surround myself with good people . . . people smarter than I." Teacher leaders confirmed that Adams supported their expertise: "He doesn't feel like you can't make decisions." A clear recognition of the critical link between all teachers and accountability was apparent in such responses as: "Everybody's input is necessary." The school's earned reputation for shared leadership was, therefore, evident. Key findings of Adams's shared leadership included these four themes: (1) communication, (2) connectedness, (3) environment of shared respect, and (4) provision of teacher resources.

Communication. Principal Adams used the KERA framework in combining communication and connectedness and fostered an environment of shared respect. Adams identified "communication" as the most important element for sharing leadership with teachers. Teacher leaders were consistently specific when they identified communication as the skill Adams most used in support of the evolution and development of shared leadership. Adams facilitated communication by working with teachers to (1) collectively craft a vision, (2) define the vision as a mission statement in operationalizing the Consolidated Plan, (3) identify clearly aligned goals, (4) affirm a shared schoolwide focus, (5) use the same vocabulary as teachers, and (6) establish priorities including time usage. Adams and teacher leaders articulated a "desire to be at the top" and described how "teachers took more responsibility because everybody wants to be a winner here."

Adams and teacher leaders consistently reported that they did not fight accountability but rather accepted it and met it head on. Responsibility for student learning fell to "Not just the teacher leaders; the role of everyone in the school is defined as to share. There is no uncertainty about anyone's role.

Everyone's purpose is known." This reference to "everyone" included Adams because he was expected to support and facilitate teachers as leaders.

Connectedness. Adams accomplished connectedness when he used data to establish a student-focused approach that teachers understood, implemented, and monitored both in classrooms and schoolwide; and when he facilitated teacher leader validation and celebration of their own knowledge and critical link to accountability. Adams and teachers at Arno School monitored data and focused on Consolidated Plan (CP) goals to elevate the essential nature of teacher leadership and to make it fundamental to success with school-level accountability. Adams and teachers designed CP methods that required teacher leadership.

The strong sense of accountability to data at Arno School was endorsed by both Adams and teacher leaders. Teacher leader responsibility often revolved around data. Adams and teacher leaders worked collaboratively. "It's like we're in a big circle working to solve problems at all times," Adams described. There are two important elements in that statement. First, the reference to "We . . . solve problems" indicated that all individuals worked together in problem solving. More important, the reference to "at all times" indicated problem solving was not an isolated event but rather an ongoing endeavor. Adams did not stay outside problem-solving interactions but was part of them. He practiced unconditional support and worked with teachers to solve problems.

The supportive manner Adams used in the context of data analysis influenced how teacher leaders worked with other teachers and was essential to collaborative associations. Adams did not make demands on teacher leaders, and teacher leaders did not make demands on their peers. Connective interactions did not stop with teacher leaders. Data supported the acceptance of responsibility by all teachers as a by-product of the connectedness.

Environment of Shared Respect. Adams shared responsibility with teachers. "[He] joins in and helps like everybody else," a teacher affirmed. Everyone was involved. "You can't be an individual here," one teacher leader reported. "Everybody has to be on two or three committees." The result was a connectedness that extended through Adams and teacher leaders to all teachers. One method of establishing the connection was with the use of data in which Adams was an active participant. His role as active participant supported an environment of shared respect.

Principal Adams observed, "Teacher leadership makes experts. Leadership is natural but not always recognized." He did recognize leaders and endorsed their efforts in ways that continually verified his respect for what they were doing. Adams validated teacher knowledge and expertise by continuously asking for their involvement. Teacher leaders reported they were continually challenged by Principal Adams to make decisions for themselves. A recurring example was captured in the oft-repeated phrase, "Use your own judgment."

Teacher leaders openly validated the knowledge of their peers and exercised their own abilities naturally during the interview sessions. Teacher interaction revealed a high level of self-assuredness and mutual respect. Adams exhibited such trust and confidence that teacher leaders emulated this behavior. A teacher described, "You know he has confidence in your judgment, and you don't feel threatened by him." By modeling confidence in teacher leaders, Adams facilitated the teacher leaders' perception of his support for them and their ability to influence student learning.

Linkage between data and classroom practice helped teachers have confidence in their ability to influence student achievement scores. Teacher leaders commented that no individual could choose to opt out of the shared efforts. A complementary extension of existing broad-based teacher involvement was teacher leadership. Because Adams joined in problem solving and supported broad-based involvement, teachers knew he shared responsibility with them.

Provision of Teacher Resources. Teacher leaders identified internal resources as the single most important contribution Adams made to increased student achievement. One of the internal resources that most vindicated teacher leadership was use of time. Adams honored teacher time as a valuable resource. Teacher leaders reported he was also astute in dealing with his own time.

Teacher decision making about resources distinguished Arno from other schools. Although all schools in the district were given the same amount of money, expenditure of resources was different at Arno School. Adams and teacher leaders worked together to identify and use all resources. Adams validated teacher expertise even when teachers selected resources he was not familiar with. This endorsement of teacher expertise affirmed Adams's confidence in teacher credibility and again supported earlier themes of communication and shared respect.

Case Analysis. These categories indicated that Adams used his own connectedness to student work to elevate the importance of classroom instruction and to drive teacher leadership. When teachers made connections between their work in classrooms and student assessment data, they sought the expertise of recognized teacher leaders. Communication was the key that kept Adams, teacher leaders, and the rest of the teachers connected. Teacher leaders had powerful knowledge tempered with the pressure of accountability and the support of Adams and their colleagues in a culture of efficacy. Adams's communication and connectedness helped teacher leaders recognize and endorse their own individual and collective critical link to accountability.

A natural by-product of the sharing of resources and knowledge was teacher leadership. Teacher leadership was valuable to Adams, and he nurtured teacher leaders and supported their role through the provision of people, money, and time. Teacher leaders were given access to outside information, professional development, and such internal resources as instructional materials, time for sharing, and access to their colleagues in a manner supportive of teacher leadership. Adams's appreciation of the value of all resources—human, fiscal, internal, and external—not only facilitated but encouraged teacher leadership. Adams and teachers designed CP methods, for example, that required teacher leadership.

Principal Barnes and Bentley Elementary School

Bentley School was located in a district of 28 schools where the surrounding small eastern-Kentucky community still flourished from the wealth that coal mining brought into the area. The school sat on a heavily traveled country road several miles from the town. One section of the well-maintained two-story structure was built in 1998, while another section dated back to 1953. The new section was added when another school was merged with the existing school. The student population was 62% poverty as defined by free or reduced lunches, and enrollment fluctuated from 852 to 960 as documented in the School Report Card. Transience is not a problem (less than five percent per year). The average daily attendance rate was 95%.

Prior to his term as principal, Barnes had been assistant principal at Bentley for 10 years and had taught high school math in the district for the 10 previous years. He had grown up in the area and expressed dedication to having students succeed in the global economy. Principal Barnes indicated he was intent on being a good principal and shared a copy of the Interstate School Leaders Licensure Consortium's Standards for School Leaders, which he and the assistant principal "live by." Three overarching themes illustrated how Barnes shared leadership with teachers: (a) culture of shared commitment, (b) teamwork, and (c) collaborative connections.

Culture of Shared Commitment. Teacher leaders credited the culture of shared commitment at Bentley School to Barnes's leadership. Barnes and teacher leaders at Bentley were characterized by purposeful collegial interactions in using the school improvement plan CP and KERA to craft a whole-school approach with big-picture connections. This shared-commitment culture was accomplished by creating an environment in which an openness with information and communication permeated the school.

Teacher leaders worked collaboratively in this environment and shared information openly. They reported that the course syllabi were written as a group and explained that if they worked collaboratively, they did not overlap materials or have to do as much review for students. Open acknowledgment of what was happening in classrooms throughout the school was often shared. The following quote best summarizes that intent: "There's not a teacher in this school who doesn't know what is going on with the assessment. If he [Barnes] didn't keep us as well informed, our scores wouldn't be as high as they are. Everyone knows what is expected of us."

Because teachers were informed, they could make decisions. One teacher leader commented, "I feel like informed people are responsible people. They have to have the information, and they will take it upon themselves to do what needs to be done."

Barnes believed in teacher expertise and proved his belief by his straightforward sharing of leadership responsibilities. Teacher leaders believed that the openness and strength of proactive information sharing facilitated their ability to lead. A teacher leader shared how Barnes used the CP to organize communication and to share leadership through clear expectations and role clarification: "Mr. Barnes communicates with us. With CP we are far ahead of other schools. Sometimes they don't know what we're talking about. You have to be organized. We build on everything everybody does." The strength of proactive communication in sharing leadership with teachers was clear when several teachers commented on how they worked with Barnes and knew what changes to anticipate. A teacher leader observed, "He's on top of what's going on in education to let teachers know what's coming down the pike." This ease of communication and information sharing at Bentley enhanced teacher leadership because the composite knowledge and expertise of Barnes and teacher leaders was shared throughout the school. Communication and openness facilitated focused collegiality.

Collegiality was deliberately focused on academics. The shared teamwork that resulted helped all teachers perceive ownership of accountability. Schoolwide goals affirmed the shared focus that permeated the school setting. Teacher leaders credited Barnes with the shared focus and schoolwide approach. "He [Barnes] keeps us all together," one said. "He doesn't refer to entities but to whole-school program." This comprehensive and totally encompassing attentiveness to the whole school alleviated isolationism and facilitated teacher leadership. Barnes and teacher leaders worked as a team, and their approach extended throughout the faculty. While teacher leaders credited Barnes with focus and goals, Barnes credited the focus on schoolwide goals to teachers because they had collaboratively set the goals. Regardless of how the collegiality was initiated, both Barnes and teacher leaders made a great effort to maintain the close connectivity at their school and expressed pride in how the resulting shared focus helped them work together.

A teacher leader linked the shared focus at Bentley School to the establishment of common goals with KERA:

> We realize KERA is about working together as a group to achieve a common goal. Teachers have to give up a lot of getting off by themselves to do their own special thing. I could probably tell you what every teacher in my grade level is doing now. We do similar activities, integrate things, it's like cooperative learning.

Barnes also linked this focused collegiality to a collaborative effort. "I told them, 'We are nearing our [KERA] assessment. [We] have to have a schoolwide effort,'" he stated. A teacher leader confirmed, "Our teachers get along well together. We work professionally together, spend our energy getting things done, have respect for each other and for him [Barnes]." This school had energy focused toward school goals in a no-nonsense approach accompanied by a sense of urgency. Further evidence of this was found in documents such as SBDM policy; faculty handbook; and CP, which were student focused and indicated shared responsibility by Principal Barnes and staff.

Instilling the Norm of Teamwork Into the School Culture. Teamwork was the second theme in this case. Teacher leaders and Barnes had reciprocal partnership expectations. One teacher leader noted, "Our principal is the type of man who makes us all feel like we are doing this together. We feel like we share." A focus group member shared, "Mr. Barnes as a leader is like a team player. A partner in this endeavor. Not like a controller, works with us." Individuals at the Bentley School were team players. They communicated easily and often offered assistance to one another.

Barnes modeled teamwork in his own professional interactions and supported teacher self-efficacy by building on strengths, by expanding leadership to include professional development, by sharing decision-making opportunities, and by focusing teamwork on academic goals. A teacher leader described how this modeling of appropriate school-level interactions had promoted teamwork and led her to teacher leadership:

> I can sum it up in one word. From being at four different schools, it's teamwork. We all work together, and the thing that amazes me about our school is that we all know what is expected of and from us, and we know how much he [Principal Barnes] thinks of us, the confidence he has in us. Mr. Barnes puts faith in all of us.

Teacher leaders supported one another and other teachers as Barnes supported them. Barnes identified individual strengths and built on them to increase teacher self-efficacy. "When he wants you to do something, he asks you as if he has the greatest amount of confidence in you," said one teacher leader.

Reports of growth in leadership characteristics were prevalent throughout the data. Teachers reported realizing strengths and abilities they had not previously been aware of until Barnes's validation of their work. One such report described Barnes as nurturing teacher-leader growth by building on teacher strengths: "Followers and leaders are always defined. It's unsaid at first. Mr. Barnes saw ability . . . helped me grow. Five years ago I wouldn't speak out at all. He pulled that out of me. Makes you feel confident."

Teachers also encouraged growth in one another because adequate leadership opportunities, including professional development, eliminated competition. A teacher summed up the frequent opportunities: "Every time we do something one person is the leader, but it changes from activity to activity. You are not the leader and responsible for everything." Because adequate leadership opportunities were afforded to all teachers, teacher leaders remained peers and were not viewed as bosses. Everyone shared responsibility from time to time so that the perception of equity was maintained.

All teachers at Bentley were part of a focused-teamwork approach to achieving targeted academic goals. Shared responsibility supported teacher leadership because all teachers were part of the team. Teacher leaders were communication "conduits" and helped with understanding KERA components while orchestrating curricular alignments. Teachers believed that by working together as a team they had control over accountability, as opposed to the state merely dictating their actions. A teacher leader revealed how teacher leaders made decisions about changes and adaptations related to KERA:

> Before KERA we were self-contained, typical traditional, so many minutes per subject. In the first year of KERA, we changed, knew we could do better. He

> [Barnes] has been so good to say, "Let's go with the change. You [teachers] see. You are in the classroom and you know."

Principal Barnes was especially intent on ensuring teacher leaders' understanding of KERA as a whole-school approach. One teacher leader summed up this intention:

> The key is that we all have shared responsibility. KERA has brought that to our attention. We are all in it together. Even though you have teachers who don't generally like to work with other teachers on a day-to-day basis or who are more independent, you just have to encourage them to become part of a team because it is a whole-school effort.

After a while the teamwork came naturally. One teacher leader responded to an inquiry about the work of teacher leaders: "We have a lot of input, work together . . . anything that comes from the state department we try to get our hands on and figure out what we can use in the classroom." Making connections between state department and classroom instruction are sometimes a rarity for teachers. Bentley teacher leaders made the connections easily and recognized the importance of focusing on the intended state guidelines including budgetary changes. "With KERA more funds are available," one teacher noted. "Teachers have more of a say now."

Collaborative Connections. Teachers recognized the power in collaborative connections between themselves and Barnes and among themselves, as required by the Consolidated Plan. When Barnes and teachers worked together through the student test data from the previous year, teachers recognized a collective, collegial sense of control when confronted with the state's accountability measures. Data analysis of student outcomes moved teacher leadership to a more concentrated and meaningful level because it supported a professional approach in which teacher expertise was prominent.

This analytic data process resulted in a shared collegial focus and approach to accountability. The teacher-leader desire to maintain pride in their school outweighed their fears of data analysis and accountability. Teacher leaders sought Barnes's expertise until everyone in the school understood data and its connection to accountability. Because all teachers were involved in data analysis and decision making, teacher leaders were not a hierarchical threat.

Barnes safeguarded the shared whole-school focus by connecting it to decision making, school outcomes, and collegial interactions. He positioned teacher leaders to maximize their support of colleagues. Both teacher leaders and Barnes deemed this positioning of key players as critical to the success of teacher leadership. Although no hierarchy of leadership existed, teacher leaders were recognized as those who had expertise with use of data analysis within the Consolidated Plan. One teacher commented that the CP provided clear direction for what had to be accomplished and made their work "flow like a flowechart. It is our Bible. It has helped us grow." A teacher leader shared how bringing everyone on board with CP helped support teacher leadership and individual teachers. "Even the weakest teacher is still accountable to the CP. With it as our guide we can pull each other along," she credited. The perception was that CP provided a tool for supporting teachers who needed help.

Classroom instructional data were fed into a whole-school approach as Barnes and teacher leaders shared information about both the individual and the combined elements of KERA. Data revealed consistent references to the organization of work within the CP. Barnes recognized that every teacher had been able to make KERA meaningful. He described how teamwork established the groundwork for teacher leadership to function:

> CP gives your staff an opportunity to see the big picture [of KERA] in the school. . . . They need to be able to answer, "What have we done this year?" We are continuously evaluating. . . . If they work with that plan [CP], they see the whole schoolwide operation, see where we are going.

Teacher leadership evolved naturally from related planning and implementation of task responsibilities.

Case Analysis. Barnes interacted collegially with teachers, accepted responsibilities not normally expected of a principal, and endorsed teacher leadership as an approach to schoolwide accountability outlined in KERA. State-mandated accountability was not perceived as problematic at Bentley School because teachers were recognized as experts capable of helping students learn at high levels. Teachers insisted on understanding data and outlining a collective, strategic, and continuous-improvement approach to the CP. Teachers then perceived control over accountability because they had proactively developed a plan of action for how to approach both present and future instruction. Teacher leaders recognized the CP as a developmental tool and spoke of how the plan would be adapted according to ongoing data collection. They perceived the CP as a way to "pull along" their peers. Together Barnes and teacher leaders planned with the entire faculty. When the planning process was accomplished, Barnes and the teacher leaders monitored and assisted with implementation. A connection to classroom instruction was realized, and educators at Bentley School lived what they had planned each day. Teachers indicated that when Barnes involved them in the planning process, he promoted teacher leadership.

Principal Calatri and Cannon Elementary School

Cannon Elementary was located in a small Kentucky community in an easily accessible location on a main highway and was opened in 1990 as the result of consolidation. Unlike most county schools located miles from town, Cannon was on the outskirts of the town it served. Enrollment fluctuated between 360 and 370 students. The school structure closely resembled a residential dwelling: a one-story brick building with a front-porch entry and white columns on either side of the front door.

The student population had a 32% transience rate, and the poverty rate was 72%. The school, one of nine in the district, served five housing projects and three low-income, rent-subsidized areas. Interview data revealed that "forty percent of families indicated difficulty in providing for food, clothing, emergency needs, utilities, etc." The daily rate of attendance (98%) exceeded both the district (97%) and nation (95%). Teacher leaders credited Principal Calatri with the high rate of attendance. Calatri indicated that she worked in multiple ways to encourage students to attend school because she felt attendance was a critical support mechanism for teacher effectiveness. Calatri was within three years of retirement and had been a teacher in the district prior to becoming principal. She was native to the area and had served as principal since the school opened in 1990.

Three main themes emerged from Cannon School data to define how Principal Calatri shared leadership with teachers and developed teacher leadership: (1) culture of shared teacher leadership, (2) purposeful partnerships and a familial approach for teacher leaders, and (3) school organization that supported teacher leadership. Teacher leadership was an expectation at the Cannon School. The supporting culture was deliberate and validated that teacher expertise and leadership was essential and natural. The culture was achieved through the promotion of a shared vision of pacesetter excellence (i.e., to become best school in the state) that resulted from collective expectations and an environment of mutual support.

Culture of Shared Teacher Leadership. For Principal Calatri at Cannon School, KERA provided tools for orchestrating teacher leadership by shifting the pyramid for leadership expectations to be more inclusive of teachers. Calatri believed mutual support was critical for teachers, and she linked this with reform in principalship responsibilities that came with KERA:

> A shifting pyramid idea could be used for changes to the principalship. Before KERA, training to be a principal was about other things. There was very little emphasis on curriculum. Now we have to understand teaching strategies and child development. We have to be the leader who knows what teachers need to know.

Calatri took advantage of the KERA pyramid shift by actively seeking shared responsibilities with teachers who then interpreted the interactions as supportive of their efforts.

When teacher leaders identified her behavior characteristic that was most closely linked to teacher leadership, they selected support. Teacher leaders provided numerous descriptions of how Calatri had provided for them in ways that facilitated their work in leadership roles, but the overwhelming message was summed up in the focus-group interview. "She's supportive," was voiced several times. Calatri repeatedly asked teachers how she could help them or what they needed. "What can I do to help you?" was her mantra and was not limited to interactions with teacher leaders but was extended to nearly everyone she encountered during the site visits.

The environment of support was further enhanced by the organizational management support through the CP. Integration of programs and people were documented in an organizational management format that provided support for teacher leadership, reduced task assignments, and maximized efficiency. The plan spelled out clear expectations. Calatri's approach to organization management within the context of the CP was inclusive, and her actions extended to all parts of the school process, with participation by all staff.

Though the CP was a state requirement, Calatri was not satisfied with merely complying with its minimum standards. She expanded on its basic requirements to organize a staffwide organization of management support. Calatri's comprehensive organization approach included acting as goal or component manager within the CP, in spite of the fact that generally teacher leaders were component managers. Corroborating interview data to support collaboration were available. "We function as a whole," was a frequent comment. One teacher leader stated, "We support each other and help each other. If I have a problem I can go to another teacher and ask for assistance." Document analysis revealed that helping other teachers was outlined as an expectation in the CP. Teachers collaborated with one another, while Calatri also collaborated with them.

Purposeful Partnerships for Teacher Leaders. Teacher leaders described how they extended the revered familial atmosphere they shared with Calatri to include peer and student relationships. Four levels of relational interactions were identified from the data to illustrate purposeful partnerships: principal and teacher, teacher and teacher, principal and student, and principal-teacher and other adult relationships. Informal interactive relationships spilled over to perceptions of concern for students as well as for one another. No hierarchy of position existed at Cannon because all individuals were valued.

Calatri was deliberate in creating purposeful partnerships among her staff. She purposefully encouraged open, informal interactions among teachers by modeling those interactions. Calatri observed, "I just want to be one of them." Teacher leaders expressed the same eagerness to be a group member. Neither Calatri nor teacher leaders wanted to be perceived as different. Equality of status was essential to their ability to lead, and familial relationships facilitated that. Calatri celebrated positive traits in every teacher, thereby alleviating competition and promoting equality among peers. The result was that the school was a comfortable place to be for everyone.

This equality of relationships helped maintain an atmosphere of harmony in the school. One teacher leader explained, "The relationships are wonderful. It goes on down to how we shared the rewards with all the people, bus drivers, cooks, secretaries, and the aides because we knew without them we couldn't run the school as well." This equity in all adult relationships throughout the school was supportive of teacher leadership because every individual was a valuable member of the purposeful partnerships and familial school approach.

The approach Calatri synthesized at Cannon School went beyond a collegial learning community to endorse the human side of educational accomplishment. Teachers believed that interactions among themselves and with Calatri made leadership easier for them. Students were ready to learn, relationships with peers were positive, and the principal was supportive. The feelings of belonging and camaraderie offset the challenging nature of being an individual in a pacesetter school. A coexisting infrastructure then sustained the purposeful partnerships.

School Organization That Supported Teacher Leadership. Principal Calatri established a school organization that supported teacher leadership as an expectation at Cannon School. Data indicated she accomplished the organization through widespread collaborative interactions, shared responsibilities, collective accountability, and academic freedom to innovate. Abundant leadership opportunities were available within the school organization that supported teacher leadership and valued teacher expertise.

Teacher leader self-confidence in problem solving and decision making were outcomes of the ease with which interactions happened. Teacher leaders perceived that their expertise was valued because Calatri supported widespread *collaborative interaction* throughout the school. Calatri was credited with facilitating interactions by giving decisions back to teachers, by valuing their expertise, by maintaining open channels of communication, by being easily accessible, and by sharing information in a clear and accurate manner. Trust in teacher decision making was affirmed with data. The result was an infrastructure of interaction that supported teacher leadership.

Calatri's best-known communication characteristic was her ability to give the decision back to teachers. Teacher leaders reported that Calatri's favorite phrase was, "Well, what do you think?" A teacher leader described, "She makes me feel like if I have a problem, I can think through it with her." Teacher leaders also mentioned "Thinking through it" with Calatri. Their supportive statements included "Always asks for input," "Always wants to know what we think," and "If there's anything coming up, she meets with us and asks for our opinion about things." Giving decisions back to teachers, helping them think through problems, and believing in their ability to make good decisions were some of Calatri's best assets as a principal. This type of communication was deliberate because she wanted teachers to be comfortable in their interactions with her and one another. Teachers perceived a balance of academic freedom to innovate and collective accountability.

The *shared responsibilities* at Cannon were broad based and provided ample opportunities for every individual to accept the leadership role. Calatri perceived the benefits of shared responsibility to be reciprocal because she gained from the expertise teacher leaders shared. Because responsibilities were shared, teachers experienced academic freedom to innovate. This could be attributed to Calatri's active involvement with teacher leadership and her sharing of responsibilities in a naturally supportive approach.

A *collective or distributed accountability* resulted from the collaborative interactions, shared responsibility, and academic freedom to innovate. The CP was used as Cannon's organization tool for the management of shared responsibility and collective accountability. Calatri summed up her perspective on shared responsibility with the following statement:

> [The] biggest thing is the CP. We took the CP and used it to organize. Took it seriously. Decided this was something to get us on the track for what we wanted to do. Something doable. Understandable. Something we could monitor.

Teachers were given decision-making authority, opportunities to accept leadership roles, and the academic freedom to innovate and improve student learning. The trade-off was a collective accountability, which was managed at Cannon School in the context of the CP process. Broad opportunities were outlined to provide involvement and leadership opportunities to all individuals who chose to accept them. Individual responsibilities, as well as collective ones, were identified. Teacher leaders reported that the CP process was an organizational tool for managing teacher leadership and lessening the threat of accountability.

Another teacher leader believed there was accountability but extended the oneness concept by stating, "We are accountable. Not as individuals but as a whole." Leadership was also extended to include everyone, as stated by Calatri: "I think everybody's got some leadership ability around here." The enlargement of leadership extended accountability naturally. Because Calatri and teachers perceived that working together was the solution, the threat of accountability seemed lessened. Within KERA they identified an organizer, the CP, that met state requirements and made KERA accountability manageable. Calatri and teachers often used the CP terminology to craft conversations.

Case Analysis. When the themes for Cannon School are combined, they indicate that Calatri deliberately and actively promoted teacher leadership and believed the collective accountability of KERA changed expectations for principals. The furtherance of leadership from teachers was evident when Calatri deliberately chose (1) to support teachers as leaders, (2) to use her role of service for their leadership, and (3) to make the jobs of all teachers easier in any way possible. Calatri integrated the opportunity for collegial interactions and resources within the CP so they became teacher-leader support mechanisms. Teacher leaders reported that Calatri provided every teacher with leadership opportunities. Because leadership was open to all teachers, there was no resentment among peers.

Calatri was deliberate in *supporting teachers as leaders* through sharing responsibility and decision making. The confidence and trust Calatri shaped through these actions augmented teacher leadership. Teacher leaders recognized her belief in them and her willingness to endorse their decisions. Reports of Calatri analytically guiding teachers toward decisions were prevalent throughout the data.

Teacher leaders used the CP as a tool to manage accountability, innovation, and their own leadership responsibilities. Calatri and teachers believed their shared pacesetter vision (to become the best school in the state) would be met by the collective expectations they had outlined in the

CP. An environment of mutual support was evident because every staff member, including Calatri, had responsibilities within the plan. Teacher leaders described the CP as an organizational tool that helped them make connections. Calatri supported the work in the CP by serving as a component manager. This gesture validated the importance of the development and implementation of the planning process. Calatri was clear that she wanted to *use her role in service for teacher leadership*.

The mutual support that facilitated teacher leadership at Cannon was bolstered by an underlying infrastructure. Widespread collaborative interaction evolved within the mutually supportive conditions and helped teacher leaders see that their expertise was valued. Shared responsibilities were then documented as tasks, using the CP as an organizer for the work.

Calatri's trust and belief in teacher leaders was offset by a collective accountability in which every person was expected to contribute to the achievement of the pacesetter excellence vision. Calatri stated that she wanted to *make the jobs of all teachers easier in any way possible*. Collective accountability made that happen. Teacher leaders held their colleagues accountable, counted on Calatri to be accountable, and expected Calatri to endorse accountability from all staff members. The result was a unified effort that demanded strong leadership beyond the principal. Both Calatri and the teacher leaders recognized that the principal could not be the sole leader. Teacher leadership was a fundamental part of how the school operated because leadership by teachers was required to maintain Cannon's shared vision of pacesetter excellence. Because the school used collective accountability to support teacher leadership, KERA was embraced rather than feared.

We now move to the cross-case analysis.

Cross-Case Analysis

Three findings emerged from the cross-case analysis: (1) accountability for student achievement made shared leadership essential; (2) the Consolidated Plan was a tool for managing partnerships, collective accountability, and shared decision making, and (3) principals were analytical guides who provided appropriate internal and external resources and supported teachers as leaders.

Accountability for Student Achievement Made Shared Leadership Essential. The ultimate intent of KERA was actualized at these schools because school-level accountability for student achievement made shared leadership essential. These three principals recognized the potential for schoolwide accountability within the KERA framework and let teachers know shared leadership was the approach they must take. Adams at Arno said, "It's like we are in a big circle, working to solve problems at all times." A Bentley teacher believed the key was "shared responsibility" that came with KERA and required a "whole school effort" for success. Teachers participated in supportive interactions and shared expectations, and teacher leaders accepted responsibilities beyond those that all teachers shared. These principals were not shy in admitting they could not meet accountability goals without shared teacher leadership. Barnes stated, "One of my strengths is the recognition of ability."

At Arno, connections between data analysis and classroom practices helped teachers see how assessment results depended on what they taught in classrooms. Teachers at both Bentley and Cannon admitted approaching the principal and requesting closer analysis of assessment results. Cannon teachers acknowledged, "We went to her [Calatri] and said, 'We have to bridge this gap in achievement.'"

The state of Kentucky required that all schools adhere to the mandates of KERA. Instead of facing these changes with fear and cynicism, Principals Adams, Barnes, and Calatri made a conscious decision to understand and implement KERA's basic tenets. This willingness to embrace change encouraged teachers to view KERA as a guide for establishing their roles as teacher leaders and for achieving pacesetter status in their schools.

The Consolidated Plan Was a Tool for Managing Partnerships, Collective Accountability, and Shared Decision Making. Assisting teachers often involved both asking questions to help them think through the numerous KERA requirements and implementing their consolidated plans. The CP was a state-mandated annual school plan based on analysis of student work and test results. Data analysis was thus used to acknowledge teacher expertise and was recognized as a critical link to accountability; the schoolwide approach indicated in KERA legislation was realized.

The CP was used as an organizational tool, which aided these principals in communicating to teachers the influence KERA could have on them as leaders in both the classrooms and the schools. Calatri stated, "Others can give you a perspective on what you won't be able to see. Therefore, I'm always encouraging teachers to take on leadership roles." She observed, "The plan tells us what goals we need to reach. It is a guideline. . . . We work together and help each other. These educators didn't just work together, however. They were all strategically focused on accomplishing common goals."

At Arno School, a teacher stated, "We have schoolwide goals, a mission statement, and everything we do is based on that." Another teacher spoke of preparing teachers to be future component managers: "We're getting ready to shadow for new component managers . . . the CP keeps us focused. I know what is expected of me and what we are accountable for."

The CP was a tool for managing collective accountability and shared decision making. Collective accountability was viewed as a manageable issue when principals used the CP as a tool for planning around data analysis. A Bentley teacher equated their planning to an integrated approach "kind of like cooperative learning." The mission statement of each of these schools included references to "accountability," and principals and teacher leaders indicated they were not threatened by accountability because they perceived a whole-school effort they could collaboratively manage.

Connections between the data analysis required for the CP and classroom practices helped teachers see how assessment results were dependent on what they taught. A Cannon teacher described that the biggest change since KERA was how the CP distributed accountability to all grade levels, not just the assessment-grade levels. KERA legislation did not specify a consolidated plan. The comprehensive-planning process was a requirement from the Kentucky Department of Education. These principals and teachers understood how the planning process could distribute accountability throughout the school. Through the planning process they helped others understand that accountability was not limited to the grade levels specified as accountability years. The CP, in brief, was viewed collectively not as an insidious "management tool" manipulated by principals but as a form of collective accountability around analysis of student outcomes.

Principals Were Analytical Guides Who Provided Resources and Supported Teachers as Leaders. Adams, Barnes, and Cilatri often responded to teacher inquiries with analytical questions that encouraged teacher decision making. One Cannon teacher was particularly insightful: "She [Cilatri] doesn't give you the answer but guides you to it. She asks you questions that make you think in a different way." These questioning techniques were found at all three schools and provided for additional teacher decision making and leadership opportunities. Teacher leadership was tapped as essential for success in an accountability environment, and principals recognized their responsibility for teacher support and for removing all barriers for teachers' self-growth. Calatri stated, "I see my job as being a service to the teachers."

Principals provided access to appropriate internal and external resources. A Bentley teacher observed, "You feel you can go to him. If funding is not available, he will find another way." Another striking commonality was how these principals accepted no barriers to providing the resources teachers needed. An Arno teacher shared, "He gets us any supplies . . . anything we need to work with in our classroom." Because supplies were plentiful at these schools, teachers shared. The sharing process underscored the collaborative approach and fostered the evolution to teacher leadership. Professional networking was encouraged both within and outside schools, and success depended on the recognition of teacher time as a valuable resource.

Time was an internal resource that was essential to professional networking. Information dissemination was efficiently handled at these schools because the principals and teachers were strategic about uses of time and used every opportunity for sharing information. These educators did not depend on formal meetings for professional networking. Informal interactions often served to share vital information.

Teacher decisions were binding even when they did not parallel those of the principal. Confidence in teacher expertise was evident in statements like the following from Principal Barnes: "They [teachers] have to have the information, and they will take it upon themselves to do what needs to be done." Support for teacher expertise tapped shared leadership as essential for success in an accountability environment. Teacher leaders shared the responsibility for goal attainment with their peers, worked collaboratively to make decisions, and recognized the importance of teacher decisions. Principals recognized powerful teacher leadership as a reward for surrounding themselves with excellent teachers. A Bentley teacher noted, "There is appreciation and support for the teachers."

These schools were successful because both principals and staff recognized the importance of appropriate resource provision and dedicated the time necessary for such discussions. Needs were openly discussed, as Adams exemplified: "All schools in the district get the same amount of money. We talk about how to use it." When time and resource identification were united, teacher leadership helped move to the forefront those issues that affected teachers in classrooms. At Cannon "[Calatri] gives us what we need to work with, supports us one hundred percent, and supports what we think needs to happen in our classrooms."

Generalizations to the Literature on School Leadership

The hypothesis grounding this study was that principals had incentives through the KERA reform package to elicit leadership from teachers. The three key findings from the cross-case analysis confirm this hypothesis and then some. Whereas many principals may be both fearful and mistrusting of mandated reform packages, Adams, Barnes, and Calatri, far from resenting "state authority," actually went beyond merely taking advantage of the opportunities for shared leadership required in the reform package. They used accountability, the consolidating planning, and their role as analytic guides to proactively craft reform measures (e.g., a focus on results, consolidated planning, classroom assessment, decentralization) in connecting themselves and teacher leaders around the common goal of improving student outcomes. Reform measures and leadership fused into one entity. The authors now make four generalizations to the school leadership literature.

First, this study's hypothesis confirms the work of Kelley (1998), who found that in successful Kentucky schools, teachers and principals worked together in ways that were "skilled and professional . . . to focus the curriculum and instruction" (p. 5). The national reform framework (e.g., site autonomy in exchange for accountability) plays into the hands of principals who both understand the conceptualization of the package and demonstrate by their actions the need to provide their schools with credible collaborative models: The source of the expertise (teacher, principal, etc.) does not matter; what matters is the quality of the expertise itself. The "indirect influence" (Glickman, 1991, p. 5) of these principals became apparent when they collaborated with teachers toward achieving common goals in a "results-through-others" approach.

Second, the three principals worked together with teachers to monitor progress toward accomplishing established goals. The critical importance of goals in school improvement has been documented for several decades (Chrispeels, Brown, & Castillo, 2000; Schmoker, 1996). Joyce, Wolf, and Calhoun (1993) best illustrated the importance of common goals when they documented that, in every successful school they studied, common goals were central to communication and school operation. These principals actualized the intent behind common goals when working with teachers to collaboratively develop and monitor common goals. Many of the goals (e.g., meeting the biennial growth targets established by the state assessment system) are done for them, freeing schools to figure how they might motivate their staffs to achieve the academic goals.

These principals interpreted KERA and the CP as "official-policy permissions" to share leadership. The critical importance of this interpretation is evident in Murphy's (1991) assertion that principals must accept the responsibility for school improvement as outlined in policy and communicate it in a way that causes teachers to accept the leadership responsibility. Good principals "accepted autonomy and accountability on behalf of the school and passed it on through the teaching staff" (Murphy, 1991, p. 26). Principals remain significant to school success in using the CP requirement as the organizer for their newfound autonomy. Moreover, they presented accountability as making shared leadership essential.

Third, principals as analytical guides providing resources complemented the culture of teacher professionalism and leadership. A major responsibility of these principals was providing an environment that nurtured teacher leadership. These principals exercised "skillful leadership to ensure that teachers can operate in an environment that values and takes advantage of what they know" (National Staff Development Council, 2000, p. 1). In addition to being analytical guides and promoters of teacher leadership, the principals were coordinators, supporters, and encouragers who knew they profited from teacher expertise. Shared leadership as a determinant for success with student achievement seemed a "core value" in these schools (Troen & Boles, 1994, p. 286). Principals acted as one player within the autonomous school unit spelled out by KERA, and they knew teachers were most intimately connected to student learning (Blase, 1989; Hallinger & Heck, 1996). Teachers were given additional recognition and responsibility and rose naturally to the occasion, as depicted by earlier researchers (David, 1994; Glickman, 1991; Kelley, 1998).

The threat of ambiguity for principals and teachers seem diminished when leadership responsibility was shared. Schmoker (1996) may be germane in his insight:

> Principals do not, at the ground level, have to implement instructional changes themselves. Teachers are vividly aware of this. Change has a much better chance of going forward when principals team up with teachers who help translate and negotiate new practices with the faculty. The combination of principals and teacher leaders is a potent combination. (p. 116)

Fourth, all three schools included shared leadership for collective accountability as a core value. The establishment of shared leadership as a practice was reviewed in individual case studies, but the common threads were relentless communication, confidence in teacher ability, and absence of hierarchy. DeBlois (2000) commented on the shared leadership model:

> Good leaders rely on the talent, commitment, and leadership of many people in the organization. Anyone who thinks that a good school is the responsibility of primarily one person is foolish. No leader or principal can be effective in overseeing, motivating, recognizing, and supporting every key individual in the school or community. (p. 26)

Because shared leadership for collective accountability was a core value, all individuals in these schools accepted the responsibility to oversee, motivate, recognize, and support.

Implications for Policy, Research, and Practice

This chapter ends with five implications based on this study. First, Adams, Barnes, and Calatri made conscious cognitive decisions to respond to KERA in a way that distributed leadership and responsibilities and openly recognized the collective influence of teachers in meeting accountability demands. This implication has a linkage to the literature on cognitive development. Spillane (2002, citing the work of Anderson & Smith, 1987; Confrey, 1990), for instance, is most instructive on this point: "Cognitive theory suggests that people use their prior knowledge and experiences to construct new understandings. Coming to know involves the reconstruction of exiting knowledge rather than passive consumption of knowledge" (p. 147). A research question emerging from this study is: How many of the 1300 principals in Kentucky have a similar grasp of the KERA conceptual framework? If they do, how did they learn about the framework? If not, they might be less predisposed to sharing the leadership with teachers than the three principals in the McDonald study. East (2003), a doctoral student at the University of Louisville, is using purposive sampling of teachers and principals in Kentucky and the interview-and-survey method to explore this question.

Second, past experiences informed each of the three principals as to what works best for continuously improving schools. (The reader may note that these three principals were seasoned veterans.) Although only one school formally participated in school-based decision making (reward schools could opt out of the statutory requirement), each principal articulated an explicit intent to share decision making. Two of the principals aligned their current leadership style with experiences in the Kentucky Effective Schools Network. A research question emerging from this study is: Are other Kentucky principals and, for that matter, principals across the United States aware of the shared-leadership opportunities emerging from the national reform framework that places immense pressure for public schools to perform at unprecedented standards (e.g., No Child Left Behind Legislation [NCLB] of 2002)?

Third, this analysis leads to another policy and research question. What about the projected massive retirement of Kentucky principals documented, for instance, by Winter and Morgenthal (2002) and by Winter, Rinehart, and Muñoz (2002)? Regarding recruitment, where can we find other candidates who welcome shared decision making, know that success with collective accountability rests in the composite knowledge of all adults, and are not threatened by assertive teacher leaders?

Fourth, it is significant that principals and teachers rarely if ever referred to their district in relation to shared leadership. This is not coincidental, because KERA made schools the center of reform and accountable for outcomes. District-level relationship building with the principal is not evident in this study's data. Because leadership from the district office did not surface, were these principals and teachers so assertive about their leadership that they could duplicate efforts (e.g., shared leadership, budget) that were traditionally the purview of the district office? Another question emerging from this study is, "How necessary is district leadership with the current reform cycle's school-based autonomy and state accountability?" We are currently investigating how one state education agency, Kentucky, provided resources and support in response to local school needs. Preliminary data from an interview with the commissioner of education identifies the need for a state agency to model the support function that districts are being asked to provide. This type of modeling is particularly warranted in high accountability environments such as those outlined in KERA and NCLB.

Last, this study reverberates with a key assertion by Fullan and Steigelbauer (1991), who claim that schools change and improve when both elements of centralization and decentralization (i.e., external pressure and internal professionalism) are applied within coherent policy frameworks. In this chapter we confirm this strong speculation: state policies, contrary to rebuttals by their critics, can have positive affects on schools as organizations. Kentucky legislators intended to implement significant changes in curriculum, instruction, and assessment through both accountability and decentralizing measures within a reasonably coherent framework. Now the task is to recruit, train, and place more principals like Adams, Barnes, and Calatri for America's 89,000 schools. This is a daunting challenge for the new millennium.

Appendix A

Kentucky Accountability for Continuous Improvement

Kentucky schools that score at least 1% above their thresholds and that move 10% of students scoring "novice" to a higher performance level receive financial rewards, which are divided according to the wishes of the majority of educators at the school. Schools not achieving their thresholds receive varying levels of assistance and/or sanctions, depending on how close they come to their threshold.

The KERA accountability index is based on a formula that weights student performance in terms of four performance standards: (1) Novice—0; (b) Apprentice—0.4; (3) Proficient—1.0; and (4) Distinguished—1.4. Novice students recall some relevant information but show minimal understanding of core concepts, for example, whereas distinguished students demonstrate in-depth understanding of concepts and/or processes and solve challenging problems using innovative and efficient strategies.

A given accountability index is calculated by multiplying the percent of students at each performance level by its corresponding weight and then adding the products. When 100% of students are proficient, the index is 100 (i.e., the concluding goal). The accountability index indicates how many students in a given school are performing in terms of the percent of novice, apprentice, proficient, and distinguished.

The graduated elevation of assessment scores every two years is referred to as the *biennial bar*. The Kentucky performance-based assessment program ensured school accountability for student achievement of the broad goals set forth in KERA. The performance assessment was first administered during the 1991–92 school year, and those results were used to determine a baseline accountability index for every school. The baseline was then used to set a progressively increased threshold (i.e., goal) that the school must reach every two years to obtain rewards or avoid sanctions.

Appendix B

Description of Teacher Leaders Used in Selection of Interview Participants

Teacher leaders are those teachers who are highly respected by other teachers and by the principal and who are involved in improving the schools in ways that reach beyond the walls of their classroom. Teacher leaders are "fully empowered partners in shaping policy, creating curriculum, managing budgets, improving practice, and bringing added value to the goal of improving education for children" (Troen & Boles, 1994, p. 276). Teacher leaders reach beyond what good teachers have always done in classrooms and share decision making with principals.

Appendix C

Initial Principal Interview

1. Please describe your vision for this school. (Smith & Andrews, 1989)

2. Has the historically established hierarchy with principal as sole leader of the school changed to accommodate teacher leadership since KERA? If so, please explain.

3. Explain the relationships among you as principal, the teacher leaders, and other teachers both prior to and following KERA? (Smylie & Denny, 1990)

4. Who are the teacher leaders in this school?

5. How did formal teacher leadership roles evolve? (Troen & Boles, 1994).

Appendix D

Initial Teacher Leader Interview

1. What guides the work of teacher leaders in this school? (Smith & Andrews, 1989)
2. What defines the support for the role of the teacher leader in this school? (Troen & Boles, 1994)
3. How is the role of the teacher leader defined in this school? (Troen & Boles, 1994)
4. What activity has the principal performed that you think most contributed to increasing student achievement? (Schmoker & Wilson, 1994)
5. How did individual teachers assume responsibility for different elements of change in this school before and following KERA? (Fullan, 1994)
6. Explain the relationships among the principal, teacher leaders, and other teachers in this school? (Smylie & Denny, 1990)
7. How do teacher leaders deal with the norms of teachers' professional independence and shared status among teachers? (Troen & Boles, 1994)
8. Explain information sharing in this school. (Schmoker & Wilson, 1994)
9. What are the weaknesses in leadership in this school? (Troen & Boles, 1994)
10. Who are other teacher leaders in this school?
11. How did formal teacher leadership roles evolve? (Troen & Boles, 1994)

References

Blase, J. J. (1989). The micropolitics of the school: The everyday political orientation of teachers toward open school principals. *Educational Administration Quarterly, 25,* 377–407.

Chrispeels, J. H., Brown, J. H., & Castillo, S. (2000). School leadership teams: Factors that influence their development and effectiveness. In K. Leithwood (Ed), *Understanding schools as intelligent systems,* Vol. 4 (pp. 39–73). Greenwich, CT: JAI Press, Inc.

Clift, R., Johnson, M., Holland, P., & Veal, M. L. (1992). Developing the potential for collaborative school leadership. *American Educational Research Journal, 29,* 877–908.

Coffee, A., & Atkinson, P. (1996). *Making sense of qualitative data: Complementary research strategies.* Thousand Oaks, CA: Sage.

Creswell, J. W. (1994). *Research design: Qualitative and quantitative approaches.* Thousand Oaks, CA: Sage.

David, J. L. (1994). School-based decision making: Kentucky's test of decentralization. *Phi Delta Kappan, 75,* 706–712.

DeBlois, R. (2000). The everyday work of leadership. *Phi Delta Kappan, 82,* 25–28.

East, M. (2003). *Teacher and principal conceptualization of the Kentucky Education Reform Act.* Unpublished manuscript.

Fullan, M. G. (1994). Teacher leadership: A failure to conceptualize. In D. R. Walling (Ed.), *Teachers as leaders: Perspectives on the professional development of teachers* (pp. 241–254). Bloomington, IN: Phi Delta Kappa Educational Foundation.

Fullan, M. G., & Steigelbauer, S. (1991). *The new meaning of educational change* (2nd ed.). New York: Teachers College Press.

Glickman, C. D. (1991). Pretending not to know what we know. *Educational Leadership, 48*(8), 4–10.

Goodlad, J. I. (1984). *A place called school: Prospects for the future.* New York: McGraw Hill.

Hallinger, P., & Heck, R. H. (1996). Reassessing the principal's role in school effectiveness: A review of empirical research, 1980–1995. *Educational Administration Quarterly, 31,* 5–44.

Hart, A. W. (1990). Impacts of the school social unit on teacher authority during work redesign. *American Educational Research Journal, 27,* 503–532.

Holmes Group. (1986). *Tomorrow's teachers: A report of the Holmes Group.* East Lansing, MI: Author.

Hunter, F. (1953). *Community power structure.* Chapel Hill: University of North Carolina Press.

Hurley, J. C. (2001, May 23). The principalship: Less may be more. *Education Week, 20*(37), 37, 39.

Joyce, B., Wolf, J., & Calhoun, E. (1993). *The self-renewing school.* Alexandria, VA: Association of Supervision and Curriculum Development.

Keedy, J. L., & Achilles, C. M. (1997). The need for school-constructed theories in practice in U.S. school restructuring. *Journal of Educational Administration, 35*, 102–121.

Kelley, C. K. (1998). The Kentucky school-based performance award program: School-level effects. *Educational Policy, 12*(3), 305–324.

Legislative Research Commission. (1994). *A citizen's handbook: The Kentucky Education Reform Act*. Frankfort, KY: Author.

McDonald, D. H. (2001). *Principal and teacher shared leadership in the Kentucky low-income high achievement schools: Accountability in a high stakes environment*. Unpublished doctoral dissertation (UMI Number 3015270). Louisville, KY: University of Louisville.

McDonald, D. H., Keedy, J. L. (2002). *Principals as teacher leaders in the Kentucky Education Reform Act era: Laying the groundwork for high-achieving, low income schools*. ERIC Digest (Document EA 031733, ERIC Publication # ED 466031) Eugene, OR: ERIC Clearinghouse on Educational Management.

Merriam, S. B. (1998). *Case study research in education: A qualitative approach* (2nd ed.). San Francisco: Jossey-Bass.

Miles, M. S., & Huberman, A. M. (1994). *Qualitative data analysis: An expanded sourcebook of new methods* (2nd ed.). Thousand Oaks, CA: Sage.

Murphy, J. (1991). *School restructuring: Capturing and assessing the phenomena*. New York: Teachers College Press.

National Staff Development Council. (2000). *Learning to lead, leading to learn: Improving school quality through principal professional development* [Online]. Available: *www.nsdc.org/leader_report.html*

Rallis, S., & Highsmith, M. C. (1986). The myth of the great principal. . . . *Phi Delta Kappan, 68*, 300–304.

Rosenholtz, S. (1989). *Teacher's workplace: A social-organizational analysis*. New York: Longman.

Schmoker, M. (1996). *Results: The key to continuous school improvement*. Alexandria, VA: Association for Supervision and Curriculum Development.

Schmoker, M. J., & Wilson, R. B. (1994). Redefining results: Implications for teacher leadership and professionalism. In D. R. Walling (Ed.), *Teachers as leaders: Perspectives on the professional development of teachers* (pp. 137–150). Bloomington, IN: Phi Delta Kappa Educational Foundation.

Smith, W. R., & Andrews, R. L. (1989). *Instructional leadership: How principals make a difference*. Alexandria, VA: Association for Supervision and Curriculum Development.

Smylie, M. A., & Denny, J. W. (1990). Teacher leadership: Tensions and ambiguities in organizational perspective. *Educational Administration Quarterly, 26*, 235–259.

Spillane, J. P. (2002). District policymaking and state standards: A cognitive perspective. In A. M. Hightower, M. S. Knapp, J. A. Marsh, & M. W. McLaughlin (Eds.), *Implementation in school districts and instructional renewal* (pp. 143–159). New York: Teachers College Press.

Troen, V., & Boles, K. (1994). Two teachers examine the power of teacher leadership. In D. R. Walling (Ed.), *Teachers as leaders: Perspectives on the professional development of teachers* (pp. 275–286). Bloomington, IN: Phi Delta Kappa Educational Foundation.

Whitaker, K. S. (1997). Developing teacher leaders and the management team concept: A case study. *The Teacher Educator, 33,* 1–16.

Winter, P. A., & Morgenthal, J. R. (2002). Principal recruitment in a reform environment: Effects of school achievement and school level on applicant attraction to the job. *Educational Administration Quarterly, 38,* 319–340.

Winter, P. A., Rinehart, J. S., & Muñoz, M. A. (2002). Principal recruitment: An empirical evaluation of a school district's internal pool of principal certified personnel. *Journal of Personnel Evaluation in Education, 16,* 129–141.

Yin, R. K. (1994). *Case study research: Design and methods.* Thousand Oaks, CA: Sage.

10

Principal Choice and Teacher Participation in Site-Based Management

Four Schools Implement One Policy

S. David Brazer

While teaching an education finance class one evening, I steered the discussion toward collaborative decision making regarding school budget allocations. By this time in the semester, most of the students had discovered that their school's budget is a closely guarded secret and were cynical about the possibility of teachers and parents influencing the allocation of resources. I turned to one student from Prince William County, Virginia, and asked, "You have site-based management in your county. Isn't your budgeting process much more open?" He acknowledged that it is, but he also explained that site-based management (SBM) did not always mean that teachers had a hand in shaping the budget. The student explained that mentioning SBM in the district was generally met with eye rolling, groaning, and claims that, although decision making may have moved from the central

AUTHOR'S NOTE: Interview-based quotations used in this chapter were reprinted with permission from their anonymous sources.

office to the school sites, it did not get much beyond the principal's office. I was intrigued to learn more about both the policy and the practice of site-based management in Prince William County.

The challenge of improving student performance generates cyclical shifts in beliefs about the appropriate roles of and relationships between school administrators and teachers in the educational process. Autocratic, take-charge leadership is embraced at one time, then replaced by SBM at other times in an effort to address student achievement, community participation, budget reductions, or other challenges. Site-based management may subsequently be replaced by a return to more centralization and greater emphasis on hierarchy when new stressors impact school districts (Murphy & Beck, 1995; Wohlstetter & Odden, 1992). The current emphases on test scores and holding administrators responsible for student achievement seem to influence school leadership away from collaboration and toward a more traditional hierarchical model (Elmore, 1993; Tyack, 1993).

Despite the cyclical nature of school management fashions, some districts still have in place strong SBM policies, which provide interesting research contexts for examining the problems and promise of principals and teachers sharing leadership. This chapter explores how SBM is implemented and practiced at the school level in a district with a sustained and long-standing SBM policy. It seeks to gain a clearer understanding of the variations in four schools implementing SBM and shared decision making under this policy. The choices that principals make in how much decision making they will share with site-based governance committees and what decision authority they will retain for themselves are critical features of policy implementation. The following research questions guide this study:

1. How is site-based management policy implemented at four school sites (one elementary, one middle, and two high schools) within one school district?
   - What committees have been established to implement SBM?
   - What kinds of decisions are made through the SBM processes?
   - To what extent do teachers at each of the four sites participate in decision making and believe they have an influence?
2. What choices do principals make in implementing shared decision making, and how do they define their decision-making role within the SBM process?

How Prince William County Defines Site-Based Management

The concept of site-based management, or SBM, has been defined differently in different settings; therefore it is important to understand the context of

SBM for this study. The Prince William County Public Schools (PWCS) have pursued an SBM policy since 1987, which means the policy can be considered a mature one that has been modified over time. Following a deliberate process of educating the school board and key teachers and administrators, visiting other school districts, and piloting SBM in selected schools, PWCS moved to district-wide implementation of SBM at all 64 comprehensive elementary, middle, and high schools in the 1990–91 academic year (Neal, n.d.; PWCS, 1990). Just a few years after full implementation, PWCS was identified in a study of SBM as one of several exemplary models in North America (Ogawa & White, 1994) and again a few years later (Robertson & Briggs, 1998).

The espoused rationale behind SBM is to improve the quality of education within the school district. Though not startling, it is interesting to see that a direct link is made between greater discretion in school management and the school district's primary goal—student achievement:

> School-based management is . . . designed to improve the quality of education for all students. It is a process through which the decisions most directly affecting the schools and the instructional process are made at the school level rather than by the central office departments. . . . The primary purpose of school-based management is to improve education by empowering schools to be more responsive and adaptive to change and to unleash productive local potential to move the division toward fulfilling its mission and goals. (PWCS, 1990, pp. 2–3)[1]

The PWCS rationale for implementing SBM is consistent with the effort to improve the quality of educational decisions that motivates implementation of this management process in school districts across the country (Beck & Murphy, 1996).

The specific context of PWCS policies and procedures defines three basic categories of decisions. First, the central office has made decisions the sites must abide by. These include (1) the policy requiring SBM, (2) the establishment of a central committee made up of school community representatives—often referred to as the Principal's Advisory Council (PAC), (3) curriculum, which includes curriculum guidelines for all subjects and grade levels and corresponding district-wide tests, (4) school achievement targets, (5) creation and periodic revision of the school plan, and (6) specialty school status (Figure 10.1). The second category is the specific decisions the district mandates schools to make, including developing a two-year school plan, drawing up a budget, and determining staff allocation. A third category of decisions is implicitly within the discretion of sites because the central office does not explicitly make them: (1) site-level curricular choices (e.g., which approved books to use), (2) instructional strategies, (3) staff development, (4) school climate, (5) technology implementation, and (6) routine procedures.

Figure 10.1 displays the three types of decisions and their relationships. Schools exist within a district context that has many influences in addition to SBM. Therefore, the school district circle is larger than SBM itself. The arrows from the box labeled "District SBM-Related Decisions" indicate that central office decisions influence individual school's SBM-related decisions. The dashed line creating the school site oval shows that the school's organizational boundaries are permeable, at least as far as the district is concerned. As mentioned earlier, school-site decisions fall into two general types—mandated and discretionary. The two exist together and influence each other but in ambiguous ways. For example, schools are required to make staffing allocation decisions, but those decisions may result in a technology specialist at one school and a reading specialist at another. The shading from gray to white in the "Site Decisions" oval conveys the distinct yet related nature of the two types of site decisions. The specific decisions named in Figure 10.1 are discussed in more detail in the "Principals' and Teachers' Perspectives on Site-Based Decision Making" section later in this chapter.

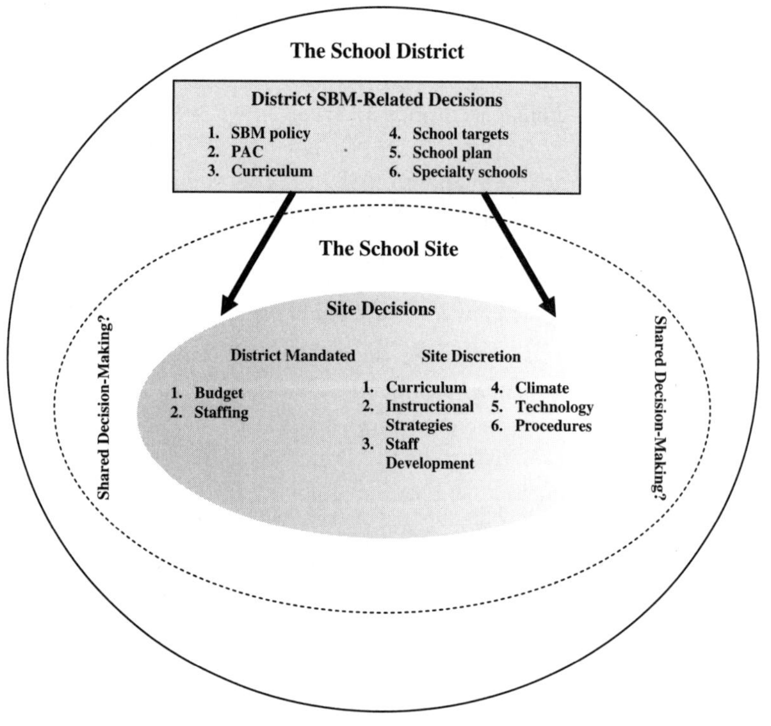

Figure 10.1 PWCS Central Office and Site Level Decisions and Their Relationships

The main purpose of engaging in SBM is to move decisions into the hands of those who understand school-site educational problems best—teachers, site administrators, and parents (Beck & Murphy, 1996; PWCS, 1990; Winter, Keedy, & Newton, 2000; Wohlstetter & Mohrman, 1994). It is often assumed that shared decision making, defined as principals sharing authority with teachers and others, is embedded in SBM. However, SBM policies frequently indicate only which decisions the district will retain and which will be made by the site. Shared decision making, in contrast, addresses the question of how much teachers, parents, and possibly students participate in the decision-making process and how much influence they have (Weiss, 1995). Whether or not shared decision making actually occurs depends largely on the choices that principals make about using it. They have substantial discretion over which decisions delegated to the sites will be addressed and how stakeholders at the site will be involved. It is possible, within a district, for principals to vary substantially in the degree to which they share decisions that the central office has delegated to them (Haskin, 1995; Weiss, 1995). Consequently, shared decision making is presented as a question in the school site oval of Figure 10.1.

Methodology and Data Sources

Six schools were recruited to participate in this study of how SBM policy is implemented in PWCS. Two declined, leaving four participating sites: two high schools, one middle school, and one elementary school. The schools represent the demographic range of students in the county and reflect the racial, ethnic, and socioeconomic diversity of the greater Washington D.C. metropolitan area. Pseudonyms have been substituted for the four participating schools and their principals. See Table 10.1 for general profiles of participating schools.

Research questions that focus on decision making are best addressed through a mixed-method approach so that both processes and outcomes may be understood. Structured interviews reveal principals' perspectives on the ways in which SBM works at specific sites. A faculty questionnaire reveals how teachers in general perceive the practice of SBM at their schools.

Interviews with all four participating principals were conducted between November 2000 and April 2001. The principal-interview data addresses both research questions by revealing which decisions principals choose to submit to their SBM processes and the ways in which they involve others in

Table 10.1 Participating School Sites and Their Unique Committees

	School			
	O'Connor High School	*Earhart High School*	*Central Middle School*	*Madison Elementary School*
Demographics	Principal: Dave Keller	Principal: Tom Riddle	Principal: Betty Grubowski	Principal: Karen Phillips
	Student Population: 2,200 (nonwhite = 47%; free/reduced lunch = 13%)	Student Population: 2,450 (nonwhite = 38%; free/reduced lunch = 20%)	Student Population: 1,100 (nonwhite = 45%; free/reduced lunch = 37%)	Student Population: 584 (nonwhite = 62%; free/reduced lunch = 22.5%)
	Number of Teachers: 155	Number of Teachers: 161	Number of Teachers: 75	Number of Teachers: 45
Unique Committees	• Staff Development Committee • Ad hoc committees • Focus groups	• Instructional Improvement Council • Committees associated with the effective schools correlates • Committees for other school needs	• Multicultural Committee	• No unique committees

making SBM decisions. The principal interviews have been transcribed and analyzed using a coding system and NVivo software. The following general areas were used in the coding process:

- Central office decisions
- Site decisions
- Decision-making committees
- Principal's role in decision making

During 2000–01 all four sites participated in a survey distributed to all staff present during a scheduled faculty meeting. The response rates were as follows: O'Connor High School, 106 teachers (68%); Earhart High School, 112 teachers (70%); Central Middle School, 52 teachers (69%); and Madison Elementary School, 34 teachers (76%).

The questionnaire completed by the faculty provides insights into the first research question by yielding data about the areas in which site-based management is active (e.g., budget, staffing, school plan, etc.) and the degree to which faculty participate in decision making. The questionnaire also permits a comparison of teacher perceptions of shared decision making to principals' descriptions of their own roles in the decision-making process—thereby addressing the second question.

Committees: Where Site-Based Management Happens

Teachers, parents, and administrators engage in the SBM process through their participation on the Principal's Advisory Council (PAC) and other committees set up for the purpose of making site-based decisions. School personnel may also engage in SBM through typical meetings involving all faculty, individual departments, department chairs, team leaders, or grade-level leaders. Each school has a somewhat different committee structure, based in part on the size of the school and based in large measure on the principal's preference. Committees serve as the arenas in which facts, opinions, perspectives, and interests come together as decisions are crafted. Examining committee and meeting dynamics is crucial to understanding how SBM really works.

Committee Structures

The Principal's Advisory Council. As indicated in Figure 10.1, the district requires schools to create a PAC or equivalent group to serve as the central decision-making committee for the school. PACs are typically composed of teachers, parents, and administrators. High school PACs may also include one or two students. Grade levels, teams, or departments may nominate teachers to serve on the PAC, or the principal may choose faculty members. The process of selecting teachers often seems to involve the principal cajoling reluctant individuals to join the group. Parents are typically invited to join as representatives of specific neighborhoods in the school's attendance area. PACs generally meet once a month to discuss an agenda that may be prepared by the principal or another member of the group.

The four participating principals agree that their PACs will make decisions regarding their budget and staffing (embedded in the school plan required by the school district), technology, and school climate. How PACs work on decisions is ambiguous, however, and seems to vary from school to school. The principal impacts the role of the PAC by writing or approving the agenda, structuring the meeting, and establishing routines for handling agenda items. Any given principal exercises different degrees of influence and control, depending on how the agenda is established and the meeting is run. In some schools, the PAC may be a discussion group, while in others it could be a rubber stamp for the principal. Furthermore, the role of the PAC appears to shift depending on the issue. A principal may discuss parent outreach in a much more open-ended way than she discusses the budget proposal she must submit to the central office. The typical PAC dynamic appears to be that the principal brings issues before the committee for general discussion and information gathering. At a subsequent meeting, the principal will present narrowed options or predetermined solutions, seeking ratification for a specific choice.

Another factor that makes the precise nature of the PAC's role in decision making difficult to pin down is the problem of expertise. PAC members are expected to represent the different interests of parents, teachers, departments, and the like, which happens naturally. Members often lack knowledge, however, on specific issues. The budget is a good example. Parents and teachers are not likely to have an in-depth understanding of the budget to match that of the principal. Furthermore, whatever budget expertise they do acquire comes from the principal and is therefore filtered by the principal to serve specific needs.

Whatever PAC members' roles and influence on the committee may be, it is clear that the PAC is a locus of power within the SBM process at all four schools. Other committees generate ideas and proposals, but major schoolwide decisions are implemented only with formal PAC approval. The PACs appear to be the gatekeepers for site-based decisions.

Other School Committees. In addition to the PAC, a range of other committees operates in participating schools. All four schools have in common typical committees found in most schools (e.g., department chairs, team or grade-level leaders, etc.), as well as a Technology Committee. Although I found no evidence for a central office mandate to establish such a committee, the principals appear to believe that a group of school-community members should guide the acquisition and use of technology. Similar to a committee of department chairs, this is the kind of committee that seems likely to be found in any school during the current period of rapid technology implementation.

The committee structure helps to drive the kinds of decisions that are made at the school site. Three of the four schools have established unique or issue-focused committees to help address identified needs. The differences among the schools are highlighted in Table 10.1. It is important to note that the high schools tend to have a more differentiated committee structure, most likely reflecting their larger size and program complexity. O'Connor reported the most flexible structure with the use of ad hoc committees to handle specific issues and focus groups for discussion with and feedback to the principal. Earhart High School has not only an Instructional Improvement Council, but also committees established to address the Effective Schools Correlates. In contrast, the only unique committee at the middle school is the Multicultural Committee, which reflects the school's current focus. Other than the Technology Committee found at all schools, the elementary school has no issue-specific committees. The smaller size of the elementary school may enable a leaner structure that ensures levels of faculty involvement similar to the larger schools.

What Committees Do

This chapter focuses on how decisions are made at school sites under the SBM umbrella. By engaging in SBM, the school district submits decision opportunities (e.g., developing a school plan and a budget) to the schools. What happens to those decision opportunities once they enter the school site is what I define as the SBM process. Committees appear to play an important role in this process, but the exact nature of that role is unclear and it seems to vary from school to school and, potentially, from decision to decision. Furthermore, committees' interactions with the principal, the PAC, and/or the faculty as a whole add greater complexity to understanding what committees do and how the SBM process works. What can be determined at this point is which committees exist (as described earlier) and teachers' perceptions regarding decisions they have either participated in making or have observed others making.

Committee structure helps to drive the kinds of decisions that are made at the school site because committee responsibilities focus attention on specific issues. Understanding teachers' awareness of the types of decisions made within the committee structure reveals their important perspective on SBM. On the questionnaire, staff were asked to indicate SBM activities that they had observed or participated in, either in committees or as a whole faculty. The results are presented in Table 10.2, with the highest percentage chosen for each school in boldface. Five major areas emerged from the questionnaire: (1) curriculum planning and material selection, (2) development of the school plan, (3) staff development planning, (4) budget planning and allocation, and (5) personnel selection. The results are generally, though not entirely, consistent with each school's committee structure.

The most consistent trends across all four schools are for one-half to two-thirds of the respondents to select curriculum planning/materials selection and development of school plan as SBM activities they know about at their school. Consistency with regard to development of the school plan is not surprising because the district mandates that school plans be written every two years. What is more unexpected is the popularity of the curriculum choice because principals discuss curriculum as a clear prerogative of the central office (see discussion in the "Curriculum" section later in this chapter). Approximately half of the teachers at the four schools also chose staff development planning, but approximately three-fourths of teachers at Madison responding to the survey selected it, suggesting a difference in the way this issue is handled at the elementary school. Personnel selection is a traditional responsibility of the principal in collaboration with the central office, making faculty participation in those decisions a less common event, and small proportions of teachers at three of the four schools selected it as an SBM activity. It is reasonable to infer from the data in Table 10.2 that PACs are addressing issues of site curricular choices, the school plan, and

Table 10.2 Site-Based Management Activities Observed/Participated In

	School				
SBM Activity	*O'Connor H.S. (N = 106)*	*Earhart H.S. (N = 112)*	*Central M.S. (N = 52)*	*Madison E.S. (N = 34)*	*Average Across Schools*
Curriculum Planning/ Materials Selection	59 (55.7%)	**72 (64.3%)**	**35 (67.3%)**	16 (47.0%)	**58.6%**
Development of School Plan	**62 (58.5%)**	56 (50.0%)	28 (53.8%)	23 (67.6%)	57.5%
Staff Development Planning	54 (50.9%)	52 (46.4%)	27 (51.9%)	26 (76.5%)	56.4%
Budget Planning and Allocation	33 (31.1%)	43 (38.4%)	30 (57.7%)	**32 (94.1%)**	55.3%
Personnel Selection	10 (9.4%)	37 (33.0%)	15 (28.8%)	19 (55.9%)	31.8%
School Averages	41.1%	46.4%	51.9%	**68.22%**	

staff development planning, but they are less likely to be involved in budget planning (with the notable exception of Madison) and personnel selection.

Table 10.2 reveals areas of difference and suggests the individual character of schools engaged in SBM. The boldfaced figures indicate the most commonly chosen activities at each school site. Teachers at Earhart and Central made curriculum planning/materials selection their most common choice, but the results at the other two schools are quite different. The highest percentage of respondents at O'Connor chose development of school plan, and teachers at Madison were nearly unanimous about budget planning and allocation. The perceptions of teachers regarding SBM decisions are most consistent with principal emphases at O'Connor, Earhart, and Madison, and they are less consistent at Central (see the following discussion) as indicated by examining prominent areas that emerged from principal interviews.

Principals' and Teachers' Perspectives on Site-Based Decision Making

The wide variation in teachers' perceptions regarding budget planning and allocation (from a low of 31.1% at O'Connor to a high of 94.1% at Madison) demonstrates how a district-mandated SBM decision can have widely varying degrees of participation associated with it. Understanding why different schools emphasize different kinds of decisions in SBM begins with the principals' perspectives.

Curriculum. Principal Riddle at Earhart was the only one who emphasized curricular issues in his interview. He has established and encouraged the Instructional Improvement Council at Earhart, a committee unique among the four schools. Consistent with Riddle's emphasis, a large proportion of Earhart teachers (64.3%) identify curriculum planning as a site-based decision in which they participate. Although the other principals did not discuss curriculum decisions in ways similar to Riddle, Central Middle School actually has a slightly higher proportion of teachers reporting curriculum planning as an SBM activity (67.3%) compared to Earhart (Table 10.2.) O'Connor High School teachers were only somewhat less likely to select curriculum planning/materials selection (55.7%), which is surprising given Principal Keller's deemphasis on curriculum and the absence of a curriculum-oriented committee in the large high school.

An apparent contradiction exists when everyone interviewed agrees that curriculum is a central office prerogative, yet large proportions of teachers believe that curriculum planning/materials selection is an activity they have either observed or participated in. Curriculum appears to have separate district and site components. The central office works with the school board to adopt an official curriculum, along with texts to support it, that is consistent with state standards and meets the needs of the school district. The central office is also responsible for monitoring that curriculum through student testing and supervision. When teachers refer to their role in curricular decisions, they probably have in mind figuring out how to meet district standards through basic planning and materials selection. Designing specific lessons and units is, naturally, the bread-and-butter of teaching. To the extent that collaborative planning within teams, departments, or committees exists, teachers will perceive curriculum planning/materials selection as a common site-based decision.

Definitions of and distinctions among the terms "curriculum," "program," and "instruction" are not entirely clear. Riddle at Earhart, for example, looks at the board-adopted curriculum as an umbrella under which he must keep the school. He can add or delete some items from the curriculum, but the basics must be there and he must not allow the school to get out from under the umbrella by trying to implement nonapproved curricula. The following portion of Riddle's interview illustrates how he used the Instructional Improvement Council to consider a curricular question:

> [Principal Riddle]: I made a recommendation [to the Instructional Improvement Council] to . . . look at re-instituting the German program. . . . I sent them a memorandum. I said I need your support or concerns about whether we should bring German back. The question I got was, Why not Latin? My response to that was that there were students taking German in the middle school. Two of our three feeder middle schools were going to start a German program. It seemed logical that we should have something in place for them when they get here. Then, perhaps, look at bringing back Latin. It was my intention to do that, but we should probably phase them in one at a time. Sent that response back to the committee. The committee said, "Oh, that makes sense."
>
> So, the Instructional Improvement Council wrote a document that said, "[W]hile we recognize the concerns of French teachers and the dwindling numbers in French and the increasing numbers in Spanish, we still think the Principal's recommendation for bringing German into the school is a good one and it does have our support from the standpoint of whatever it would cost to hire a new teacher for German." So, that went to the School Planning Council [a.k.a. the PAC] as a discussion item in preparation for the School Plan and the budget process, and one drives the other. Suddenly from the floor, without any word . . . I had no idea this was going to happen, somebody said, "Rather than bring German or Latin, we should institute a sign language program." (Riddle interview, 12/04/00)

When we discussed my view that Riddle was working on curriculum, he argued that the foreign language decision is a program decision, not curriculum. Riddle's point was that he would never try to alter the board-adopted curriculum for a particular subject (informal meeting with Riddle, 1/25/02). The term "curriculum" is ambiguous and may be interpreted differently by principals and teachers alike.

Keller at O'Connor is even more emphatic in his expression of the belief that curriculum questions are out of bounds for school committees.

> [Interviewer]: You were talking about initiatives, though, in the last part. I assume you're speaking of curricular initiatives. We want to make, perhaps, some changes in the way in which we teach or what we teach?
>
> [Principal Keller]: I think pedagogy, or the methodology that we use with our students. The curricula throughout the school are developed at a [district] level, but that development employs teachers from each of the sites. (Keller interview, 01/30/01)

Keller's adamancy on this point is somewhat at odds with his faculty's perception of their involvement in curricular decisions.

Staff Development. Principal Keller at O'Connor High School has chosen to address instructional strategies through a Staff Development Committee—an emphasis that did not come out in other principal interviews. This item is among the top three most frequently chosen SBM activities at O'Connor, and likewise across the four schools (Table 10.2). Keller explains the significance of the Staff Development Committee:

> [Interviewer]: [T]he faculty . . . decided that you wanted to have your own site-based staff development in addition to what the county provides?
>
> [Principal Keller]: That was more of the Staff Development Committee, with the approval of the PAC, which is our Principal's Advisory Council.
>
> [T]eachers are the ones that are going to be involving themselves in staff development. If they are subjected to sit-and-get-it type opportunities or they register for a class or they go to hear this person speak. . . . That's not the end-all of staff development. Action research or working with a colleague, mentoring, mapping of instruction—there are other ways that we develop ourselves professionally as teachers that probably have a greater impact on our ability to teach kids than going to a conference, than going to these other [passive activities]. . . . [Our plan] says here are four different ways to learn, basically, that you could develop your own plan. . . . If I can do my own little mini-research on failure rates in my Algebra I class and I can share those results with my colleagues who are teaching Algebra I, that may spur some ideas in their heads as to how to remedy that. (Keller interview, 01/30/01)

As clear as Keller may be about his emphasis on staff development, the faculty appear to have a somewhat different perspective because staff development planning doesn't stand out to the extent that budget planning and allocation does at Madison or curriculum does at Earhart. Keller's emphasis on the school plan may overshadow specific decision-making areas when it comes to the formation of teachers' perspectives.

Although the other three principals did not emphasize staff development in their interviews, large proportions of their faculties selected staff development planning as an activity they had either observed or participated in, Madison at a far greater rate than O'Connor. Riddle at Earhart and Grubowski at Central did not discuss staff development, while Phillips at Madison mentioned it only as a budget issue. Teachers may be given opportunities to plan staff development activities outside of the SBM committee structure (e.g., in teams or departments) and yet regard staff development decisions as part of SBM because they are involved in making site-level decisions about it. Principals, on the other hand, may be less inclined to think of staff development as part of SBM if it does not emerge on PAC agendas as an issue. Keller was the only principal who made any indication that staff development might be a topic of discussion in the PAC. The staff development data suggest that principals and their teachers may not have consistent perceptions about all of the SBM activities taking place in their schools.

Cultural Diversity. Although all of the principals discuss school climate issues that could be addressed through SBM (most of them speaking in specific terms about attendance and discipline), Betty Grubowski at Central Middle School uniquely emphasizes cultural diversity—a subset of school climate—as an area of site decision making. Her goal is to make all students and their families feel welcome in her school. Grubowski's discussion of cultural diversity appears consistent with her establishment of the Multicultural Committee:

> [Principal Grubowski]: I have an emerging Hispanic population. We have felt a strong need to figure out a way to bring that culture into our school on a regular basis. So, we designed a bilingual parents' academy. For five sessions, we bring an entire family. We teach ESOL [English Speakers of Other Languages] . . . skills. We give them an opportunity to understand how to set up homework. Then we split the families up. We take our children and give them an individualized education program for reading and math. We take the parents who have limited English and we begin some basic English as a Second Language instruction. (Grubowski interview, 02/04/01)

It is difficult to gauge the faculty's perceptions relative to their principal on the importance of climate because neither school climate nor cultural diversity were choices on the teacher survey.

Budget. During her interview, Principal Phillips at Madison Elementary speaks frequently about budget issues. She begins when describing the district's entry into SBM:

> I remember . . . the associate superintendent [showing] us piece-by-piece how central office money was assigned to our school-based budget. . . . It was almost like a graduate course in how [the budget] was built from all of the money really being spent centrally to it being moved to [the sites]. . . . We also had to learn how to really be budget holders. Some principals had not had that much experience in managing and balancing . . . creating, managing, and balancing a budget. (Phillips interview, 11/15/00)

Phillips also describes the budget-making process when asked about the kinds of decisions addressed in SBM:

> Well, it's just almost everything in the sense that certainly the forming of the budget is a huge part that starts in February—January to February—and really does not play out until we get the final count on September 30th. So, we spend a huge amount of the year talking either about the upcoming budget or managing the current budget. I would say the budget piece—the amount of money that we're given per student to really run and staff the school—is a huge part of it. (Phillips interview, 11/15/00)

The perception that budget dominates SBM at Madison is confirmed by teacher survey data. Although budget planning is only the fourth most commonly chosen SBM activity across the four schools, it ranks first at Madison with 94.1%—all but two teachers—indicating that they have either observed or participated in this activity. Despite a small amount of discretionary revenue in the budget, the power associated with allocating resources may be a source of the greater sense of influence teachers perceive at Madison (see "Teachers' Roles in Decision Making" section).

The "School Averages" row in Table 10.2 shows the possible influence of school size on teacher experiences of the site-based management process. The high schools are more than twice the size of the middle school, with enrollments between 2,200 and 2,500 students. The average percentage selection of the five items listed in the questionnaire is noticeably smaller for the two high schools than it is for Central Middle School and Madison Elementary School. Central, in turn, is approximately twice as large as Madison and has an overall lower selection rate. Smaller school size may be

Table 10.3 Principals' Mention of Unique Site Decisions

O'Connor H.S.	*Earhart H.S.*	*Central M.S.*	*Madison E.S.*
Specific staff allocations (i.e., modifying class sizes at different grade levels)	Attendance policies	Saturday Scholars Structure of Signet (gifted program) Discipline Bilingual parents academy Every teacher teaching reading in small groups once per week	Looping Reading Recovery (although this was later mandated by the central office) Procedural issues such as how students enter and exit the building Discipline plan

associated with teachers being more aware of SBM decisions because of greater ease of communication. Furthermore, smaller schools appear to have greater collaborative potential because they have a greater proportion of teachers participating in decisions on fewer committees that address a greater number of decisions.

In addition to the principal's specific decision-making emphasis at each school, other decisions emerged in interviews. Table 10.3 displays these more minor decisions to demonstrate how different each site can be in the decisions it addresses through SBM.

The differences among the school sites shown in Tables 10.2 and 10.3 demonstrate in a manner similar to the variety in committees that principals make choices about which decisions schools can or should make. Figure 10.1 illustrates both the areas in which the central office requires site decision making and the specific decisions that appear to be at the discretion of the sites—collectively referred to by Ogawa and White (1994) as the "domain in which power is delegated" (p. 61). Principals in PWCS play a major role in determining whether or not specific decisions are shared with teachers and the degree to which teachers will influence those shared decisions.

Shared Decision Making: What Teachers and Principals Do

Teachers' Roles in Decision Making

Having examined the committees that exist at participating schools, the kinds of decisions taken up as part of SBM, and similarities and differences

Table 10.4 Teacher Participation and Influence on Committees

	School			
	O'Connor	*Earhart*	*Central*	*Madison*
Teachers on Committees	(N = 104) 40 (38%)	(N = 111) 35 (32%)	(N = 52) 22 (42%)	(N = 34) 20 (59%)
Level of Influence on Committees(4 or 5; on a scale of 1 to 5)	(N = 43) 14 (33%)	(N = 55) 17 (31%)	(N = 30) 6 (20%)	(N = 21) 8 (38%)
Opportunities to Influence Schoolwide Decisions (4 or 5; on a scale of 1 to 5)	(N = 98) 19 (19%)	(N = 108) 23 (21%)	(N = 50) 11 (22%)	(N = 34) 10 (29%)

between principals' and teachers perceptions about SBM, I turn now to the issue of the roles teachers play in the decision-making process. The kind of committee structure described earlier is common to SBM implementation nationwide (Johnson & Logan, 2000; Winter, Keedy, & Newton, 2000), making committee membership a reasonable measure of the SBM participation level at a school site. I asked teachers to report through the survey whether or not they serve on committees, in order to estimate the proportion of teachers who actually engage in SBM. The results show a consistent pattern with school size: the smaller the school, the higher proportion of teachers reporting that they serve on committees. Table 10.4 displays the number and percentage of respondents reporting that they serve on one or more SBM committees.

Central and Madison, the two smaller schools in the study, are structured for a higher proportion of teacher participation because of the leadership positions Grubowski and Phillips have created. For example, Grubowski has both department heads and team leaders who serve on the department head–type committee. Likewise, Phillips has grade-level leaders, the school counselor, two administrative assistants, a special education teacher, and a librarian serving on the School Leadership Team. The appointed or elected leaders in the middle and elementary schools represent a much larger percentage of the faculty than they do in the high schools. Yet, the greatest proportion of teachers participating in committees is just over half at Madison. Consequently, one-half to two-thirds of the teachers at any given school do not participate directly in the SBM process.

Apart from merely sitting on a committee, teachers' perceptions of the degree of shared decision making depend on whether or not they believe they have influence over committee decisions. Table 10.4 shows the percentages of committee members at each site who, on a scale from 1 to 5, reported their level of influence on committees to be a 4 or a 5, with 5 being the highest rating.

Of the one-third to one-half of teachers serving on committees, comparatively few rate their committee influence high (either 4 or 5). Thus, out of all survey respondents, a low of 6 of 52 (11.5%) teachers at Central and a high of 8 teachers out of 34 (23.5%) at Madison believe they have a strong influence on their committees. It appears that a small proportion of the faculty at each of the four schools perceives strong influence in SBM. The data also indicate that Phillips at Madison is more democratic than she described herself in the interview and Riddle at Earhart is less so.

Not all influence on decisions is exercised through committee work. Informal relationships within a school can be powerful channels of teacher influence. Looking at the influence over schoolwide decisions that all teachers perceive themselves to have provides additional insight into the degree to which decisions are shared. The third row of Table 10.4 shows the percentages of teachers responding to the survey who rated their opportunities to influence important schoolwide decisions either 4 or 5 on a scale from 1 to 5. The size trend is apparent once again with the smallest school, Madison, displaying the highest level of perceived teacher influence over schoolwide decisions. Although the committees may differ somewhat in the degree of shared decision making they employ from school to school, the schools in general show similar profiles, with the smaller schools demonstrating slightly greater propensities for shared decision making.

The relationship between size of school and decisions made, decision-making participation, and influence was unexpected and has not been identified in other studies I have found. The relationship suggests that teachers at smaller schools play a larger, more influential role in decision making. An important implication for larger schools may be that they ought to be more deliberate in their efforts to include decisions in SBM processes and more persuasive in their invitations to teachers to participate in those processes.

If principals are able to increase teacher participation and influence in decision making, they still face a serious problem with the decision domain. Evidence from principal interviews and teacher surveys suggests that the decision domain in schools is tightly constrained and probably does not have much direct relationship with teaching and learning. Under present circumstances in PWCS, small proportions of teachers participate and have influence in decision making about issues that are only indirectly related to the classroom. Now the reasons for the groaning about SBM that my student reported before my study began seem obvious.

Teacher perceptions and school size do not complete the entire picture of SBM implementation, however. As noted early in this chapter, principals play a key role in determining how SBM is practiced. Understanding how principals' preferences and behaviors shape the roles they stake out for themselves fills in some implementation-picture details.

The Principal's Role in Decision Making

Principals, through their thoughts, words, and deeds, choose the roles they wish to play in the decision-making process. Based on self-descriptions from interviews, I have designated three broad roles principals might play. A Decision Maker decides what is best for the group or the school, a Decision Engineer structures the information and/or alternatives a committee might consider, and a Facilitator works as a peer who keeps the decision-making process functioning as it should. Table 10.5 presents these roles and the complementary rules that seem likely to govern behavior in those roles in a manner similar to that which March (1994) describes.

As one would expect, roles and rules are not necessarily discreet or mutually exclusive. Principals describe themselves as playing different roles in the decision-making process at different times. Furthermore, it would be best to think of the role of the principal as fitting somewhere on a continuum with Decision Maker at one end and Facilitator at the other.

Table 10.5 Principal Decision-Making Roles and Rules

	Definition	*Rules*
Decision Maker	The principal decides what the outcome will be.	The principal takes in information formally and/or informally, then makes the "best" decision under the circumstances and informs faculty.
Decision Engineer	The principal structures the decision by presenting a constrained set of choices to others.	The principal uses committee structure to ratify the "best" choice presented.
Facilitator	The principal is the steward of the decision-making process.	The principal functions as a peer within committees and helps others to reach consensus through SBM processes.

Principal as Decision Maker. All four principals describe themselves as, at least potentially, encountering situations in which they would be the one person to make a decision. There are two basic circumstances in which this might be true: (1) the principal is the person most competent to make a judgment about a specific issue; and (2) collaborators cannot agree and therefore the decision falls to the principal. Principal Phillips is the most outspoken about the need to step in and make a decision under specific conditions:

> [Principal Phillips]: [Superintendent] Kelly never really did ask us to give away our authority in a building under site-based management. There are times when we will come to a crossroad and there might be a decision to be made in which . . . we've got about 50 percent of the people thinking this and 50 percent thinking that. Under those circumstances what I have to do is I have to be sure that everyone's been heard. Then I step forward and make the decision. (Phillips interview, 11/15/00)

Principal Keller explains that he needs to make personnel decisions that are required for overall school operations and that it is important for him to keep collaborative groups informed about his decisions and the rationale behind them:

> [Principal Keller]: The hiring of a secretary, or the decision that we need an additional secretary in guidance. They're aware of it and I'll present the justification to the department chairs and to the PAC because it's certainly going to have an impact on the budget. I'm not really looking for their approval as much as I'm just helping them to understand why this is a need. (Keller interview, 1/30/01)

The least likely to be the lone decision maker, Riddle decided to put German into the curriculum because his committee could not agree and because the committee came to a consensus that he should be the one to make the decision.

Principal as Decision Engineer. Both Grubowski at Central and Phillips at Madison display reasonably strong tendencies toward decision engineering. They describe cases in which they carefully structured information so that collaborative groups could make a choice within a tightly bounded framework.

> [Principal Grubowski]: So, what we did is got the best literature available on best practices in reading. At a faculty meeting had each group—sixth grade,

> seventh grade, PE, music—read a different article. We asked each group to come up and present to the [whole] group in a round-robin kind of thing. . . . We put all those on a chart. Before they left, they had a green dot and a yellow dot, and we asked them to determine what the priority was. From there we developed two ad hoc committees. One that would look at a specialized reading program that had children in small groups on a regular basis. The second was content strategies for content teachers to use. Those two committees met over the summer. What we came back to in the school community was, in 15:1 ratio, everyone in this building for one hour a week teaches reading. (Grubowski interview, 02/04/01)

> [Principal Phillips]: When I think of the Advisory Council meeting last night, I spent a good portion of the day preparing for that meeting. Copying the new piece of the budget that I wanted everybody to have. Looking at some information about the school data—the test results, whether we're provisionally accredited or not, the report from the State, and all of that. It's important information and Advisory Council needs to know where this school stands. (Phillips interview, 11/15/00)

Although Keller's vignette describes him in a decision maker mode, I've chosen to characterize him as a decision engineer because that appears to be his greater tendency. More typical for Keller is the following story about working with school leaders to provide resources for a specific program:

> [Principal Keller]: We were in dire straits up in Business with the computers. The computer labs we had up there. They could not teach the curriculum. They had been let go to the point where we just needed new labs. Well, that's $30,000, so in the first month of school, we had to come to consensus and say from each department we're going to have to throw back into the pot to accommodate this need in our building, which means that you may do without a little bit for this year, but folks, we're all on the same team. We're teaching the same kids. These kids. . . . We need to do this so that these kids can have the curriculum taught to them. (Keller interview, 01/30/01)

Keller decided that the computers needed to be purchased, thus narrowing the scope of the decision, but he enlisted the cooperation of department chairs to find the money.

Principal as Facilitator. All four principals describe themselves as facilitators when asked to indicate their primary role in SBM. But Grubowski and Phillips refer to what I have called decision engineering behaviors as facilitative behaviors. Riddle at Earhart High School articulates the clearest vision of himself as a facilitator. In addition to letting school-community members decide which decisions should enter the SBM arena, Riddle explains that, in the name of the greater good for the school and the process, he strives not to impose his will on decisions submitted to a collaborative process. When I asked him what the principal's role in SBM is, he replied:

> [Principal Riddle]: Guide on the side, I think. My role is to . . . keep our eye on the ball. To make sure that students are achieving and to help the process. I have a very controlling personality. No doubt about it. After all these years, it is still a struggle for me to keep my mouth shut, to not get in there to give a stump speech to shut it down and move on. . . . My job is to try to make [collaborators] feel like this is all worthwhile, that all of this extra work that we're doing to manage this building in a collaborative process has a payoff. . . . I try to counsel, I try to guide, I try to facilitate, I try to remind. . . . I try not to control the meetings. The most I do is slip the chairman a note, "You might want to get us back on track." (Riddle interview, 12/06/00)

The Principal's Role: Summary. Whatever role the principal strives to fulfill in the decision-making process, personalities are likely to feel more or less comfortable with different choices. Principal choice may be constrained to a considerable degree by their perception that accountability for school results rests with them. This is probably the most important factor pushing the principals toward decision making and decision engineering. Yet, there is a built-in contradiction between principals being held accountable and an implied expectation that the decision-making process involves teachers and parents as experts. Riddle describes how he strives to compromise the dilemma between accountability and participation:

> [Principal Riddle]: I guess I try to see myself as one of the collaborators, understanding that, ultimately, I make a decision. Understanding that this really is an advisory council to the principal. Understanding that, ultimately, I *cannot* take a recommendation of the Council. All I need to do is call a faculty meeting and explain my rationale for why I would ignore something that the School Council had suggested to do. That's never happened. I think that we just promote an arena of respect between each other. We can respectfully disagree. But we also need to understand that we can come to an agreement if we work hard enough, we can do it. (Riddle interview, 12/06/00)

Riddle and the other principals know they have the power to make all of the decisions. The fundamental choice they make is how much to focus their attention on the SBM process and how much on the ultimate decision. This choice is a critical influence on how site-based decisions are made.

Conclusions: The Site-Based Management Process Revealed

Within a variety of committee structures, four areas of decision making predominate at school sites in Prince William County schools—curriculum planning/materials selection, development of the school plan, staff development planning, and budget planning and allocation. Some variation occurs as different schools emphasize one or more areas over others. Teacher influence, a measure of the degree of shared decision making, varies somewhat according to school size, with only small proportions of teachers perceiving themselves to have a high degree of influence in SBM.

Principals make critical choices that shape implementation of SBM policy in PWCS. They determine committee structure beyond the PAC, decide which questions the committees will address, and play specific decision-making roles within SBM. The choices that principals make in these areas shape how each school experiences SBM, in terms of both the decision-making domain and the decision-making process.

The central office has not been the focus of this chapter, but it is a major player in SBM. PWCS has placed several significant constraints on decisions subject to SBM. With control over curriculum and school accountability mechanisms, for example, the central office retains substantial power over the sites. Virginia statewide testing and accountability requirements reinforce the power of the central office. As a result, schools in Prince William County are expected to provide essentially the same services to their students (with the exception of the Specialty Schools program), no matter what the unique student needs may be at any given site. Principals appear to tinker at the edges of improving the quality of teaching and learning by planning professional development to meet district and state expectations, deciding which foreign languages to offer, making more of the school community feel welcome, or determining how to spend a small proportion of the site budget. If principals and their staffs set their own priorities, they might be misaligned with district-determined targets, which could have negative consequences on state testing or other district accountability measures. Principals no doubt consider central office and state influences as they make choices about decision-making processes in SBM.

Opportunities for meaningful shared decision making seem to be relatively rare among the four participating schools. With between one-third and one-half of teachers at any given school working on SBM-related committees, teacher participation appears moderate at best. Teachers need to participate in order to have the possibility of influencing site-based decisions.

Yet, among those teachers who actually serve on committees, only small numbers rate their influence as high. Schoolwide, the number of faculty who believe they have a strong influence on decisions grows slightly, but the proportions shrink.

Moderate participation and weak influence at all four schools suggest that SBM decisions are not widely shared in the participating schools. Despite the establishment of various committees to work on decisions and principals' espoused beliefs in shared decision making, school size seems to trump structure and values, but just barely. Teachers at the smaller schools have a tendency to select more SBM activities that they have either observed or participated in. Furthermore, the smallest school in the study, Madison, has teachers reporting both higher rates of participation in SBM and a greater degree of perceived influence over decisions.

Principals cannot choose the size of their schools, but they do make meaningful choices about how to structure decision making. If decisions are to be widely shared in order to "empower schools to be more responsive and adaptive to change and to unleash productive local potential to move the division toward fulfilling its mission and goals" (PWCS, 1990, p. 3), then principals need to find ways to broaden both participation and influence in decision making. The large schools could learn from the smaller by creating more teacher leadership positions and opening up decision making to a larger degree.

An important caution is required here. Thus far in this study, the nature of teacher participation and influence in decision making is only vaguely understood. Gaining a clearer understanding of the roles that teachers and principals play in SBM requires, at a minimum, observation of teachers, parents, and administrators engaged in the SBM process. Future research will focus on observing committee meetings to discover how principals actually behave, how different kinds of decisions are handled, and how teachers influence the decision-making process. A follow-up survey will also be conducted to test the validity of propositions contained in this chapter.

At least three factors are inhibiting principals who might wish to involve teachers more deeply in decision making: (1) more participation means more time devoted to decision making, and teachers are reluctant to take time away from teaching and other concerns (Johnson & Logan, 2000; Winter, Keedy & Newton, 2000); (2) involving more people in decision making makes running the school more complex and dilutes principal control; and (3) the central office may be reluctant to relinquish meaningful decision-making power.

The three potential barriers to fuller implementation of SBM are directly related to the issue of improving the quality of education for all students.

They would need to be cleared away or mitigated for SBM to make a more substantial difference for students. This examination of SBM in PWCS has thus far (with the notable exception of the Central Middle School reading program) turned up very little mention of improved classroom practices resulting from SBM. The pattern of SBM implementation revealed at this point in PWCS is consistent with Leithwood and Menzies' (1998) "Administrative Control" (p. 238) model of SBM—that is, site administrators have greater control over resources than they did prior to SBM policy, but teachers do not. Leithwood and Menzies argue that SBM in Administrative Control mode has little impact on the classroom. Principals acting single-handedly may not have sufficient power, influence, and/or knowledge to orient SBM more toward teaching and learning.

Advocating SBM alone will not make a difference in site decision making unless real power is given to decision-making groups—a situation that is rare within most SBM policies (Wohlstetter & Odden, 1992), including that in PWCS. As long as the central office maintains primary control over curricula, unilaterally establishes accountability targets for schools, and holds principals solely accountable for school results, then SBM remains only partially implemented because school-site committees are missing key elements of power over teaching and learning. To achieve full implementation would require further shifts of decision-making power from the central office to the sites and a reorientation from merely giving greater control to site administrators to making teachers more influential decision makers, moving from the SBM strategy with the least impact on classrooms to that with the greatest impact (Leithwood & Menzies, 1998). Then, both the superintendent and principals would need to step back and "trust the process" (in the words of Principal Riddle) to achieve greater benefit from SBM.

Head shaking and eye rolling similar to what my student related to me when I raised the issue of SBM is likely to continue as long as key decisions remain outside the school site. By revealing how site-based decision making actually occurs, this study indicates ways in which SBM processes could be improved. Teachers require more extensive professional development in SBM processes and deeper knowledge of the content of site decisions in order to be effective collaborators with their principals (Beck & Murphy, 1996; Mohrman, 1994). Principals must be more conscious of their decision-making profiles and more deliberate in their enhancement of shared decision making if they intend to use SBM to improve teaching and learning. The kind of training that teachers and principals require to engage in SBM as an engine of school improvement will be effective only if and when school districts like PWCS demonstrate the courage to allow those who actually teach children to make important decisions about what and how students will learn. In today's context of greater centralization and heightened accountability, this is not an easy road.

Note

1. The PWCS language specifies "school-based management." I have opted for the more commonly used term "site-based management." The meaning is the same.

References

Beck, L. G., & Murphy, J. (1996). *The four imperatives of a successful school.* Thousand Oaks, CA: Corwin Press.

Elmore, R. F. (1993). School decentralization: Who gains? Who loses? In J. Hannaway & M. Carnoy (Eds.) *Decentralization and school performance* (pp. 33–54). San Francisco: Jossey-Bass.

Haskin, K. *A process of learning: The principal's role in participatory management.* Paper presented at the Annual Meeting of the American Education Research Association (San Francisco, April 18–22, 1995).

Johnson, P., & Logan, J. (2000). Efficacy and productivity: The future of school-based decision-making councils in Kentucky. *Journal of School Leadership, 10*(4), 311–331.

Leithwood, K., & Menzies, T. (1998), A review of research concerning the implementation of site-based management. *School Effectiveness and School Improvement, 9*(3), 233–285.

March, J. G. (1994). *A primer on decision making.* New York: The Free Press.

Mohrman, S. A. (1994). High involvement management in the private sector. In S. A. Mohrman & P. Wohlstetter (Eds.) *School-based management: Organizing for high performance* (pp. 25–52). San Francisco: Jossey-Bass.

Mohrman, S. A., & Wohlstetter, P. (1994). Introduction: Improving school performance. In S. A. Mohrman & P. Wohlstetter (Eds.) *School-based management: Organizing for high performance* (pp. 1–21). San Francisco: Jossey-Bass.

Murphy, J., & Beck, L. G. (1995). *School-based management as school reform: Taking stock.* Thousand Oaks, CA: Corwin Press.

Neal, R. G. (n.d.). *School based management: An effective approach to reform. Executive summary.* Written report. Prince William County Public Schools, Virginia.

Ogawa, R. T., & White, P. A. (1994). School-based management: An overview. In S. A. Mohrman & P. Wohlstetter. (Eds.) *School-based management: Organizing for high performance* (pp. 53–80). San Francisco: Jossey-Bass.

Prince William County Public Schools, Virginia. (1990). Executive summary.

Robertson, P., & Briggs, K. (1998), Improving schools through school-based management: An examination of the process of change. *School Effectiveness and School Improvement, 9*(1), 28–57.

Tyack, D. (1993). School governance in the United States: Historical puzzles and anomalies. In J. Hannaway & M. Carnoy (Eds.) *Decentralization and school performance* (pp. 1–32). San Francisco: Jossey-Bass.

Weiss, C. H. (1995). The four "I's" of school reform: How interests, ideology, information, and institution affect teachers and principals. *Harvard Educational Review, 65*(4), 571–592.

Winter, P. A., Keedy, J. L., & Newton, R. M. (2000). Teachers serving on school decision-making councils: Predictors of teacher attraction to the job. *Journal of School Leadership, 10*(3), 248–263.

Wohlstetter, P., & Mohrman, S. A. (1994). Establishing the conditions for high performance. In S. A. Mohrman & P. Wohlstetter. (Eds.) *School-based management: Organizing for high performance* (pp. 165–183). San Francisco: Jossey-Bass.

Wohlstetter, P., & Odden, A. (1992). Rethinking school-based management policy and research. *Educational Administration Quarterly, 28*(4), 429–549.

11

Successful Leadership in Schools Facing Challenging Circumstances

No Panaceas or Promises

Alma Harris

The educational reform agenda in many countries reflects a renewed interest in school leadership as a panacea or "cure-all" for raising standards of attainment and performance.[1] There is a strong belief in the ability of school leaders to promote and generate school improvement. This is reinforced in the research literature, which consistently emphasizes the powerful relationship between leadership and school development (e.g., Hopkins, 2001a; Van Velzen, Miles, Elholm, Hameyer, & Robin, 1985; West, Jackson, Harris, & Hopkins, 2000). Hallinger and Heck (1996) report that principals have an indirect, but highly measurable, effect on student achievement, explaining up to a quarter of the school level variance in student achievement. The dominant message is unequivocal: effective leaders exercise an indirect but powerful influence on the effectiveness of the school and on the achievement of students (Leithwood & Jantzi, 2000). The research evidence consistently demonstrates that the quality of leadership determines the motivation of teachers and the quality of teaching in the classroom (Fullan, 2001; Sergiovanni, 2001). In summary, the contribution of leadership to school effectiveness and school improvement is significant (Wallace, 2002).

Interestingly, the basis for much of the theorizing about leadership and school improvement has tended not to focus on schools in high-poverty areas or schools with above-average levels of deprivation. With some important exceptions (e.g., Barth, Haycock, Jackson, Mora, Ruiz, et al., 1999; Borman, Rachuba, Datnow, Alberg, Mac Iver, et al., 2000; Leithwood & Steinbach, 2002), the contemporary school-improvement literature has not been overly concerned with leadership in schools facing difficult or challenging circumstances. Only relatively recently have researchers focused their expertise and attention upon leadership in "failing" or "ineffective" schools (e.g., Gray, 2000; Harris & Chapman, 2002; Hopkins, 2001b; Myers & Stoll, 1998; Reynolds, Hopkins, Potter, & Chapman, 2001). Gray (2000) contends that, "We don't really know how much more difficult it is for schools serving disadvantaged communities to improve because much of the improvement research has ignored this dimension: that it is more difficult, however, seems unquestionable" (p. 33). In addition, relatively few of these studies have focused exclusively on leadership practices or forms of leadership that have contributed directly to improving schools facing challenging circumstances (SFCCs).

The reason for this lack of attention resides predominantly in the inherent sensitivity and complexity of the terrain. Schools that face multiple forms of disadvantage are least likely to be open to critical scrutiny or exposure because they are most often the schools where academic performance is below average. While social disadvantage may not be an excuse for poor achievement in academic terms, it certainly is a powerful factor and source of explanation. As Power, Warren, Gillborn, Clark, Thomas & Coate (2002) conclude in their study:

> [Educational] outcomes in deprived areas are worse than those in non-deprived areas, whether they are measured in terms of qualification, attendance, exclusions or "staying on" rates. Inner-city areas in particular feature as having low outcomes. (p. 26)

These authors also point to the need to reduce the "compositional effects that appear to result from high concentrations of disadvantaged students" (Power et al., 2002, p.65).What is being described here is a paucity of "cultural and social capital," which significantly increases the difficulty for schools in challenging circumstances to improve.

The terms *cultural capital* and *social capital* derive from the work of Bourdieu (1987), who highlights the way that practices are infused (unequally) with social legitimizing so that not all cultural practices are viewed as having equal value. Both cultural and social capital are primarily concerned with the way in which social position is transformed into social advantage. Lamont and Lareau (1988) define cultural capital as "widely shared high status cultural signals used for social and cultural exclusion" (p. 156). Implicit in this definition is the notion of inherent disadvantage perpetuated by a class system. Similarly, social capital refers to the social networks and relationships that give certain groupings advantages over others. These social networks provide advantages in a highly differentiated social space and maintain deep divides within and between schools. In short, cultural and social capital are concerned with sustaining power relations and patterns of social and cultural domination. They provide middle-class families with invisible benefits not so readily available to working-class and poor families.

Schools located in areas of high socioeconomic deprivation are also more likely to be populated with students typically categorized as "disadvantaged" or "at risk." They generally face a greater risk of school failure by comparison with their more affluent counterparts and have significantly lower levels of social and cultural capital. Parenthetically, with disadvantage comes diversity, and the more severe the disadvantage the greater the diversity within the student population (Harris & Chapman, 2004). In short, schools facing challenging circumstances have students who vary tremendously from one another and also from their teachers in outlook, experience, and other attributes directly linked to success at school. In these schools, the social stratification or class of students may be relatively homogeneous while differences in race, ethnicity, religion, and language may vary considerably. These variations expand disproportionately the lower down the socioeconomic scale schools go. Consequently, these schools are facing two inherent and, some would argue, intractable problems. The first is the influence of social mix on a school's ability to generate the social and cultural capital necessary for higher levels of performance (Thrupp, 1999). The second is the complexity of the teaching task presented by a less affluent student population.

Students from disadvantaged backgrounds can challenge teachers' conceptions of what to teach, what to expect of students, and even how to communicate with them (Knapp, 2001). This is not to suggest a deficit model of teaching in schools in difficult circumstances but simply to acknowledge the extent of the task in securing levels of performance that schools in more affluent areas achieve with relative ease. Recent research has shown that, in order to achieve and sustain improvement in such schools, teachers must exceed what might be termed as "normal efforts" (Maden, 2001, p. 16). They have to work much harder and be more committed than their peers in more favorable socioeconomic circumstances. In addition, "they have to maintain that effort in order to sustain improvement as success can be short-lived and fragile in difficult or challenging circumstances" (Whitty, 2002, p. 109).

It cannot be denied that there is a strong negative correlation between most measures of social disadvantage and school achievement. However, this should not translate into a deterministic position of believing that there is little that can be done to raise attainment in schools in difficult or challenging contexts. Although it is important to recognize the sociocultural factors that sustain inequalities in educational achievement, cultural deficit models underestimate the potential of schools, teachers, and students to "buck the trend." There is increasing evidence that schools facing difficult and challenging circumstances are able to add significant value to levels of student achievement and learning (Maden & Hillman, 1996). Evidence also shows that these schools can and do improve levels of student performance and achievement (Gray, 2000; Harris & Chapman, 2004).

In schools that are in difficult or challenging circumstances, but that nevertheless are improving, the quality of leadership has been shown to be a major contributory factor (Hopkins, 2001b; Reynolds, Hopkins, Potter, & Chapman, 2001). However, few in-depth studies exist that have explored successful leadership practices in SFCCs. This chapter outlines the findings from a contemporary study of successful leadership in both secondary and primary (elementary) schools in England that were considered to be in difficult or challenging circumstances. This chapter outlines the key features of successful leadership practice in SFCCs; it highlights some of the strategies for improvement adopted by head teachers,[2] or principals, in each school; and it considers the long-term prognosis for improving schools that face difficult or challenging circumstances. This study points toward the centrality of distributed leadership practice and the importance of focusing on community building both within and around the school. It also points to the importance of a multiagency and differentiated approach to improving schools in challenging circumstances.

Context for the Study

The research project (funded by the National College for School Leadership in England) investigated leadership within a group of schools, geographically spread across several areas of England, that were designated by the Department for Education and Skills (DfES) as "facing challenging circumstances." Schools in which 25% of students, or fewer, achieve success at external examinations by the age of 16 are placed in this category. This also includes a number of schools in which more than 25% of their students achieve success but where more than 35% of the students receive free school meals. Approximately 8% of secondary schools in England are in this grouping. Many of these schools are also in the DfES categories of "Special Measures" or "Serious Weaknesses" which identifies them as "failing" and places then under the regime of regular external inspection. Not surprisingly, within the "schools facing challenging circumstances," grouping are a high representation of schools with students of low socioeconomic status, urban areas, schools with falling enrollment, and schools serving inner-city communities (Gray 2000).

The research study consisted of three phases.[3] Phase one involved a literature review and generation of research questions and propositions. Phase two involved data collection at 10 school sites; this included semi-structured interviews with key stakeholders (heads, senior teachers, teachers, pupils), the collection of a wide range of documentary evidence (inspection reports, performance data, development plans, etc.), and general observations within each school. Phase three incorporated case analysis and the testing of initial findings with head teachers from a group of schools facing challenging circumstances that were not involved in the study. The selection of case-study schools was informed by two factors. First, care was taken to ensure that the schools represented a wide range of contexts and were geographically spread. Second, inspection reports were scrutinized to ensure that there was evidence of successful leadership and an upward school-improvement trajectory. Consequently, the sample included:

- Schools located within a range of socioeconomic and cultural situations (inner city, urban, rural, and those with predominantly one ethnic group and also mixed and multiethnic groups).
- Schools that were demonstrating improvement; that is, there was evidence of sustained improvement in performance as shown through external examination results, inspection reports, and other assessment and benchmarking data.

Within a small scale, the possibilities for generalization are inevitably limited. However, the volume and range of data collected in this study provided a basis for the researchers to draw some preliminary findings about leadership in SFCCs. The study aimed to explore whether and how far leaders in SFCCs shared similar approaches to leadership and the extent to which the particular demands of the school context shaped or influenced their leadership style. Research has shown that authoritarian forms of leadership are most prevalent in failing schools and particularly in those in the early stages of their recovery; for example in the first or second year (Gray, 2000). In a failing-school context, immediate action is required, and hence leadership approaches are often very directive and task focused to secure immediate changes. In schools that are not desperately failing but are on an upward incline, however, the potential for alternative leadership styles and leadership approaches clearly exist.

The evidence collected in the study suggests that head teachers or principals adopt leadership approaches that match the particular stage of a school's development. While the principals acknowledged that they had all adopted autocratic leadership approaches at critical times when firm direction was needed, they also agreed that this leadership approach was least likely to contribute to sustained school improvement. All the heads favored a leadership approach that empowered others to lead by enabling teachers to engage in real leadership tasks that contributed to improvements in teaching and learning. This "distributed" form of leadership in many ways covers a similar terrain to transformational leadership, in both its orientation and aspiration (Leithwood & Jantzi, 2000). However, the particular emphasis given by the heads to teacher participation and involvement would suggest an approach to leadership that has both democratic and transformational principles at its core.

The study found that in all 10 schools forms of distributed leadership prevailed and that this leadership approach directly influenced approaches to organizational problem solving and decision making. Head teachers' responses to problems varied, depending on the circumstance or situation, but their value position remained consistently one of involving students, staff, and parents in seeking solutions to the problems facing the school. This also extended to other agencies outside the school (e.g., social services), as heads were aware that many of the difficulties they encountered with young people originated from circumstances outside the school. The findings from the research study suggest that leadership in SFCCs is primarily concerned with creating a culture of high expectations where young people feel valued and where high-quality teaching and learning is of paramount importance. This form of leadership is people centered and centrally concerned with generating improvement capacity within the organization by encouraging others to lead.

Successful Leadership in Schools Facing Challenging Circumstances

Vision and Values

Of central importance to leaders in SFCCs were the cooperation and alignment of others to their set of values and vision. The heads communicated their personal vision and belief systems by direction, words, and deeds. All of the head teachers in the study had chosen to work in an SFCC. Their vision and values emanated from a core belief in the ability of all children to learn and in the school's potential to offset the effects of disadvantage on student performance. Their vision was regularly communicated to staff and parents. The data showed that their vision was shared both within and outside the school. Through a variety of symbolic gestures and actions, they were successful at aligning staff, parents, and students to their particular view of what the school stood for and how it should operate. They had great optimism around learning, and all subscribed to the view that within their school was huge potential for student growth and development. They respected others and treated each person as an individual. They trusted others and required trust from others. They recognized the need to be actively supportive, caring, and encouraging as well as challenging and confrontational when necessary. "I lead through making my values explicit to others and motivating them to believe in the same vision of what the school could be" (Head S 1 [School 1]). "The head's values are clear and made explicit in his actions. He leads through his values and these are pretty well shared within the school" (Teacher S 5 [School 5]).

Vision was an inherent part of their leadership relationships in that it helped them communicate a sense of direction for the school. The vision and practices of these heads were organized around a number of core personal values concerning the modeling and promotion of respect (for individuals), fairness and equality, caring for the well-being and whole development of students and staff, integrity, and honesty. It was clear from everything said by the heads that their leadership values and visions were primarily moral (i.e., dedicated to the welfare of staff and students, with the latter at the center) rather than primarily instrumental (for economic reasons) or noneducative (for custodial reasons). Their values and visions both constructed their relationships with staff and students and were constructed within them.

The heads displayed people-centered leadership in their day-to-day dealings with individuals. Their behavior with others was premised on respect and trust and their belief in developing the potential of staff and students commonly held. "The head's main aim is to allow others to flourish and grow, whether staff or students, it doesn't matter. The aim is to develop others and to generate self-belief and self-esteem in those that currently lack it" (Teacher S 9). "People are your greatest asset and I firmly believe, therefore, that the staff and the students in this school are my best resource for change" (Head S 4).

Their ability to invite others to share and develop their vision was frequently commented on by staff and students alike. Alongside these qualities, however, were examples of heads being firm (in relation to values, expectations, and standards) and occasionally making very tough decisions, such as initiating competency proceedings against teachers who consistently underperformed. These heads did not gently cajole staff and students toward success but recognized that balancing pressure and support while building positive relationships was of prime importance. In many respects, the way they interacted with others was the common denominator of their success. The human qualities they possessed enabled them to lead others effectively and to establish confidence in others that their vision was worth sharing.

Distributing Leadership

The heads adopted highly creative approaches to tackling the complex demands of implementing multiple changes. The decision to work with and through teams as well as individuals was a common response to the management of change. The heads used a number of strategies for bringing out the best in staff. In addition to formal development opportunities, these strategies included the power of praise, involving others in decision making, and giving professional autonomy. Although the heads tended to concentrate on teaching staff in the first instance, they used similar approaches when dealing with parents, and to some extent students. All the heads invested in others in order to lead the school. From the perspectives of others, the overarching message was one of the head building the community of the school in its widest sense, through developing and involving others.

> The head has given real leadership responsibilities to others. It's not a case of just delegating headship tasks. (Teacher S 3)

> The middle managers now have greater responsibility and authority for leading. The days of being in charge of stock cupboards are over. (Department Head S 10)

Heads in the study and their constituencies consistently highlighted the importance of possessing a range of leadership strategies to address the diverse sets of issues and problems they faced. They also emphasized the contingent nature of many of the decisions they made and how different leadership strategies would be used in different contexts. The majority of schools in the study had at some stage emerged from the DfES categories of special measures or serious weaknesses. The heads commented on the importance of careful planning for the external inspection that all schools deemed to be failing must undergo. All the heads acknowledged that they adopted a more autocratic leadership style during the preinspection phase.

This included paying special attention to issues such as policy implementation and consistent standards of teaching (Chapman, 2002). During the inspection the heads adopted a more supportive leadership style in order to assist staff through the process. Leaders in SFCCs took this role very seriously and consciously demonstrated high levels of emotional responsibility toward their staff during the inspection period. An important contributory factor to achieving a positive outcome was considered to be how the heads' leadership style matched the situation or circumstance facing the school at different times.

> It's a learning curve all the time. I think leadership styles have to match the needs of that school at that particular point in time. (Head S 2)

> The head displays a range of leadership styles really; much depends on the situation or circumstance. (Teacher S 4)

> I don't think there is one leadership style or approach, is there? Anymore than there is a single teaching style. You need breadth and diversity in both. (Department Head S 5)

In particular, the heads emphasized that, although they adhered to a broad set of values, they did not consider this to be a fixed leadership approach. They felt strongly that they could switch to a leadership style that suited the situation and could behave in ways that did not reflect their core beliefs, if necessary.

Leading Learning

For these heads, effective leadership was centrally concerned with building the capacity for improved teaching and learning. The heads were quick to dispel the "cultural deficit" notion prevalent in many SFCCs, and were committed to the belief that every child can learn and succeed. They made decisions that motivated both staff and students and placed an emphasis on student achievement and learning. The heads talked about "creating the conditions that would lead to higher student performance," and they were deeply concerned about the welfare and the educational experiences of minority children. They set high expectations for students, emphasized consistency in teaching practices, and provided clear rules about behavior and stressed discipline. Their developmental focus was on improving the quality of teaching and learning. In this sense, they were instructional leaders, as the emphasis was on student attainment and achievement.

> The head has reoriented our attention to the classroom level. We are encouraged to share ideas and to talk about teaching rather than how individuals behave in class. (Teacher S 9)

> The predominant culture in this school was one where teachers discuss issues of teaching and learning very rarely. In fact everything else but that! The head has changed that. He has positively encouraged debate and discussion around on classroom issues, which has been a welcome change. (Department Head S 7)

The heads created learning opportunities for both students and teachers. They focused their strategic attention on the classroom and engaged staff in dialogue about teaching and learning issues rather than issues of behavior or classroom management. They were able to make clear links between their core values and their vision for improved student achievement and learning.

Investing in Staff Development

A primary concern for heads was one of maintaining staff morale and motivation. In a number of the schools, staff morale had been low and individual self-esteem had been eroded by successive criticism of the school. Consequently, the heads consistently and vigorously promoted staff development whether through in-service training, visits to other schools, or peer-support schemes. It was noticeable, also, that such development did not focus only on those needs that were of direct benefit to the school but also those that were of direct benefit to the individual. The development needs of nonteaching staff were also included. The emphasis heads placed on the continuing development of their staff was an endorsement that teachers were their most important asset and that, particularly in difficult times, it was important to maintain their own sense of self-worth by valuing them:

> Teachers in this school have had their morale eroded and chipped away by successive inspection. It is important to invest in them and their capabilities, to raise morale and to foster "can do" culture. (Head S 6)

> If you are constantly told you are failing, you believe it. You are a failed teacher. (Teacher S 7)

The emphasis placed on the continuing development of their staff reflected the recognition among heads that the teachers were their most important resource. Consequently, they were highly skilled at using a combination of pressure and support to promote the efforts of teachers, particularly when working with the most difficult students. They encouraged teachers to take risks and rewarded innovative thinking.

The heads set high standards for teaching and teacher performance. The focus and emphasis on improving teaching and learning was common across all case-study schools. Time was provided to ensure that teachers met to discuss teaching approaches and were able to observe each other teaching. In addition, teaching performance was monitored and individual assessments made. Poor teaching was not ignored or tolerated within the schools. Where it did exist, it was challenged and strategies were agreed for improvement. Where this did not occur, the necessary steps were taken by the head teacher to deal with the problem. In the majority of cases, a combination of structured support, monitoring, and an individual development program addressed the problem of poor-quality teaching. For these heads, effective leadership was about capacity building in others and investing in the social capital of the school.

Relationships

The heads were good at developing and maintaining relationships. They were considered to be fair and were seen as having a genuine joy and vibrancy when talking to students. They generated a high level of commitment in others through their openness, honesty, and the quality of their interpersonal relationships. The heads engaged in self-criticism and were able to admit to others when they felt they had made a mistake. They placed a particular emphasis on generating positive relationships with parents and fostering a view of the school as being part of rather than apart from the community: "It is important that staff and students are involved in the life of the school and relate to each other in a positive way" (Head S 1). "The head has ensured that we work more in teams and work across our subject areas. This has made us build broader relationships and work together" (Teacher S 8).

Stoll and Fink (1996) describe *invitational leadership* as a form of leadership where leaders place a high premium on personal values and interpersonal relationships with others. Heads in the study did reflect many of the dimensions of invitational leadership. They placed an emphasis on people rather than systems and invited others to lead. It was clear that, although they possessed a range of leadership strategies to address the diverse sets of issues and problems they faced, at the core of their leadership practice was a belief in empowering others.

> Ultimately, the job of the leader is to give others the confidence and capability to take on new responsibilities. It's really about giving power to others rather than keeping it at the top. (Head S 10)

> In many respects we have more power than before. We are involved in decision making, we are able to take ideas forward and to challenge new ideas and developments. I guess we are more involved, more part of the decision-making process than before. (Teacher S 6)

> The head has deliberately devolved leadership to others. I was concerned at first that this would mean we would lose control over the management of the school but it has generated much more interest from the staff in being involved in decisions. There is less apathy and less resistance to change. (Department Head S 5)

Although the heads emphasized the contingent nature of many of the decisions they made and how different leadership strategies would be used in different contexts, the central belief in distributing leadership to teachers remained unaltered. This form of leadership starts not from the basis of power and control but from the ability to act with others and to enable others to act. It places an emphasis on allowing and empowering those who are not in positions or responsibility or authority to lead.

Community Building

A distinctive feature of schools that are improving is the extent to which they work as *a professional learning community*. A climate of collaboration existed in the schools in the study, and there was a commitment among most staff to work together. However, this climate was the result of lengthy discussion, development, and dialogue among those working within and outside the school. It was deliberately orchestrated through the provision of opportunities to build social trust. This included providing opportunities for dialogue between staff and parents. The heads emphasized the need to establish an "interconnectedness of home, school, and community." This also involved adopting a multiagency approach to problem solving and understanding the wider needs of the community. West and Pennell (2003) note that multiple forms of inequality do not exist separately but coalesce and operate collectively. The implication here is that schools cannot operate in isolation from other agencies or the community they serve.

Recent research has reinforced the importance of school leaders connecting with the community (Harris, Muijs, Chapman, Stoll, & Russ, 2003) and of hearing and taking account of parent (and student) voices (Chrispeels, Castillo, & Brown, 2000). The head teachers in this study were acutely aware of the need to engage with their community. They visited homes, attended community events, communicated regularly with the parents about successes, and engendered trust by showing genuine care for young people. They understood the forces within the community that impeded learning, they were aware of the negative forces of the subcultures, and they listened to parents' views and opinions regularly. The heads tried to create integral relationships with the families in the communities they served. They recognized that family, school, and community relationships directly affected student outcomes; hence, the need to connect with the community was of paramount importance to the success of the school.

> The first thing I recognized that needed to be done was to get the parents into the school, so we screened World Cup games on parents' evenings. (Head S 10)

> This school is located on the edge of a large predominantly white, working-class estate. There is long-term unemployment, low aspirations, high levels of crime, and drug abuse. The biggest problem we had was getting the community to see us as a resource rather than the enemy. (Department Head S 3)

The heads were also highly responsive to the demands and challenges placed on their school by other external forces. Schools facing challenging circumstances are often in receipt of much more attention and intervention from the district and central-government level than schools in more affluent circumstances. Hargreaves (2002) has suggested that there is an "apartheid of professional development and school improvement" (p. 190), which has been generated by default rather than design by educational policymakers in England. He argues that although schools that are performing well enjoy "earned autonomy," those categorized as "failing or close to failing have prescribed programmes and endlessly intrusive monitoring and inspection" (p. 190). Often SFCCs are in receipt of multiple innovations, "while the cruising schools with coasting teachers who ride in the slip stream of middle class academic achievers get off scot free" (Hargreaves, 2002, p. 190).

The schools in this study were under constant scrutiny and pressure to implement numerous innovations and interventions. The heads saw their role as protecting teachers from unnecessary intrusion or burdens by acting as gatekeepers to external pressures. Although each school did have innovations and new initiatives, these had been carefully selected to ensure that they would enhance the development program of the school and would not simply compete for teachers' classroom time and energy.

Strategies for School Improvement

Across the schools in the study, it was evident that the heads had adopted particular strategies for improvement. The combination of these strategies depended on the particular context and circumstance of the school, but in each case there was evidence that a number of these strategies had been successfully put in place and had made a positive difference. This finding reinforces the view that differential school improvement strategies are required for schools at different stages of their growth and development (Hopkins, Harris, & Jackson, 1997). In SFCCs the problems are much more immediate and pressing, and therefore the strategies adopted by the schools combined short-term "tactical" approaches to change (Hopkins, 2001a) and longer-term strategies aimed at changing the culture of the school. This study identified eight strategies for improvement: improve the environment, generate positive relationships, set a clear vision and expectations, provide time and opportunity for teacher collaboration, place a relentless focus on teaching and learning, engage the community, evaluate and innovate, and distribute leadership.

Improve the Environment

The majority of schools in the study were located in positions that meant that their immediate surroundings were often very poor. A number of schools were located on council estates or in inner-city contexts that presented a run-down and at times hostile school environment. The physical condition of the majority of the schools was initially very poor, with leaking classrooms, broken windows, graffiti-covered furniture, and litter-covered corridors. Consequently, one of the first actions taken by heads was to improve the immediate environment in which students and staff worked. Resources were allocated to painting and repair work, to new furniture, to a new reception area, to display boards and refurbishment of the staff room. Emphasis was placed on litter removal, and students were given the task of sanding down desks to eradicate graffiti. This strategy had a symbolic and real purpose as it demonstrated to staff, students, and parents that the school was changing and improving.

Generate Positive Relationships

Within all the schools in the study, the heads acknowledged that a major difficulty resided in the quality of the relationships between staff and also among staff, students, and parents. In many cases relationships had deteriorated over time, resulting in a negative culture within the school characterized by low expectations and a high degree of mistrust. The heads invested a great deal of time in creating opportunities for more positive relationships to be developed. For staff, opportunities were provided to work together and to work across teams and within teams. Social events were organized, and staff-development activities included the expertise and involvement of those within the school. For students, staff-student committees were organized, student councils were established, lunch-time and after-hour clubs were set up, and trips were planned. For parents, there were evening classes and "drop in sessions." All parents' evenings included a social component, and more opportunities were created to give parents positive feedback and to invite them into the school. An emphasis was placed on breaking down social barriers and creating a climate within the school where staff, students, and parents had more opportunities to talk.

Set a Clear Vision and Expectations

Schools facing challenging circumstances often have low expectations of what students can achieve. Many reflect a cultural deficit notion of schooling and expect little from the community and little from the students. One of the central tasks of the leader faced with low expectations from staff and students is to generate belief in a culture of improvement. A first step in achieving this is to set clear expectations with students and staff, to share a vision of improvement, particularly with students, and to reaffirm this on a regular basis. Students, staff, and parents need to know what the school has to offer them and what part they play in its development. When heads set clear expectations, create a vision, and share this vision with others, the possibility for improvement is significantly enhanced. The heads were able to establish a more positive climate for learning within their school by "talking up" the school, setting clear expectations (e.g., behavior, truancy, attendance), and encouraging respect for others. They imparted a sense of urgency for maintaining high academic standards and exerted pressure on staff and students to excel.

Provide Time and Opportunities for Teacher Collaboration

Schools facing challenging circumstances have often suffered from a lack of attention, emphasis, and investment in staff development over time. The erosion of professional confidence and capability can be a major barrier to improving schools in difficulty. In many cases, teachers feel devalued and deskilled, particularly if the school is a member of the DfES "special measures" category, because teachers can become the prime focus of blame. It is important, therefore, that the leadership within the school ensures that teachers have the time and opportunity to collaborate. There need to be opportunities for new approaches to professional development, such as mentoring, coaching, and peer review. Where teaching practices are poor, improvements can be achieved simply through investing in forms of professional development and collaboration that raise teachers' self-esteem and acknowledge that they can share important dimensions of their work. Providing groups or teams of teachers who have not worked together before with a specific task or an area for improvement has been shown to result in benefits not only to the school but also to the individuals involved.

Place a Relentless Focus on Teaching and Learning

Schools that find themselves in difficulty can be subject to a wide range of external interventions that can compete for time, energy, and resource. The demands of numerous initiatives can prove to be counterproductive in securing school improvement, particularly in schools that have additional problems of social disadvantage. One way of rationalizing and focusing improvement efforts is to locate them strictly in the area of teaching and learning. Teachers in SFCCs need to acquire skills to be successful with students with particular sets of needs. They will need to use a variety of teaching approaches to ensure that all children have access to learning in the most efficient and effective manner. It is also important that they provide opportunities for student-initiated and student-directed learning activities and that teachers relate instruction to practical and meaningful student experiences. By providing staff-development opportunities that focus directly on effective teaching strategies and approaches, the possibility for improved teaching and learning is enhanced. Additionally, by placing a consistent and continual emphasis on teaching and learning, improvement at the classroom level will more likely occur.

Engage the Community

Schools in difficulty are often located in communities of extreme poverty and deprivation. As a consequence, they have to deal with problems that are a by-product of the socioeconomic context in which the school is located. Indeed, the school may be viewed with mistrust and suspicion by the community. It may be seen as having relatively little to do with the lives and aspirations of those within the community it serves. A main task of the leadership of SFCCs must be to build bridges with the outside community and to form relationships with families that extend beyond just getting students and parents into the school. Schools that are in difficulty but are improving have a strong desire to get parents involved in the educational process. Community and families are perceived as assets that should be capitalized on and integrated into the school in a manner that values and seeks their contribution.

Schools that have built solid and lasting links with the local community are more likely to gain its support and loyalty in difficult times. This means providing opportunities for parents to come into school, talk to teachers, use the facilities, and see the school as a resource for them and their children. This means breaking down traditional barriers between the school and the community by seeking ways to integrate and involve parents in school life. Social, sporting, and charitable events offer some points of entry for parents, but evening classes and community meetings can also encourage parents to view the school as an important part of the local community. It is important that schools celebrate and value a diversity of languages and cultures as community assets and see them as being of intrinsic worth. Also, it is important that schools openly support educational equity and excellence for all students.

Evaluate and Innovate

One of the main difficulties facing SFCCs is recognizing that there is a problem and knowing how to deal with that problem most effectively. For many schools in difficulty, a culture of denial predominates that prevents meaningful change from taking place. One way of breaking this cycle is to put in place robust evaluation mechanisms that highlight strengths and weaknesses. By providing an internally driven means of diagnosing developmental needs, the possibility of change is increased. If staff recognize that evaluation mechanisms and data gathering offer them powerful ways of planning development and change, they are more likely to use the information for developmental purposes.

Schools facing challenging circumstances can be data rich and information poor, so it is imperative that evaluation focuses on areas of importance and intrinsic value to teachers. By providing feedback on issues directly connected to teaching and learning, evaluation is more likely to be viewed as a means to an end and not simply as another form of accountability. It will be necessary for schools in difficulty to manage change and innovation effectively. Leaders will need to have optimism in the face of failure, to pursue all goals with energy and persistence, and to have the ability to find common ground and to build rapport with others. To manage change effectively requires relying on others and generating a shared belief among staff and students that change is achievable.

Distribute Leadership

The importance of clear and purposeful leadership is recognized as being important in SFCCs. In many cases, schools in difficulty suffer from a sustained lack of leadership at both the district and school level and have been left to drift or spiral downwards. Hence, strong leadership is an important prerequisite for enabling a school in difficulty to move forward. The study showed that although the provision of firm, directive leadership is necessary to turn around a school in difficulty, it is insufficient to sustain improvement over time. It would appear that a more democratic form of leadership is needed as the school moves from the visibly failing stage and into the capacity building phase. This is not well-developed territory, but the research that does exist points toward the need for a fit between the leadership or improvement approach and developmental phase or cultural state of the school (Hopkins, Harris, & Jackson, 1997). If the goal of raising performance in SFCCs is to be achieved, leadership approaches that neglect to address or match the different growth states of schools will be unlikely to succeed. There are no easy answers or neat solutions to improving SFCCs, but it is clear that undifferentiated leadership approaches are unlikely to raise student performance and results.

In addition, leadership approaches that fail to involve or engage others in leadership activity are equally at risk of failing. Schools facing challenging circumstances often experience an overdependency on the head to lead and a reluctance among teachers to take leadership responsibility. However, this research has shown that where teachers are given leadership responsibility, work together in teams, and are empowered to lead instructional development, they have a greater sense of ownership and involvement. In this sense, leadership is a shared entity and is primarily concerned with building the capacity for improvement. In the 10 schools in this study, leadership was not the preserve of the head teacher but was a distributed form of agency among teaching staff given responsibility to take innovation forward. This distributed view of leadership requires schools to "de-centre" the leader (Gronn, 2000, p. 5) and to subscribe to the view that leadership resides not solely in the individual at the top but in every person at entry level who in one way or another acts as a leader (Goleman, 2002, p. 14).

Distributed leadership, therefore, means multiple sources of guidance and direction, following the contours of expertise in an organization, made coherent through a common culture. It is the "glue" of a common task or goal—improvement of instruction—and a common frame of values for how to approach that task (Elmore, 2000, p. 15). Evidence from this study suggests that forms of distributed leadership lead to greater capacity for change and improvement at both the school and classroom level. It also highlights that where teachers share good practice and learn together, the possibility of securing better quality teaching is significantly increased. In short, distributing leadership equates with maximizing the human capacity within schools and increasing the possibility of individual agency.

Distributing Leadership: Panacea, Promise, or Possibility?

School-improvement advocates have suggested that schools that are improving "do and should operate as a *professional learning community*" (Hargreaves, 2002, p. 2; emphasis added). This term not only implies a commitment to teachers sharing learning but also to the generation of a schoolwide culture that makes collaboration an expectation. A professional learning community is a community where teachers participate in decision making, have a shared sense of purpose, engage in collaborative work, and accept joint responsibility for the outcomes of their work (Harris & Lambert, 2003). In their review of successful school improvement efforts, Glickman, Gordon, and Ross-Gordon (2001, p. 49) construct a composite list of the characteristics of what they term the "improving school," a "school that continues to improve student learning outcomes for all students over time." At the top of this list appears "varied sources of leadership, including distributed leadership" (p. 49). Research by Silns and Mulford (2002) has also shown that student outcomes are more likely to improve when leadership sources are distributed throughout the school community and when teachers are empowered in areas of importance to them. This implies a changing view of structures away from command and control. It suggests viewing the school as a learning community chiefly concerned with maximizing the achievement capacities of all those within the organization (Gronn, 2000). The evidence from this research study similarly points in the direction of distributed forms of leadership but recognizes that there are some inherent difficulties in adopting this approach within schools.

First, distributed leadership requires those in formal leadership positions to relinquish power to others. Apart from the challenge to authority and ego, this potentially places the head or principal in a vulnerable position because of the lack of direct control over certain activities. In addition, there are financial barriers, as formal leadership positions in schools carry additional increments. Consequently, securing informal leadership in schools requires heads to use other incentives and to seek ways of remunerating staff who take on leadership responsibilities. Second, the "top-down" approaches to leadership and the internal school structures offer significant impediments to the development of distributed leadership. The current hierarchy of leadership within both primary and secondary schools means that power resides with the leadership team; that is, at the top of the school. As a consequence, leadership is viewed as the preserve of the few rather than the many. In addition, the subject or department divisions, plus the strong year groupings, present significant barriers to teachers working together. These structures militate against teachers attaining autonomy and taking on leadership roles within the school.

Finally and most important, distributed leadership poses the challenge of *how* to distribute responsibility and authority and, more important, *who* distributes responsibility and authority. If it remains the case that the head distributes leadership responsibilities to teachers, then distributed leadership becomes nothing more than informed delegation. A distributed view of leadership "incorporates the activities of multiple groups or individuals in a school who work at guiding and mobilizing staff in the instructional change process" (Spillane, Halverson, & Diamond, 2001, p. 20). It implies a social distribution of leadership where the leadership function is *stretched over* the work of a number of individuals where the leadership task is accomplished through the interaction *of multiple leaders* (Spillane et al., 2001, p. 20). It implies interdependency rather than dependency, embracing how leaders of various kinds and in various roles share responsibility. Although distributed leadership does not equate with "delegation," it also does not represent a form of leadership that is so diffuse that it loses its distinctive qualities. As this study has shown, there will inevitably be a relationship between those in formal leadership positions and those who are involved in leadership activities at other levels. It is clear that certain tasks and functions would have to be retained by those in formal leadership positions but that the key to successful leadership resides in the involvement of teachers in collectively guiding and shaping instructional development.

It remains the case that schools located in contexts of multiple disadvantages have levels of performance that, in most cases, fall short of national averages. This not only presents them with a range of practical difficulties but asks a great deal of those who lead the school to "buck" this particular trend. There is little doubt that it would be simpler to pass off responsibility to other sectors or to the government and claim there is little schools can do. Similarly, it is easier to diminish any school-improvement efforts as naïve than it is to attempt to assist schools with strategies and approaches that could help their teachers and students. As Myers and Stoll (1998) note, there are no "quick fixes" for schools facing challenging circumstances, but there is an emerging evidence base to suggest that distributing leadership is a powerful means of engaging and empowering teachers in the process of school renewal and improvement.

We undoubtedly need to know much more about leadership in schools facing challenging circumstances and how such schools improve and sustain improvement over time. Increasingly, the evidence base is pointing toward the possibilities and potential of distributed leadership in building the capacity for school improvement (Gronn, 2000; Harris & Lambert, 2003; Spillane et al., 2001). This offers, at present, little more than an alternative way of viewing leadership practice and generating opportunities for teachers to work together. The empirical base remains thin. However, leaders in schools facing challenging circumstances cannot wait for educational policy to catch up or for inequities in the system to be eradicated before new practices are adopted or new programs trialed. The daily task they face is too immediate, too pressing, and too relentless. As the long-term patterning of educational inequality looks set to remain, leaders in schools facing challenging circumstances must look for strategies and approaches that might assist their school, in their context with their students. Although distributed leadership is certainly no panacea, it does provide schools with an alternative way of conceptualizing leadership practice and the possibility for greater improvement potential. For this alone it merits serious consideration.

Notes

1. I am grateful to the National College for School Leadership and to my co-researcher Christopher Chapman for allowing me to draw upon the evidence from the research project in order to write this chapter. I am also grateful to the heads, teachers, and students in the schools facing challenging circumstances who are currently working with me. They continue to impress and inspire. Thanks also to Janet Chrispeels for her comments on an earlier version of this chapter.

2. References to "head" or "headmaster" equate to the term "principal".

3. A full account of this study can be obtained from the National College for School Leadership at *www.ncsl.org.uk*

References

Barth, P., Haycock, K., Jackson, H., Mora, K., Ruiz, P., Robinson, S., & Wilkins, A. (1999). *Dispelling the myth. High poverty schools exceeding expectations.* Washington, DC: US Department of Education, Office of Educational Research and Improvement [ED 1.310/2:445140].

Bourdieu, P. (1987). Forms of capital. In J. G. Richardson (Ed.). *Handbook of theory and research for sociology of education* (pp. 241–258). New York: Oxford University Press.

Borman, G. D., Rachuba, L., Datnow, A., Alberg, M., Mac Iver, M., & Stringfield, S. (2000). *Four models of school improvement. Successes and challenges in reforming low-performing, high poverty Title 1 schools.* Baltimore: Johns Hopkins University, Center for Research into the Education of Students Placed At Risk.

Chapman, C. (2002, January). *School improvement in challenging circumstances: The role of external inspection.* Paper presented at the symposium on School Improvement in Challenging Circumstances, ICSEI 2002. Copenhagen, Denmark.

Chrispeels, J. H., Castillo, S., & Brown, J. (2000). School leadership teams: A process model of team development. *School Effectiveness and School Improvement, 11*(1), 20–56.

Elmore, R. (2000). *Building a new structure for school leadership.* Washington, DC: The Albert Shanker Institute.

Fullan, M. (2001). *Leading in a culture of change.* San Francisco, CA: Jossey-Bass.

Glickman, C., Gordon, S., & Ross-Gordon, J. (2001). *Supervision and instructional leadership: A developmental approach.* Boston: Allyn & Bacon.

Goleman, D. (2002). *The new leaders: Transforming the art of leadership into the science of results.* London: Little Brown.

Gray, J. (2000). *Causing concern but improving: A review of schools' experience.* London: DfEE.

Gronn, P. (2000). Distributed properties: A new architecture for leadership. *Educational Management and Administration, 28*(3), 317–338.

Hallinger, P., & Heck, R. (1996). Reassessing the principal's role in school effectiveness: A critical review of empirical research 1980–1995. *Educational Administration Quarterly, 32*(1), 5–44.

Hargreaves, A. (2002). Professional learning communities and performance training sects: The emerging apartheid of school improvement. In A. Harris, C. Day, M. Hadfield, *Effective leadership for school improvement* (pp. 180–195). London: Routledge Falmer.

Harris, A. (2002, January). Leadership in schools facing challenging circumstances, presented at *International Congress of School Effectiveness and School Improvement.* Copenhagen.

Harris, A., & Chapman, C. (2002). *Effective leadership in schools facing challenging circumstances,* Final Report, National College for School Leadership (NCSL). Nottingham.

Harris, A., & Chapman, C. (2004, forthcoming). Improving schools in difficult contexts: Towards a model of differentiated intervention. *Educational Research.*

Harris, A., & Lambert, L. (2003). *Building leadership capacity for school improvement.* Milton Keynes, U.K.: Open University Press.

Harris, A., Muijs, D., Chapman, C., Stoll, L., Russ, J. (2003). *Improving schools in disadvantaged areas—A review of the research evidence.* London: Department for Education and Skills.

Hopkins, D. (2001a). *School improvement for real.* London: Falmer Press.

Hopkins, D. (2001b). *Meeting the challenge: An improvement guide for schools facing challenging circumstances.* London: Department for Education and Skills.

Hopkins, D., Harris, A., & Jackson, D. (1997). Understanding the school's capacity for development: Growth states and strategies. *School Leadership and Management, 17*(3), 401–411.

Knapp, M. S. (2001). Policy, poverty and capable teaching. In B. Biddle (Ed.) *Social class, poverty and education.* New York: Routledge Falmer.

Lamont, M., & Lareau, A. (1988). Cultural capital: Allusions, gaps and glissandos. *Sociological Theory, 6,* 153–168.

Leithwood, K., & Jantzi, D. (2000). The effects of transformational leadership on organisational conditions and student engagement. *Journal of Educational Administration, 38*(2), 112–129.

Leithwood, K., & Steinbach, R. (2002). *Successful leadership for especially challenging schools.* Unpublished manuscript.

Maden, M. (Ed.). (2001). *Success against the odds: Five years on.* London: Routledge.

Maden, M., & Hillman, J. (Eds.). (1996). *Success against the odds: Effective schools in disadvantage areas.* London, England: Routledge.

Myers, K., & Stoll, L. (1998). *No quick fixes: Improving schools in difficulty.* London: Falmer Press.

Power, S., Warren, S., Gillborn, D., Clark, A., Thomas, S., & Coate, K. (2002). *Education in deprived areas,* London: Institute of Education.

Reynolds, D., Hopkins, D., Potter, D., & Chapman, C. (2001). *School improvement for schools facing challenging circumstances: A review of research and practice.* London: Department for Education and Skills.

Sergiovanni, T. (2001). *Leadership: What's in it for schools?* London: Routledge Falmer.

Silns, H., & Mulford, B. (2002). Leadership and school results. In K. Leithwood & P. Hallinger (Eds.), *Second international handbook of educational leadership and administration.* Dordecht, the Netherlands: Kluwer.

Spillane, J., Halverson, R., & Diamond, J. (2001). *Towards a theory of leadership practice: A distributed perspective.* Evanston, IL: Northwestern University, Institute for Policy Research Working Article.

Stoll, L., & Fink, D. (1996). *Changing our schools: Linking school effectiveness and school improvement.* Buckingham, UK: Open University Press.

Thrupp, M. (1999). *Schools making a difference: Let's be realistic! School mix, school effectiveness and the social limits of reform.* Ballmoor: Open University Press.

Van Velzen, W., Miles, M., Elholm, M., Hameyer, U., & Robin, D. (1985). *Making school improvement work.* Leuven: Belgium ACCO.

Wallace, M. (2002). Modelling distributed leadership and management effectiveness: Primary school senior management teams. *England and Wales' School Effectiveness and School Improvement, 13*(2), 163–186.

West, M., Jackson, D., Harris, A., & Hopkins, D. (2000). Leadership for school improvement. In K. Riley & K. Seashore Louis (Eds.). *Leadership for change.* London: Routledge Falmer.

West, A., & Pennell, H. (2003). *Underachievement in schools.* London: Routledge Falmer.

Whitty, G. (2002). School improvement and social inclusion: Limits and possibilities. In G. Whitty (Ed.). *Making sense of education policy.* London: Sage.

PART IV

Preparing School Leaders for Shared Leadership

12

Supporting Teachers' Leadership

What Can Principals Do?

A Teachers' Perspective From Research

David Frost

Judy Durrant

This chapter presents teachers' ideas, views, and practical suggestions about what can be done within schools to empower teachers as leaders and to provide day-to-day support for their leadership. The chapter begins with a rationale for teacher-led development work, by which we mean school change initiated and led by teachers who may or may not have designated leadership roles. It centers on the agency of teachers as a key to school improvement, drawing on a recent research project designed to focus on the impact of teachers' leadership. Interviews with teachers who were experienced in leading school change contained powerful messages for school principals who may be interested in sharing leadership in their schools. Recommendations from teachers include the following: recognizing and understanding the potential for leadership in teachers; developing a culture that is conducive to teacher-led development; providing time and access for external support; ensuring the existence of facilitative organizational structures; and providing critical friendship to teachers.

In this chapter we focus on how teachers can take the lead in improving the quality and effectiveness of teaching and learning, and on what principals can do both to facilitate this and to maximize its impact. The final part of the chapter suggests how this activity can be supported through partnerships with universities and other external agencies.

The current policy discourse on school leadership is peppered with concepts such as *shared leadership, distributed leadership, dispersed leadership, collective leadership,* and *parallel leadership* (e.g. Crowther, Kaagan, Ferguson, & Hann, 2002; Harris & Muijs, 2002). The differences between these concepts hinge on the question of whether teacher leadership is genuine leadership or merely a commodity that can be distributed or shared by the head teacher or principal. Some writers avoid this conceptual problem by talking about *leadership density* (Sergiovanni, 2001) or a *leader-rich culture* (Mitchell & Sackney, 2000). We take a pragmatic view that recognizes the inevitability of principals continuing to have a disproportionate degree of power, but we argue that they can choose to use that power to create the conditions in which teacher leadership can flourish.

Teacher Leadership and Capacity Building

Improvement in teaching and learning ultimately depends on the action taken by teachers, whether the impetus for change arises from national reforms, school development priorities, or a teacher's belief that something could be better. In the case of "top-down" initiatives mandated by policy, the compliance of teachers can be secured, as recent numeracy and literacy strategies in England have demonstrated, but it is not possible to enforce the commitment and enthusiasm on which real and sustained improvement depends. So our central concern here is the development of the capacity of individual teachers, who may or may not have formal management responsibility, to exercise leadership and take greater responsibility for deep and lasting improvement of professional practice.

Theories that assume a hierarchical model of organization suggest that the organizational conditions in schools are the result of interactive processes through which the tensions between *top-down* and *bottom-up* power are resolved. Such theories draw from the structuralist tradition in which leadership styles are underpinned by values such as control, predictability, and efficiency. The assumption within this view of organizations is that principals or head teachers and others with management responsibility (now often called "the leadership team") take strategic action, and that teachers respond by exercising *bottom-up power* in different ways. For example, teachers may be compliant if there is a high level of trust between them and their managers, or if there happens to be a very high level of consensus within the school. On the other hand, they may resist change by passive inertia, or challenge it more actively by articulating and voicing their opposition to practices introduced precipitously by those in formal leadership positions.

Teachers may not see themselves as powerful, of course, but principals and head teachers who have attempted to lead their schools through a process of change are likely to be in no doubt that members of their staff exercise power. Clearly both pedagogical practice and the organizational conditions in the school are shaped by factors associated with the school's culture. We take the term *culture* in this context to mean the complex patterns of habitual behavior, expectations, and entrenched beliefs and values of teachers, expressed through the power relations that result from the school's particular history (Hargreaves, 1995). Principals and head teachers also know that the process of micropolitical negotiation is unpredictable and difficult to manage and can result in a level of organizational chaos that is unproductive and damaging to the school's effectiveness. They may therefore be tempted to embrace an authoritarian model of leadership in the attempt to promote effectiveness. This may well show short-term gains, but research suggests that long-term and sustained improvement depends on what is often referred to as *capacity building* (Gray, Hopkins, Reynolds, Wilcox, Farrell, & Jesson, 1999). "Capacity building" is a term used increasingly in the school improvement literature to refer to the school's capacity to improve itself. Foremost among British researchers who have contributed to the development of capacity-building strategies is John MacBeath, whose work tends to rely on the sort of generic definition outlined by Stoll: "Internal capacity is the power to engage in and sustain continuous learning of teachers and the school itself for the purpose of enhancing pupil learning" (Stoll, MacBeath, Smith, & Robertson, 2001, p. 171).

We find this definition helpful but, like Mitchell and Sackney (2000), want to extend it to include collegial decision making. The organizational capacity of schools depends on both the personal and interpersonal capacity of teachers (Mitchell & Sackney, 2000); that is, the extent to which they can develop their professional knowledge and skill, and the extent to which they can form and sustain collaborative relationships with their colleagues. It is through collaboration that schools can develop the coherence of values and the consistency of practice that characterize effectiveness (Sammons, Hillman, & Mortimore, 1995). It is this collegiality that is essential for a school that aspires to be a learning community.

We argue that the concept of *teacher leadership* is the key to capacity building within the organization. It has the potential to help us avoid the limitations of the hierarchical model of school organization. Teacher leadership is consistent with a view of organizations that draws on Giddens's (1984) sociology to support the argument that teachers can play a significant part in shaping the organizational structures, rules, procedures, and cultures that shape their lives. Teacher leadership is about the cultivation and use of power, but the term *bottom-up power* used by Giddens and others is not appropriate. It is important that teachers are able to exercise leadership within a coherent collegial framework rather than as a response to the exercise of power applied from the top down.

We argue here that most teachers are likely to need practical support to enable them to deploy power in ways that are both more strategic and more responsible to ensure that their pupils' life chances are improved as a result.

Leadership: Values, Vision, and Strategy

We need to be clear about what the term *leadership* implies. For us, there are three key concepts: *values, vision,* and *strategy*. Our assumption is that the process of leadership begins with the clarification of values and the articulation of a vision underpinned by those values. Vision we take to be the result of imagining what could be and what ought to be. In addition, the exercise of leadership necessarily entails strategic action intended to realize those values in practice and to narrow the gap between that vision and the current reality of professional practice. Although an organization in which so many people are promoting their own vision and acting strategically could be impossibly chaotic, comfort can be drawn from Fullan's arguments about complexity and moral purpose (Fullan, 1999); he draws on Stacey's work (1996a, 1996b) to support the view that schools are inevitably complex and that we have no choice but to work to foster the sort of human interaction that leads to the growth of empathy and the pursuit of mutual interest. Research suggests that effective schools have a high degree of coherence of values and consistency in practice (Sammons et al., 1995), but this cannot be achieved by suppressing dissenting voices and failing to recognize individual capacity. Instead, schools need to embrace the tensions between the personal vision building of individual teachers and the priorities of the school as an organization, and they need to work toward resolution through collaboration and dialogue.

It is axiomatic, therefore, that principals and head teachers need to adopt a model of leadership that facilitates such capacity building: so-called *transformational leadership* (Leithwood & Jantzi, 1990). Some have expressed misgivings about this: Mitchell and Sackney (2000), for example, have suggested that transformational leadership is still focused on the exercise of power at the apex of the organization where the concern is to engage teachers in consultation and decision making as a means to "get them on board." For them, the problem remains that power is not distributed equitably; as we have said, however, we consider it inevitable that principals and head teachers have more of a grip on the levers of power and that the building of organizational capacity rests on their ability and willingness to use their power to that end. Angus (1989) is among those who have argued along these lines:

> Those who hold administrative positions need to realize that their best contribution to educational reform may be to use the authority of their position to facilitate the exercise of agency of those of their staff who, for one reason or another, have begun to examine critically, and engage in dialogue about, educational issues and educational purposes so that they are rendered problematic and subjected to scrutiny. (p. 86)

He suggests here that the first stage of this process is to engage in critical reflection challenging practice and purpose, and that this is a collective activity. Dialogue enables individuals to articulate their ideas and perceptions and to move to a deeper shared understanding. Michael Fullan (1993) promotes the view of Peter Senge, who says that "a shared vision is a vision that many people are truly committed to because it reflects their own personal values" (Senge, 1990, p. 206). This is not to say that the school's development goals are to be based on some kind of amalgam of the personal values of its staff, but rather that they are fashioned and tempered collectively through the kind of discourse within which values are clarified and examined.

Morale and Agency

Arguably the reforms of the past decade or so have achieved a great deal, but one of the costs has been the undermining of teacher morale. We have found the concept of human *agency* most helpful in illuminating this pervasive problem. Bruner (1996) argues that agency is a fundamental aspect of selfhood and that humankind is distinguished not simply by the capacity to initiate and sustain activity of our own volition, but most crucially by the capacity to construct a narrative: "a record that is related to the past but that is also extrapolated into the future—self with history and with possibility" (Bruner, 1996, p. 36). This capacity to narrate necessarily involves moral choice about our actions and a sense of responsibility for them. Our actions require "skill and know-how" and consequently involve self-evaluation, which has a major impact on self-esteem. In the current climate of performativity, teachers are judged by simplistic measures of students' academic performance, and so the opportunities for experiencing failure overwhelm the opportunities for experiencing success through their own actions. Their self-esteem is lowered and their individual agency is frustrated, with inevitable consequences for morale.

The impact on the morale of teachers is evident in the prevailing difficulties with staff recruitment and retention. Research for the National Union of Teachers in the United Kingdom (Horne, 2001) confirms that more than 10 years of top-down reform has led not only to intolerable work loads but, more fundamentally, to a demolition of a sense of agency. There has been a dramatic increase in the use of counseling help lines (*Times Education Supplement* [TES], 1999a) and claims made against Local Education Authorities (LEAs) by teachers who have suffered stress-related breakdowns. These have been attributed variously to heavy workloads, external accountability, and draconian management styles (Evans, 1998; TES, 1999b, 2000; Webb & Vulliamy, 1996). Therapeutic strategies such as counseling and stress management may well be necessary *at present,* but in the long run they are not the answer. They are patronizing and ineffective in tackling such a fundamental malaise. Over the past 10 years we have been developing an approach and strategies for individuals and for schools and external agencies that address the matter of teachers' sense of agency in pursuit of school improvement (Frost & Durrant, 2003). In short, our approach offers practical support for teacher leadership.

Leadership for Learning

Teacher leadership is often talked about in terms of the extent to which teachers can be persuaded to take on management roles such as department chair or a short-term responsibility such as chair of a working party or school improvement group of some kind. Our view of teacher leadership is more inclusive in that we are addressing the need to encourage all teachers to be "change agents" (Fullan, 1993) whether or not they have such formal roles or positions (Frost & Harris, 2003). Furthermore, we are interested in teachers' leadership of *development work,* which has an explicit focus on improvement and learning. For us, this is an essential dimension of *leadership for learning* or *learner-centered leadership* (MacBeath, 2004). We suggest that teachers' leadership of learning-centered development work has three essentially interrelated dimensions, as expressed in Figure 12.1.

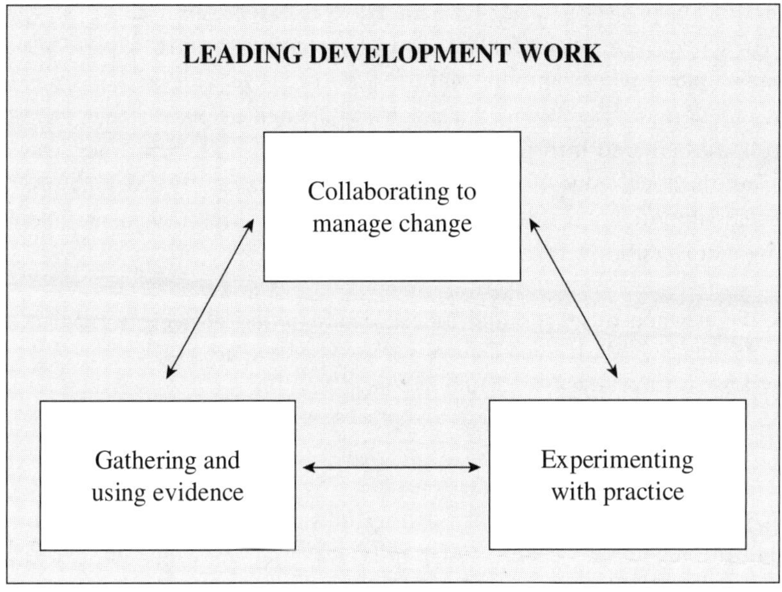

Figure 12.1 A Model of How Principals Can Lead and Facilitate Teacher Development Work

A growing body of evidence suggests that it is through the leadership of such development work that teachers can make a major difference to the personal and interpersonal capacities of themselves and their colleagues, to pupils' learning, and to the organizational structures and cultures of their schools (Frost & Durrant, 2002). In addition, they can make a significant contribution to wider professional discourse and professional knowledge creation and transfer. Our previous research (Frost, 1999; Frost & Durrant, 2002; Frost, Durrant, Head, & Holden, 2000; Holden, 2002a, 2002b), however, shows that teachers are unlikely to be able to engage in such leadership without a framework of support and expectations, at least not in large numbers.

In 2001 we carried out a small-scale investigation to examine how teachers think about the impact of their development work. Through a series of interviews we explored a conceptual framework and also learned a great deal to reinforce our experience and extend our understanding about the things that principals and head teachers can do to facilitate and support teacher-led development work. We interviewed a sample of teachers who were known to have initiated and sustained development activity in their schools. This work took place in the context of externally supported school improvement projects, some of which led to the award of a master's degree. Four teachers were selected from each of three programs to which we were already linked. The common characteristic of these programs is that they were all designed to support teachers as change agents in their schools. Universities entered into partnerships with schools and with other agencies such as the local education authority (school district) in order to provide external support for teachers' leadership and school improvement. The role of these universities was to provide the following:

- Frameworks of support and critical friendship for leadership of change
- Guidance in the methodology of school-based enquiry
- Links with wider research and discourse
- Expertise related to pedagogy and process where relevant

The style of the interviews with teachers was exploratory, so as to enable us to apprehend the complexity of the links among teacher development, organizational development, and pupils' learning. Having established the focus of the development work and learned something about the institutional context for it, we sought to elicit a rich narrative that would push at the boundaries of our informants' thinking about the focus, context, and process of development, but most crucially would tell us about its possible impact. The interviews also included questions about how the teachers had gathered evidence of the impact of their development work and explored their thinking about the issue of monitoring and evaluation. A fuller account of the methodology can be found elsewhere (Frost & Durrant, 2002).

What the Impact Project Told Us About the Role of Principals and Head Teachers

The teachers interviewed emphasized the importance of creating the right conditions within schools to enable them to exercise leadership and maximize the impact of their work. They were in no doubt as to the crucial role that principals and head teachers have in this respect, and they offered a range of both positive and negative experiences to illustrate their views. Teachers suggested that internal support is needed in the following areas:

- Cultural and structural support
- Planning and research support
- Extension of internal and external networks
- Recognition and celebration of leadership and voice

The detailed points extracted from a fuller analysis of the interview data are presented below under these four headings. Clearly some of the points fall within more than one category, but this set of advice is offered as the basis for reflection and discussion through which the links can be made.

Cultural and Structural Support

Recognize and Understand the Potential For Leadership in Teachers. We now have a body of evidence that clearly demonstrates that there is massive and largely untapped potential: teachers have ideas, enthusiasm, and expertise, but exercising leadership and taking action may require a change of attitude for those used to "training." One of the teachers interviewed describes her reaction after a support group meeting:

> I realized this was actually to do with us and not to do with us being lectured at; it is something we are actually going to do.

Principals/head teachers play a pivotal role in releasing this energy and in nurturing self-esteem and confidence to enable teachers to assume leadership roles.

Build a Culture Conducive to Teacher-Led Development Work. This is clearly a complex and long-term endeavor. Some teachers described "a climate where staff are willing to learn and participate" and spoke of the threat (e.g. from external judgment and inspection) being removed. They felt able to work with ideas, contribute to school development, and influence school policy. Others felt pressured and stifled, unable to discuss work in progress or present outcomes of their development work in school. Teachers presented a consistent view of the kind of support that is most effective; they praised head teachers who were strong but "gentle" managers, "unleashing potential," giving "freedom to experiment," motivating, setting an example, and having high expectations of staff.

Provide Opportunities for Teachers to Tap Into Their Own Enthusiasm. Given the right conditions, teachers can reflect on their circumstances, values, and beliefs in the context of their current responsibilities and school development priorities, and in so doing identify personal development priorities. Sometimes this can be complex, as in the case of this teacher who was prompted by literature accessed through a school improvement scheme to address a professional concern:

> I was tracking this bottom-set group which I found really challenging—they were very hard work [for teachers] and I just wanted to . . . try something

> different to motivate them, so that they would enjoy the lessons and I would enjoy teaching them. The literature said to try out these formative assessment ideas—there's quite a lot to gain for the low attainers—so I thought I'd give it a go.

Working ideas through and developing action plans with proper support enable teachers to achieve a strong sense of conviction about the development work that follows and ensures maximum energy and commitment.

Ensure the Existence of Facilitative Organizational Structures. For teacher-led development work to have maximum impact, organizational structures need to be in place for the purposes of collective deliberation and decision making, sharing good practice, and embedding good practice in the fabric of the school. A review of such structures may well reveal obstacles to the maximization of impact. This may be at the most basic level: in one school, the teachers interviewed regretted that colleagues were unwilling or unable to meet in the staffroom at break and lunchtimes so that even day-to-day opportunities for discussion, sharing, friendship, and support were missed.

Use Communications Structures to Keep Everyone Informed and Elicit Support. Our data contains examples of development work being undermined because members of the senior management team are not always aware of the range of development work going on in the school. One teacher spoke about participating in an "open discourse," whereas others felt that there was no forum at all for their ideas and that their participation in a master's program was perceived as an individual professional development exercise, despite the focus on support for school improvement. Well-informed senior managers are well positioned to make powerful links between strands of development.

Provide Access to External Frameworks of Support. Our data demonstrates how valuable external support can be. This may include the input of particular knowledge and expertise, the provision of a researcher to gather data, the provision of critical friendship, the provision of networking opportunities, and the provision of a framework for reflection and inquiry. All the teachers interviewed were members of facilitated groups, and they valued this support highly. Some commented that it is vital to have long-term support and continuity within partnership arrangements, rather than taking part in a succession of "projects."

Make Time Available for Development Work. The single most consistently mentioned obstacle to teacher-led development work is the lack of time for development activities for both teachers and those supporting the development work. Tiredness, busyness, and overload were frequently mentioned in our interviews, particularly by those working in schools in the most challenging circumstances who said it was "exhausting" even to remain "calm and friendly" in relationships with pupils. Principals and head teachers are clearly pivotal in allocating resources to a development project; they may also have to convince teachers that it is acceptable and valuable to take time out of the classroom. Our data includes good examples of teachers being allowed time—either built into the timetable in advance or provided through substitute teaching—to carry out development activity. Some head teachers served as the substitute teachers themselves, which demonstrated a personal commitment that was highly appreciated and valued by the teachers concerned, and also reassured the teachers that their classes were being properly looked after. Where there are problems of recruitment and retention, however, it is increasingly difficult for teachers to be released from their classes, and more creative solutions may need to be found, such as more flexible use of staff professional development time and imaginative timetabling.

Planning and Research Support

Focus Development Work in High Priority Areas With Greatest Potential Benefits. Some starting points for development are more productive than others. Research can be used to identify the strands of development that have the highest effect size, such formative assessment. Principals and head teachers need to assess the energy input against the potential effect size and ensure that teachers do not wear themselves out for little reward (see Hargreaves, 2001, for a discussion about "leverage").

Set Priorities and Coordinate Initiatives to Prevent Overload and Fragmentation. The teachers interviewed saw multiple initiatives as a major problem and commented that they did not appear to be "joined up" at policy level. Teachers' energy was divided and their attention diverted and fragmented. They recognized that their development work gained support if linked to national initiatives or school priorities (e.g., addressing weaknesses identified through inspection), but many had sketchy knowledge of school and district development plans and planning processes. It is up to the principal/head teacher, who has better knowledge of internal and external plans and priorities, to protect teachers from conflicts over multiple initiatives and to help them to reconcile their personal priorities with school priorities. Principals and head teachers can interpret and channel external pressures and ensure that, once a teacher-led development project has been agreed upon, it is supported and given appropriate priority.

Ensure That Development Work Is Well Planned for Maximum Impact. Planning is a crucial aspect of development work. It is up to principals and head teachers to set high standards and to support teachers in their planning. Teachers said that frameworks and time scales, particularly in accredited programs, increased the effectiveness of their leadership, helping them to clarify focus, structure their planning and action, and evaluate systematically. Senior managers should be involved in this planning to ensure that (1) they are consulted over action plans; (2) action plans take into account the full range of possible impact factors; (3) they include a collaborative element to draw colleagues in; (4) they are linked to, and compatible with, previous and concurrent work; and (5) they are realistic in terms of time and energy. This active involvement enables managers to give practical as well as moral support for teachers' strategic action.

Ensure That Monitoring and Evaluation Are in Place. It is important to ensure that the school's arrangements for monitoring and evaluation include development work led by teachers. This may be threatening to the teachers concerned, but senior managers have a key role to ensure that (1) the success criteria used reflect the full range of possible impact, (2) the gathering of evidence is planned, and (3) evidence is generated throughout the development work rather than just at the conclusion. Teachers in our study were enthusiastic in describing evidence of the impact of their development work, particularly where pupils had started to find a language to discuss their own learning, but they were reticent about the significance of their "findings." Principals and head teachers may need to take the lead in reassuring teachers about the value of different kinds of evidence, particularly where there is a pervading emphasis on test results and other quantitative data.

Document, Archive, and Share the Processes and Outcomes of Development Work. In addition to the support strategies already outlined, the school can derive maximum benefit when the development work is documented and archived. Benefits include expanded institutional memory; better follow-up on projects; effective dissemination through discussion; professional development activities for other staff; and internal publications. One experienced leader of change wanted to see a culture where this became normal:

> I think if we can try and create a culture of learning which includes recording, researching . . . evaluating, identifying good bits of work, then it's got to have an effect.

It is important that such use and dissemination of evidence is repeated and reinforced to take account of the fact that people move on and change roles, so that organizational learning as well as individual learning are nourished.

Extension of Internal and External Networks

Provide Space to Talk About Teaching and Learning Rather Than Just Results. Our data clearly shows that many teachers are still enthusiastic about learning and care deeply about pupils' experience. One teacher was delighted to observe the impact of changes in teaching strategy:

> It was lovely to see them excited about writing and they couldn't get to the table fast enough.

Teachers find discussion about learning satisfying but talked about tensions in their role; for example, one teacher said that higher test scores had been achieved "at the expense of creativity, enjoyment, and investigation." Some described an overt discourse about learning in their schools, but this was not always the case. Where teachers have a strong desire to find ways of making learning and teaching more satisfying for all concerned, principals and head teachers need to have faith in this possibility.

Facilitate Collaboration and Sharing With Colleagues From Other Schools. Our interviewees report that even modest collaboration with colleagues in another school is powerful:

> We've had one conference and that's been really good, if for no other reason than just to talk to people and hear what's going on.

The sharing and contrasting of practice leads to new ideas, teachers "have credibility with other teachers," and the reciprocal expectation gives development work momentum. Teachers find it valuable to belong to a community of practice with a feeling of shared values and purpose. For example, they may have a focus on improving pupils' learning; a recognition that teachers, too, need to learn; a belief in the value of inquiry as the basis for change. These learning communities need careful coordination and monitoring to ensure that they are meeting the needs of teachers and schools. They should be responsive and are likely to evolve over time.

Provide Critical Friendship. Teachers who may have relatively little experience of development work need to learn about leadership as they go. This may be best achieved through the provision of critical friendship (e.g. MacBeath, 1998; MacBeath, Schratz, Meuret, & Jakobsen, 2000), which is difficult for senior managers to provide in a very hierarchical organization. Although an external consultant may have the advantage of being independent and the teacher's peer may have the advantage of not having power over the teacher, the senior manager has the advantage of having an overview of the school as an organization. Some of the teachers interviewed talked about offering critical friendship to colleagues; one said he had learned in his leadership role that "being a friend" is more important than "missionary zeal."

Encourage Teachers to Disseminate Beyond the School. When teachers are encouraged to share their work beyond the school and the school examines the work of other teachers, not only are teachers recognized but also the school secures fresh professional knowledge. Some teachers were surprised by the interest shown in their work; others were reluctant to share, but at the same time they said that they found the experience and evidence of colleagues in other schools very valuable. The knowledge given away through such dissemination is repaid not only by the personal and professional development of the teacher concerned but also by the knowledge that travels back along the line of dissemination.

Recognition and Celebration of Leadership and Voice

Enable the Student/Pupil Voice to Be Heard. Teachers tend to see this starting point for the identification of problems and opportunities for development as more legitimate and acceptable than external inspection. One teacher had talked in depth with pupils over time about their learning, and this had given rich insights and demonstrated pupils' expertise as witnesses. As another teacher reported:

> They will talk over and over again about how they hate worksheets . . . copying questions . . . responding to questions in textbooks . . . they don't learn anything. And what comes out so strongly is that learning's all about autonomy, authority, engagement, democracy. . . . Their perception is quite scary sometimes. They quite often see things that the teachers don't see and understand.

This teacher was convinced of the value of listening to pupils, but clearly this has to be done sensitively and with appropriate support. School self-evaluation in which pupils are listened to can provide stimulus and a source of evidence to support teachers' development work, and some schools have taken this much further to establish pupils themselves as researchers and leaders of development work (Fielding, 2001).

Ensure That the School Derives Maximum Benefit From Teachers' Involvement With an External Source of Support. Some teachers were frustrated that their schools took little notice of their endeavors and therefore stifled the impact that their development work could have: "The senior management team are very pleased, very supportive in terms of, 'Yes, we think it's a very good thing, but please don't tell us anything about it, please don't agitate.'" This kind of nominal support is unlikely to be of strategic or practical help as the development work proceeds. Where teachers have undertaken a master's degree program or participated in a scheme supporting their development work, principals and head teachers need to express their expectations by asking for reports, asking for active interventions, and drawing the teacher into collaboration during the life of the project rather than waiting for a final product in the form of a report or thesis.

Celebrate and Praise the Development Work. Our data sometimes points to the inadequacy of support from the senior management team in celebrating and supporting development work, as in the previous example. The reduction of self-esteem and deprofessionalization described by some teachers, particularly under punitive inspection regimes, was noteworthy:

> It's not very nice to be told that what you're doing isn't very good . . . really I think people on the whole are very talented and I think we've lost some of the sparkle in people, in individual flair and skills.

Encouragement, praise, and recognition, therefore, are as important as active, practical support from senior managers.

Recognize Emerging Expertise and Professional Capacity. Teachers who have put their energy into the leadership of development work will be encouraged when they are provided with opportunities to share their insights, articulate their views, and acquire expert status. Most of the teachers interviewed described in great detail their sophisticated approaches to the management of change (characteristically raising awareness; being approachable; taking small steps; providing examples, materials, and checklists; demonstrating success; and building on existing good practice). They also demonstrated enormous commitment and "a bit of faith and staying power." This capacity to manage change can be of great value to a school if recognized by the principal or head teacher. These emerging teacher leaders can be invited to act as critical friends to others who may be undertaking the leadership of development work. They can be consulted on other proposals for change, and they can be involved in school-based professional development activities in place of or alongside expensive external "experts."

Working in Partnership

All of the suggestions just mentioned rely on support for teacher leadership from within the school and from external sources. In order for this support to be coherent, consistent, and complementary, we suggest that schools and external agencies need to work in partnership. Partnerships with external agencies are important because they can bring to bear a range of different expertise and value orientations. External agents are also relatively untrammeled by the particular history and micropolitics of the school and can offer impartial critical friendship. University departments or faculties of education (UDEs) are particularly well placed to play a part in such partnerships because of their expertise in research, but just as important is their experience in providing structures to support teachers' reflections and their presentation of accounts of practice. This is not straightforward, however, because the emphasis in some UDEs on academics' own research may well stand in the way of an orientation toward such work. Stenhouse's argument in the 1970s about the role of such bodies is more relevant than ever and one that has been echoed more recently by David Hargreaves (1998). Stenhouse (1975) was concerned with issues of authority and status, validation, and accountability. He argued that members of UDEs should recognize that teachers are best placed to understand classrooms and therefore the university staff should offer their skills in support of teachers' inquiry-based development work.

The interviews with teachers in our study revealed how they had been supported through partnerships involving the university and other agencies such as the local education authority (school district). Table 12.1 shows how the different aspects of internal support can be strengthened as schools work in partnership with external support.

The list discussed in this chapter shows the importance of both internal and external support, but the responsibility for balancing this lies mainly with the principal. While universities and other supporting agencies need to adopt flexible approaches that are responsive to school needs, principals must ensure that schools gain maximum benefit from partnerships and other external arrangements. In particular, our research suggests that the impact of teacher-led development work can be radically transformed when senior colleagues work with teachers to ensure that the initial planning of such work addresses a wide range of possible outcomes, including the development of teachers' personal capacity, the school's organizational

Table 12.1 Relationship Between Internal and External Supports Needed for Teacher-Led Development Work

Internal Supports	*External Supports*
Cultural and structural support	• Assist the school to examine and alter the organizational structures, system, and culture to enable teachers to exercise leadership and manage change. • Provide guidance materials and frameworks to support teachers' leadership. • Devise monitoring, evaluation, and research strategies to ensure partnership arrangements are effective and responsive to changing circumstances.
Planning and research support	• Provide access to published literature • Provide guidance on planning, data collection and analysis, documentation, and reflection • Encourage on linking theory and practice • Facilitate collaboration and sharing of process and outcomes • Encourage a critical approach to all forms of evidence
Extension of internal and external networks	• Establish a program/group to support discourse that is critical and authentic. • Provide opportunities and support for networking and internal and external critical friendship so that teachers can engage in collaboration, dialogue, and the sharing and contrast of evidence from different contexts.
Recognition and celebration of leadership and voice	• Provide flexible award-bearing frameworks that directly support teachers to improve their schools while achieving academic goals. • Help teachers celebrate their work through sharing and disseminating results within and beyond the school. • Provide opportunities for teachers to make contributions to professional knowledge and influence policymaking at school, district, and national levels, thereby enhancing agency and self-esteem.

capacity, and pupils' learning (Frost & Durrant, 2002). Principals have a crucial role to play in seeing that such planning is followed through with effective monitoring and evaluation. A key outcome of our impact project is a conceptual framework that can be used as a foundation for such planning, monitoring, and evaluation; a number of tools derived from this framework are presented in *Teacher-led Development Work* (Frost & Durrant, 2003).

We argue that schools should engage with the values of higher education; this includes putting a high premium on inquiry, evidence, scholarship, and critical debate. However, we also believe that this is likely to be most effective when it takes place, in part at least, on the school site rather than solely within the cloistered world of the university. When teachers attend courses designed by university staff and held on the university campus, there is little sense of partnership. The partnership between schools and external agencies has to be a genuine one based on mutual respect for different values, missions, expertise, and experience. It is important, therefore, that, where schools control the funding, they should flex their muscles and negotiate a set of arrangements that fit their own agenda, are adjusted to suit local circumstances, and make best use of the expertise and agenda of potential partners.

Policymakers, practitioners, and academics have a responsibility to work together to develop a climate in which professional knowledge is created and transformed. Teachers must have a central and active role in this process, which in practice means creating the right climate for teacher participation at the local and district level. In *Teacher-led Development Work,* we put forward a model that goes far beyond the provision of training or staff development activities, toward the creation of professional learning communities—networks of critical discourse based on inquiry, evidence, reflection on experience, comparison, and contrast from a range of educational perspectives. This happens most effectively when teachers experience a sense of belonging and shared values and purpose, encouraging them to make contacts, develop relationships, and explore and test practice through inquiry and discussion. Principals and partners should work to maximize the conditions supporting teacher involvement and mutual learning within these communities so that all the partner organizations—not just the schools—are able to develop a better understanding of learning and teaching and the processes of school improvement, so as to build powerful capacity for change.

References

Angus, L. (1989). New leadership and the possibility of educational reform. In J. Smyth (Ed.) *A socially critical view of the self-managing school* (pp. 63–92). London: Falmer Press.

Bruner, J. (1996). *The culture of education.* Cambridge, MA: Harvard University Press.

Crowther, F., Kaagan, S., Ferguson, M., & Hann, L. (2002). *Developing teacher leaders: How teacher leadership enhances school success.* Thousand Oaks, CA: Corwin Press.

Evans, L. (1998). *Teacher morale, job satisfaction and motivation.* London: Paul Chapman Publishing.

Fielding, M. (Ed.). (2001). *Forum, 43,* p. 2.

Frost, D. (1999). *Teacher-led school improvement: The development through action research of a school-based, award-bearing form of support.* Unpublished doctoral dissertation Centre for Applied Research in Education, University of East Anglia, U.K.

Frost, D., & Durrant, J. (2002). Teachers as leaders: Exploring the impact of teacher-led development work. *School Leadership and Management, 22*(2).

Frost, D., & Durrant, J. (2003). *Teacher-led development work: Guidance and support.* London: David Fulton Publishers.

Frost, D., Durrant, J., Head, M., & Holden, G. (2000). *Teacher-led school improvement.* London: Routledge Falmer.

Frost, D., & Harris, A. (2003). Teacher leadership: Towards a research agenda. *Cambridge Journal of Education, 33*(3), 479–498.

Fullan, M. (1993). *Change forces: Probing the depths of educational reform.* London: Falmer Press.

Fullan, M. (1999). *Change forces: The sequel.* London: Falmer Press.

Giddens, A. (1984). *The constitution of society.* Cambridge: Polity Press.

Gray, J., Hopkins, D., Reynolds, D., Wilcox, B., Farrell, S., & Jesson, D. (1999). *Improving schools: Performance and potential.* Buckingham, UK: Open University Press.

Hargreaves, D. (1995). School effectiveness, school change and school improvement: The relevance of the concept of culture. *School Effectiveness and Improvement,* 6(1), 23–46.

Hargreaves, D. H. (1998). A new partnership of stakeholders and a national strategy for research in education. In J. Rudduck and D. McIntyre (Eds.), *Challenges for educational research: New BERA dialogues* (pp. 114–136). London: Paul Chapman Publishing.

Hargreaves, D. (2001). A capital theory of school effectiveness and improvement. *British Educational Research Journal,* 27(4) 487–503.

Harris, A., & Muijs, D. (2002). *Teacher leadership: A review of research.* Nottingham, UK: National College for School Leadership.

Holden, G. (2002a). Towards a learning community: The role of mentoring in teacher-led school improvement. *Journal of In-service Education, 28*(1).

Holden, G. (2002b). *Changing stories: The impact of teacher-led development work on teacher, school and student learning.* Unpublished doctoral dissertation, Canterbury Christ Church University College, University of Kent at Canterbury, U.K.

Horne, M. (2001). *Classroom assistance: Why teachers must transform teaching.* London: Demos.

Leithwood, K., & Jantzi, D. (1990). Transformational leadership: How principals can help reform school cultures. *School Effectiveness and School Improvement 1*(4), 249–280.

MacBeath, J. (1998). I didn't know he was ill: The role and value of the critical friend. In L. Stoll & K. Myers (Eds.), *No quick fixes: Perspectives on schools in difficulty*. London: Falmer Press.

MacBeath, J. (2004). Democratic learning and school effectiveness: Are they by any chance related? In L. Moos & J. MacBeath (Eds.), *Democratic learning: The challenge to school effectiveness*. London: Routledge Falmer.

MacBeath, J., Schratz, M., Meuret, D., & Jakobsen, L. (2000). *Self-evaluation in European schools: A story of change*. London: Routledge Falmer.

Mitchell, C., & Sackney, L. (2000). *Profound improvement: Building capacity for a learning community*. Lisse, Netherlands: Swets and Zeitlinger.

Sammons, P., Hillman, J., & Mortimore, P. (1995). *Key characteristics of effective schools: A review of school effectiveness research* (Report for the Office of Standards in Education). London: Institute of Education.

Senge, P. (1990). *The fifth discipline: The art and practice of the learning organization*. New York: Doubleday.

Sergiovanni, T. (2001). *Leadership: What's in it for schools?* London: RoutledgeFalmer.

Stacey, R. (1996a). *Strategic management and organizational dynamics* (2nd ed.). London: Pitman.

Stacey, R. (1996b). *Complexity and creativity in organizations*. San Francisco: Berrett-Koehler.

Stenhouse, L. (1975). *An introduction to curriculum research and development*. London: Heinemann.

Stoll, L., MacBeath, J., Smith, I., & Robertson, P. (2001). The change equation: Capacity for improvement. In J. MacBeath & P. Mortimore (Eds), *Improving school effectiveness*. Buckingham, UK: Open University Press.

Head of Year wins £47,000 for stress. (1999a, October 21). *Times Education Supplement*, p. 1.

The downward spiral of stress. (1999b, November 12). *Times Education Supplement*, p. 12.

Record payout for school stress. (2000, May 12). *Times Education Supplement*, p. 5.

Webb, R., & Vulliamy, G. (1996). Impact of ERA on primary management. *British Educational Research Journal, 22*, 441–458.

13

Promoting Leadership Development and Collaboration in Rural Schools

Joseph I. Castro

This chapter focuses on the challenges faced by school leaders, particularly those in rural areas. It describes how one professional-development program for school leaders—the University of California, Merced, San Joaquin Valley School Leadership Program—was developed to provide quality support for school leaders that enhanced their effectiveness in a range of leadership areas. Prominent among these skills is collaborating with teachers and other stakeholders. This professional-development program was designed to help principals, vice principals, and district office leaders deal effectively with the challenges they face.

California and other states have joined the paradigm shift in education that swept the United States in the 1990s: the move from providing schooling for all children to holding schools accountable for meeting high standards for all children. To meet these changed expectations, educators are beginning to change the ways they work so they can effectively support student-learning needs for the knowledge society. The requirements for new ways of teaching so that all children will learn also necessitate new leadership and extensive opportunities for significant professional development for all (Tucker & Codding, 2002). These challenges are difficult for all districts to meet but remain especially acute for those educators serving students in rural communities because of their isolation and limited resources. This chapter will describe a model from the University of California, Merced, San Joaquin Valley School Leadership Institute that has helped prepare school leaders in rural areas to better understand this new paradigm and to function more effectively within it. Although the model developed was specifically designed to meet the needs of administrators in the San Joaquin Valley area, it provides a useful framework for all universities, school districts, and service providers.

Key Issues and Challenges Facing Rural Schools

Rural school districts have the responsibility for educating about one-fifth of the nation's students (Martin, Williams, & Hess, 2001). This job is not easy considering the significant and often unique challenges faced by rural school districts. These challenges include the following:

- *Recruiting and Retaining Qualified Teachers and Administrators.* Rural school districts generally struggle to attract and retain the most talented and experienced teachers and administrators (Jimerson, 2003). This often results in a disproportionate number of underprepared (noncertified) and less experienced teachers relative to suburban and many urban school districts.

- *Increasing Student Achievement.* Many rural school districts, particularly in California, have large numbers of students who are not experiencing academic success. These students are generally not performing well on standardized tests, and too many are dropping out before they graduate from high school (Kaufman, Alt, & Chapman, 2001). This challenge is complicated by the relatively large number of students, particularly from migrant farm-worker families, who are struggling to learn English while also trying to master high academic standards.

- *Securing Adequate Financial Resources.* Rural schools generally lack sufficient resources to serve adequately the educational needs of their students and are less successful in securing federal grants (Dewees, 2000). This challenge is a result of relatively high levels of poverty, underemployment, and unemployment that exist in many rural communities. Due to the severe economic constraints facing many rural areas, families have less discretionary income available to contribute to schools than those in suburban and many urban areas.

• *Being Geographically Isolated.* Rural schools are located in geographic areas that are isolated from resources that assist them in addressing the challenges just described (Perroncel, 2000). For example, rural schools are usually located relatively far from higher education institutions, major public libraries, and professional-development centers for teachers and administrators. Geographic isolation is one root cause of lower levels of human and cultural capital found in many rural communities.

Professional-Development Needs of Rural Educators

In light of the country's movement toward expanded teacher accountability and new curriculum standards, many administrators and teachers find themselves desperately searching for those practices that are most likely to raise achievement levels for all students. This cannot happen, however, if teachers lack the knowledge or the time to implement these practices (Darling-Hammond, 1997). Raising student achievement can only occur when teachers are adequately prepared to support student learning. As Linda Darling-Hammond has found in her extensive research on schools, the problem is not that teachers do not want to meet the demands of reform, but that they do not know how (Darling-Hammond, 1997). This finding supports strongly the need for professional development to be a high priority for schools. Professional development is a welcome, even desired opportunity for teachers. Such opportunities rank higher than salary incentives and paid educational opportunities for attracting and retaining rural teachers. Furthermore, research has shown that school administrators are critical in helping to equip their teachers with effective teaching strategies through professional-development activities (Mitchell & Sackney, 2000).

Problem of Attracting and Retaining Qualified Administrators

Although it is clear that effective administrative leaders are critical to the success of effective teaching and learning, in California and other states schools are facing myriad challenges in attracting qualified persons to hold leadership positions. A paper produced by the California Postsecondary Education Commission, titled *In Pursuit of Educational Leaders* (Sallee, 2001), found evidence that K–12 school leaders are serving for shorter periods of time, and fewer qualified people are interested in pursuing such positions. Research studies in the past (Boyer, 1986) have found that school administrators suffer from high levels of stress, and many were considering early exits from their positions. This stress, it appears, may be compounded by recent national and state reforms that have put into place stricter accountability measures for principals and teachers (Sallee, 2001). This situation makes it even more critical that policies and programs are implemented to provide support for existing school principals, particularly those in rural areas and that serve large populations of socioeconomically disadvantaged students. Any support provided in this area must take into consideration the unique needs, beliefs, and values of the community of which the school is part (Bolman & Deal, 1992; Sergiovanni, 1999).

Importance of Providing Quality Professional Development

Research indicates that professional-development programs for teachers and administrators are most beneficial when they are on-going as opposed to short, stand-alone training days (Joyce, 1992; Joyce & Showers, 1988). Professional development needs to be followed up; the needs of the students must be evaluated first in order to strategize; and the training and actual implementation of the ideas need to involve both administrators and teachers working together in a collaborative environment, similar to professional development for any administrator. Identifying and validating best practices, which will increase academic achievement levels and result in higher test scores, should be the focus of professional development for administrators and teachers in rural schools. Leadership roles must be shared to promote effective professional development so that student achievement improves. Yet administrators have had little preparation in how to collaborate and share leadership.

Designing a Leadership Institute for Rural School Leaders

In 1997, the University of California established a new academic center in Fresno; its overall goal was to serve the educational needs of working professionals, including school administrators and teachers. The new center was strategically located in Fresno so that the university could make its programs more accessible to communities throughout the San Joaquin Valley, particularly rural areas. The center was a key part of an overall strategy to plan for and build the first research university in the region, University of California, Merced.

Forming a Partnership to Design the Institute

A needs assessment conducted by the university in 1998 identified school teachers and administrators among those professionals in the area who most needed accessible and quality professional-development support. In a follow-up to the needs assessment, university academic program officers convened meetings in 1999 with county school superintendents, district superintendents, and principals throughout the region to discuss the most effective ways to serve the professional-development needs of these school administrators and teachers. School leaders from rural areas were well represented at these meetings because they were the most in need of professional-development programs. One immediate outcome of these meetings was the decision to design together a new professional-development program for school leaders.

Because no one organization or institution in the region had the capacity to carry out successfully a quality school leadership institute on its own, a consortium of partner organizations with mutual goals, under the leadership of UC Merced, was established to implement the school leadership institute.

The partners that UC Merced brought together came from throughout the region and included the following:

- *Experienced school administrators* from rural school districts, some of whom were graduates of a Joint Doctoral Program in Educational Leadership sponsored by the University of California and California State University, Fresno.

- *The president of a local community college (Merced College),* who was a former school teacher, principal, and district superintendent.

- *Faculty and staff members from local comprehensive universities* (California State University, Fresno, and California State University, Bakersfield), currently the largest public universities in the region.

- *The Academic Program Director for the first research university planned for the region* (University of California, Merced), who had recently completed doctoral study in educational leadership at a major research university.

- *The Director of Professional Studies from the University of California, Merced,* who had a graduate degree in education and the skills and interest to organize and implement the program.

- *Prominent scholars of educational leadership from throughout the University of California system and other research universities.* Several of these scholars had personal ties to the region and were interested in contributing to its development.

After considering the needs of regional school leaders, the program was designed to include two primary components:

1. *A five-day summer institute* serving initially about 25 school leaders, which took place at the University of California Center in Fresno in 2000 and 2001 (and at the University of California Center in Bakersfield in 2001). Participants were given the option of staying in a hotel across the street from the center during the institute or to commute from their homes.
2. *One-day workshops* each quarter during the following academic year. All summer-institute participants were invited to attend the workshops.

Institute Participants

The institute was open to school principals, vice principals, and district leaders throughout the San Joaquin Valley region. A written application was required from each leader prior to admission; however, all eligible applicants who submitted the required information in a timely way were admitted to the program. A participation fee was charged, but in virtually all cases the school or district with which the applicant was affiliated covered the fee. UC Merced provided full or partial scholarships to applicants from school districts that were unable to cover this fee, including many rural school districts.

The approximately 40 to 50 leadership-institute participants as a group were rich in diversity. This diversity is illustrated through the following characteristics:

- *Gender.* 60% were female and 40% were male.

- *Race/Ethnicity.* 53% were Latino, 40% were white, and 7% were African American.

- *Experience.* Many of the administrators were relatively new to their position at the time of the interview. About 93% of the administrators had served fewer than five years, and 60% had served fewer than three years in their current position. The maximum number of years of service in their current position was five years.

- *Educational Background.* Approximately 75% of the administrators had earned at least a master's degree, and 25% had a bachelor's degree only. However, all administrators with a bachelor's degree were enrolled in a master's program. One of the administrators had also received a doctoral degree in educational leadership.

- *Type of School.* Approximately 67% of the administrators worked in middle or high schools, and 33% worked in elementary schools.

Institute Topics

As determined in previous discussions, the institute focused on (1) the content of areas that were of greatest interest to the administrators, and (2) enhancing the leadership skills they possessed to deal effectively with the challenges they faced. The institute curricula included the following topics:

- The characteristics of effective leadership, shared leadership, and collaboration with teachers and other stakeholders
- Financial and management issues facing school leaders
- Improving educational equity for students
- Identifying and accessing educational resources via the Internet
- Building and sustaining partnerships with community-based organizations and higher education institutions

Institute Faculty

In recognition of limited resources in the region, it was essential to recruit faculty members from other institutions to help provide instruction. The institute faculty included scholars from throughout the state and country, including UC Berkeley, UC Santa Barbara, Stanford University, the University of Washington, and the University of Texas, El Paso. University faculty members were invited to make presentations of their research on the topics noted in the curricula above. The presentations were organized to complement one another. The institute participants were asked to review materials in advance of these presentations and were encouraged to ask questions and engage in dialogues with the faculty members.

Working Collaboratively with Colleagues and Veteran School Leaders

In addition to exposing participants to prominent scholars and their most recent research findings, the institute also helped to facilitate new relationships among and between themselves and with more experienced administrators from throughout the region. This was accomplished through the design of break-out sessions where smaller groups of administrators (five to eight) worked together on case studies that focused attention on leadership issues facing the participants. Senior administrators from the region served as facilitators of these discussions and assisted in building networks.

Assessing the Quality and Benefits of the Leadership Institute

Data Collection

After completing two years of the institute, 15 of the participants were interviewed for one hour at their school sites. All institute participants were invited to participate in the interviews, but their busy work schedules coupled with the distance between the participants and the project's time and resource constraints resulted in some administrators not being able to participate in an interview. The interview protocol, which was approved by the UC Santa Barbara Human Subjects Committee, included questions asking each participant to assess the quality of the institute and how it specifically provided them with new skills and a heightened awareness of important issues. The interview also asked them to relate the skills they acquired at the institute to new and on-going challenges that they were facing.

Generally, the administrators rated the institute highly and believed that it helped them in many important ways. Almost all of the participants felt that the institute either helped them to rethink their job in some manner or reinforced their current practices. The following are some areas that institute participants found most helpful:

- *Shared Learning.* Virtually all of the administrators said that the institute provided them with a great opportunity to meet and interact with other administrators facing similar challenges. They learned new ways of thinking about similar issues by engaging in formal and informal dialogue with school-site and district-office leaders. One participant, a middle school principal who had completed his first year on the job just prior to the institute, remarked "Networking (during the institute) allowed me to see that I was not the only one facing certain issues, and I learned about issues that I am likely to face in the future." Another principal said that the institute enabled her to better appreciate "different perspectives from administrators in other districts and the challenges that they face."

- *Policy Awareness and Research Skills.* Participants became more aware of educational policy issues and more sensitive to the need to use "data-driven" research to make decisions. "I learned . . . how to be a better school leader and to make decisions based on research. I was encouraged to read more books and to use research to be a more effective principal," said one middle school principal who had been in the position for three years prior to the institute. Another participant, a continuation high school principal, commented "I cannot [any longer] make decisions based only on experience and feelings. I should make decisions based on data."

- *Technology Training.* Participants were more apt to use computers after the institute and were more aware of resources available on the Internet and the usefulness of different technologies in schools. "The institute caused me to be more aware and open to technology. My school is ahead of others in meeting the requirements for a CTAP [California Technology Assistance Program] grant because the institute provided this awareness," noted an elementary school principal. Another principal found that the level of emphasis on technological skills during the institute was helpful and appropriate. "Principals should have computer skills to do their jobs effectively."

All but a few institute participants interviewed for this study believed that the skills they gained were important. According to an elementary school principal who had just completed his first year on the job, "The institute inspired my enthusiasm about leadership and got me 'pumped.' It validated that I need to get things moving (in my school)." Some participants found the unit on "emotional intelligence" so powerful that they planned to implement those ideas, in collaboration with teachers, immediately in their schools. Emotional intelligence refers to how leaders handle themselves and their relationships (Goleman, McKee, & Boyatkis, 2002).

The institute benefited participants in a variety of ways. Many participants found it to be a transformative experience that resulted in a reformulation of how they do their jobs. They also began to view leadership in a broader way, considering new ways to share responsibility and authority with teachers and other key stakeholders. When interviewed six months after the institute was completed, a high school principal captured the essence of shared leadership by stating that "principals should be visionaries who can also work well with parents, students, teachers, and the community."

Leadership Challenges in Rural Schools

The institute participants returned to their schools feeling better equipped to address myriad challenges. When interviewed after the completion of the second institute, the principals and vice principals expressed a strong commitment to sharing leadership responsibilities with teachers. Working collaboratively with teachers and other stakeholders was a consistent theme in their comments regarding what knowledge and skills are necessary to be effective school leaders. These issues are critical in informing future UC Merced institutes, and also provide important information for others who direct administrative preparation programs and provide ongoing professional development for administrators. Too often preparation and the training agenda are set by outsiders and not those on the frontline of school leadership work. Furthermore, the institute participants also identified the following areas as the most important challenges they faced and wanted assistance with in the coming year:

- *Supporting Teachers.* Many administrators were concerned about how best to support their teachers so their schools could achieve district and state expectations. They wished to support teachers' interest in expanded technology training and to provide them with feedback about their teaching through more classroom observation. An elementary school principal remarked, "I want to focus in and improve instruction by helping unsatisfactory teachers become satisfactory teachers. I want to make sure that teachers have the tools they need to be successful." Also of concern to the administrators was making sure that the curriculum used by teachers is appropriate for the grade level and to meet the standards-based requirements.

- *Managing Relationships.* Another major challenge cited by administrators was the need to deal with a wide range of personnel issues within their schools. The administrators found themselves trying to manage complicated relationships with personnel at their schools and in the districts. Some administrators felt unsupported by their district, citing a lack of leadership or a tendency to micromanage issues. The administrators generally felt ill-equipped to deal with the range and complexity of these issues. A veteran elementary school principal asked rhetorically, "How can I deal effectively with so many different people, including parents and teachers? You can't please everybody." This perspective was most often shared by those administrators who had been in their positions for fewer than two years.

- *Strategic Planning and Setting Priorities.* Several administrators felt challenged by the need to have strong organizational and multitasking skills to achieve their goals. Many of them expressed a need to better prioritize tasks and learn how to delegate actions so that they might be more effective in their positions. This was an area where most of the administrators said they needed to improve their skills. A vice principal with many years of prior teaching experience noted that she "needed to be better prepared for future challenges and opportunities by engaging in strategic planning . . . school leaders must be talented in a variety of ways to be successful."

• *Understanding School/Community Culture.* One of the last types of major challenges mentioned by administrators was the need to relate better to their school and community culture and to the attitudes held by students, teachers, and families. Some of these attitudes included overcoming uninformed or negative preconceived notions regarding the academic achievement of certain groups of students. A high school principal observed that one of the main challenges she faces is "changing the school culture from one that believes demographics dictate educational achievement and commitment to one that respects and appreciates diversity." An elementary school principal put it succinctly: "I want to bring parents, students, and teachers together so we all know what to expect from a K–6 education."

A Case Study of a Rural School District Using the Institute to Model Shared Leadership

One rural school district in the San Joaquin Valley—Parlier Unified School District—demonstrated an unusually high level of participation in the leadership institute. The district is typical of other districts in the region in the student achievement challenges it faces. The STAR 2002 district summary reports reveal that Parlier does not currently meet California state standards. In English/Language/Arts, only 9.3% of its students in grades 2–11 scored at the proficient or advanced levels (a drop of 2.8% from 2000), whereas in Mathematics 13.2% of the students in grades 2–7 are classified at the proficient or advanced levels (a drop of 2.7% from 2000). This means that 89.7% and 86.8%, respectively, of the current Parlier students are at basic, below-basic, or far-below-basic test levels in English/Language/Arts and in Mathematics. Much hard work must occur to bring these students up to state standards. These statistics prompted UC Merced to reach out to Parlier and prompted the superintendent to respond assertively to the offer to participate. The district participated as a team in both years of the institute, sending all of their principals and vice principals and one district office representative. The superintendent required their participation and visited the institute each day to observe the discussions and participate in some meetings. The district also required that their leaders participate in follow-up sessions throughout the academic year and gave release time to attend the meetings. Although there was resistance from a few principals during the first summer institute, this resistance dissipated as the principals engaged with others facing similar challenges and received support in addressing "their" issues.

To build on the district's strong commitment to professional development, UC Merced, UC Santa Barbara, and the district submitted and were successful in securing a grant from the California Policy Research Center that enabled the leadership team to be broadened to include teachers from each school in the district. In 2002, the district's entire leadership team of administrators and teachers, including the superintendent, enthusiastically met for a two-day forum at UC Santa Barbara.

The decision to include teachers in the forum was part of a deliberate strategy to enhance shared leadership skills. The teachers were selected by each principal, in consultation with the superintendent. Although they had not participated in the leadership institutes with the administrators, several had worked in the district for many years and had already developed a trusting relationship with them. However, that relationship was based on a more traditional paradigm of school leadership that included less frequent involvement of teachers in school and district decisions. At the forum, the teachers were full participants in all of the sessions, and they were asked to contribute to discussions regarding issues facing the district as well as new policies and practices to address these issues.

The forum participants identified a range of challenges they faced in effectively sharing leadership. The primary challenges include the following:

- *Creating an Environment That Fosters Shared Leadership.* School leaders want an environment that fosters professional growth in teaching strategies, honest two-way communication between administration and faculty, and shared team leadership development. Explicit requests were made for additional strategies that promote shared leadership.

- *Finding Time for Administrators and Teachers to Work Together.* Because new mandates and standards require educators to learn new knowledge and skills, the forum participants expressed the need for administrators and teachers to spend more time together engaged in strategic planning and professional development than is currently allocated. Existing school calendars and class schedules keep teachers isolated and allow little time or flexibility for professional collaboration related to goals, objectives, content standards, and professional development.

- *Securing Additional Resources to Overcome Isolation.* Many of the school leaders expressed the need for both external expertise to help them improve as well as the need to facilitate and draw on internal teacher expertise. They expressed a desire to see in action school models for curriculum development, research-based effective teaching strategies, and implementation of standards-based content units and lessons. Given the isolation of these school districts and potential distance from such models and expertise, careful attention needs to be paid to providing both time and creative professional development that might facilitate exchanges between schools and that will enhance teacher and administrative skills. Participants also recognized the potential for facilitating their own professional development through learning how to conduct their own action research on their classroom and school practices. Such teacher-led school development has shown to be a powerful incentive for school improvement and increased student achievement (Frost, Durrant, Head, & Holden, 2000).

- *Balancing State Mandates With Local Autonomy.* It was agreed that more collaboration needs to occur between state policymakers and school administrators so that educational goals could be jointly negotiated and established in ways that would increase consistency between policymakers' agendas and pressing local needs. Educators in rural communities often face considerable challenges in just meeting the demands of facilities, acquiring the basic supplies they lack, recruiting and retaining highly qualified staff, as well as serving high-needs students compared to their affluent counterparts in suburban districts. Participants felt pressured by the push and pull of enforcing state mandates as well as meeting local needs such as promoting school change and professional development.

Conclusion

Educators in rural schools, similar to their counterparts in urban areas, face a daunting task in improving the achievement of students, particularly those from low-income backgrounds and those who are still learning English. These challenges are shaped by a paradigm shift in education occurring nationally, which holds schools accountable for meeting high standards for all children. The UC, Merced, San Joaquin Valley School Leadership Institute was designed as a new partnership model of professional development to assist rural school leaders. The current shift in education requires school leaders to work in closer collaboration with teachers to serve the needs of students. The institute provided school leaders with strategies to work with teachers and other stakeholders, emphasizing that leadership for their schools be shared with teachers and other stakeholders.

The institute's design process was an example of how shared leadership can bring about positive results. Several different partners, who had not worked together before, joined as a team to serve the needs of educational leaders. The institute could not have been carried out independently by any one of the partners because of the social and economic constraints facing the region. By sharing leadership and resources, the partners were able to deliver together a quality professional-development program.

Parlier Unified School District demonstrated its commitment to shared leadership by inviting teachers to join their team during a forum that followed the completion of the two summer institutes. During this forum, teachers were empowered to participate actively in discussing the most significant challenges facing the district and proposing solutions to address those challenges.

In future institutes, it would be advantageous to include teachers as full participants. Doing so would affirm the critical importance of collaboration between administrators and teachers, strengthen the personal and professional relationships among and between these groups, and model new ways to structure shared leadership and collaboration within their schools.

At the time of this first institute, California and other parts of the nation were experiencing an economic downturn that was, in many respects, more severe than the economic downturn of the early 1990s. Rural areas of the state and country generally had a less diverse economic base and were especially hard hit during this period (Danenberg, Jepsen, & Cerdan, 2002). At the time of this writing, this fiscal crisis has led to significant cuts to education that could be devastating to efforts to ensure that all children master high standards. School leaders will be responsible for working with teachers, school board members, and other stakeholders to assess how these cuts will affect their schools and to identify options that help preserve effective programs and people. It is critically important that professional-development programs remain available to support rural school administrators and teachers as they address these formidable challenges. By enhancing the skills of school leaders, particularly skills required to facilitate shared leadership and closer collaboration with teachers, professional-development programs of this kind provide a valuable way to help rural schools overcome their most difficult challenges.

References

Bolman, L. & Deal, T. (1992). Leading and managing: Effects of context, culture and gender. *Educational Administration Quarterly, 28,* 314–329.

Boyer, E. (1986) *High school: A report on secondary education in America.* Stanford, CA: Carnegie Foundation for the Advancement of Teaching.

Danenberg, A., Jepsen, C., & Cerdan, P. (2002). *Students and school indicators for youth in California's Central Valley.* San Francisco: Public Policy Institute of California.

Darling-Hammond, L. (1997). *The right to learn.* San Francisco: Jossey-Bass.

Dewees, S. (2000). *Participation of rural schools in the comprehensive school reform demonstration program: What do we know?* Charleston, WV: Rural Laboratory Network Program.

Frost, D., Durrant, J., Head, M., & Holden, G. (2000). *Teacher-led school improvement.* London: Routledge Falmer.

Goleman, D., McKee, A., & Boyatkis, R. (2002). *Primal leadership: Realizing the power of emotional intelligence.* Cambridge, MA: Harvard Business School Press.

Jimerson, L. (2003). *The competitive disadvantage: Teacher compensation in rural America.* Washington, D.C.: Rural Trust Policy Series on Rural Education.

Joyce, B. (1992). Cooperative learning and staff development: Teaching the method with the method. *Cooperative Learning, 12*(2), 10–13.

Joyce, B., & Showers, B. (1988). *Student achievement through staff development.* New York: Longman.

Kaufman, P., Alt, M. N., & Chapman, C. (2001). *Dropout rates in the United States: 2000.* Washington, D.C.: National Center for Education Statistics.

Martin, S. M., Williams, J. M., & Hess, R. (2001, March). *Personnel preparations and service delivery issues in rural areas: The state of the art.* Conference proceedings from Growing Partnerships for Rural Special Education, San Diego, CA.

Mitchell, C., & Sackney, L. (2000). *Profound improvement: Building capacity for a learning community.* Lisee, The Netherlands: Swets & Zeitliner.

Perroncel, C. B. (2000). *Getting kids ready for school in rural America.* Charleston, WV: The Rural Specialty.

Sallee, J. (2001). *In pursuit of educational leaders.* Working paper prepared for the California Postsecondary Education Commission.

Sergiovanni, T. J. (1999). *The lifeworld of educational leadership.* San Francisco: Jossey-Bass.

Tucker, M. S., & Codding, J. B. (2002). *The principal challenge: Leading and managing schools in an era of accountability.* San Francisco: Jossey-Bass.

14

Problem-Based Learning and Its Role in Preparing School Leaders for Collaboration

Edwin M. Bridges

Universities that prepare educational leaders confront at least three major, interrelated challenges:

1. How to combine theory, research, and practice
2. What knowledge, skills, and values to emphasize
3. How to facilitate the acquisition of the particular knowledge, skills, and values

How universities choose to meet these challenges largely determines the kind and quality of the educational leaders who graduate from these programs.

The historical record of universities' efforts to meet these challenges paints a disappointing picture. Although the literature in the field of educational leadership underscores the importance of combining theory, research, and practice, few universities have seriously confronted this challenge and even fewer have met it. With respect to the second challenge, universities have generally emphasized the knowledge domain and have neglected, if not ignored, skills and values. Finally, universities have typically used a limited number of instructional approaches—namely, lecture and discussion—to prepare educational leaders.

This chapter discusses how I and some of my colleagues at Stanford University chose to confront these three challenges when designing a program for preparing prospective school principals. The discussion will focus primarily, though not exclusively, on preparing future educational leaders to engage teachers, staff, and parents in shared decision making. From the outset, preparing leaders for this particular style of leadership figured prominently in our design of the program. Details about the program content, structure, and outcomes can be found in Bridges and Hallinger (1992).

A Critical Ingredient: Problem-Based Learning

Problem-based learning (PBL) provided the primary vehicle for our addressing the three aforementioned challenges. This instructional approach originated in the field of medical education as a response to numerous criticisms of how physicians were being trained. Recognizing the potential power of this approach, we created our own version of PBL for preparing educational leaders. It is now being used by a number of universities in the United States, Australia, Asia, and Canada, as well as the New York City public schools.

Although PBL comes in various versions, each rendition includes the following elements:

1. The starting point for learning is a problem. These problems are ones that students are likely to face as future professionals.
2. Theory, research, and knowledge are organized around problems rather than the disciplines.
3. Students, individually and collectively, assume considerable responsibility for their own learning and are active learners, not passive ones.
4. Students learn in the context of small groups rather than lectures.
5. Instructors act as coaches; they are a "guide on the side, not a sage on the stage."

In the version of PBL that we incorporated into our program for prospective principals, we assign students to a project team. Each team usually consists of six members. We designate one member as the leader of the team for the life of the project. Projects usually last for four or five class sessions. Each class session, approximately three hours in length, is viewed as a meeting of the project team. The team leader and meeting facilitator plan the agenda prior to each meeting. During the meetings of the team, members engage in a variety of activities: defining the problem, reviewing resources provided by the instructor and other team members, deciding how to solve the problem that is the focus of the project, and providing feedback to the leader and other team members. Students must implement their solution rather than just discuss how they intend to solve the problem. The product or performance that represents their solution to the problem is an authentic one and enables students to experience the consequences of their chosen solution (Bridges & Hallinger, 1992, pp. 29–57).

Conceptual Underpinnings of PBL

Numerous theoretical grounds exist for expecting students who have been trained using PBL to differ in important ways from students prepared in traditional methods—information theory, contextual learning, cooperative learning, self-determination theory, control theory, motivational, and functional (Albanese, 2000; Bridges & Hallinger, 1997). We have found information theory, motivational theory, and functional grounds to be the most compelling. Based on these three theoretical grounds, we expect that students in PBL programs should be more likely than students in traditional programs to do the following:

1. Retain, access, and apply their newly acquired knowledge.
2. Master leadership skills and understand what it feels like to be a leader.
3. Exert more effort while learning.
4. Display a more favorable attitude toward their preparation.
5. Make more informed decisions about school leadership as a career and to be more satisfied if they choose to become a school leader (Bridges & Hallinger, 1997).

Information Theory. According to Schmidt (1983), PBL creates three optimal conditions for learning. First, students *activate their prior knowledge* while processing new information. Problem-based learning facilitates the activation of prior knowledge by the selection and sequencing of problems in the curriculum, which in turn facilitates understanding of the new material. Second, PBL *creates a context that resembles the situation* in which students will later apply their knowledge. The similarities in context supply cues that stimulate recall and use of the knowledge. Third, PBL encourages students to *elaborate their newly acquired knowledge* at the time it is initially learned. During a PBL project, students read to acquire the knowledge, test their understanding of the material with their team members, grapple with how to apply the knowledge to the problem they face, and prepare reflective essays about what they have learned and how they plan to use it in the future.

Motivational Theory. Problem-based learning stimulates a high level of intrinsic motivation. Students view the learning environment as meaningful and relevant because it is structured around problems they are likely to face in their professional careers. In addition, PBL includes several features that motivate learners—namely, active roles for students, peer interaction, emphasis on higher-order thinking skills, authentic products, and simulations (Good & Brophy, 1991).

Functional Theory. Unlike conventional instruction, PBL provides a realistic job preview of school leadership. While learning new knowledge and skills, students also learn what a leader does and how it feels to be in a leadership position. This added insight into the nature of leadership occurs in various ways. Students work on problems like the ones they will encounter in the future, the products and performances they fashion to solve the problems are authentic, and they occupy leadership roles in PBL projects. Clearly, the work of a student in PBL more closely parallels the work of school leaders than does the work of students in more traditional forms of instruction. This job preview provides students with more realistic conceptions of a school leader's role and enables them to test their fitness for it. As a result, they should be less likely to make a wrong occupational choice and to experience the disillusionment produced by excessively unrealistic expectations (Bridges & Hallinger, 1992, 1997).

Effectiveness of Problem-Based Learning

Research on the effectiveness of PBL has been conducted most extensively in the field of medical education. Four major reviews of this research (Albanese, 2000; Albanese & Mitchell, 1993; Colliver, 2000; Vernon & Blake, 1993) comparing PBL with traditional instruction show that the satisfaction scores of PBL students are consistently and substantially higher than those students taught by more traditional methods. Students in PBL programs tend to have slightly greater clinical knowledge and higher clinical ratings of performance than traditionally trained students. Scores on basic science examinations, however, are slightly higher for traditionally trained students than PBL students.

In the field of educational leadership, research on PBL is much more sparse. The most rigorous studies have been conducted by Copland (2000, 2003). His first study compared three groups of students who had varying degrees of exposure to PBL. After controlling for scholastic aptitude, he found that all three cohorts of students differed significantly in problem-framing skills—the greater exposure to PBL, the greater the skill in problem-framing ability. In his second study, he studied a single group of students at two points in time. This longitudinal study showed that students increased their problem-framing skills as they gained greater exposure to problem-based learning. The subskills in problem-based learning that Copland (2000) studied included the following (p. 605):

1. Definition of the Stated Problem

Descriptor

- Clear recognition of the stated problem.

2. Reflection on the Stated Problem

Descriptors

- Identification of the importance of formulating a clear interpretation of the problem prior to considering possible solutions.
- Identification of the importance of approaching a problem without holding to a preconceived solution.
- Cognition and review of personal assumptions about the problem situation.
- Consideration of the views of others in the problem situation.
- Identification of preexisting solution(s) embedded in the initial problem situation.

3. Reframing of the Problem (If Necessary)

Descriptors

- Restatement of the problem in solution-free terms.
- Identification and reliance on personal values related to a problem-solving process in restating the problem.
- Anticipation of the obstacles likely to arise during the problem-solving process.
- Anticipation of ways to address obstacles should they arise.

An Abbreviated Example: Safety and Order

Members of a typical project team in our program are confronted with the following problem scenario:

For more than 50 years Monroe City High School has been the pride of the community. Last spring a skirmish occurred on campus. Six students suffered injuries, hired an attorney, and sued the former principal and the school district for negligence. The school board fired the principal and mandated the newly appointed principal to restore safety and order at Monroe City High School. The principal appointed a committee chair and five others to attack the problem. Her charge to the committee chair, a newly appointed assistant principal, was as follows:

To: M. Jones, Assistant Principal for School Discipline

From: T. Smith, Principal

The Board has asked us to restore safety and order at M.C.H.S. Before drafting our plan for achieving this objective, I want to know how terrible things actually are here. It is conceivable that the skirmish last spring, serious as it was, isn't really a good indicator. I am providing you with the disciplinary database for the first semester of last year. If you find any other information or data that might provide insight into how serious the problems are here, by all means use them.

I want to have a clear picture of the situation with respect to student discipline and a tentative plan for restoring safety and order at M.C.H.S.

The other two assistant principals and I will react to your committee's work at our meeting next week.

Note to project team members: Some additional information about the problem is available upon request. If the information is available, we will provide it. Team members must ask for specific types of information, not general ones like "What additional information is available?" or "May I have the rest of the information?" [Important pieces of information supplied: gang activity and discipline incidents for second semester.]

As the members of the project team ponder how to respond to the principal's memo, their attention turns to additional information they want to request that may be relevant to understanding the problem fully.

The Role of Collaboration in PBL

In the process of acquiring new knowledge to deal with real-world challenges like the one above, students learn the knowledge, skills, and values needed by principals who lead by facilitating collaboration and building consensus rather than by exerting formal authority. Because the context for learning is a small problem-solving and decision-making group, students inevitably must deal with the array of challenges inherent in such groups: limited resources, time constraints, value conflicts, diverse personalities and styles, and varying perspectives on what the problem is and how to solve it.

By marrying PBL and an emphasis on collaboration, we sought to produce a multiplier effect. To optimize performance in self-directed group work that involves decision making as well as learning, students need to master skills in running meetings, solving problems, and building consensus. These related skills also form the same skill set for administrators who engage their staffs in shared decision making. In line with our intent to exploit this potential multiplier effect, we have consciously sequenced the first few PBL projects so that each successive project draws on the knowledge and skills developed in preceding projects. The spiraling character of this curriculum provides students with repeated opportunities to practice and refine their collaborative skills.

Content

To prepare students for collaboration, we emphasize the following content:

1. A systematic approach to problem solving
2. A method for managing meetings
3. A set of tools and techniques for group problem solving and decision making
4. A method for resolving conflict and building consensus
5. An appreciation of the value of shared decision making

Approach to Problem Solving. Numerous models exist for solving problems; we chose one that has worked for us in a variety of situations.

The components of this problem-solving process typify most rational approaches:

1. Identify the pertinent facts
2. Define the problem
3. Specify the criteria for evaluating solutions to the problem
4. Generate possible solutions
5. Evaluate each solution in terms of the criteria
6. Choose a solution
7. Foreshadow potential problems and plan to deal with them

As we later discuss, student mastery of this problem-solving approach proved much more difficult and required considerably more practice and coaching than we had anticipated.

Meeting Management Method. Although administrators spend much of their work day in meetings, this time is often wasted. Numerous problems plague these meetings. Discussions wander aimlessly, one or two people dominate the discussion, feelings are hurt, and group members complain about a lack of accomplishment. Most leaders and group members lack an understanding of the ingredients of an effective meeting; even fewer have been trained to run their meetings effectively.

In order to increase our students' knowledge and understanding of how to run effective meetings, we introduce them to the Interaction Method (Doyle & Straus, 1981). A key feature of this method centers around clarification of four roles: leader, facilitator, recorder, and group members. Facilitators, not the leader, run the meetings. It is their responsibility to move the meeting along smoothly, to suggest process tools for dealing with the content items on the agenda, to handle conflict and disruptive behavior in the group, to prevent people from dominating the discussion, and to bring the group to closure on action items. In short, facilitators focus on group process and refrain from participating in resolving the items on the agenda.

Tools for Group Problem Solving and Decision Making. To make meetings run smoothly, facilitators, as well as other group members, require knowledge and understanding of various tools and when they might be used during the problem-solving process. As part of their training, students become acquainted with fourteen tools that have proven useful in group problem solving and decision making. Most of these tools are discussed in Doyle and Straus (1981); we cite several examples below:

> *Brainstorming.* Generating ideas without evaluating them.
>
> *Straw voting.* Getting a sense of how the group feels about an issue or solution.
>
> *Rating ABC.* The group examines a list of statements arrived at through brainstorming. The facilitator asks members to rate each item on the list with an A, B, or C. A is the highest rating, C the lowest. The rating of each item by each member is recorded for all to view. The facilitator tallies the results. Items with the most As and Bs rise to the top of the list.

Resolving Conflict. During the process of making decisions as a group, two or more members may become enamored with their positions, and these differences may lead to destructive conflict unless skillfully handled by the facilitator. To prepare students to deal with conflict when it arises within the group, we introduce them to the work of Fisher and colleagues' *Getting to Yes* (1991). A central tenet of their approach to conflict resolution is the importance of probing and surfacing the major interests or concerns underlying the positions of the parties in conflict. When these underlying interests or concerns have been identified, the facilitator works with the group to arrive at a solution that satisfies all of these interests. This approach stimulates creative problem solving and usually, though not always, a win-win outcome.

Appreciation of Shared Decision Making. Knowledge and skills are necessary, but insufficient, prerequisites for shared decision making. School leaders who use this approach will inevitably discover that group decisions take longer than ones made unilaterally. Moreover, building consensus requires patience, a tolerance for others' viewpoints, and an appreciation of its value. After serving in the leader's role, one of the students in the prospective principals program wrote this about her experience:

> The value of group work was reinforced through this experience. Working as a group provided opportunity to capitalize on multiple strengths and viewpoints. Reflecting back, I think the decisions made by the group were better overall than individual decisions. The group memo was better, in my opinion, than my own or any other individual memo. The final plan of action determined by the group was also better than my plan alone.
>
> I gained a new perspective on the role of the leader. Midway through the project I realized I was feeling very stressed about the project. Reflecting on

> this, I concluded that wasn't my responsibility as the leader. Problem-solving was the group's responsibility. Reflecting on past leadership experiences, I surmised that this misplaced sense of responsibility might account for my dissatisfaction with other group experiences. If I didn't want to revert to autocracy, my role was to facilitate, clarify, and guide the process. (quoted in Bridges & Hallinger, 1992, p. 70)

Another student in the program wrote:

> The affective outcomes of the process are the amazing camaraderie, the sensitivity to others, the change of intolerance to tolerance to acceptance to appreciation of different viewpoints. All of these are important to the operational goal of the program, and in developing a new breed of administrator who won't settle for the isolation so characteristic of the principalship. (quoted in Bridges & Hallinger, 1992, p. 68)

Instructional Process

To facilitate student learning of the aforementioned content and mastering of the skills in using this content, we rely primarily on a strategy consisting of the following components:

1. Explicit focus on the importance of process
2. Expectation that the content and skills we introduced students to should be practiced during meetings of the project team
3. Student modeling of the interaction method, problem solving skills, and process tools
4. Feedback regarding students' use of the interaction method, skills, and tools

Focus on Process. To underscore the importance of process, we created a problem-based learning project on meeting management. In this project, students read *How to Make Meetings Work* and familiarized themselves with the problem-solving process and related tools. We intentionally chose a problem with no educational content, the Desert Survival Exercise, to increase the likelihood that students would focus on process, not content. (See Lafferty, Clayton, & Pond, 1974, for more details on this exercise.) Students were expected to practice the targeted skills as they worked on solving the problem embedded in the Desert Survival Exercise. The instructions for this exercise were as follows:

> Your plane has crash landed in the Sonoran Desert. Before the plane caught fire your group was able to salvage the 15 items listed in the hand-out, "Desert Survival Situation." Your task is to rank these items according to their importance to your survival, starting with "1" as the most important, to "15" as the least important. Complete the 11 steps described on the hand-out.
>
> Before completing the group ranking of the 15 items, you may find it useful to discuss, define, and solve the problem facing your group. When discussing, defining, and solving the problem, you may wish to follow the problem-solving process.

Students discover through this exercise that applying the interaction method, the problem-solving process, and the various tools presents much more of a challenge than they had expected. Their realization stimulates them to work on mastering this material during the succeeding projects.

Stated Expectations. We communicate our expectations that students demonstrate mastery of these skills by the end of the third summer orally and in writing. We also explain the reasoning behind our expectations; namely, that administrators spend a great deal of time in meetings. Moreover, administrators often complain that these meetings are a waste of time because they have not been trained to run them effectively. Many students experience a sense of awkwardness when trying to learn these skills; to them it just doesn't feel right. Over time these feelings disappear as students become more familiar with the techniques and observe growth in their ability to use them.

Use of Student Models. By the beginning of the third summer, students have increased their skills in using the interaction method, the problem-solving process, and the process tools. We identify the most proficient leaders, facilitators, and recorders and designate them to perform these roles in teams consisting of second- and third-year students. Our use of these third-year students to model how to perform these roles skillfully accelerates the learning process of second-year students. They, in turn, become role models for the next group of students. Second-year students consistently remark about how much they have learned from the third-year group about using the process skills.

Feedback. We rely heavily on feedback to promote students' mastery of the skills. Initially, the instructor models how to provide feedback by making specific rather than general comments. Instead of saying something like, "I thought you did a good job of facilitating the group," we would comment, "I particularly was impressed with your choice of tools during the problem-solving process. When your group brainstormed a long list of criteria, you appropriately used the ABC tool." Gradually, we encourage students to provide specific feedback to the leader, facilitator, and recorder about how each has performed his or her role, noting what they appreciated and what he or she might consider doing in the future. After students have become accustomed to providing unsolicited feedback, we suggest to members of the team that they solicit the feedback they want. By this time, students have developed a sense of where they need to improve and desire feedback on their progress. We devote the end of each session to feedback, and it plays an important role in the students' development.

Problems Encountered

Although students in the program eventually mastered the knowledge and skills associated with consensus decision making, the learning process consumed much more time than we had anticipated. In subsequent problem-based learning projects, we observed a number of learning problems that surprised us. Looked at another way, we, as instructor-coaches, gained insight into the learning process and had to create new learning and assessment activities to facilitate the students' mastery of the material. In the discussion that follows, we describe how we coped with these initially baffling situations.

Conceptual Confusion. After introducing students to the interaction method, problem-solving process, and process tools during the first summer of the three-quarter practicum, we discovered that they made sparing use of these concepts in the second summer. Puzzled by what happened, we met over lunch with students and said, "We are somewhat baffled by your reluctance to use the concepts that you were introduced to last summer. We wonder if you would share with us why this seems to be happening." In the ensuing discussion, we learned that students had little or no sense of how and when to use these various concepts during their meetings. Consequently, we developed a structured activity around a classroom assessment technique recommended by Cross and Angelo (1988, pp. 26–28). Our modification of their memory matrix took the following form:

The purpose of this activity is to assist you in clarifying and consolidating the concepts to which you have been exposed in the practicum. We have discovered that participants often understand most, but not all, of the pieces but don't grasp how they fit into the larger picture. We designed this activity to move you toward greater understanding of these key concepts.

We have provided you with a matrix or grid and 21 items. Please follow these directions:

1. Review each of the 21 items and star those whose meanings are unclear. Jigsaw the starred items and report back what team members have learned about these items.
2. Sort the 21 items into two categories (one category consisting of seven items and the other consisting of 14 items).** Label each of your categories. [*Hint:* As a group, you may find it easer to work with these 21 items if you tape these to the board and then move them around as you categorize them.]
3. Determine whether the items in either category should be sequenced; if so, sequence the items. Explain the basis for sequencing the items.
4. Determine if a relationship exists between any of the items in one category with one or more items in the other category. If you see a relationship, use an X to depict the relationship between the items in the two categories. Explain why you see a relationship between the items in the two categories.
5. How might the group use the completed grid in the future, either in the practicum or in your own work situation?

Discussion Question: How does the above relate to the meeting management method (Interaction Method) that we have introduced you to in the practicum?

NOTE: Please bring Doyle and Straus and the other meeting management materials that we distributed earlier in the practicum.

**AUTHOR'S NOTE: The seven items in this category are steps in the problem-solving process. The remaining fourteen items are tools that can be used in one or more steps of this process.

We appointed two students—one as facilitator and the other as recorder—for the three-hour session allotted to this activity. The facilitator guided team members through the activity. Team members universally found the activity extremely helpful in clarifying how and when the process tools could be used in the problem-solving process. We subsequently observed facilitators reviewing the grid as they prepared for team meetings. During these meetings, they employed a greater variety of tools and used them appropriately. As a result, we inserted this activity midway through the first-year practicum. One of the students in the program, Michael Milliken, drew on this activity to generate his own matrix featuring the elements of the problem-solving process and the tools that might be used at various stages of this process (see Figure 14.1).

Troublesome Concepts. As we observed students endeavoring to use the problem-solving process, we noticed that group after group had difficulty applying three important concepts: the nature of a problem, criteria for evaluating solutions, and presented versus discovered problems. Without any clear conception of a problem or criteria, students inevitably experienced difficulty in stating problems and criteria. To assist them in judging the adequacy of a problem statement, we drew heavily on the work of Cuban (2001). In his book *How Can I Fix It?: Finding Solutions and Managing Dilemmas,* Cuban discusses some of the common mistakes problem solvers commit when stating problems. Two of these often appeared in students' problem statements: embedding a solution and placing blame on others. To counteract these tendencies, we encouraged students to evaluate the adequacy of their problem statements in terms of the following:

- Is it solution-free?
- Is it blame-free?
- Does it contain a single problem?
- Is there supporting evidence?

Initially, we supplied feedback on their problem statements by asking them questions based on this list. For example, we asked, "Have you embedded a solution in your problem statement?" After several sessions, we invited students to state the basis on which they would evaluate the adequacy of their problem statements and then to evaluate them in light of what they had stated. When students encountered difficulty in doing so, we pointed out their errors of commission or omission and explained the reasoning behind our judgments. Gradually, we withdrew our questions as students developed the habit of evaluating their own problem statements.

With respect to criteria for evaluating solutions, we noted that students often generated too many criteria, and many of the criteria represented elements of a solution to the problem. To clarify the meaning of criteria, we

Step	*Comments*	*Tools*
1. Identify the Facts		5 W's (Who, what, when, where, why) Relevant positions and interests for each party; constraints, and resources
2. Define the Problem	Is the cause of the problem crucial to dealing with it? Four important q's: • Is there a solution embedded? • Is there more than one problem stated? • Does it lay blame? • Is there evidence that it is a problem? Possible forms: a question, a declarative statement; or a goal and the obstacles preventing that goal.	Is/Ought (focus on "Is" items that are undesirables) Is/Is Not (a pinpointing tool for What, When, Where, Extent) Generating ideas: Brainstorming, idea cards, small groups Narrowing: Lasso, measles, ABC, spend a dollar, pros and cons Decisions throughout can be made using thumbs (straw vote), fist to five, majority vote, executive decision or consensus
3. Establish Solution Criteria	Solution criteria should focus on the state of things once the problem is solved. Sol. criteria should not have solutions embedded in them. Sol. criteria can be negative, e.g., "We do not want a police state."	Generating: Brainstorming, idea cards, small groups Narrowing: Lasso, measles, ABC, spend a dollar, pros and cons
4. Generate Possible Solutions		Brainstorming, idea cards, small groups
5. Evaluate Solutions		Checkerboard, pros and cons
6. Choose a Solution		Lasso, measles, ABC, spend a dollar, pros and cons, cut and paste
7. Anticipate Obstacles and Plan to Deal With Them	This step in the process often is glossed over. Make an effort to imagine what could go wrong. Is it preventable? If not, how will you deal with it if it happens?	Brainstorm; individual idea cards; think, pair, share

Figure 14.1 Problem-Solving Process and Tools

SOURCE: Student-generated matrix. Reprinted with permission from Michael Millikin.

decided to use Kepner and Tregoe's (1961) definition of objectives, which is synonymous with criteria. For them, objectives are the *results* expected to come from a solution. To clarify this concept, we related the following anecdote:

> This winter my car stalled nearly every time I stopped at a red light or stop sign. Frustrated by my car's poor performance, I took it to the dealership where I had purchased the car. Later that day I picked up my car. The service manager proceeded to tell me what they had done to the car: cleaned the carburetor, changed the spark plugs, installed a new wire set, and changed the battery. The bill for this work was $450. On the way home, my car started to stall again. The result or main criterion I had for judging the adequacy of the dealer's solution was not satisfied; my car continued to stall whenever I came to a stop. So, when you generate criteria, think of the *results* you want accomplished by your solutions, including unwanted results like lawsuits, excessive costs, and so on.

Subsequently, we observed students generating fewer criteria and omitting elements of a solution in the criteria which they generated.

In the practicum, we purposely included two major types of problems: presented and discovered. Presented problems confront the decision maker with a predefined problem that has no clear solution. Discovered problems, however, confront the problem solver with a problematic situation in which both the problem and solution are unclear. These two types of problems appear in different forms (Bridges with Hallinger, 1992). For example, a presented problem may take the form of an *implementation problem* (the administrator is assigned a new policy or program to implement and must figure out how to ensure the successful implementation of this policy or program; Bridges and Hallinger, 1992, p. 96). Discovered problems also come in multiple forms such as *the agenda for leadership* (sizing up a new situation, synthesizing the information that he or she has acquired, and using this information to create a pathway or vision for the future; Bridges with Hallinger, 1992, p. 95).

Initially, we introduced students to discovered problems, a situation requiring them to use all seven steps of the problem-solving process. When students later were faced with presented problems, they inappropriately wasted time trying to define the problem. After observing them struggling with this step of the problem-solving process, we apprised them of the distinction between presented and discovered problems. Furthermore, we pointed out that when confronted with presented problems, one started with step 3 in the process, establishing solution criteria. Following this clarification, we observed them identifying the type of problem they faced before proceeding with the problem-solving process.

Shot Gun Approach to Information Gathering. In one of our projects, *Safety and Order,* we modified the way in which students acquired information about the problematic situation. Instead of providing students with all the information as generally happens in a written case, we withheld some key information. We told students that there was more information available; however, they would obtain this information only if they asked the right questions. When students generated questions to which they wanted answers, we were surprised to see that their questions elicited irrelevant information. In response to their questions, we asked, "If you had the answers to all of the questions on your list, would you have any greater insight into the nature of the problem you are facing?" With our question in mind, they looked at their lengthy list of questions and replied, "We need more time to rethink our questions." At the next session, they asked six questions, all of which were relevant to enhancing their understanding of the problem they faced.

Unequal Participation. In heterogeneous groups, there is the ubiquitous tendency for white males to talk more than females and people of color. To counteract this inclination, we tally the number of comments made by each individual during the first two sessions. Ordinarily, we record this information several times during the session for periods lasting 10–15 minutes. At the end of the session we say to students, "At the beginning of the session your group established the norm of equal participation. Do you believe that you lived up to this norm?" Students generally reply, "Yes." At that point we introduce the data we had recorded and ask, "What story do the data we tallied tell?" They are startled by what we have revealed and often discuss how this pattern of interaction corresponds to what they have witnessed in other groups. In subsequent meetings of the team, we observe a more even distribution of participation. Moreover, there is no evidence that the group suffers a relapse.

Free-Riders. During group activities, it is not uncommon for group members to vary in the effort they put forth on behalf of the group. Unless group members are held accountable for their performance, the free-rider problem is apt to flourish. We hold group members accountable in several ways. Because the group jigsaws the reading assignments, members prepare a written summary of their material and orally report how, if at all, it applies to the problem the group is trying to solve. If the final product is written, we require each member to submit it in writing. If the final product is a performance, we roll the die a few minutes before the scheduled performance. The person with the winning number makes the presentation on behalf of the team. To commemorate this occasion, one student posted a sign on our door that read, "For whom does the die roll? It rolls for thee." The die roll certainly raises the level of performance anxiety and sense of accountability for the team's product. Presenters want to represent their group's effort as well as they can and come well prepared.

Conclusion

Problem-based learning offers a powerful learning strategy and approach to building a curriculum for school leaders. It represents a solution to one of the persistent, perplexing problems in the profession—how to combine theory, research, and practice. PBL also creates a setting in which school leaders can acquire, practice, and master the array of skills essential to collaborative decision making. Finally, PBL provides instructors with insight into the nature of the difficulties students encounter when striving to understand new knowledge and learn how to apply it in practical situations.

Despite its potential power in preparing school leaders, PBL presents instructors with a set of unique challenges. Students have been socialized to teacher-centered approaches, and the transition to a more student-centered learning environment can be initially frustrating. Students may direct their frustration at the instructor who, unaccustomed to this behavior, may be crippled by it. Problem-based learning also requires a level of preparation prior to the beginning of a course that surpasses the preparation for more teacher-directed classes. The amount of preparation can be reduced if the instructor uses or modifies existing PBL projects. Lastly, PBL instructors who choose to emphasize collaborative skills may lack the requisite process skills.

We, as well as others, have found that the power of PBL trumps the challenges. It creates a more satisfying and meaningful learning environment for both instructors and students than other instructional approaches that we have used. We would, however, wish to add a caveat to this observation.

The learning that derives from this approach is enhanced substantially by the integration of the various components that we have discussed. For example, the development of students' skills in problem solving not only prepares them for more effective professional practice, but it also enables them to gain more from the learning method. Other instructors and schools that implement PBL in a more piecemeal fashion should not expect to mine the full richness of PBL. It is the systematic integration of the PBL method with an emphasis on collaborative skills in a spiral curriculum that creates the powerful learning that we have observed in our students.

References

Albanese, M. (2000). Problem-based learning: Why curricula are likely to show little effect on knowledge and clinical skills. *Academic Medicine, 34,* 729–738.

Albanese, M., & Mitchell, S. (1993). Problem-based learning: A review of literature on its outcomes and implementation issues. *Academic Medicine, 68,* 52–80.

Bridges, E. M., with Hallinger, P. (1992). *Problem based learning for administrators.* Eugene, OR: ERIC Clearinghouse on Educational Management.

Bridges, E. M., & Hallinger, P. (1997). Using problem-based learning to prepare educational leaders. *Peabody Journal of Education, 72*(2), 131–146.

Colliver, J. A. (2000). Effectiveness of problem-based learning curricula: Research and theory. *Academic Medicine, 75*(3), 259–266.

Copland, M. A. (2000). Problem-based learning and prospective principals' problem-framing ability. *Educational Administration Quarterly, 36*(4), 585–607.

Copland, M. A. (2003). Problem-based leadership development: Developing the cognitive and skill capacities of school leaders. In Hallinger, P. (Ed.), *Reshaping the landscape of school leadership development: A global perspective* (pp. 101–118). Lisse, the Netherlands: Swets & Zeitlinger.

Cross, K. P., & Angelo, T. A. (1988). *Classroom assessment techniques: A handbook for faculty.* Ann Arbor: Board of Regents of the University of Michigan for the National Center for Research to Improve Postsecondary Teaching and Learning.

Cuban, L. (2001). *How can I fix it?: Finding solutions and managing dilemmas.* New York: Teachers College Press.

Doyle, M., & Straus, D. (1981). *How to make meetings work.* New York: Playboy Press.

Fisher, R., Ury, W., & Patton, B. (Eds.). (1991). *Getting to yes: Negotiating agreement without giving in.* New York: Penguin Books.

Good, T., & Brophy, J. (1991). *Looking in classrooms.* New York: Harper & Row.

Kepner, C. H., & Tregoe, B. B. (1961). *The rational manager: A systematic approach to problem solving and decision making.* New York: McGraw Hill.

Lafferty, J., Clayton, J., & Pond, A. (1974). *The desert survival situation.* Plymouth, MI: Human Synergistics.

Schmidt, H. G. (1983). Problem-based learning: Rationale and description. *Medical Education, 17,* 11–16.

Vernon, D. T. A., & Blake, R. L. (1993). Does problem-based learning work? A meta-analysis of evaluative research. *Academic Medicine, 68,* 550–563.

PART V

Conclusions

15

Sharing Leadership

Learning From Challenge—Aiming Toward Promise

Janet H. Chrispeels

We can make the train of school reform go faster and faster around the track with technical know-how. But what we need is a radically different form of transportation to reach all kids: not a train, but a rocket ship; not a technical solution, but an adaptive change . . . something we have never had to do before, and our schools are not designed to do that. This is really an important point . . . that no one should be ashamed or feeling like he or she is failing. We are running a system that no longer is adequate to meet the needs of our current aspirations. . . . We are at work on a very hard problem; not just running our systems better, but re-inventing our system; the moment that is interesting is as the train leaves the tracks at the edge of the cliff; where are we going? It is like going to the moon.

—Comments by Robert Kegan, 2003[1]

The case studies presented in this volume describe varied contexts and unique circumstances where shared leadership has succeeded, and the results have been increased student learning and greater teacher collaboration. Each case presents leaders (principals, teachers, community) "who are at work on a very hard problem." These leaders seem to recognize that normal efforts and standard practices will be insufficient if all children are to achieve at the academic levels expected and needed for a knowledge society. They have recognized that the system is no longer adequate, and they are trying to bring about adaptive and fundamental changes. As Harris reminds us in Chapter 11, for schools facing extremely challenging circumstances (that is, both high levels of poverty as well as racial, linguistic, and ethnic diversity), the work of teachers and school leaders is doubly difficult. She argues that two inherent, and possibly intractable, problems face these schools:

> The first is the influence of social mix on a school's ability to generate the social and cultural capital necessary for higher levels of performance (Thrupp, 1999). The second is the complexity of the teaching task presented by a less affluent student population.

Facing these challenges has meant learning new ways to work together and to share leadership. Some schools seem to have reached a point of take-off; others are still traveling around the track of school reform, engaged in incremental or technical change but unable to cross the threshold and create a new mode of transportation that will enable all students to achieve proficiency of the high standards now set for them. Although each case has its nuances and reveals unique lessons to be learned, together they collectively augment the knowledge about shared leadership and the factors that support and constrain its implementation. Furthermore, the longitudinal nature of these studies illustrate the power of expert leadership distributed widely throughout the system, especially to teachers, to bring about school change and improve outcomes for students. The length of the processes described in many of the cases (Chapters 2 through 6) also provides insights into *how* shared leadership can be achieved. Across the cases, seven important themes emerge that can help others who wish to share leadership and work collaboratively to profoundly confront the challenges facing schools and those who work and learn in them:

1. Policymakers and leaders at national, state, district, and school levels need a clear understanding of the reasons for shared leadership and the benefits that can accrue to students, teachers, and the broader community.

2. The attitudes, beliefs, and skills of leaders in positions of power are critical to achieving shared leadership. Providing preparation programs and professional development opportunities that develop administrators' ability

to work collaboratively with others can greatly facilitate shared leadership in schools and districts.

3. Leaders need to recognize that shared leadership is an adaptive change that requires new mental models and has significant consequences for district leaders.

4. Schools and their leaders need some degree of autonomy from the larger educational system within which they are embedded if shared leadership is to be successfully implemented.

5. Policies can be important levers for site leaders to implement shared leadership, especially if they provide districts and schools with some autonomy; encourage experimentation and innovation, not just conformity; and seriously begin to address the social, cultural, and financial capital inequalities among schools.

6. Systems thinking is essential to implement an adaptive change such as shared leadership, especially given the complex organizational world of schools.

7. Our current mental models of how schools should be organized will need to shift if shared leadership is to become a reality and no child is to be left behind. Hierarchical and bureaucratic structures do not seem to fit the learning needs of teachers or children in a democratic knowledge society.

Reasons and Rationale for Shared Leadership

Through a cross-case analysis, four primary reasons and rationales for sharing leadership emerged, which represent different disciplines and traditions. The reasons, some explicit and others implicit, provide a rationale and purpose for the shared leadership processes described in the cases. Understanding these multiple perspectives and bases for shared leadership can ground the thinking of leaders and other stakeholders as they work to establish leadership teams and collaborative work environments. Clearer thinking about the rationale for shared leadership could have helped the district in Chapter 5 formulate a less vague and convoluted policy and provided more concise guidance to the leadership team. More active discussion and engagement with an enacted policy, such as in Prince William County (Chapter 10), could have expanded the choices for principals as they worked to implement the policy in their particular context. The principals in Park School District, Chapter 8, might have experienced much less frustration if there had been open discussion and debate with the superintendent about the changes they were trying to collaboratively implement with their staff and the district policies that ran counter to shared decision making at the site. The cases also suggest that preparation and professional development programs as outlined in Chapters 12, 13, and 14 are important opportunities to explore the reasons for sharing leadership and to develop the skills needed for its implementation.

The Rational/Utilitarian Argument

Policymakers and system leaders often base shared leadership on a rational, utilitarian or efficiency argument: the principal cannot do all the work alone. The Prince William County Board of Education policy on site based management suggests increased efficiency if decisions are made closer to the site where they must be enacted. The Kentucky Education Reform Action (KERA; Chapter 9) also recognized that, unless teachers were involved in the decision-making process, it was unlikely that learning could be improved for students. Through shared leadership, others can be enabled to assist and lighten the workload of the principal and more effectively change classroom practice.

The Psychological Argument

A second rationale is grounded in a psychological argument: through shared leadership the members of the organization will gain a greater commitment to organizational goals and a sense of belonging. Teacher isolation will be lessened and job satisfaction will be increased. This shared commitment enables the school to achieve goals that, if individually pursued, could not be reached. The validity of the psychological argument often did not emerge until teachers, principals, and parents actually began working together, as was most evident in the schools facing challenging circumstances in Chapter 11 and in the cases presented in Chapter 2 and 3. The emergence of a strong sense of commitment and shared purpose, not just among teachers and principal but with the whole school community, has been identified as essential if truly adaptive changes are to occur (MacBeath & Mortimore, 2001; Waters, Marzano & McNulty, 2003). By sharing leadership and distributing responsibility for improvement throughout the system, there is a greater likelihood that the school or district will reach a "take-off point to launch the train of school reform into a new orbit."

A Democratic Argument

A third rationale derives from democratic traditions of participation and engagement in decisions that affect the community. This argument was put forth implicitly in the site-based decision-making policy adopted by the board in Prince William County (Chapter 10). However, none of the cases seems to explicitly argue the importance of teachers and administrators modeling democratic practices for their students. The minimal reference to democratic or ethical values as a rationale for implementing shared decision making and distributing leadership reflects the hierarchical and bureaucratic nature of most districts in which these schools are embedded. Only in Chapter 3, the case of the Learning Together Charter School, and Chapter 11 was there evidence of a real commitment to involving parents and teachers in significant governance issues that went beyond shared leadership for pedagogical purposes. The charter school case, the Amherst Middle School (Chapter 2), the Australian high school (Chapter 4), and English secondary schools (Chapter 11) also present evidence that students were beginning to be recognized as important participants who need meaningful opportunities to be involved and take responsibility for their school and own learning.

A Social Constructivist Perspective of Shared Leadership

Finally, the social constructivist perspective is important for understanding the process of shared leadership, although this perspective is not explicitly identified in the cases. Shared leadership structures can be implemented through policy, but it is only through the interactions of the actors in dialogue, deliberation, and debate that shared leadership comes into being. In other words, through coming together as a leadership team, teachers and principals jointly construct the knowledge that enable the schools to solve problems of practice and move forward to implement adaptive changes. These changes are not possible without a common language and shared sense of purpose. This shared language evolves through purposeful conversations and discussions in formal and informal settings. Even in the cases where the full benefits of shared leadership needed for adaptive changes to promote significant student learning gains were not fully realized (Chapters 5 and 6), teachers and principals exhibited shared knowledge that enabled them to collaborate on important technical problems at the school.

The Critical Role of Leaders in Positions of Power

The stories sketched in this book confirm that leaders count and their leadership is critical to organizational growth and development that leads to student learning (Murphy & Datnow, 2003; Waters, Marzano, & McNulty, 2003). Leaders, with positional power at the top of the hierarchy in districts and schools, play a powerful role in influencing and shaping the actions of the actors throughout the system, especially the involvement of others in the process of leadership. As one of the principals in Chapter 7 commented, shared leadership will only happen if the principal wants it. Chapter 5 confirms that the superintendent also needs to endorse it.

The cases of both successful and less successful practice of shared leadership show that leaders must have a clear mental model of shared leadership and the knowledge and skills to bring it to fruition (Senge, 1990). Principals Cavalier in Chapter 2, Santos in Chapter 3, and Burke in Chapter 4 illustrate that with clear guiding ideas about shared leadership and collaboration, they were able to involve their staff in significant leadership roles. These chapters also document that, as teachers and principals gain skills in sharing leadership, their attitudes and beliefs about the benefits of sharing leadership are reinforced and new structures and behaviors are implemented to ensure its continuance. Chapters 5, 6, and 8, in contrast, demonstrate the challenges that can arise when guiding ideas about shared leadership are not aligned with those of the district.

Importance of Professional Development for Shared Leadership

Establishing a clear rationale for shared leadership can be an essential first step. Providing professional development for administrators and teachers to develop the knowledge and skills needed for shared leadership is an important second step in the process of learning to lead together. Typically neither principals nor teachers participate in the kinds of activities that facilitate shared leadership during their preparation programs. Principals often do not know how to engage in practices that teachers indicate will support their leadership work such as creating a culture and structures that facilitate collaboration, linking teachers with external resources, and rewarding and recognizing teachers for their collaborative efforts to improve student learning (Chapter 12). The lack of these skills is often exacerbated through district practices. For many principals, especially those in large districts, their own administrative meetings with district leaders consist of *informational dumps* and do not give principals time to work collaboratively or practice group process skills with their own colleagues. In other words, the hierarchical model of leadership is reinforced at most district administrative meetings.

One promising approach for preparing principals to share leadership is problem-based learning as described in Chapter 14. Through collaborating with classmates to tackle real problems of practice, future administrators learn valuable skills needed to lead and guide teamwork and collaborative problem solving. Chapters 5, 6, and 13 illustrate how ongoing professional development can help principals and teachers discover how to share leadership. Although the principal and teachers at the schools described in these chapters still had not perfected the collaborative process, the team training they were receiving enabled district and school leaders as well as the leadership teams to undertake significant problem solving tasks that most likely would not have been considered prior to the training. As Harris reminds us in Chapter 11, however, we still do not know much about the leadership for schools facing extremely challenging circumstances and how to go about preparing leaders for these schools.

Shared Leadership as Adaptive Change

A major theme that emerges from these cases is that shared leadership needs to be viewed as an adaptive, fundamental, or second-order change (Argyris & Schön, 1978; Cuban, 2001; Heifetz & Laurie, 1997). This means that if shared leadership is fully implemented, which was reflected in only some of the cases in this book (Chapters 2, 3, 4, 9, and 11), underlying beliefs, attitudes, and patterns of interaction would be significantly altered. Schools would be pursuing not only technical changes such as phonics instruction but would also be altering the ways students and teachers interact in the learning process (e.g., conversing, discussing, debating about ideas, and jointly producing stories and other products). A second-order change would not be a coach in the classroom helping a teacher to implement a prescribed curriculum, but teachers working together to design and continuously refine a lesson so that *all students* attain proficiency.

Sharing leadership runs counter in many respects to the hierarchical structures operating in most school districts (as illustrated in Chapter 5 through 8) and is rarely acknowledged as an adaptive change. This failure seems likely to have caused many of the schools and districts to underestimate the implementation challenges. For example, in the case of Prince William County Schools, although that district adopted path-breaking site-based management as a district-wide policy before many other districts in the country, collaborative decision making in each school was constrained considerably by how principals interpreted the policy. There is little evidence that the principals were given the professional development needed to effectively practice shared leadership. Chapter 5 and 6 also illustrate the conflicts that can arise if districts and their schools do not recognize the system-changing potential of shared decision making and shared leadership.

Unless there is agreement that shared leadership is the desired direction, the adaptive benefits that can lead to substantial learning gains for students are unlikely to be realized.

In the cases where shared leadership was most fully implemented (e.g., the charter school, the Amherst Middle School, the high school in Australia, the three schools in Kentucky, and the secondary schools in England), the schools gained considerable autonomy from district guidelines, rules, and procedures even as they remained generally within the district structure. Where this degree of autonomy was not achieved, principals and committed teachers struggled with only limited success against the homeostatic pull of the bureaucratic traditions and expectations of other teachers within the school and the administrators in the larger district context. In other words, the hierarchical power structure of the district/state remained generally intact.

The Importance of Autonomy for Shared Leadership

The cases in this volume strongly suggest that school-level autonomy may be an essential precursor for adaptive changes. Cuban (2001) has observed that many potentially second-order reforms (ungraded classes, vouchers, parent-run schools, online high schools, and profound restructuring movements such as the Coalition of Essential Schools) are usually squeezed to the margins of the system. Part of the reason for the failures of these adaptive changes to take hold is the inability and/or unwillingness of schools and districts to address the underlying hierarchical power relationships among the participants (Sarason, 1982). As illustrated in Chapter 7, however, some of the counter-forces to shared leadership may not be fully recognized. Within the seeds of one change, a contradictory mandate may also be operating. For example, many of the reforms enacted within the past 10 years frequently call for teacher involvement in site-based comprehensive reform models; more recently in the U.S. federal No Child Left Behind legislation, reforms call for parental choice if the school does not make adequate yearly progress. Parents in England also have considerable choice options if they consider their child's school to be underperforming. However, as Cuban (2003) notes, although students and parents currently have more choice of schools through charter and magnet schools, overall, "the type of schooling children receive has narrowed considerably" (p. 14). To get results, many districts are adopting *teacher-proof, prescriptive curricula*. Teachers are expected to deliver this curriculum, often through traditional pedagogical patterns of teacher question/student response/teacher judgment of the correctness of student response. These approaches allow little time for classroom discussions or joint productive work that will lead to deeper student learning and the development of complex problem-solving and thinking skills (Rueda, 1998). The role of parents is to make sure that their children attend school ready to learn and to support their students to do their homework. "It is a schooling in which administrators, teachers, and students are held responsible for performing better than they did the previous year" (Cuban, 2003, p. 14), with little say about how teaching is enacted. The frustrated voice of one principal in Chapter 7 is not atypical: *What is there to share?*

Three of the case studies—Amherst Middle School, the California charter school, and the story of the 16-year effort of David Burke to transform his high school into a learning community—suggest that teaching can be significantly transformed through consistent and sustained shared leadership. Collaborative processes were established in these schools that engaged teachers in deep conversations about teaching and learning. One of the primary tasks of leadership distributed to grade levels and departments is to guide and facilitate extensive staff professional development that involves everyone in the process. The data suggest that these three schools are engaged in adaptive and second-order change. Teachers in these schools are working hard on important first-order or technical changes in teaching practices. Burke, in Chapter 4, chronicled several instructional strategies that teachers were testing to increase learning and improve the outcomes for their students. A fundamental difference in these three cases as compared to many other schools, however, is that the teachers appear to be succeeding in implementing important adaptive changes in the way they work together, work with their students, and work with their administrators to implement these changes. In two of the cases—Amherst and the charter school—parents are also an important part of the equation.

The examples provided by the school leaders suggest it is possible to engage in transformative work and to create places that are positive environments for students and teachers to work and learn. They also illustrate how demanding the work is, however, and how challenging it is within bureaucratically organized school systems. Teachers have valuable insights about the support they need to engage in adaptive work. These suggestions are captured in Chapter 12 and provide specific actions that leaders can pursue to help build "a new form of transportation" that may enable student learning to soar.

The Role of Policy as a Lever for Shared Leadership

Federal, state, and district policies often drive educational change. Although policymakers may envision their policies as system changing (McDonnell & Elmore, 1987), policy studies have frequently shown that local implementers have a natural tendency to turn fundamental changes into incremental ones (Cuban, 2001). Homeostasis, or maintaining the status quo, is a natural response of most systems, and local school responses to policy mandates are no exception. Educational policies played multiple and important roles in several schools as they worked to implement shared leadership.

School Leaders Use Policy as a Lever for Change

The Kentucky case showed that in the hands of capable leaders, state policy became a lever for both technical and adaptive change in the three schools.

The authors of Chapter 9 confirm this strong speculation: state policies, contrary to rebuttals by their critics, can have positive affects on schools as organizations. Kentucky legislators intended to implement significant changes in curriculum, instruction, and assessment through both accountability and decentralizing measures within a reasonably coherent framework.

The principals of the case schools reacted positively to the Kentucky Educational Reform Act and saw its potential for empowering teachers and altering relations among staff. It is clear that not all schools in Kentucky responded in the ways that these leaders and their schools did; nevertheless, this case study is critical in helping to illustrate the power that policy can have in guiding change.

Chapter 3 illustrates a second example of a policy being seized by a principal as an opportunity. Without the California Charter School legislation, it is unlikely this principal could have guided the school through the transformative process of uniting a tracked and divided school into one where teachers and parents share equally in the governance of the school. The charter status opened the door for the principal to build a common vision with the staff and community and to find resources that enabled the faculty to consistently and collaboratively work in grade-level teams by altering traditional school schedules. Further exploration is needed to understand the factors that enable some educators to see the possibilities of system transformation in policies.

Understanding Policy Implications

The example of Prince William County once again confirms findings in the policy literature that a single policy becomes *policies* as it is interpreted and translated in each individual school context by the local actors. What remain unanswered in these cases are the consequences for students and teachers when policies are interpreted differentially. These studies suggest that districts and their schools may spend insufficient time in exploring what meaning the policy has for each level of the system and how varying interpretations may support or undermine the policy intent.

Chapters 5 and 8 illustrate the negative consequences for principals and school leadership teams when there is a rapid policy change in the district. In Chapter 5, the shifting definition of site-based management and shared leadership—caused by the change in superintendents—created considerable consternation, role conflict, and ambiguity for the principal and the leadership team. The quick change in district policies about the teaching of writing caused similar dismay and confusion for the schools described in Chapter 8. Because in the policy arena competing values and interests are debated, negotiated, and decided, it is not surprising in a democratic society to have shifting and even contradictory policies in place. Without an understanding of the policy world and the importance of policy in distributing valued goods and resources, leaders can miss opportunities to use policies to their advantage or help colleagues make sense of policy contradictions.

Second, policies are often enacted without understanding how they will impact each local and individual case where local policies may already be in place that are contradictory to the new policy. The school consolidation and amalgamation policy, perceived as financially essential at the state level in Victoria, Australia, had considerable disruptive impact on the process of technical and adaptive change underway at one of the schools to be amalgamated. In this instance, the change proved to be only a "time out" period until a new culture could be molded and the sense of loss overcome.

The Role of Systems Thinking in Guiding Change

Wherever important adaptive changes were occurring, the leaders showed that they were able to reflect on their practice. Through the reflexive accounts of these leaders, we see that they are, in the words of Heifetz and Laurie (1997), able to "get on the balcony" and perceive and reflect on the pattern of action and change occurring in their schools, thus enabling them to help their teachers in the process (p. 125). In other words, they were able to take a systems perspective.

> Without the capacity to move back and forth between the field of action and the balcony, to reflect day to day, moment to moment on the many ways in which an organization's habits can sabotage adaptive work, a leader easily and unwittingly becomes a prisoner of the system. The dynamics of adaptive change are far too complex to keep track of, let alone influence, if leaders stay only on the field of play. (Heifetz & Laurie, 1997, p. 125)

Several of the leaders were able to step back from the daily activities, get on the balcony, and see the interaction of the parts to the whole; that is, engage in systems thinking (Senge, 1990). As they pursued their individual quests to improve instruction in their middle schools, the four principals in Park School District, described in Chapter 8, began to understand the strengths and limits of the system. Through collective action they helped the board of education understand the unique needs of middle schools. They pressed hard on the district system to have their place within the larger context realized. They also, at times, felt thwarted by the perceived lack of system coherence.

Chapter 5 helps to illustrate the negative impact when leaders at the district and the sites do not have a clear systems perspective. The superintendent wanted the principal to understand that it was her role to take the district's perspective. It is critical to realize, however, that the district view is not necessarily a systems perspective. Neither superintendent nor principal fully grasped the forces and interrelationship that were shaping the behavior of the school leadership team as it received training on collaboration and problem solving and was being urged to address learning needs of students at the school. The right balance between site autonomy and district direction does not seem to have been addressed.

A significant component of systems thinking that emerges in this volume is the role of the reinforcing and balancing loops (Kim, 1994; Senge, 1990). The idea of a balancing loop is explicitly addressed in Chapter 2. When Mary Cavalier recognized the "overload" of innovations on her faculty, she and the coach agreed "to nurture the faculty through the spring and allow time for the new structures to provide evidence of positive change to the faculty." David Burke also recognized the need for "time out" periods for the faculty to regroup and consolidate changes. These rest periods from the adaptive change process were especially important when confronted with other external pressures and mandates.

Another related element of systems thinking is identifying core values and beliefs and their link to sustainability of change. For example, in the business world, Collins and Porras (2002) found that companies that endured over time were those that were founded on a set of core beliefs. Several of the principals in Chapters, 2, 3, 4, 8, 9, and 11 explicitly showed the ability to identify their core beliefs and goals. Mary Cavalier found she had to look inward and know what her core beliefs were before she could lead outward. Creating rich learning opportunities for students and collaborating with colleagues to better understand how students learn were key values that guided David Burke in his 16-year journey to build a learning community. He was able to turn to these values as they were expressed in the school's charter to help the staff return to its core purpose during a period of transition and turmoil. In Chapter 3, Principal Santos's deep commitment to shared leadership, collaboration, and teaming enabled her to lead her school in ways that were counter to district policy. And in her study (Chapter 11), Harris found that head teachers of schools in extremely challenging circumstances who were raising achievement held a firm belief that all students could learn and that the school had the potential to offset students' disadvantaged status.

The Need for New Mental Models

The public school systems in democratic countries would appear to reflect our democratic ideal and mental model of providing schooling for all children. These systems were developed at a time of rapid economic expansion and industrialization and were patterned on the bureaucratic and hierarchical models of industry. In many respects, public schools have fulfilled their mission and many children are receiving a good education. As Jim Collins (2001) reminds us, however: "Good is the enemy of great" (p. 1). As twenty-first-century societies are undergoing rapid changes to keep pace with the knowledge society, and as information from the cognitive sciences about how children learn expands exponentially, new models of education are emerging. Several schools described in chapters of this book reflect these new models. Others are still trapped in the old mental model, struggling against the hierarchy of district bureaucracies that prevent collaboration and shared leadership. However, our goal as a society has become not just to provide schooling for all but to ensure learning by all. This shift to learning, especially learning to high standards, requires schools not to be good but to be great. The paradox reflected by the cases in this volume is that true democratic models occur in smaller, autonomous communities where there is sufficient access to power and resources by all members of the community and opportunities for collective thinking by teachers, administrators, students, and parents. If we truly want learning by all, then we will need to change our mental model of what education looks like in a democratic society. It will require us to learn to lead together.

Note

1. Robert Kegan's remarks were presented at the Gevirtz Graduate School of Education (University of California, Santa Barbara), Center for Educational Leadership, Fall Institute, entitled, *No Child Left Behind: A Role for All Stakeholders.* Santa Barbara, California, October 9, 2003.

References

Argyris, C., & Schön, D. A. (1978). *Organizational learning: A theory of action perspective.* Reading, MA: Addison-Wesley.

Collins, J. C. (2001). *Good to great.* New York: Harper Collins.

Collins, J. C., & Porras, J. I. (2002) *Build to last: Successful habits of visionary companies.* New York: HarperCollins.

Cuban, L. (2001). *How can I fix it? Finding solutions and managing dilemmas.* New York: Teachers College Press.

Cuban, L. (2003). *Why is it so hard to get good schools?* New York: Teachers College Press.

Heifetz, R. A., & Laurie, D. L. (1997). The work of leadership. *Harvard Business Review, 75*(1), 124–135.

Kim, D. H. (1994). *Systems archetypes I: Diagnosing system issues and designing high leverage interventions.* (Toolbox Reprint Series). Cambridge, MA: Pegasus Communications, Inc.

MacBeath, J., & Mortimore, P. (Eds.) (2001). *Improving school effectiveness.* Buckingham, UK: Open University Press.

McDonnell, L. M., & Elmore, R. F. (1987). Getting the job done: Alternative policy instruments. *Educational Evaluation and Policy Analysis, 9*(2), 171–178.

Murphy, J., & Datnow, A. (2003). *Leadership lessons from comprehensive school reform.* Thousand Oaks, CA: Corwin.

Rueda, R. (1998). *Standards for professional development: A sociocultural perspective.* (Research Brief #2). Santa Cruz, CA: Center for Research on Equity, Diversity, & Excellence (CREDE).

Sarason, S. B. (1982, 2nd ed.). *The culture of the school and the problem of change.* Boston: Allyn & Bacon.

Senge, P. (1990). *The fifth discipline: The art and practice of learning organizations.* New York: Doubleday.

Thrupp, M. (1999). *Schools making a difference: Let's be realistic.* Ballmoor, UK: Open University Press.

Waters, T., Marzano, R. J., & McNulty, B. (2003). *Balanced leadership: What 30 years of research tells us about the effect of leadership on student achievement.* Boulder, CO: Mid-Continent Regional Educational Laboratory (McREL).

Name Index

Subject Index